progressive muslims

ON JUSTICE, GENDER AND PLURALISM

"These are among the more lucid essays in any field of scholarship. Superbly edited by Omid Safi, [they] are essential reading for anyone concerned with the most vital global issue of our time. This book is immensely readable, for specialists and non-specialists alike, crystalline in its scholarly integrity, and explosive in its implications."

MICHAEL SELLS, HAVERFORD COLLEGE, PENNSYLVANIA

RELATED TITLES FROM ONEWORLD

Approaches to Islam in Religious Studies, edited by Richard C. Martin,
ISBN 1–85168–268–6
Defenders of Reason in Islam, Richard C. Martin, Mark R. Woodward and
Dwi S. Atmaja, ISBN 1–85168–147–7
Islam and the West, Norman Daniel, ISBN 1–85168–129–9
The Legacy of Arab–Islam in Africa, John Alembillah Azumah,
ISBN 1–85168–273–2
The Mantle of the Prophet, Roy Mottahedeh, ISBN 1–85168–234–1
On Being a Muslim: Finding a Religious Path in the World Today, Farid Esack,
ISBN 1–85168–146–9
The Qur'an: A Short Introduction, Farid Esack, ISBN 1–85168–231–7
Qur'an, Liberation and Pluralism, Farid Esack, ISBN 1–85168–121–3
Revival and Reform in Islam, Fazlur Rahman, edited and with an introduction by
Ebrahim Moosa, ISBN 1–85168–204–X
Speaking in God's Name: Islamic Law, Authority and Women, Khaled Abou El
Fadl, 1–85168–262–7
What Muslims Believe, John Bowker, ISBN 1–85168–169–8

progressive muslims

ON JUSTICE, GENDER AND PLURALISM

EDITED BY
OMID SAFI

ONEWORLD
OXFORD

Oneworld Publications
(Sales and Editorial)
185 Banbury Road
Oxford OX2 7AR
England
www.oneworld-publications.com

ISBN 1–85168–316–X

Cover design by Design Deluxe
Cover illustration by Michael Green
Typeset by LaserScript Ltd, Mitcham, UK
Printed and bound in Britain by Bell & Bain Ltd, Glasgow, UK

CONTENTS

CONTRIBUTORS

KECIA ALI is the Senior Research Analyst responsible for Islam with the Feminist Sexual Ethics project at Brandeis University (www.brandeis.edu/departments/nejs/fse). Her work focuses on marriage and divorce in Islamic jurisprudence, particularly on the interdependent but unequal rights of spouses. Current projects include an article on slave marriage in classical Sunni law and a study of how the Prophet's own practice is utilized in jurisprudence. Aside from her research and writing on Islamic law, she lectures frequently on topics related to women and gender in Islamic discourses and Muslim communities.

KHALED ABOU EL FADL received his B.A. from Yale University, his J.D. from the University of Pennsylvania School of Law, and Ph.D. from Princeton University. He teaches Islamic law, Immigration law, and national security law. He is the author of several books on Islamic law, including *Rebellion and Violence in Islamic Law* (Cambridge: Cambridge University Press, 2001); *And God Knows the Soldiers: The Authoritative and Authoritarian in Islamic Discourses* (Lanham, MD: University Press of America, 2001); and *Conference of the Books: The Search for Beauty in Islam* (Lanham, MD: University Press of America, 2001). He is the Omar and Azmeralda Alfi Distinguished Fellow in Islamic Law, and Professor of Law at the UCLA School of Law.

FARID ESACK is a South African Muslim Theologian who studied in Pakistan, the U.K. and Germany. He has written *Qur'an, Liberation and Pluralism, On Being a Muslim* and *The Qur'an: A Short Introduction*, all with Oneworld Publications. He has published on Islam, gender, liberation theology, interfaith relations, and qur'anic hermeneutics. Esack served as a

Commissioner for Gender Equality in the South African government and has taught at the Universities of Western Cape, Ohio, and Hamburg, and Union Theological Seminary (New York). He is currently Brueggemann Chair in Interreligious Studies at Xavier University in Cincinnati. Email: Faridesack@hotmail.com. Web-page: www.faridesack.com/

MICHAEL GREEN is an artist who draws inspiration from a wide range of Eastern, Sufi, and Native American spiritual traditions. He has generously contributed the beautiful calligraphic illumination you see on the cover of this book. His work has been previously featured in best-sellers such as *The Illuminated Rumi*, and *The Illuminated Prayer*. He has been a long time devotee of the Sufi master Bawa Muhaiyaddeen. More information about his art can be found at http://artstribe.com/green

MARCIA HERMANSEN is Professor of Theology at Loyola University, Chicago where she teaches courses in Islamic studies and world religions. She received her Ph.D. from the University of Chicago, where she was a student of Dr. Fazlur Rahman. Her book, *The Conclusive Argument from God*, a study and translation (from Arabic) of Shah Wali Allah of Delhi's *Hujjat Allah al-Baligha* was published in 1996. She has also contributed numerous academic articles in the fields of Islamic thought, Sufism, Islam and Muslims in South Asia, Muslims in America, and women in Islam. Email: mherman@orion.it.luc.edu

AMIR HUSSAIN is a member of the Religious Studies Department of California State University, Northridge. Born in Pakistan, Amir was raised and educated in Canada, doing his graduate work at the University of Toronto's Centre for the Study of Religion. Amir's doctoral dissertation was on Muslim communities in Toronto. He has published in the areas of Islam and Muslim communities in North America, religion and literature, and religion and film. Amir has been involved for over a decade with interfaith dialogue, most notably with the World Conference on Religion and Peace, and the Fellowship of Reconciliation. Email: amir.hussain@csun.edu Webpage: www.csun.edu/~ah34999/

AHMET T. KARAMUSTAFA (Ph.D., McGill University, 1987) is associate professor of history and religious studies at Washington University in St. Louis, where he also directs the Religious Studies Program. He specializes in pre-modern Islamic intellectual and social history. His most recent book, *God's Unruly Friends* (University of Utah Press, 1994), is a study of ascetic movements in medieval Islamic mysticism. His current research focuses on the history of Islamic mysticism, conceptions of the individual in the Islamic world during the thirteenth century, and Islamic perspectives on the concept of religion. Email: akaramus@artsci.wustl.edu

TAZIM R. KASSAM is Director of the Graduate Studies Program of Religion and Associate Professor of Islamic Studies at Syracuse University. A historian of religions specializing in the Islamic tradition, her research and teaching interests include ritual, devotional literature, gender, and the cultural heritage of Muslims particularly in South Asia. Her book *Songs of Wisdom and Circles of Dance* (SUNY, 1995) explores the religious songs of the Ismaili Muslims of the Indian Subcontinent. She has twice co-chaired the Study of Islam section of the American Academy of Religion, and is on the editorial board of the Journal of the American Academy of Religion. Email: tkassam@syr.edu

SCOTT KUGLE is an American Muslim who also goes by the name Siraj al-Haqq. He is an Assistant Professor in the Department of Religion, Swarthmore College. His research focuses on the intersections between Islamic law, ethics and mysticism. He has written articles on gender and sexuality in Islamic societies: "Sultan Mahmud's Make-Over: Colonial Homophobia and Persian-Urdu Poetics" in Ruth Vanita (ed.), *Queering India: Same Sex Love and Eroticism in Indian Culture and Society* (New York: Routledge, 2001), and "*Haqiqat al-Fuqara*: Poetic Biography of 'Madho Lal' Hussayn" and "The Mirror of Secrets: Akhi Jamshed Rajgiri" in Ruth Vanita and Saleem Kidwai (eds.), *Same Sex Love in India: Readings from Literature and History* (New York: St. Martin's Press, 2000): 136–140 and 145–156. He has written on ethical issues in Islamic law ("Framed, Blamed and Renamed: the Recasting of Islamic Jurisprudence in Colonial South Asia," *Modern Asian Studies* 35(2) (May 2001) 257–313), in addition to articles on Islamic society in South Asia and North Africa. He is currently writing a study of the Sufi jurist from Morocco, Shaykh Ahmad Zarruq, entitled "Rebel Between Spirit and Law." Email: skugle1@swarthmore.edu

EBRAHIM MOOSA teaches Islamic Studies in the Department of Religion at Duke University and has interests in Islamic law and ethics. He is author of the forthcoming book, *Ghazali and the Poetics of Imagination*, which reflects his interests in medieval Islamic thought. He has written a range of articles on topics dealing with the Qur'an, Islamic law, and contemporary Islamic thought. His publications include editing and introducing the late Fazlur Rahman's *Revival and Reform: A Study of Islamic Fundamentalism* (Oxford: Oneworld, 1999); "Allegory of the Rule (Hukm): Law as Simulacrum in Islam," *History of Religions* 38(1) (August 1998) 1–24; "The Poetics and Politics of Law after Empire: Reading Women's Rights in the Contestations of Law," in *Journal for Islamic and Near Eastern Law* (*JINEL*), UCLA Law School, 1(1), (fall/winter 2001–2) 1–46; "Languages of Change in Islamic Law: Redefining Death in Modernity," *Islamic Studies* 38(3) (1999) 305–42. Email: moosa@duke.edu

AHMAD S. MOUSSALLI is Professor of Political Science at the American University of Beirut. He was visiting Professor at the Center for Muslim–Christian Understanding at Georgetown University (USA) and University of Copenhagen (Denmark). He received his Ph.D. in Government and Politics from the University of Maryland, M.A. in Liberal Arts from Saint John's College, Santa Fe, New Mexico, and B.A. in Islamic Studies and Languages from Al-Azhar University, Cairo. He is the author of numerous publications, including the following books: *The Islamic Quest for Human Rights, Pluralism and Democracy*; *Historical Dictionary of Islamic Fundamentalist Movements in the Arab World, Iran and Turkey*; *Moderate and Radical Islamic Fundamentalism: The Quest for Legitimacy*; *Modernity and the Islamic State, Myths and Realities of Islamic Fundamentalism: Theoretical Aspects and Case Studies*; *Radical Islamic Fundamentalism: The Ideological and Political Discourse of Sayyid Qutb*; *A Theoretical Reading In Islamic Fundamentalism*; *Discourse, Islamic Fundamentalism: A Study in Sayyid Qutb's Ideological and Political Discourse*; and *World Order and Islamic Fundamentalism*. Email: asmouss@aub.edu.lb

FARISH AHMAD-NOOR is a Malaysian political scientist and human rights activist. He has taught at the Centre for Inter-Civilisational Dialogue, University of Malaya and the Institute for Islamic Studies, Freie University of Berlin, and has been a visiting academic fellow at the Institute for the Study of Islam in the Modern World (ISIM), Leiden, Netherlands. He has served as the Secretary-General of the International Movement for a Just World (JUST). Author of *Terrorising the Truth: The Demonisation of the Image of Islam and Muslims in Global Media and Political Discourse* (JUST, 1997). He is also a columnist for a number of newspapers and Islamist journals in Malaysia, Pakistan, Britain, and the United States. Email: korawa@hotmail.com

OMID SAFI is an Assistant Professor of Philosophy and Religion at Colgate University. He is a member of the Steering Committee for the Study of Islam at the American Academy of Religion. He specializes in the study of the Islamic mystical tradition (Sufism), pre-modern history of the Eastern Islamic world, and post-modern Muslim thought. His forthcoming translation of Ayn al-Qozat Hamadani's *Tamhidat* is to be published in the Classics of Western Spirituality Series of Paulist Press. He served as the planner and editor of this volume. Email: omidsafi@hotmail.com. Web-page: http://classes.colgate.edu/osafi

SA'DIYYA SHAIKH is a South African Muslim woman. She is a doctoral candidate in the Department of Religion at Temple University. Her research interests in Islamic studies include areas of feminism, qur'anic studies, Sufism and interfaith dialogue. From 1999 to 2001, she was involved in directing and facilitating interfaith programs focusing on social justice issues for emerging religious leaders under the auspices of the National Conference for Community and Justice based in New York City. She is a long-standing member of the Circle of Concerned African Women Theologians and the Gender Desk of the Muslim Youth Movement in South Africa. She is currently teaching at the University of Cape Town. Email: sshaikh@nimbus.ocis.temple.edu

GWENDOLYN ZOHARAH SIMMONS is an Assistant Professor of Religion at the University of Florida. She obtained her Ph.D. in Islamic Studies along with a Graduate Certificate in Women's Studies from Temple University. Her primary areas of research and teaching include Islamic progressive reform; the contemporary impact of Islamic law on Muslim women; and women, religion and society. She also teaches in race, religion and rebellion; and African-American religious traditions. She is a Sufi Muslim who studied for over seventeen years with the renowned Sufi mystic, Sheikh Muhammad Raheem Bawa Muhaiyadeen. She has been a social activist for all of her adult life, beginning with full time work in the Civil Rights Movement during the 1960s and 1970s. Her domestic work for justice for African Americans has blossomed over the years into a concern for international justice especially as it concerns the gross inequities between the Western world and so-called Third World nations and their people.

AMINA WADUD is Associate Professor of Islamic Studies in the Department of Philosophy and Religious Studies at Virginia Commonwealth University. Best known for her book, *Qur'an and Woman: Rereading the Sacred Text from Woman's Perspective*, she is a core member of Sisters in Islam, Malaysia, a group engaged in policy reforms on issues of gender.

INTRODUCTION:
THE TIMES THEY ARE A-CHANGIN'
– A MUSLIM QUEST FOR JUSTICE, GENDER
EQUALITY, AND PLURALISM*

Omid Safi

Inna 'l-laha ya'muru bi 'l-'adl wa 'l-ihsan
Indeed God commands justice (*'adl*)
and the actualization of goodness, realization of beauty (*ihsan*)
Qur'an 16:90

Come gather 'round people
wherever you roam
and admit that the waters
around you have grown
and accept it that soon
you'll be drenched to the bone.

If your time to you
is worth savin'
then you better start swimmin'
or you'll sink like a stone
for the times they are a-changin'.
Bob Dylan[1]

Evoking the sacred message of the Qur'an and the revolutionary spirit of Bob Dylan's lyrics, this book represents the collective aspirations of a group of Muslim thinkers and activists. We realize the urgency of the changin' times in which we live, and seek to implement the Divine injunction to enact the justice (*'adl*) and goodness-and-beauty (*ihsan*) that lie at the heart of the Islamic tradition. It is the urgency of realizing that in so many places the waters around

Muslims have grown (Palestine, Bosnia, Afghanistan, Kashmir, Iraq, Gujarat, sub-Saharan Africa, and now the United States). It is time to start swimming in these turbulent waters, to save both ourselves and the variety and vibrancy of the Islamic tradition. It may not be an exaggeration to state that unless we succeed in doing so, the humanity of Muslims will be fully reduced to correspond to the caricature of violent zealots painted by fanatics from both inside and outside the Muslim community.

It is time to start a-changin'. It is time to acknowledge the complicated mess around us, and to aim for the implementation of the vision of justice and goodness-and-beauty that is rooted in the Qur'an. We start by admitting that it is not just our time that is worth saving, but also our very humanity, the most precious blessing we have been given by God. The conversations in this volume are an open-eyed move in that direction, one that is simultaneously optimistic and critical. What brings us together is a deep distrust of all simplistic solutions, since we are aware that complicated problems call for equally complicated analyses and answers. This book is not about arriving at convenient solutions, but rather about starting the process of getting to a viable destination. Before one gets to the destination, however, one needs to get on the path. Before one gets to the shore, one has to swim. In Dylan's prophetic words, it is time to start swimming. The progressive Muslim movement is above all an attempt to start swimming through the rising waters of Islam and modernity, to strive for justice in the midst of society.

THE MULTIPLE CRITIQUE UNDERTAKEN BY PROGRESSIVE MUSLIMS

Feminist scholars have introduced the useful concept of "multiple critique," an idea with great relevance for Muslims committed to social justice, pluralism, and gender justice. In short, multiple critique entails a multi-headed approach based on a simultaneous critique of the many communities and discourses that we find ourselves positioned in.[2] As we will document shortly, an important part of being a progressive Muslim is the determination to hold Muslim societies accountable for justice and pluralism. It means openly and purposefully resisting, challenging, and overthrowing structures of tyranny and injustice in these societies. At a general level, it means contesting injustices of gender apartheid (practiced by groups such as the Taliban) as well as the persecution of religious and ethnic minorities (undertaken by Saddam Hussein against the Kurds, etc.). It means exposing the violations of human rights and freedoms of speech, press, religion, and the right to dissent in Muslim countries such as Saudi Arabia, Turkey, Iran, Pakistan, Sudan, Egypt, and others. More specifically, it means embracing and implementing a different vision of Islam than that offered by Wahhabi and neo-Wahhabi groups.[3] A vital corollary component of our multiple critique entails standing up to increasingly hegemonic Western political, economic, and intellectual structures that perpetuate an unequal distribution of resources around the world. This hegemony comprises a multitude of forces, among them the oppressive and environmentally destructive forces of multi-national corporations whose interests are now linked with those of neo-imperial, unilateral governments. Together they enforce policies through overwhelming military force, hammering down at the poorest people in the world with disturbing frequency. And yes, as much as it makes some Muslims uneasy to hear this, it does mean challenging certain policies of the United States and other countries that put profit before human rights, and "strategic interest" before the dignity of every human being.

At the heart of a progressive Muslim interpretation is a simple yet radical idea: every human life, female and male, Muslim and non-Muslim, rich or poor, "Northern" or "Southern,"[4] has exactly the same intrinsic worth. The essential value of human life is God-given, and is in no way connected to culture, geography, or privilege. A progressive Muslim is one who is committed to the strangely controversial idea that the worth of a human being is measured by a person's character, not the oil under their soil, and not their flag. A progressive Muslim agenda is concerned with the ramifications of the premise that all members of humanity have this same intrinsic worth because, as the Qur'an reminds us, each of us has the breath of God breathed into our being.[5]

Many people today who come from a whole host of religious, political, and ethnic backgrounds describe themselves as "progressives." There is, furthermore, a nascent community of Muslim activists and intellectuals who readily identify with the term "progressive Muslims" and publicly embrace it. "Progressive," in this usage, refers to a relentless striving towards a universal notion of justice in which no single community's prosperity, righteousness, and dignity comes at the expense of another. Central to this notion of a progressive Muslim identity are fundamental values that we hold to be essential to a vital, fresh, and urgently needed interpretation of Islam for the twenty-first century. These themes include social justice, gender justice, and pluralism. Of course, the kind of Islamic interpretation one comes up with is largely determined by who undertakes the interpretation.

In talking about social justice, gender issues, and pluralism, we are mindful to avoid the trap in which "Islam" becomes a façade for some contemporary political ideology such as Marxism. Rather, ours is a relentless effort to submit the human will to the Divine in a way that affirms the common humanity of all of God's creation. We conceive of a way of being Muslim that engages and affirms the humanity of all human beings, that actively holds all of us responsible for a fair and just distribution of God-given natural resources, and that seeks to live in harmony with the natural world. To put it slightly differently, being a progressive Muslim means not simply thinking more about the Qur'an and the life of the Prophet, but also thinking about the life we share on this planet with all human beings and all living creatures. Seen in this light, our relationship to the rest of humanity changes the way we think about God, and vice versa.

Throughout this book, we will time and again challenge, resist, and seek to overthrow the structures of injustice that are built into Islamic thought. These challenges cannot be conducted haphazardly, however. They must be undertaken patiently and critically. Yet the necessary and contingent element of being a progressive Muslim is the will to resist the structures of injustice that are built into the very societies in which we live. That goes for the Muslim world as well as the United States and Europe. In all cases, we strive to be social critics, rather than outright revolutionaries. We criticize not because we have stopped being Muslim (or American, or South African, or Turkish, or . . .) but precisely because we want to see all the various communities of which we are a part rise up to their highest potential of justice and pluralism.

In crucial ways, being a progressive Muslim also means being mindful and critical of the arrogance of modernity. What we mean by arrogance of modernity is an alleged teleology that posits a Hegelian, unidirectional, and inevitable march towards the end game of modern Western civilization. Progressive Muslim interpretations share this critique of modernity with other thinkers who are now commonly described as post-modern.[6] Indeed, this is one important way in which progressive Muslims differ from the host of "modernist" Muslim thinkers in the late-nineteenth and much of the twentieth century. We no longer look to the prevalent notion of Western modernity as something to be imitated and duplicated *in toto*. In fact, we direct our critique just as much to the West as to Muslim societies. This is particularly the case in response to arrogant voices in the West that insist on the inevitability of a global march towards modernity.

It is disturbing that these arrogant voices are not only coming from certain corners of the academic community (Francis Fukuyama, Bernard Lewis, Samuel Huntington, etc.), but are also now being echoed by the most powerful government in the world. A recent policy paper released by the United States White House titled *The National Security Strategy of the United States of America*, for example, is riddled with disturbing instances of hubris. According to the very first sentence of this document, there is now "a single sustainable model for national success," based on the essential components of freedom, democracy, and free enterprise. Not many people would argue against freedom and democracy, but many progressive Muslims would point out that the foreign policy record of the United States is less than stellar in its support of democracy around the world. Time and again, the United States has supported and armed tyrannical rulers who have oppressed their own pro-democracy citizens. One could point to the U.S.-led overthrow of the pro-democratic Mossadegh in Iran in 1953, the U.S. support of the Mujahidin fighters (including Osama bin Laden) in Afghanistan during the 1980s, or the U.S.$1.5 billion given to Saddam Hussein's brutal regime during the Iran–Iraq War. To these, one could add the more recent examples of U.S. support of anti-democratic Parvez Musharraf in Pakistan, and support for Hosni Mubarak's regime when the Egyptian government imprisoned the noted pro-democracy reformer Dr. Saad Eddin

Ibrahim. Democracy would indeed be a worthy goal if we in the United States actually pursued it globally, and if we truly believed that other people should have the choice to decide for themselves as to whether or not they should embrace it. As Gandhi himself stated, "I would heartily welcome the union of East and West provided it is not based on brute force."[7]

It is the third component of this "single sustainable model," an element benignly called "free enterprise," that drives much of *The National Security Strategy of the United States of America*. Later on, the document further boasts, "Free trade and free markets have proven their ability to lift whole societies out of poverty." Where are these "whole societies" that have allegedly been lifted out of poverty? Nowhere is there an acknowledgement of or engagement with North/South divisions, or the myriad ways in which globalization has worked to make some of the rich super-rich, and the super-poor even poorer.

Another equally disturbing example of the essential arrogance that (mis)-informs *The National Security Strategy of the United States of America* is the call for a single system of morality. The President of the United States is here quoted as stating, "Some worry that it is somehow undiplomatic or impolite to speak the language of right and wrong. I disagree. Different circumstances require different methods, but not different moralities."[8] Just whose system of morality is it that we are to abide by here? That of the President of the United States? Right-wing evangelical Christians? Tibetan Buddhists? Catholics? Secular Humanists? The implication is clear: according to this document, just as there is now (or so we are told) one sustainable model of national success, there is now one single acceptable system of morality. And it is the President of the United States (and his advisors) who get to determine what that is. It is precisely such a hegemonic discourse that progressive Muslims would challenge, in the same way that we reject the arrogant authoritarian discourse of Muslim literalist-exclusivists.[9]

PROGRESSIVE MUSLIMS AND THE ENGAGEMENT
WITH TRADITION IN LIGHT OF MODERNITY

The attempt to reflect critically on the heritage of Islamic thought and to adapt it to the modern world is of course nothing new. At the opposite ends of the spectrum of contemporary Muslims grappling with tradition one finds rigid extremes – on one side a steadfast conservative traditionalism, and on the other a knee-jerk rejectionism of the traditional Muslim heritage by certain Muslim modernists. Conservative traditionalism sees all Muslims as bound by what it deems the authoritative juridical or theological decisions of the past. The rejectionist perspective argues that there is now an epistemological rupture with the past so severe as to warrant throwing out the baby with the bathwater. Among other points, this modernist perspective calls for abolishing the Islamic legal and theological schools of thought (*madhahib*, sing. *madhhab*).

Most Muslims today recognize that neither extreme is fully viable. The two positions represent above all idealized camps from which the adherents of the two schools of thought shout at each other. Most of us find ourselves in the gloriously messy middle where real folks live and breathe. One of many commonalities between the conservative traditionalists and the modernists is that they both have had a difficult time attracting many ordinary Muslims, especially at a communal level. The edicts of those who would wish to see twenty-first-century Muslims bound by all medieval juridical decisions have seemed too restrictive to many. On the other hand, many modernists have simply not appeared authentically "Muslim" enough to most Muslims. This has had less to do with their personal piety (or lack thereof), than with the fact that their interpretations have not sufficiently engaged Islamic sources.

Progressive Muslims seek to learn from the deficiencies of both of these ideologies, in order to get past the slogan games. The challenge is not to find some magical, mythical middle ground, but rather to create a safe, open, and dynamic space, where guided by concerns for global justice and pluralism, we can have critical conversations about the Islamic tradition in light of modernity.[10] A wonderful Jewish friend of Muslims, Rabbi Zalman Schachter, perhaps said it best: "Tradition has a vote, not a veto."[11]

It is our hope that the book you hold in your hand marks a new chapter in the rethinking of Islam in the twenty-first century. Our aim has been to envision a socially and politically active Muslim identity that remains committed to ideals of social justice, pluralism, and gender justice. The aim here is not to advocate our own understanding as uniquely "Islamic" to the exclusion of the past fourteen hundred years of Islamic thought and practice. This is not a tyrannical attempt to insist that standing here at the threshold of the twenty-first century, we finally "got it right"! No, warts and all, from its glorious nobility to misogyny, there has always been a spectrum of interpretations in Islam. We seek to locate ourselves as part of that broader conversation, not to collapse the spectrum. But ours is not a passive, relativist locating of our own voices. Being progressive also means to issue an active and dynamic challenge to those who hold exclusivist, violent, and misogynist interpretations. Traditions do not arrive from heaven fully formed, but are subject to the vicissitudes of human history. Every tradition is always a tradition-in-becoming, and Islam is no exception. Our aim is to open up a place in the wider spectrum of Islamic thought and practice for the many Muslims who aspire to justice and pluralism. This will entail both producing concrete intellectual products and changing existing social realities.

Progressive Muslims are concerned not simply with laying out a fantastic, beatific vision of social justice and peace, but also with transforming hearts and societies alike. A progressive commitment implies by necessity the willingness to remain engaged with the issues of social justice as they unfold on the ground level, in the lived realities of Muslim and non-Muslim communities. Vision and activism are both necessary. Activism without vision is doomed from the start. Vision without activism quickly becomes irrelevant.

Allow me to elaborate what I understand to be the key agenda items of progressive Muslims. But before I get to that, let me shatter any illusion that the following is meant as a "progressive Muslim manifesto." While it is the case that the fifteen contributors to this volume have been involved in many intense and fruitful conversations, I wish to make it very clear that there are substantial differences of opinion among us. This is as it should be. I cannot – and do not – advocate my own understanding of progressive Islam as canonical. Indeed, that notion runs against the progressive Muslims' model of the fluid exchange of ideas and the acknowledging of a wide spectrum of interpretations. The following, therefore, represents my own reflections on being a progressive Muslim. Others in this volume would no doubt add many more items, and would perhaps take exception to some of my formulations.

ESSENTIAL CONCERNS OF PROGRESSIVE MUSLIMS

Engaging Tradition

Progressive Muslims insist on a serious engagement with the full spectrum of Islamic thought and practices. There can be no progressive Muslim movement that does not engage the very "stuff" (textual and material sources) of the Islamic tradition, even if some of us would wish to debate what "stuff" that should be and how it ought to be interpreted. The engagement with the weight of the tradition might be uneasy at times, occasionally inspiring, now and then tedious, and sometimes even painful. Still, we believe that it is imperative to work through inherited traditions of thought and practice. In particular cases, we might conclude that certain pre-existing interpretations fail to offer us sufficient guidance today. However, we can only faithfully claim that position after – and not before – a serious engagement with the tradition. To move beyond certain past interpretations of Islam, we have to go critically through them.

It is not difficult to find progressives from a Muslim background who tackle issues of social justice, disparate distribution of wealth, oppression of Muslim women, etc. However, it has been our experience that too often such activism lacks the necessary engagement with the specifics of Islamic tradition. Such programs for social reform could just as easily come from Christian, Jewish, Hindu, Buddhist, Secular Humanist, or agnostic progressives. Perhaps this partially explains why the progressive agenda has held little appeal for many Muslims worldwide, who have correctly detected that those who espouse these otherwise valuable teachings are simply giving an "Islamic veneer" to ideologies such as Marxism. Some have leveled charges in the past that Muslim voices speaking up for justice are simply parroting the secular ideology of socialism dressed up in Qur'an and *hadith*. To state the obvious, a progressive Muslim agenda has to be both progressive and Islamic, in the sense of deriving its inspiration from the heart of the Islamic tradition. It cannot survive as a graft of Secular Humanism onto the tree of Islam, but must emerge from within that very entity. It can receive and surely has received inspiration from other spiritual and political movements, but it must ultimately grow in the soil of Islam.

We hold that some interpretations of Islam in both the past and the present have been part of the problem. We also assert that ongoing interpretations and implementations of Islamic ethics guided by justice and pluralism can be part of the solution. To introduce an Islamic term, one might state that the progressive Muslim project represents an ongoing attempt at an Islamic *ijtihad*, or committed critical thinking based on disciplined but independent reasoning, to come up with solutions to new problems. This progressive ijtihad *is* our jihad. In the aftermath of September 11, 2001, the term "jihad" is all too familiar to most people. To both the Muslim fanatic and the Muslim-hating xenophobe, jihad is simply "holy war" declared by Muslims against Westerners. For the Muslim apologist, jihad is instead purely the inner struggle against one's own selfish tendencies. Neither interpretation takes into consideration the possibility of engaging and transforming the social order and the environment in a just and pluralistic fashion that affirms the humanity of us all.

It is vitally important to recognize that "jihad" is etymologically related to the concept of *ijtihad*. In Arabic, concepts that share the same triliteral etymological derivation are essentially linked to one another. "Jihad" and *ijtihad* both come from the root *ja-ha-da*, meaning "to strive," "to exert."[12] For progressive Muslims, a fundamental part of our struggle (*jihad*) to exorcise our inner demons and bring about justice in the world at large is to engage in a progressive and critical interpretation of Islam (*ijtihad*).

An essential part of the progressive *ijtihad* is to account for and challenge the great impoverishment of thought and spirit brought forth by Muslim literalist-exclusivists. Groups such as the Wahhabis have bulldozed over not just Sufi shrines and graveyards of the family of the Prophet in Arabia, but also whole structures of Islamic thought. As some of the essays in this volume – especially that by Khaled Abou El Fadl – make clear, there is an urgent need for progressive Muslims to problematize, resist, and finally replace the lifeless, narrow, exclusivist, and oppressive ideology that Wahhabism poses as Islam. I view Wahhabism – amplified by hundreds of billion dollars in petrodollars and supported by the same U.S. government that claims to support democracy and freedom in the Muslim world – as the single greatest source of the impoverishment of contemporary Islamic thought. Yet ours is not simply an "anti-Wahhabi" Islam. That would be to remain in the realm of the polemical and oppositional. There is no option of going back to the eighteenth century prior to the rise of the Wahhabis, nor would that be desirable. As with all other modes of injustice and oppression, we have to identify Wahhabism and oppose it before we can rise above it. This aspect of the progressive Muslim agenda yet again identifies the necessity of remaining engaged with the very stuff of Islam, past and present.

One should add here that Wahhabism is not the only brand of Islamic literalism-exclusivism, and our task as progressives is to resist all of them. In doing so, it is imperative for progressive Muslims to resist the oppressive ideology of Wahhabism, but equally important to avoid the trap of dehumanizing the Wahhabi-oriented human beings. If we dehumanize and demonize them, we have lost something valuable in our quest to acknowledge the humanity of all human beings. Gandhi was right: "It is quite proper to resist and attack a system, but to resist and attack its author is tantamount to resisting and attacking oneself, for we are all tarred with the same brush, and are children of one and the same Creator."[13] This is a great challenge.

Social justice

There have, of course, long been Christians, Jews, Buddhists, Hindus, agnostics, avowed atheists, and others involved in many social justice issues. Increasingly, they now find themselves standing shoulder to shoulder with new Muslim friends. The term "social justice" may be new to some contemporary Muslims, but what is not new is the theme of justice in Islam. Justice lies at the heart of Islamic social ethics. Time and again the Qur'an talks about providing for the marginalized members of society: the poor, the orphan, the downtrodden, the wayfarer, the hungry, etc.

It is time to "translate" the social ideals in the Qur'an and Islamic teachings in a way that those committed to social justice today can relate to and understand. We would do well to follow the lead of Shi'i Muslims who from the start have committed to standing up for the downtrodden and the oppressed. Everyone knows that Muslims have always stood for the theme of Divine unity. Yet how many people have also realized that the Mu'tazilites (who have greatly affected Shi'i understandings of Islam) so valued justice that they identified themselves as the folk of "Divine Unity *and* Justice" (*ahl al-tawhid wa 'l-'adl*)?[14] In the Sunni tradition, there is a vibrant memory of the Prophet repeatedly talking about how a real believer is one whose neighbor does not go to bed hungry. In today's global village, it is time to think of all of humanity as our neighbor. The time has come for us to be responsible for the well-being and dignity of all human beings if we wish to be counted as real believers. To borrow a metaphor from our Christian friends, we are all our brothers' and our sisters' keepers now.

The time has come to stand up and be counted. As Muslims and as human beings, we stand up to those who perpetuate hate in the name of Islam. We stand up to those whose God is a vengeful monster in the sky issuing death decrees against the Muslim and the non-Muslim alike. We stand up to those whose God is too small, too mean, too tribal, and too male. We stand up to those who apologetically claim that the beautiful notions of universal brotherhood and sisterhood in the Qur'an have somehow made Muslim societies immune to the ravages of classism, sexism, and racism. To all of these, we say: not in my name, not in the name of my God will you commit this hatred, this violence. We stand by the Qur'anic teaching (5:32) that to save the life of one human being is to have saved the life of all humanity, and to take the life of one human being is to have taken the life of all humanity. That which you do to my fellow human beings, you do to me.

And yet again we recall that ours is a multiple critique, one of engaging and challenging all the ideologies and institutions of injustice and inequality in the various communities in which we find ourselves. This means standing up to those who support and benefit from the Western hegemony over the rest of the world. The time has come for us to stand up to those who look at the world not as a single human family, but as "us" versus "them." The time has come to stand up to those who look down at others through an imperialist lens, those who favor a "globalization" that works to the exclusive benefit of multi-national corporations at the detriment of ordinary citizens. The time has come to stand up to those who proliferate the structures whereby five percent of the world's population consumes twenty-five percent of its resources, while tens of millions perish in agonizing starvation. The time has come to stand up to drug companies who clutch their patents of HIV drugs while untold millions die of AIDS in Africa and elsewhere. The time has come to stand up to those who are rightly outraged at the murder of innocent civilians in the U.S.A. and allied countries, but easily dismiss the murder of innocent civilians in other countries as "unfortunate collateral damage." To all of them, we say: not in my name will you commit these acts of violence that result in the death of so many innocents. That which you do to my fellow human beings you do to me.

The time has come, and that time is now. We cannot start committing to social justice tomorrow, because the tomorrow of social justice is the tomorrow of "I will lose fifteen pounds": it will never come. There is only today. We are, as the Sufis say, children of the present moment (*ibn al-waqt*). It is in this present moment we live, and in this present moment we have the choice to be fully human. It is for our decisions in this very present that we are held cosmically accountable, and will answer to God Almighty. Justice starts now, starts at this present moment, and it starts with each of us.

Gender Justice

Progressive Muslims begin with a simple yet radical stance: the Muslim community as a whole cannot achieve justice unless justice is guaranteed for Muslim women. In short, there can be no progressive interpretation of Islam without gender justice.

Let us be clear that by "gender" we are not just talking about women. Far too often Muslims forget that gender injustice is not just something that oppresses women, it also debases and dehumanizes the Muslim males who participate in the system.

Let us be clear that by "gender" we don't mean to focus exclusively on the *hijab* (head covering worn by some Muslim women). The hijab is, no doubt, one important marker of identity for many Muslim women who choose either to wear or not to wear it. It is also an important marker of social regulations when many Muslim women are forced to wear it. But it is futile to engage in conversations about gender that reduce all of women's religiosity and existence to the *hijab*. There are many more fundamental issues at stake in the social constructions that affect the lives of both men and women, and we aim here to engage many of them.

Some of the essays in this volume probe exactly what we mean by gender justice. The essays by Sa'diyya Shaikh, Zoharah Simmons, Scott Kugle, and Kecia Ali break new ground here. Muslim feminism is the radical notion that Muslim women are full human beings. The human and religious rights of Muslim women cannot be "granted," "given back," or "restored" because they were never ours to give – or take – in the first place. Muslim women *own* their God-given rights by the simple virtue of being human.

Gender justice is crucial, indispensable, and essential. In the long run, any progressive Muslim interpretation will be judged by the amount of change in gender equality it is able to produce in small and large communities. It is for this reason that I have placed "gender" as the lynchpin of our subtitle for the whole volume. Gender equality is a measuring stick of the broader concerns for social justice and pluralism.

No doubt this heavy emphasis on issues of gender – issues that far too many Muslims would rather shove under the rug, or at least deal with in the happy and unhappy confines of their own communities – will strike some as unbalanced. We are mindful of the ways in which conversations about gender are at the center of group dynamics and politics in Muslim communities. But it is way past the time to be squeamish.

There have of course been feminist movements in the Muslim world which have drawn inspiration largely from secular sources. Those movements have opened some doors, and we look to open still others. We strive for what should be legitimately recognized as Islamic feminism. If that strikes some people as an oxymoron, we unapologetically suggest that it is their definition of Islam that needs rethinking, not our linkage of Islam and feminism.

Pluralism

In 1967, Martin Luther King, Jr. published a monumental essay titled "Where Do We Go From Here: Chaos Or Community?" Dr. King ended this essay by stating. "We still have a choice today: nonviolent coexistence or violent coannihilation."[15] We too believe that as members of a single humanity, as people of faith, and as progressive Muslims, we have a choice, a choice we need to make today and every day.

Pluralism is the great challenge of the day not just for Muslims, but for all of humanity: can we find a way to celebrate our common humanity not in spite of our differences but *because* of them, through them, and beyond them? Can we learn to grow to the point where ultimately "we" refers not to an exclusivist grouping, but to what the Qur'an calls the *Bani Adam*, the totality of humanity?[16] Challenging, undermining, and overthrowing the pre-Islamic tribal custom of narrowly identifying oneself with those who trace themselves to the eponymous founder of a tribe, the Qur'an here describes all of humanity as members of one super-tribe, the human tribe. This is a great challenge, and yet what choice do we have but to rise up to meet it?

Can we live up to the challenge issued to us by the Prophet Muhammad, and rephrased so beautifully by the Persian poet Sa'di? Can we envision each other as members of one body, to feel the pain of another as our own? Only then will we be worthy of the name "human being."

> *Human beings are like members of one body*
> *created from one and the same essence.*
> *When one member feels pain,*
> *the rest are distraught.*
> *You, unmoved by the suffering of others,*
> *are unworthy of the name human!*[17]

These days, of course, a lack of pluralism goes far beyond simple disagreement. All too often, fanatic bigotry finds expression in brutal violence. At times, this violence is deployed by paramilitary terrorist groups. At other times, it is unleashed by nation-states and their armies. Along with the overwhelming majority of Muslims, progressive Muslims stand firmly against all attacks on civilians, whether that violence comes from a terrorist group or a nation-state. Does it matter to those who have lost loved ones whether the instrument of death was held by a terrorist or a state-sponsored army? The twentieth century was by far the bloodiest in the history of humanity. May it be that in the twenty-first century – admittedly already off to a rocky start – we find a path to pluralism and a peace rooted in justice. I am often inspired by the courageous words of Martin Luther King, Jr., who stated:

> *The ultimate weakness of violence is that it is a descending spiral, begetting the very thing it seeks to destroy.*

> *Instead of diminishing evil, it multiplies it... Through violence you may murder the hater, but you do not murder hate. In fact, violence merely increases hate....*

> *Returning violence for violence multiplies violence, adding deeper darkness to a night already devoid of stars. Darkness cannot drive out hate; only love can do that.*

Muslims no less prominent than the incomparable Rumi have also echoed this emphasis on nonviolence, "Washing away blood with blood is impossible, even absurd!"[18] The humane vision of pluralism articulated so eloquently above is a powerful issue for contemporary Muslims. It is no exaggeration to say that Muslims, for so long members of a pluralistic civilization that turned everyday interpersonal ethics into a choreographed exchange of civility, kindness, and generosity, are in real danger of losing their manners. It may seem odd to hear activists talk about the importance of manners, but I firmly hold that one of the most important measuring sticks of pluralism for us Muslims is the way that we treat each other. It is past time for us to restore the humaneness of interpersonal ethics (*adab*).

Years ago, I had the pleasure of running one of those errands that graduate students in top-notch university programs are called upon to perform: drive a famous speaker to the airport. The speaker in this case was the renowned French expert on religious fundamentalism, Gilles Kepel, who had just given a great lecture comparing Jewish, Christian, and Islamic fundamentalisms. We had some time before his plane took off, so we sat in a café at the airport, and talked for a while. He was reminiscing about his travels to many parts of the world, and his interactions with various Abrahamic fundamentalists. At one point he leaned over and said, "You know what all three groups have in common?" I feverishly raced through my mind to find the most up-to-date theoretical articulation, but fortunately decided to remain silent and yield to this wise expert. He leaned over and said (in a wonderfully thick French accent), "They all have such bad adab!"

Ah, adab... that most essential, basic, and glorious of Muslim interpersonal codes. Adab is the compassionate, humane, selfless, generous, and kind etiquette that has been a hallmark of refined manners in Muslim cultures. Almost anyone who has ever traveled to areas that have been profoundly influenced by Muslim ethics has no doubt seen great examples of this wonderful way of being welcomed and put at ease.

It is precisely this compassionate humaneness that is missing from so much of contemporary Islam. Sadly, some of us Muslims are often quite rude to one another: not only do we brand each other as infidels, we oppress each other, we also cut each other off in speech, and are quick to anger. Words like *kufr* (infidelity), *shirk* (associating partners with God, i.e. polytheism), and *bid'a* (heretical innovation) flow far too easily from our tongues. The finger that used to point up at the end of prayers towards the Heavens now points most frequently at another Muslim. That same index finger that used to be a reminder of Divine Unity (*tawhid*) is now a symbol of accusation and *takfir* (branding another an infidel). What we are losing in all of this incivility is our very humanity. Here again Gandhi had a keen observation: "As soon as we lose the moral basis, we cease to be religious. There is no such thing as religion over-riding morality."[19]

I suggest that this is one example where one of the strands of Islamic thought and practice, Sufism, has much to offer us. *Al-tasawwuf kulluhu al-adab*: All of Sufism is adab. Here I am not talking about formal initiation into Sufi orders, or elaborate cosmological speculations about the reflection of the loftiest heavenly realities in the very soul of humanity. Though there are many of us who are drawn to those aspects of Sufism as well, what I am pointing to here is something much simpler, and perhaps ultimately much more urgent. As much as any group of Muslims, the Sufis have attempted to cultivate this interpersonal ethic at a communal level, and we would do well to cherish their *adab* yet again.

There is a lovely story that I recall from my childhood, a tale told of the great Sufi master Bayazid Bistami. Bayazid's abode was flanked by a Zoroastrian (thus, non-Muslim) on one side, and a rather fanatical Muslim on the other. The Zoroastrian was quite fond of Bayazid and his gentle manners. The fanatic Muslim, on the other hand, never tired of bothering the Zoroastrian, and would periodically challenge him by saying, "If you like Bayazid so much, you should become Muslim!" One day the poor Zoroastrian snapped back,

"If being a Muslim is what Bayazid is,
then I am not worthy of that.

But if being a Muslim is what you are,
Then I don't want to be that!"

Part of pluralism is measured by openness to engage sources of compassion and wisdom, no matter where they originate. No less a figure than Hazrat 'Ali, the first Shi'i Imam and the fourth Sunni Caliph, has stated that one should evaluate a statement based on what it says, not who says it. The great Muslim philosopher al-Kindi stated, "We should not be ashamed to acknowledge truth and to assimilate it from whatever source it comes to us, even if it is brought to us by former generations and foreign peoples. For him who seeks the truth there is nothing of higher value than truth itself; it never cheapens or abases him who reaches for it, but ennobles and honors him."[20] At times it is easier to hear first other wisdom traditions that have elaborated on certain themes before returning "home" to seek out long marginalized and exiled sub-traditions. Studying Christian liberation theology, for example, might ultimately help us recover voices that speak out on behalf of the oppressed in Islam. Taking a close look at Taoist teachings might remind us of long-forgotten Islamic teachings on the necessity of living in harmony with nature. I am not here talking about becoming a liberation theologian of Christianity, or a Taoist. Rather, we sometimes need a refresher course to remind us that such concerns have also been part of the spectrum of interpretation in Islamic thought. Our task could then consist of bringing back to the foreground concerns that have fallen off the radar, so to speak.

Living in the twenty-first century, I urge Muslims to consider that it is no longer sufficient to study only the Qur'an and *hadith*. In addition to those essential founts of wisdom, we need to be conversant with Rumi and Ibn al-'Arabi, Plato and Ibn Sina, Ghazzali and Hazrat 'Ali, Chomsky and Abu Dharr, Gandhi and Arundhati Roy, Rabi'a and Maya Angelou, Robert Fisk and Edward Said, His Holiness the Dalai Lama and Elie Wiesel, Martin Luther King, Jr. and Malcolm X, Sa'di and Hafez, Qawwals of South Asia and Eqbal Ahmed, and of course Bob Dylan and Bob Marley.[21] A friend was joking with me about the above, saying that we are all going to need bigger desks, bigger book shelves, bigger CD cases, bigger mp3 files.... Yes, all these things must be expanded. And bigger hearts, and bigger intellects too. As big as humanity.

IS THIS AN "ISLAMIC REFORMATION"?

When confronted with the challenging issues that we engage in this volume, some people have asked us if we envision this as a sort of "Islamic reformation." The question is usually asked seriously, and it deserves a serious answer. The answer is both yes and no.

There are progressive Muslims, like the courageous scholar Abdullahi an-Na'im, who argue passionately for the usefulness of the term "Islamic reformation."[22] It is undeniably true that there are serious economic, social, and political issues in the Muslim world that need urgent remedying. It is equally true that these changes will take time, and it is also likely that they will be extremely difficult to achieve, as the recent experiences of the courageous reformers in Iran so amply demonstrates. Much of the Muslim world is bound to a deeply disturbing economic structure in which it provides natural resources (most importantly in the Middle East, of course, oil) for the global market, while at the same time remaining dependent on Western labor, technological know-how, and staple goods. This economic situation is exacerbated in many parts of the modern Muslim world by atrocious human rights situations, crumbling educational systems, and worn out economies. If one is talking about a reformation that would address all of those levels, then I would suspect that most progressive Muslims would readily support that usage of the term.

However, at least in some people's usage the term "reformation" carries considerably more baggage than that. Based on these connotations, there are good reasons to resist the language of "Islamic reformation." In speaking of the "Islamic reformation," many people have in mind the Protestant Reformation, initiated by Martin Luther. It is this understanding that leaves many of us uneasy. Ours is not a project of developing a "Protestant" Islam distinct from a "Catholic" Islam. I for one am very dubious about thinking that other religious traditions (in this case Islam) must necessarily follow the historical and cultural course of action laid out by the Christian tradition. Many of us insist that we are not looking to create a further split within the Muslim community so much as to heal it and to urge it along. Furthermore, embedded in the very language of "Reformation" is the notion of a significant break with the past. I would suggest that the progressive Muslim project is not so much an epistemological rupture from what has come before as a fine-tuning, a polishing, a grooming, an editing, a re-emphasizing of this and a correction of that. In short, it is a critical engagement with the heritage of Islamic thought, rather than a casual bypassing of its accomplishments. In some of the essays in this volume you will notice authors spending a great deal of time working through passages of the Qur'an, medieval legal texts, political philosophers, and contemporary writings. It might be an easier task to start with a *tabula rasa*, but that would not be an Islamic project. Being a progressive Muslim, at least in the view of this group, mandates a difficult, onerous, critical, uneasy engagement with the tradition.

None of the attempts to add nuance to the term "reformation" has prevented some members of the media from using the term to describe certain Muslim progressives. One, the Iranian progressive Muslim thinker Abdolkarim Soroush, was even branded the Iranian Luther![23] Comments like this tell us a great deal about the reporters who create such leaps of logic, revealing their fanciful wishes that a single intellectual can (as the title of the above article on Soroush reads) "shake the foundations of Islam." At least in our group of progressive Muslims, there are no would-be Luthers. There *are*, however, Ebrahim Moosa and Zohara Simmons, Sa'diyya Shaikh and Farish Noor, etc., and that is what matters here. Let us engage issues, not attempt to mold one another into the shape of long dead icons.

There is one other reason that I do not favor the language of "Islamic reformation." Not long ago, I was asked to give a talk on Islamic aesthetics at a leading liberal arts college in North America. After a wonderful reception from the audience, the talk turned – as it invariably does – to contemporary politics, and more specifically to the agenda that progressive Muslims might have to offer as a way forward. A well-intentioned person in the audience asked what I thought of the fact that many economic and social factors (rise of the middle class, increase in literacy, etc.) had to be in place *before* the Protestant Reformation could occur in Europe. The answer came clear to my heart: we cannot wait. There are clearly far too many places in the Muslim world that suffer from an appalling lack of literacy, huge and ever-growing socio-economic gaps between the "haves" and the "have nots," political tyranny, religious exclusivism, gender injustice, etc. In some cases, prognosticators have predicted that it may take decades, if not centuries, for the Muslim world to "catch up." As progressive Muslims, we simply cannot wait. We do not have the luxury of sitting idly by in the vague hope that changes will take place *before* we start dealing with these difficult issues. In my reading of the Qur'anic call, we are all held accountable by God for the opportunities we are given in this life, and asked to answer for how we responded to them. Our responsibility of *khilafa* (vicegerency, stewardship) deals with the here and now, not twenty years from now, not two hundred years. We are children of this moment (*ibn al-waqt*), and have to work within the societies in which God has placed us.

Having gone into some depth about the salient features of progressive Muslims, let me also take some time to describe what progressive Muslims are not about.

PROBLEMS WITH THE TERM "PROGRESSIVE"

Since I know some are going to make this same criticism, let me beat them to the punch. All of us who have contributed to this volume realize that the term "progressive" Muslim is far from perfect. Let us be honest, and admit that it has been a very abused term.

The real issue with "progressive," of course, is that problematic "progress" embedded so deeply in it. Progress towards what, one may ask? Progress has all too often been conceived of as a Hegelian, unilateral march towards post-Enlightenment, rational, male, Euro-American civilization. Wasn't the twentieth century allegedly the century of progress? While no doubt it witnessed the rise of many technological wonders, it also turned out to be among the most hateful and bloody in human history.

In the past 150 years of Islamic thought, a number of people have called for a whole host of "reform"- and "progress"-oriented interpretations of Islam, but in many cases these have proven to be nothing more – nor less – than a simple aping of the most recent Western trends. Furthermore, the term "progressive," at least in the minds of some people, has a slightly elitist connotation, implying that the "progressives" are somehow better, smarter, or more advanced than the alleged "non-progressives."

So why use the term? Can't we find something better? Well, actually we tried. Unfortunately, none of the alternatives was totally problem-free.

Some suggested the label "liberal Muslim." It is certainly true that on many social issues most of us find ourselves on the "left," so to speak. But many progressive Muslims also do not agree with the connotation of liberal as "loose, not strict," as if progressives are only *loosely* Muslim, and they can be progressive only because they are not *strictly* following Islamic teachings. Furthermore, in our view many self-declared "liberal Muslims" have been too enamored with modernity, too eager to identify themselves wholeheartedly with European and American structures of power. In the end, they have proven unable and unwilling to adopt a critical stance against the injustices of *both* Muslim societies *and* Western hegemony. It is precisely such a critical stance that we have identified here as multiple critique.

Another suggestion was "critical Muslims," which has the great appeal of calling attention to the desperate need for critical thought. The problem is that in many non-academic circles, the term "critical" is taken to refer to those who criticize. It is certainly true that we critique many contemporary and historical

Islamic practices and interpretations, but we always do so with an eye toward more just and pluralistic alternatives. "Critical Muslims" can sound like a bunch of whiners who sit around and complain. For some, the term "critical Muslim" also implies pontificating about Islam without the attempt to change realities in Muslim societies on the ground level.

It is not just that the other terms had problems. There is something about this term "progressive." It is more than anything else an umbrella term that signifies an invitation to those who want an open and safe space to undertake a rigorous, honest, potentially difficult engagement with tradition, and yet remain hopeful that conversation will lead to further action.

We felt adamant that the title of this work should be "Progressive Muslims," and not "Progressive Islam." The distinction may be irrelevant to some, but it matters a great deal to us. On one hand, as one of the contributors to this volume has stated, "Islam has always been progressive. It is Muslims that have not always been so." On the other hand, we are also wary of falling into the easy dichotomy of "I love Islam, it is those darn Muslims that I have a problem with." For better or worse, in truth and ignorance, in beauty and hideousness, we call for an engagement with real live human beings who mark themselves as Muslims, not an idealized notion of Islam that can be talked about apart from engagement with those real live human beings. Even if we take Islam in the most ordinary sense of submission to the Divine, there can be no Islam without the humanity who is doing the submitting. Take humanity out of the equation, and all we are left with is the God who stands prior to and beyond Creation. About that understanding of God no human being is perhaps qualified to speak, since for them to speak they would have to exist, thus implying by necessity the very act of creation. But in terms of a relationship between humanity and the Divine, Islam cannot be interpreted, experienced, or articulated without engaging with real live human beings. To keep the focus on the responsibilities of human beings, we have titled this volume "Progressive Muslims," rather than "Progressive Islam."

WHERE DID THIS PARTICULAR GROUP OF PROGRESSIVE MUSLIMS COME FROM?

The volume you hold in your hand is the result of almost an entire year of conversation, dialogue, and debate among the fifteen contributors. It had its real genesis in the aftermath of September 11, 2001, in what we saw as the urgent need to raise the level of conversation, and to get away from the standard apologetic presentations of Islam. During the past year, we have exchanged some six hundred email messages and spent countless hours on the telephone in an effort to harmonize our endeavors.

One of the key points about this volume is that it represents Muslim intellectuals and activists whose understanding of Islam has been shaped by the academic study of Islam in Western institutions. To understand the significance of this point, it is important to recognize the wider ramifications for the Muslim world of the decline of the traditional Islamic universities (*madrasas*).

One of the real challenges facing Muslim communities around the world has been the marked decline of the madrasa system. Many scholars have directly attributed this decline to the impact of European colonialism, positing that the colonial system undermined the relevance and prestige of Islamic education in favor of more technological and scientific institutions. In places like North Africa, the colonial powers actually shut down some of the most prestigious institutions of higher Islamic learning. This much is certainly clear: in many places around the Muslim world, madrasa institutions are no longer the center of creative, critical thinking. In the pre-modern world, the very brightest Muslim minds (at least the male ones, since the females were usually relegated to education at home[24]) were to be found in the madrasas. The traditional curriculum was based on the memorization of the foundational texts (Qur'an, etc.), and learning the rigorous methodology by which one could arrive at a religious opinion. How strange it must seem to many modern Muslims to read a pre-modern theologian like Ghazzali offer an opinion in such a fashion: The following group holds this opinion, while group 2 states something to the contrary. Group 3 is still different, holding to such-and-such a belief, while group 4 follows this practice. As for myself (i.e., Ghazzali himself), I find myself in accordance with the views of the third group.

How refreshing! How intellectually honest, to summarize the perspectives of various schools of thought, to legitimize a range of opinions and to acknowledge a spectrum of interpretations! It is then, and only then, that a learned scholar like Ghazzali would situate himself in that wider spectrum. Such a willingness to undertake self-positioning may not have been the norm, but it was utilized by some of the leading pre-modern Muslim thinkers. How different is this attitude from so many contemporary Muslim pundits who hijack an entire tradition, claiming to be a one-man (and it is almost always a man) spokesperson for all Muslims: "Islam states...." No debate, no discussion, no spectrum of perspectives. The Almighty Islam has spoken, or so we are told, and the conversation is over.

It is above all the rigor displayed by pre-modern thinkers like Ghazzali that is sorely missing from contemporary madrasa training. With few exceptions (Iran, for example), the brightest minds in the Muslim world are no longer found in madrasas. Instead, they are training to be doctors, engineers, computer scientists, and lawyers. Good for them. And bad for us. It is a sad reality that in many places in the Muslim world, the madrasas now attract many of the weaker students who could not make it into more competitive schools of higher education. In other places, such as Pakistan, many of these madrasas have become at best institutions of social welfare providing free room and board, and at worst a breeding ground for the most virulent type of fanaticism.

The decline of the traditional Islamic educational system has had another important consequence: many of the leading Muslim intellectuals in the world today have achieved their intellectual and spiritual understanding of Islam largely outside the traditional madrasa curriculum. That is certainly the case for the contributors to this volume. While a few of us (Ebrahim Moosa, Khaled Abou El Fadl, and Farid Esack) have studied in traditional madrasas, all of us have grown in our understanding of Islam through Ph.D. programs in Islamic studies at Western (or Western-style) universities. Without the benefit of a traditional madrasa curriculum, there are surely some limitations to our arguments. No doubt there are many advantages as well, since we have enjoyed the room and latitude to approach old problems from new perspectives. In a real sense, lay Muslim intellectuals and activists are now stepping into the vacuum created by the marginalization of the traditional Islamic madrasas. This is particularly the case given that many of the products of the contemporary madrasa system have failed to address issues of social justice, pluralism, and gender justice.

Yet the same gap that in a sense has created room for us also makes our task much more difficult. So many contemporary conversations about Islam in the crucial realms of law and theology would be laughed out of any medieval madrasa, with the accusations of superficiality and lack of rigor. As Khaled Abou El Fadl has pointed out, this has also resulted in a situation where pseudo-scholars and quasi-muftis now issue "Islamic verdicts" that often follow authoritarian tendencies. Examples could include Osama bin Laden's *fatwa* calling for the murder of American civilians. All of this makes the task of progressives speaking as contemporary Muslims to both Muslims and non-Muslims alike much more difficult.

PROGRESSIVES SPEAKING AS CONTEMPORARY MUSLIMS

So now we have some notion of what progressives are and are not. But precisely how is their version of talking different from other Muslim discourses? Let me offer a few key features.

Beyond apologetics

Here is a newsflash, courtesy of progressive Muslims: God is doing just fine. God doesn't need any help. God doesn't need any defenders. It is humanity that needs help, especially the oppressed, the downtrodden, the marginalized, and the all-but-forgotten who desperately need champions and advocates.

I bring this up to underscore that being a progressive Muslim means self-consciously moving beyond apologetic presentations of Islam. Our apologism does God no good, and it solves none of our real problems. And it is no exaggeration to say that the overwhelming majority of writings that dominate Islamic centers fall into the realm of apologetics. Why do apologetic writings hold such appeal to religious folks, including Muslims?

The past few years have been a challenging time for nearly all people of faith. For Muslims, this has meant an urgent imperative to define what we stand for and, just as importantly, what we reject. For Catholics, it has meant coming to terms with the catastrophic sexual abuses in the Church. For Jews and Hindus, it has meant confronting the brutal violence committed or tolerated by nation-states that claim to represent them. It has been a time of a great deal of vocal but vexing public conversation about all religions, including Islam.

Part of the challenge is to recognize that there are many ways of talking about all religions, including Islam, in the public sphere. Two of them seem to have gained prominence in the post-9/11 world. One level is the normative, theological way, when self-designated (or selected) representatives speak with the weight of authority, and feel perfectly entitled to make statements like "Catholicism states...," "Judaism teaches us that...," and of course, "Islam states...." The other way of talking about religion is more historical and descriptive, less theological, and more people centered. The followers of this perspective are likely to say, "This Jewish group practices the following ritual, while other Jewish groups practice otherwise..."; "These Muslim groups hold this interpretation of *jihad*, while their interpretations are opposed by the following groups..."

I find myself increasingly on the side of the second way of talking. Regarding many issues, the majority of Muslim scholars have formed a clear enough consensus *(ijma')* to allow us to speak of near unanimity. On other issues – precisely those that many contemporary Muslims and non-Muslims would be interested in hearing about and debating – there has been and remains a wide range of interpretations and practices among Muslim scholars and within Muslim communities. Our task as progressive Muslims is to begin by honestly chronicling the spectrum of Muslim practices and interpretations for both ourselves and society at large. We cannot and should not single out only sublime examples that are likely to be palatable to a non-Muslim public, just as we would not want the xenophobes to focus exclusively on the fanatical fringe of Muslim societies. It is imperative for all of us to demonstrate the full spectrum of interpretations, particularly in dealing with the "difficult" issues (gender constructions, violence, pluralism, etc.).

Furthermore, I find myself being less and less patient and satisfied with assertions that "Islam teaches us..." This seems to me to be an attempt to bypass the role of Muslims in articulating this thing called Islam. Let me be clear, and perhaps controversial here: "Islam" as such teaches us nothing. The Prophet Muhammad does. Interpretive communities do. I would argue that God does, through the text of the Qur'an. But in the case of texts, there are human beings who read them, interpret them, and expound their meanings. Even our encounter with the Prophet is driven by different (and competing) textual presentations of his life, teachings, and legacy.[25] In all cases, the dissemination of Divine teachings is achieved through human agency. Religion is always mediated. To drive this message home, I usually offer this intentionally irreverent comment to my students: "Islam" does not get up in the morning. Islam does not brush its teeth. Islam does not take a shower. Islam eats nothing. And perhaps most importantly for our consideration, Islam *says* nothing. *Muslims* do. Muslims get up in the morning, Muslims brush their teeth, Muslims shower, Muslims eat, and Muslims speak.

Is this just semantics? I do not believe so. My experience, at the level of both devotional and academic communities, has been that many people simply ascribe their own (or their own community's) interpretations of Islam to "Islam says..." They use such authoritative – and authoritarian – language as a way to close the door on discussion. And closing discussions is something that we cannot afford.[26]

No more "Pamphlet Islam"

Walk into any Islamic center, and there is likely to be a table in the hallway or in the library that features a wide selection of pamphlets. The pamphlets bear titles like "The Status of Women in Islam," "Concept of God in Islam," "Concept of Worship in Islam." Printed in pale yellow, pink, and green shades, they promise truth in black and white. I hate these pamphlets.

I think we are in imminent danger – if we are not there already – of succumbing to "pamphlet Islam," the serious intellectual and spiritual fallacy of thinking that complex issues can be handled in four or six glossy pages. They simply cannot. The issues involved are far too complicated, and the human beings who frame the issues are even more so. I recently saw a bumper sticker that proclaimed, "Islam is the answer." If Islam is the answer, pray tell, what is the question? Modernity? Existence? God?

A few years ago, when I started teaching at an undergraduate college in New York, I was the only Muslim faculty member there. I was predictably appointed as the advisor to the small group of Muslim students on campus. There were about six of them at that time, vastly outnumbered by the other students on campus whom the Muslim students (perhaps rightly) considered to be woefully ignorant of even the basics of Islam. As we went around introducing ourselves, one of the students in the group gushed: "What I love about Islam is that it is so simple!" That comment spurred a great debate, which we are still having four years later. To me, Islam has never been simple. I remember having worked my way through some of the most important Muslim primary sources such as Ghazzali's *Ihya'* and Rumi's *Masnavi*, as well as the masterpieces of scholarship on Islam like Marshall Hodgson's *The Venture of Islam* and Harry Wolfson's *The Philosophy of Kalam*. "Simple" is not exactly a word that comes to mind in describing any of them.

"Islam is simple" is a slogan used all too often as an excuse to avoid discussion, disputation, and even disagreement. After all, if Islam is simple, how can reasonable and intelligent people disagree over it? Do these disagreements occur because some are deluded away from the simple truth? Not so! Islam is not simple because Muslims are not simple. Surely our identities in these virulent and turbulent post-colonial times are far from simple. Muslims are every bit – not an ounce more, and not an ounce less – as complicated as all of the other members of humanity. We argue, we discuss, we disagree, we joke, we laugh, we walk away mad, we come back, we compromise. But we do not, have not ever, and will not ever all agree on one interpretation of Islam.

This is why I so dislike "pamphlet Islam" – and what seems to be taking its place now, "web Islam."[27] I do not want to hear about Islam from an authoritarian who hides his or her own views under a grand title like "The Islamic Position on Jesus." I would prefer each author to tell me about her or his own position, identify his or her own argument and sources, and mention where they fit in a wider intellectual spectrum. When I mentioned this to some intellectual friends, they replied, "You have become too corrupted by post-modern thinking. That type of self-positioning only comes up in late modernity." Is that so? I do not dispute that many schools of anthropology, post-colonial theory, and feminist hermeneutics have advocated such self-positioning. Indeed, many of us progressive Muslims have benefited from the fruits of those disciplines. But this self-positioning also seems to me to be one of the characteristic markers of the writings of many, though not all, pre-modern Muslim scholars like the famed Ghazzali.

We can do better than "pamphlet Islam." We must. From time to time, of course, there is a need for concise articulation of Islam for ourselves and others. But let us do it honestly, without burying the dazzling array of interpretations that have always existed in Muslim thought and life.

Let me demonstrate how urgent a non-apologetic, progressive presentation of Islam can be by tackling two of the most pressing issues that have dominated the public discourse on religions in general and Islam in particular: the need for tolerance, and the positing of Islam as a religion of peace.

Islam beyond "tolerance"

Since September 11, 2001, we have been told time and again that our task as global citizens is to increase tolerance towards one another and to achieve a more tolerant society. Many Muslims have also emphasized that there are great strands of tolerance in Islam that must be articulated more clearly.

I beg to differ. I am not interested in teaching or preaching "tolerance." Naturally I don't want to see us kill and oppress each other. But words are powerful vehicles in shaping our thoughts, and there are often many layers of meaning embedded in words. The connotations of "tolerance" are deeply problematic. Allow me to elaborate this point: the root of the term "tolerance" comes from medieval toxicology and pharmacology, marking how much poison a body could "tolerate" before it would succumb to death. Is this the best that we can do? Is our task to figure out how many "others" (be they Muslims, Jews, blacks, Hindus, homosexuals, non-English speakers, Asians, etc.) we can *tolerate* before it really kills us? Is this the most sublime height of pluralism that we can aspire to? I don't want to "tolerate" my fellow human beings, but rather to engage them at the deepest level of what makes us human, through both our phenomenal commonality and our dazzling cultural differences. If we are to have any hope of achieving anything resembling a just peace in the future, that examination needs to include both the greatest accomplishments of all civilizations, and also a painful scrutiny of ways in which the place of privilege has come at a great cost to others. That goes equally for both the Islamic civilization and for the Western powers of today.

In short, progressive Muslims do not wish for a "tolerant" Islam, any more than we long for a "tolerant" American or European society. Rather, we seek to bring about a pluralistic society in which we honor and engage each other through our differences and our commonalities.

Islam beyond "religion of peace"

After September 11, 2001, almost every Muslim I know, including myself on a number of occasions, found himself or herself repeating something akin to this phrase: "Islam is a religion of peace. The actions of these terrorists do not represent real Islam." And yet for some reason, I – speaking not on behalf of any other progressive Muslims, just myself – am less and less satisfied with this mantra.

Let me be clear here: at a fundamental level, I believe that the Islamic tradition offers a path to peace, both in the heart of the individual and in the world at large, when the Islamic imperatives for social justice are followed. Yet there is something pathetically apologetic about turning the phrase "Islam is a religion of peace" into a mantra. It is bad enough to hear Muslim spokespersons repeat it so often while lacking the courage to face the forces of extremism in our own midst. It is just as bad to hear a United States President reassure us that he respects Islam as a "religion of peace" as he prepares to bomb Muslims in Afghanistan and Iraq, or support the brutal oppression of Palestinians. In both of the above senses, "Islam is a religion of peace" has become to my ears a hollow phrase, full of apologism and hypocrisy.

As Muslims, we owe it to ourselves to come to terms with the problems inside our own communities. All societies have their beautiful and noble citizens, along with their share of hateful and extremist ones. Muslims are human, not an ounce less and not an ounce more than any other people. We too have our saints and sinners, our fanatical zealots and compassionate exemplars. At this stage of history our primary responsibility is to come to terms with the oppressive tyrants and fanatics inside our own communities, our own families, and our own hearts. Hiding behind the simple assertion that "Islam is a religion of peace" does not solve our problems.

There is another reason that I have come to detest this slogan. It seems to me that we have lost sight of the real meaning of "peace," just as we have lost a real sense of "war." Many have come to think of peace as simply the absence of war, or at least the absence of violent conflict. Yet, as progressives, we must preserve the possibility of upholding resistance to well-entrenched systems of inequality and injustice through non-violent conflict. This is one of the great challenges of our time: affirming the right of a people who have been dehumanized and oppressed to resist, while encouraging them to do so non-violently. This is a great challenge indeed.

The very concept of "peace" can be and has been co-opted and adopted by hegemonic powers to preserve the unjust *status quo*, as we have seen in both Israel and apartheid-era South Africa. At times like this, a progressive can and perhaps must reject the superficial appeals of an unjust peace, and insist instead on a peace that is rooted in justice. This is precisely the sentiment echoed by His Holiness the Dalai Lama. In his Nobel Peace Prize lecture, he stated, "Peace, in the sense of the absence of war, is of little value to someone who is dying of hunger or cold ... Peace can only last where human rights are respected, where the people are fed, and where individuals and nations are free."[28] Similarly, Bob Marley's former partner in reggae, Peter Tosh, sang, "We don't want no peace – we want equal rights and justice!" Marley himself sang a powerful song called "War," which captures this sense well. In the lyrics below, "war" is seen as more than a violent military conflict. It is, rather, a declaration that one will fight systems of prejudice, injustice, and inequality.

> *Until the philosophy which holds one race superior*
> *and another inferior*
> *is finally and permanently*
> *discredited and abandoned –*
> *Everywhere is war –*
> *Me say war.*

> *That until there is no longer*
> *first class and second class citizens of any nation*
> *until the colour of a man's skin*
> *is of no more significance than the colour of his eyes –*
> *Me say war.*

> *That until the basic human rights*
> *are equally guaranteed to all,*
> *without regard to race –*
> *Dis a war.*

That until that day
the dream of lasting peace,
world citizenship
rule of international morality
will remain in but a fleeting illusion
to be pursued, but never attained –
Now everywhere is war – war.[29]

The statement that "Islam is a religion of peace" must not be allowed to become a license to avoid dealing with the grinding realities of social, political, and spiritual injustice on the ground level. To do so is to sell out our humanity, and to abandon our cosmic duty to embody the Qur'anic call for implementing justice (*'adl*) and realizing goodness-and-beauty (*ihsan*). Our great challenge as progressive Muslims is to find a non-violent means of resisting the powers that be, and to speak truth to them. At the same time, we must aim to bring about a just and pluralistic society in which all of us can live and breathe, and realize the God-given dignity to which we are entitled as human beings. We do not *grant* this dignity to one another: it belongs to all of us simply because, as the Qur'an teaches us, all of us have the Divine spirit breathed into us.

CONCLUSION

It is superficial to talk about a conclusion to the progressive Muslim project, since it is clearly only at its beginning. Yet let me offer a final thought here: in the visionary song that frames this essay, Bob Dylan talks about how the "waters around you have grown." The Qur'an likewise talks about a prophet, Noah, who found his community surrounded by rapidly rising waters. Like Noah, we must accept that we will soon be drenched to the bone. And like Noah, we repeat the prayer:

wa qul rabbi: anzilni munzalan mubarakan,
wa anta khayru 'l-munzilin
And say: "O My Lord, lead me to a blessed landing,
for you are best of deliverers."[30]

Let us remember that Noah's task did not end when he got on the ark, but continued after he landed on the ground. We ask God to lead us to a blessed landing station, one from which our work will continue. The road *there* starts here, at this very moment, with every one of us.

   May we all have the courage, the vision, and the compassion to heal this fractured world.[31]

Wa ilayhi raji'un
"And we are perpetually returning to God"

ENDNOTES

*I am deeply grateful to all the friends who have looked over this essay in its various incarnations, and provided me with invaluable suggestions for refining it. Rob Rozehnal took time out of a very busy phase of his life to unselfishly provide me with not one but two sets of comments. Kecia Ali, Scott Kugle, Tara van Brederode, and Tazim Kassam all provided very insightful feedback. Nasrollah Pourjavady graciously pointed out the quotes from Rumi's *Masnavi* and Hazrat 'Ali. Their friendship and kindness is a constant reminder of the fact that none of us walks alone on this path.

1. Lyrics are from Bob Dylan's official web site, http://www.bobdylan.com/. This song appeared in Dylan's 1964 album, also titled *The Times They Are A-Changin'.* That version is classic, revolutionary, and powerful. Also worth listening to is the more tender live version on Dylan's *The Bootleg Series, Vols. 1–3* (released 1991). In the second version Dylan sings, "If your spirit to you is worth savin'. . . ."
2. I am here indebted to miriam cooke's discussion of "multiple critique" in her insightful work *Women Claim Islam: Creating Islamic Feminism through Literature* (New York: Routledge, 2000). Sa'diyya Shaikh's essay in this volume also brings up this concept, and I am grateful to both of them.
3. Wahhabism is a reactionary theological movement that originated in eighteenth-century Arabia. It remained an undistinguished intellectual movement for a long time, until it was adapted as the ideology of the ruling Sa'ud family, who came upon the incredible wealth of oil resources. Subsequently, this previously trivial ideology was armed with the financial resources to export its vision all over the Muslim world. The essay by Khaled Abou El Fadl in this collection is very useful in demonstrating the ways in which Wahhabism and Salafi reformist movements have not always been in agreement, although many tend to conflate the two today. For more information on Wahhabism, refer to Ahmad Dallal, "The Origins and Objectives of Islamic Revivalist Thought, 1750–1850," *Journal of the American Oriental Society* 113 (3), 1993, 341–59; Michael Cook, "On the Origins of Wahhabism," *Journal of the Royal Asiatic Society* 3(2), 1992, 191–202; and Hamid Algar, *Wahhabism: A Critical Essay* (Oneonta: Islamic Publications International, 2002).
4. "North" and "South" evoke the language of those who point out the hypocrisy and injustice of the global inequalities in the distribution of resources and consumption. The "North" represents those who consume more than their fair share, at the expense of the "South." Many have favored using this terminology in place of the explicitly hierarchical language of "First World" and "Third World" (as if there is more than one world), or other euphemisms like "developed" and "underdeveloped" countries (as if "development" is unequivocal, or quintessentially positive).
5. As the Qur'an states in two separate passages, *wa nafakhtu fihi min ruhi.* God states, "I breathed into humanity something of My own spirit." (Qur'an 15:29 and 38:72)
6. Post-modern critiques of modernity were developed in a whole range of academic disciplines, including feminist scholarship, anthropology, literary criticism, and post-colonial studies. The corpus of post-modern scholarship is truly vast, and often bewildering. A good starting point is the collection of essays by Habermas, Lyotard, Jameson, Eco, Rorty, and others in Thomas Docherty, ed., *Postmodernism: A Reader* (Columbia: Columbia University Press, 1992). Also useful is Ania Loomba, *Colonialism/ Postcolonialism* (New York: Routledge, 1998).
7. Shalu Bhalla, *Quotes of Gandhi* (New Delhi: UBS Publishers, 1995), 143.
8. *The National Security Strategy of the United States of America,* released by the White House of George W. Bush in September 2002. Available on-line at: http://www.whitehouse.gov/ nsc/nss.pdf.
9. I have deliberately avoided the term "fundamentalist," since that term is open to so many interpretations and abuses. The groups that I address here combine a literal reading of

select texts with an exclusivist understanding to arrive at what in any other time in Islamic history would be seen as an extreme position on the spectrum of Islamic interpretations. Yet, contrary to what is often stated, their response is also a distinctly modern one, in the sense that it requires modernity as a foil against which it articulates itself. It is not, as its advocates might claim, simply "traditional," or "the way things have always been." Living as we do in these terrible days of Islam-phobia, it is important to point out that just as is the case in the Christian and Jewish traditions, one can be a literalist-exclusivist without necessarily resorting to violence. To put it in a shorthand fashion, not every Wahhabi (or Jama'at Islami) is a terrorist. However, the communal enforcement of literalist-exclusivist ideologies such as Wahhabism so dehumanize entire groups both inside and outside the Muslim community that they narrow the gap to violence against both other Muslims and non-Muslims. So many places in the Muslim world where violence is a fact of life also feature these literalist-exclusivist interpretations of Islam.

10. For insightful reflections on tradition and modernity as related epistemic fields rather than binary oppositions, see Marilyn Robinson Waldman, "Tradition as a Modality of Change: Islamic Examples," *History of Religions* 25, 1986, 318–40; Daniel Brown, *Rethinking Tradition in Modern Islamic Thought* (Cambridge: Cambridge University Press, 1996).

11. Rabbi Zalman Schachter, cited in Roger Kamenetz, *The Jew in the Lotus* (San Francisco: HarperSanFrancisco,1994), 43. I am deeply grateful to Reb Zalman for reminding me in a conversation that as one commits to undertaking the transformation and reformation of the social and spiritual order, it is also necessary to mourn the injustices that we have willingly and unwillingly participated in. Failure to do so always runs the risk of reformers getting caught in arrogance and self-righteousness.

12. In Arabic, as in other Semitic languages, most nouns are based on a triliteral root system which is then applied to different forms to yield slightly different shades of meaning. Both *jihad* and *ijtihad* come from the triliteral root *ja-ha-da.*

13. *Quotes of Gandhi,* 99.

14. It is significant that in this Mu'tazili interpretation, '*adl* did not stand for an abstract principle of justice, but rather was seen as being directly related to human free will. If human beings were not free to choose between good and evil, then God would be unjust in punishing us for actions that we are not ultimately responsible for. See W. Montgomery Watt, *The Formative Period of Islamic Thought* (Oxford: Oneworld, 1998), 231.

15. Martin Luther King, Jr., "Where Do We Go from Here: Chaos or Community," in *A Testament of Hope: The Essential Writings and Speeches of Martin Luther King, Jr.*, ed. James M. Washington (San Francisco: HarperSanFrancisco, 1986; reprint, 1991), 633.

16. The Qur'an uses the phrase *bani adam*, literally "children of Adam," on at least seven separate occasions to refer to the totality of humanity: 7:26, 7:27, 7:31, 7:35, 7:172, 17:70, and 36:60. "Thus we have honored the children of Adam..."

17. *The Rose Garden.* Shaykh Muslih al-Din Sa'di, *Gulistan*, ed. Muhammad Khaza'ili (Tehran: Intisharat-i Javidan, 1361/1982), 190. Translation is mine.

18. Mawlana Jalal al-Din Balkhi Rumi, *Masnavi-yi Ma'navi*, ed. R.A. Nicholson (Tehran: Intisharat-i Nigah, 1371/1992), 532. This line is found in the third book of the Masnavi, line 4726 of the Nicholson Persian edition.

19. *Quotes of Gandhi,* 25.

20. Translation is from R. Walzer, "Islamic Philosophy," cited in Seyyed Hossein Nasr, *Three Muslim Sages* (Delmar, NY: Caravan, 1964), 11. This same sentiment is echoed by many other Muslim philosophers.

21. Only half jokingly, I like to refer to these last two figures as "the two holy Bobs."

22. Abdullahi A. an-Na'im, *Toward an Islamic Reformation: Civil Liberties, Human Rights and International Law* (Syracuse, NY: Syracuse University Press, 1990).

23. Robin Wright, "An Iranian Luther Shakes the Foundations of Islam", *The Guardian*, February 1, 1995 (quoted from the *Los Angeles Times*, January 1995). Available online through Soroush's own website: http://www.seraj.org/guard.htm.

24. There were of course some exceptions, and there are records of women teachers and students at madrasas who were usually still required to teach from behind a screen to an audience of male pupils.
25. I am here referring to the different corpus of *hadith* collections that contain the statements of the Prophet Muhammad.
26. Among contemporary Muslim authors, one of the most eloquent critics of authoritarian tendencies has been Khaled Abou El Fadl, particularly in his *Speaking in God's Name: Islamic Law, Authority, and Women* (Oxford: Oneworld, 2001) as well as his *And God Knows the Soldiers: The Authoritative and Authoritarian in Islamic Discourses* (Lanham, MD: University Press of America, 2001).
27. To be fair, one has to admit that the very nature of the web does allow for greater flexibility of scholarly and activist presentations of Islam than in the realm of pamphlets, which tend to be dominated by neo-Wahhabi interpretations. Despite what has been called the "digital divide," there are great opportunities for Muslim communities and individuals to place their views on the web, even if they do not have access to costly printing and distribution resources. Today we find Muslim websites devoted not just to literalist interpretations of Islam, but also to women's groups, social justice organizations, peace movements, gay and lesbian Muslim groups, and Sufi communities.
28. The Dalai Lama, *A Policy of Kindness*, ed. Sidney Piburn (Ithaca: Snow Lion, 1990), 17.
29. Bob Marley, "War." Lyrics are from Bob Marley's official website, http://www.bobmarley.com/. The words to Marley's song are actually from a speech made by Haile Selassie to the United Nations. The song is featured on the third disk of the four-CD compilation of Marley's songs, entitled *Bob Marley: Songs of Freedom*.
30. Qur'an 23:29
31. I am here reminded of the similarity of this Islamic perspective to the Jewish mystical concept of *Tikkun olam*, which calls humanity to be responsible for healing the world through concrete acts of righteousness and goodness, alongside mystical meditation on the Divine spheres. May this be one bridge that we can use to bring like-minded and like-hearted Muslims and Jews together to heal our communities, as we seek to heal this world. *Amin....*

part I

PROGRESSIVE MUSLIMS
AND CONTEMPORARY ISLAM

I

THE UGLY MODERN AND THE MODERN UGLY: RECLAIMING THE BEAUTIFUL IN ISLAM

*Khaled Abou El Fadl**

Around the middle of March 2002, Saudi newspapers reported an incident that took place in Mecca, the Prophet Muhammad's birthplace, that should have caused a public outcry, investigations, and prosecutions. Instead, nothing happened, and the incident is now all but forgotten. According to the official count, at least fourteen young girls burned to death or were asphyxiated by smoke when an accidental fire engulfed their public school. Parents who arrived at the scene described a horrific scene in which the doors of the school were locked from the outside, and the Saudi religious police, known as the *mutawwa'un*, forcibly prevented girls from escaping the burning school and also prevented firemen from entering the school to save the girls, by beating some of the girls and several of the civil defense personnel. According to the statements of parents, firemen, and the regular police forces present on the scene, the *mutawwa'un* would not allow the girls to escape or be saved because they were not properly covered, and the *mutawwa'un* did not want physical contact to take place between the girls and the civil defense forces. The governmental institution that is responsible for administering the *mutawwa'un* (known as the Committee for the Promotion of Virtue and the Prevention of Vice)[1] denied beating any of the girls or civil defense workers, and also denied locking the gates of the school and trapping the girls inside. But witnesses told Saudi newspapers that the *mutawwa'un* yelled at the police and firemen to stay back, and beat several firemen, as they commanded the girls to go back into the burning building and retrieve their veils (known as *'abaya* and *niqab* in Saudi Arabia) before they might be allowed to leave the school. Several parents told journalists that they saw at least three girls being beaten with sticks and kicked when they attempted to argue with the *mutawwa'un*. Several girls did obey the *mutawwaʿun*, and returned to the school in order to retrieve their veils, only to be found dead later.[2]

In recent times, Muslim societies have been plagued by many events that have struck the world as offensive and even shocking. This has reached the extent that, from Europe and the United States to Japan, China, and Russia, one finds that Islamic culture has become associated with harshness and cruelty in the popular. When one interacts with people from different parts of the world, one consistently finds that the image of Islam is not that of a humanistic or humane religion. In fact, for many non-Muslims around the world, Islam has come to represent a draconian tradition that exhibits little compassion or mercy towards human beings. From this perspective, the event described above ought not give us pause; it simply becomes yet another inhumane incident in the history of modern Islam that borders on the incomprehensible and insane. Placed in the context of many other morally offensive events, such as *The Satanic Verses* and the death sentence against Salman Rushdie, the stoning and imprisoning of rape victims in Pakistan and Nigeria, the treatment of women by the Taliban, the destruction of the Buddha statues in Afghanistan, the sexual violation of domestic workers in Saudi Arabia, the excommunication of writers in Egypt, and the killing of civilians in terrorist attacks, this event seems to be just another chapter in a long Muslim saga of ugliness. This saga of ugliness has forced Muslims who are embarrassed and offended by this legacy to adopt apologetic rhetorical arguments that do not necessarily carry much persuasive weight. One of the most common arguments repeated by Muslim apologists is that it is unfair to confuse the religion of Islam with the deeds of its followers. The fact that the followers commit egregious behavior in the name of the religion does not in itself mean that the religion commands or sanctions such behavior. A similar, often repeated argument is that one must distinguish Islamic religious doctrines from the cultural practices of Muslims, the implication being that it is culture and not religion that is the culprit responsible for immoral behavior. Another more subtle argument, but one that surreptitiously betrays the same feelings of discomfort and embarrassment, is simply to remind the world that only a very small percentage of the Muslim world is Arab. Although this is factually correct, Muslims would not have been keen about reminding the world of this fact if the behavior of Arabs or their image was honorable. It is exactly because Arabs suffer from a troubled image in today's world that many Muslims feel the need to distance Islam from the Arab identity or Arab culture.

I call these arguments unpersuasive not because they are inaccurate – in fact, all the defensive points mentioned above are logical or factually correct. Nonetheless, I call them unpersuasive because they fail to take account of a variety of counter veiling arguments and problems. For instance, they ignore the role of history in understanding the present, and they also ignore the fact that it is not always possible to separate with surgical accuracy a system of belief from the social practices that have grown around it. Specifically, these arguments fail to take account of the role of human subjectivities in determining and acting upon doctrine. For example, it is true that Arabs constitute twenty percent of the sum total of Muslims in the world today. But it must be remembered that the very racial category of Arab was socially constructed and re-invented in different periods and places of the world. In certain times and places, whoever spoke Arabic eventually became an Arab, or, at least, came to be perceived as an Arab. The very classification of an Arab was the product of a dynamic and creative socio-linguistic process. The Arabic language, itself, demonstrated a remarkable ability to spread to new nations, and, eventually, to Arabize them. Consider, for instance, the complaint of the Bishop of Cordoba, Alvaro, in ninth-century Spain. He states,

> Many of my coreligionists read verses and fairy tales of the Arabs, study the works of Muhammedan philosophers and theologians not in order to refute them but to learn to express themselves properly in the Arab language more correctly and more elegantly. Who among them studied the Gospels, and Prophets and Apostles? Alas! All talented Christian young men know only the language and literature of the Arabs, read and assiduously study the Arab books... If somebody speaks of Christian books they contemptuously answer that they deserve no attention whatever (*quasi vilissima contemnentes*). Woe! The Christians have forgotten their own language, and there is hardly one among a thousand to be found who can write to a friend a decent greeting letter in Latin. But there is a numberless multitude who express themselves most elegantly in Arabic, and make poetry in this language with more beauty and more art than the Arabs themselves.[3]

One notices that, at least for conquered Spain, the relation between Arab and Muslim is far more fluid. According to Alvaro, young men were eager to learn the language of the Islamic culture of Andalucia because in that age the Arab was not considered a symbol of reactionism or barbarity. One doubts that a Muslim living back then would have had much incentive to differentiate between Arabs and Islam. Even in countries, such as Persia and India, that preserved their native languages after the Islamic invasions, scholars continued to write most books on theology and law in Arabic.[4] Alvaro's statement is significant in another respect; it reminds us of the shifting fortunes of the reputation of Muslims in the world. There is no doubt that Islam and Europe have had a long and unpleasant tradition of mutual vilification and demonization, but these processes of the past were materially different from the present.[5] In my view, the Western attempts to vilify Islam in the past were inspired by fear and respect, and Western perceptions of Muslims were not based on any realistic understanding of Muslim socio-political circumstances. Most of the vilifications were nothing more than the anxieties, fears, and aspirations of Westerners projected onto the dominant force at the time without any foundation in reality. At the intellectual, commercial, and scientific levels, one finds that Westerners borrowed heavily from Muslim social and legal thought and scientific inventiveness. By contrast, today, whatever bigotry exists against Muslims, it is based in the unfortunate socio-political realities experienced by Muslims, which the West perceives, generalizes, and exaggerates, and which then become the basis for stereotypes. Today's prejudices against Muslims are not based on fear and respect, but on the worst and most cruel type of bigotry, and that is the type that is displayed against those whom the West dominates and controls. Pre-modern bigotry was directed at Muslims, as the masters of the world. Today's bigotry is directed at those who are seen to be at the bottom of the human hierarchy – people who politically and socially live in a dependent and bonded status, like that of slaves.

Hate and bigotry are often based on what social psychologists have called the binary impulse in human beings – the primitive and vulgar tendency to define the world in terms of "us versus them." This binary impulse first attempts to find an "us," and then associates that "us" with all that is good and virtuous. At the same time, "them" becomes associated with all that is counter to the "us," and therefore, the "other" is presumed to be not good, and even evil. What disrupts and challenges this simplistic primitive paradigm is "social need." Although human societies gravitate towards this binary instinct, the need for interaction and cooperation between different societies and nations acts as a force often inducing human societies to define themselves a way that does not exclude the "other." With a sufficient amount of overlapping interests, interactions, and conscientiousness, the paradigm could shift from an "us versus them" to an "us–us" perspective.[6] In the pre-modern age, although there is clear evidence of a strong binary impulse pervading both the Muslim and Western worlds, given the scientific and intellectual achievements of Muslims, Christian and Jewish bigotry towards Muslims had to be tempered by the element of need. Both Jews and Christians could not help but be influenced by Muslim intellectual products, and this made the dynamics with Islam complex and multi-faceted.[7] In the modern age, however, the binary perspective of Muslims is no longer one that is undertaken from a position of strength: the relative self-sufficiency of the West is matched by the economic dependency of the Muslim world. Muslim nations are underdeveloped and economically and political dependent, and in the contemporary age there is little that Muslim cultures are able to contribute to the West, other than the Muslim faith.[8] But offensive incidents, such as those mentioned above, greatly impact upon the way that this faith is understood in the West, and further feed into binary constructs vis-à-vis Islam and Muslims.[9] Put simply, such incidents of stark ugliness lead many to believe that the Islamic tradition and civilization is fundamentally at odds with the Judeo-Christian tradition, and that a civilizational showdown or confrontation between Islam and the West is inevitable.[10]

My point in this article is not to examine the "Clash of Civilizations" thesis, and I am also not interested in assessing the reasons for the Western bias and prejudice against Islam or Muslims. I am interested, however, in exploring what might be called the vulgarization of contemporary Islam.[11] By "vulgarization" I mean the recurrence of events that seem to shock the conscience of human beings or to be contrary to what most people would identify as moral and beautiful. As noted above, Islam in the modern age has become associated with violence, harshness, and cruelty, and although mercy and compassion are core values in Islamic theology, these are not the values that most people identify with Islam. As argued below, Islam in the modern age has become plagued by an arid intellectual climate and a lack of critical and creative approaches, which has greatly hampered the development of a humanistic moral orientation. In my view, in order for an intellectual tradition to develop morally, and to vigorously confront renewed moral challenges, a rich and critical intellectual discourse is necessary. But the contemporary Islamic world has been intellectually impoverished, and so there have been far too few influential philosophical or critical intellectual movements emerging from the Muslim world in the modern age. As I argue later, even the most puritan and literalist movements within contemporary Islam have remained largely reactive and intellectually dependent.

BEARING WITNESS TO VULGARITY IN THE AGE OF MODERNITY

The incident recounted above regarding the schoolgirls and religious police in Mecca ought to give all Muslims a long conscientious pause. If the event did in fact take place as witnesses alleged that it did, then, in my view, it ought to mark a point for Muslims to rethink much of their experience in the contemporary age. This incident symbolizes not only the abysmal condition of women within certain theological orientations in Islam, but also the gross misuse of the doctrines and traditions of Islamic law in the contemporary age. At the most basic level, even if one assumes that Islamic law does command strict adherence to rules of seclusion and veiling, the necessity of preserving human life would trump any such rule.[12] Furthermore, the Qur'an, itself, clearly states that whatever rules of seclusion might have been commanded, at one time or another, for women, had one justification and one justification only, and that is the safeguarding of women from molestation or harm.[13] The death of these girls was contrary to the very *raison d'être* and every possible rational basis for the laws of seclusion. One even wonders, if the preservation of the life of these girls had any value whatsoever to the Saudi religious police, why this police did not do something as simple as unlocking the gates of the burning schools, and then withdrawing all the men from the area so that the girls could escape to safety without being seen by men. If the religious police were sufficiently concerned, they could have even removed their own head gear (known as the *ghutra*) and placed it on the heads of the escaping girls, thus allowing them to survive.[14] The point, however, is not the Saudi religious police's lack of creative problem solving, or their abnormal obsession with the seductive power of women, or even their callous disregard for the value of human life, especially the lives of women. The point is that this event symbolizes a truly troubling level of moral degeneration in the collective life of contemporary Islam. This incident follows in the wake of a series of events, all of which are symptomatic of something gone awfully wrong in our Muslim system of belief. These events have ranged from the highly visible and infamous such as the 9/11 suicide mass slaughter of mostly non-Muslims, to less visible and lesser-known incidents. For instance, a lesser-known, but equally horrific, incident involved the beheading of a Syrian citizen, 'Abd al-Karim al-Naqshabandi, on December 13, 1996, for allegedly practicing witchcraft against his Saudi employer, Prince Salman bin Sa'ud bin 'Abd al-'Aziz, a nephew of King Fahd. The primary evidence warranting the execution of al-Naqshabandi was an amulet, with Qur'anic verses inscribed on it, found in his desk drawer at work. According to al-Naqshabandi, the amulet was given to him by his mother in Syria, in the belief that it would ward off envy and evil spirits. The Saudi government, however, considered the possession of the amulet and some books on Sufism allegedly found in the defendant's home to be grievous acts of heresy (a'mal bid'iyya wa shirkiyya) that warranted nothing less than death.[15]

The consistent commission of repulsive acts of injustice by people who believe that they are acting in the name of Islam must give all Muslims serious pause. From the perspective of a believing Muslim, I must worry about God's covenant with the Muslim people, especially that the Qur'an is full of warnings to Muslims that if they fail to establish justice and bear witness to the truth, God owes us, Muslims, nothing, and is bound to replace us with another people who are more capable of honoring God through establishing justice on this earth.[16] The covenant identified in the Qur'an and given to Muslims is not an entitlement. The Qur'an consistently emphasizes that the covenant given to Muslims is contingent, and that the failure to do it justice will lead God to abandon those once entrusted with the Divine covenant to their own vices and the consequences of their evil deeds.[17] Looking at the sheer amount of ugliness perpetuated in the past twenty years in Islam's name, only the most deluded or self-absorbed Muslim would remain unconcerned. In this context, it is important to note that tragic incidents, such as the murder of al-Naqshabandi, or the 9/11 terrorist attacks, cannot safely always be attributed to an aberrational fanaticism that can be considered marginal and unrepresentative. From a sociological perspective, the commission of violently repulsive acts is often the byproduct of ongoing social malignancies that fester for a long time before manifesting in publicly visible acts. It is risky, and quite foolish, to wave away socially and politically pathological behavior as marginal corruptions in society. Put rather bluntly, people do not just wake up one day and decide to commit an act of terrorism, or decide to kill a person for practicing witchcraft; rather, such acts are preceded by social dynamics that desensitize and deconstruct society's sense of moral virtue and ethics. Especially, as far as theological constructs are concerned, the commission of and social responses to acts of cruelty typically undergo a long process of indoctrination and acculturation that both facilitate the commission of such acts and mute or mitigate the sense of social outrage upon the commission of offensive behavior. Much of this process of indoctrination and acculturation can be gleaned from the relatively apathetic and muted Muslim responses to the commission of socially and politically abusive acts. Furthermore, a probing and conscientious Muslim ought to be concerned at the evidence of the emergence of a consistent pattern and practice of such abusive conduct. When one finds that Islam is repeatedly and consistently being exploited to justify immoral behavior, this must be considered as a pattern of practice that ought to give Muslims cause for serious concern. This is all the more so because, in many ways, it is history that sets the future in motion. Each abusive act committed in the name of Islam becomes a historical precedent, and each precedent could carry normative weight, and therefore influence the meaning of Islam in the future. Even when one is considering Divinely revealed values, such values acquire meaning only within evolving and shifting contexts. Functioning within different and particularized contexts, interpretive communities coalesce around revealed injunctions and values, and then endow them with meaning. Put differently, there is a socio-historical enterprise formed of various participants that partake in the generation of meaning. The participants in these various socio-historical enterprises are known as interpretive communities – groups of people who share common hermeneutical methodologies, linguistic skills, and epistemological values and coalesce around a particular set of texts and determine the meaning and import of these texts. The determinations of the participants in a socio-historical enterprise become precedents that help set the meaning, and practical applications, of a text, even if the text is sacred, such as the Qur'an. Therefore, when we speak about the meaning of Islam today, we are really talking about the product of cumulative enterprises that have generated communities of interpretation through a long span of history.[18]

In my view, it is imperative for Muslim intellectuals to engage the various precedents set in the name of Islam, and to negotiate the meaning of their religion. Shirking away from this responsibility, or dealing with it in an irresponsible apologetic fashion, would be tantamount to the abandonment of Islam, and a violation of the solemn obligation to promote what is good in life, and reject what is wrong. As Muslims, we are well aware of the Islamic obligation placed upon every Muslim man and woman to enjoin the good and forbid the evil (*al-amr bi'l ma'ruf wa al-nahy 'ann al-munkar*).[19] In fact, according to the Qur'an, the merit of the Muslim nation is hinged on its discharging of this obligation of bearing witness, on God's behalf, to goodness and justice.[20] Naturally, testifying to the injustice committed by non-Muslims against Muslims is infinitely easier than testifying to the injustice committed by Muslims, whether it be against fellow Muslims or non-Muslims. This is why the Qur'an explicitly commands Muslims to bear witness for truth and justice, even if the testimony is against themselves or against loved ones. Furthermore, the Qur'an specifically identifies such truthful testimony against self-interest as testimony rendered on God's behalf.[21] In my view, truthful testimony is rendered on God's behalf because silence in the face of a wrong committed in the name of Islam is a form of suborning the corruption of the religion. Considered from this perspective, the worst injustice, and the one most worthy of Muslim outrage, is that committed by Muslims, in Islam's name, because that is more deprecating to God and God's religion than any supposed heresy or legal infraction. It is out of concern for the sanctity of their own religion that one would imagine that Muslims would be the most boisterous and vigilant in protesting injustices committed in Islam's name, whether against Muslims or non-Muslims. But in the atmosphere of rampant apologetics and defensiveness that plagues Muslim cultures, one finds that it is exactly this type of thinking that is conspicuously absent from current Muslim activism and intellectual discourses.

When it comes to the issue of self-critical appraisals, Muslim discourses, for the most part, remain captive to the post-colonial experience. These discourses are politicized and polarized to the extent that a Muslim intellectual who takes a critical approach to the Islamic tradition often feels that he is stepping into a minefield. It is difficult for a contemporary Muslim scholar to take a critical position on such matters as Islam and violence or Islam and women without becoming the subject of suspicion, and even accusations as to his or her loyalties and commitments. In addition, it has become a rather powerful rhetorical device to contend that the West is perpetuating false universalisms, and to accuse Muslim critics of being deluded into accepting these universalisms as a God-given truth. These Muslim critics, it is claimed, then project the West's truth onto the Islamic tradition, as if what the West sees as true and good must necessarily be so, and therefore must be adopted by all Muslims.[22] Most often, this type of accusation is leveled against Muslim critics with feminist agendas, but also it has been utilized rather widely against Muslim intellectuals calling for self-critical re-evaluations post-9/11. It is a powerful rhetorical device because the user of such a device is positioning himself or herself as the guardian of integrity and authenticity, while positioning his or her opponents as gullible and even simple-minded.[23] In addition, as an extension of the relativism argument, it is often argued that it is immaterial whether the West, or anyone else in the world, is offended or shocked by the legal and social practices of Muslims. Islam, it is argued, has its own set of standards for justice and righteousness, and it is of no consequence if those standards happen to be inconsistent with the moral sensitivities of non-Muslims. This argument was repeated often in the context of justifying and defending the Salman Rushdie affair, the destruction of the Buddha statues in Afghanistan, and the treatment of women by the Taliban. On face value, this argument is attractive because it seems to affirm a sense of Islamic autonomy and authentic uniqueness that is arguably consistent with the notion that God is sovereign and that the Divine law is not in any way contingent upon the whim of human beings.[24]

The issue of, what is now commonly described as, cultural relativism versus universalism is very complex, and this is not the place to delve into it. I will note only that this whole discourse becomes rather incoherent unless one clearly identifies what specific value is being identified as relative or universal. Unless one is explicit and specific about the particular value that is claimed to be unique, this whole discourse stops making any sense. In addition, Islam itself, like all religions, is founded on certain universals such as mercy, justice, compassion, and dignity.[25] The Qur'an itself consistently uses terminology that presupposes the existence of universal values, and presumes such values to be recognizable by human beings universally. Much of the Qur'anic discourse on values such as justice, mercy, truth, kindness, and generosity would make little sense if one rejected the existence of universal values.[26] Furthermore, claims of ontological truth, whether based on reason or revelation, are not anathema to Islam.[27] From an Islamic perspective, Muslims are not forbidden, and in my opinion are even encouraged, to search for moral universals that could serve as shared and common goals with humanity at large.[28] This seems to me to be an essential characteristic of a universal religion that is addressed to humanity at large, and not to an exclusive cultural or social group. The Qur'an insists that it is the bearer of a message to all humankind, and not to a particular tribe or race.[29] If this is so, Muslims cannot afford to claim that they are not concerned with how the rest of the world sees and evaluates their actions. A universal religion must be accessible and accountable to others so that it can remain pertinent to humanity at large. A universal religion that is neither accessible nor accountable to humanity at large becomes like a private and closed club with bylaws and practices that make sense only to its members.

It seems to me that commentators who respond to shocking incidents such as those mentioned above, by engaging in a knee-jerk reaction of protesting false Western universals, and rejecting introspective self-critical approaches, play well into the hands of a siege mentality that seems to pervade much of contemporary Muslim thought. If critical approaches to the tradition will be consistently dismissed as Western influenced, or as a form of Westoxification,[30] it is difficult to imagine how Muslims will be able to emerge out of what might be described as a state of intellectual dissonance, and into a more constructive engagement with modernity. By "intellectual dissonance," I mean a state of social and cultural schizophrenia in which Muslims experience simultaneously the challenge of modernity, a severe alienation, and evasiveness towards the Islamic intellectual experience, and, at the same time, a symbolic identification and an idealization of that experience.[31] While we suffer this state of intellectual dissonance, there is the very real risk that in our defensive effort to expunge the moral universals of the West, Muslims will also end up dismissing the moral universals of Islam itself. For instance, when contemporary Muslim scholars rise to emphasize the numerous moral and humanistic aspects of the Islamic tradition, and they are accused by their fellow Muslims of seeking to appease the West, the real danger is that in this highly polarized and politicized climate much of what is authentically Islamic and genuinely beautiful will be lost or forgotten for a long period to come. This, in turn, points to a basic and very serious fallacy, and that is the tendency, usually exhibited by religious fundamentalists and ideological purists, to presume that moral values have a pure lineage that can be precisely identified as Western or non-Western. Whether Muslims or not, purists tend to classify particular values as squarely Judeo-Christian while others are Islamic. It is as if values have a genealogy that can be clearly and precisely ascertained, which then can be utilized in classifying what properly belongs to the West and what belongs to Islam. But the origin and lineage of values are as much of a socio-historical construct as are claims about racial genealogical purity. Considering the numerous cultural interactions and intellectual transmissions between the Muslim world and Europe, it is highly likely that every significant Western value has a measure of Muslim blood in it.[32] This is not merely a matter of acknowledging the Muslim contribution to Western thought. Rather, if we recognize the mixed lineage of ideas, a simple and straightforward taxonomy of moral values and civilizations, and what civilizations are supposed to stand for, becomes much more problematic. As for racial categories, one ought to recognize that civilizational categories are artificial political constructs that do not necessarily fit comfortably with socio-historical realities, and that many moral values do not carry a manufacturer's label or an owner's tag.

Confronted by extreme acts of ugliness, there is no alternative for a Muslim who is interested in reclaiming the moral authority of Islam but to confront the quintessential questions of: Is this Islam? Can this be Islam? And, should this be Islam? It is far too easy for contemporary Muslims to avoid taking responsibility for the extreme acts of ugliness committed by zealots in our midst, and instead cast all the blame upon Western imperialism and colonialism. It is far too easy to engage in the morally evasive strategy of complaining about false universals, and to blame everything and everyone else, but refuse a confrontation with one's own conscience. With every major human tragedy committed in the name of Islam, I think that it is imperative for every Muslim to put aside, for a while, the various intellectual methods by which responsibility is projected, transferred, diluted, and distributed, and to engage in a conscientious pause. In this pause, a Muslim ought to critically evaluate the prevailing systems of belief within Islam, and reflect upon the ways that these systems of belief might have contributed to, legitimated, or in any way facilitated the tragedy. In my view, this is the only way for a Muslim to honor human life, dignify God's creation, and uphold the integrity of the Islamic religion.

If one engages in this conscientious and self-reflective pause, I believe that one would realize that a supremacist and puritanical orientation in contemporary Islam shoulders the primary responsibility for the vast majority of extreme acts of ugliness that are witnessed today in the Islamic world. In my view, Muslims must come to terms with, and reclaim their religion from a supremacist puritanism that has been born of a siege mentality – a mentality that this supremacist puritanical orientation continues to perpetuate as the primary mode of responding to the challenge of modernity. Importantly, this orientation is dismissive of all universal moral norms or innate ethical values, regardless of the identity of their origins or foundations. In this orientation, the prime and nearly singular concern is power and its symbols. Somehow, all other values, traditions, and normativities are made subservient. As argued below, this orientation, which I will call Salafabism, was, and remains, uninterested in critical historical inquiry. It has responded to the challenge of modernity by escaping to the secure haven of the text, but it has treated rational moral insight as fundamentally corrupting of the purity of the Islamic message. As a result, it has ended up undermining the integrity and viability of the Islamic texts and, in the process, it has arrested and stunted the development of Islamic normative ethical thinking.

THE SIEGE MENTALITY AND THE EMERGENCE OF SUPREMACIST PURITANISM

The real challenge that confronts Muslim intellectuals today is that political interests have come to dominate public discourses to the point that moral investigations and thinking have become marginalized in modern Islam. In the age of post-colonialism, Muslims have become largely pre-occupied with the attempt to remedy a collective feeling of powerlessness and a frustrating sense of political defeat, often by engaging in highly sensationalistic acts of power symbolism. The normative imperatives and intellectual subtleties of the Islamic moral tradition are not treated with the analytic and critical rigor that the Islamic tradition rightly deserves, but are rendered subservient to political expedience and symbolic displays of power. Elsewhere, I have described this contemporary doctrinal dynamic as the predominance of the theology of power in modern Islam, and it is this theology that is a direct contributor to the emergence of highly radicalized Islamic groups, such as the Taliban or al-Qaeda, and the desensitization and transference with which Muslims confront extreme acts of ugliness.[33] Far from being authentic expressions of inherited Islamic paradigms, or a natural outgrowth of the classical tradition, these groups, and their impulsive and reactive modes of thinking, are a byproduct of colonialism and modernity. These highly dissonant and defensive modes of thinking are disassociated from the Islamic civilizational experience with all its richness and diversity, and they invariably end up reducing Islam to a single dynamic – the dynamic of power. They tend to define Islam as an ideology of nationalistic defiance to the "other" – a rather vulgar form of obstructionism to the hegemony of the Western world.[34] Therefore, instead of Islam being a moral vision given to humanity, it becomes constructed into the antithesis of the West. In the world constructed by puritan modes of thinking and their groups, there is no Islam; there is only opposition to the West. This type of Islam that the puritan orientations offer is akin to a perpetual state of emergency where expedience trumps principle, and illegitimate means are consistently justified by invoking higher ends. In essence, what prevails is an aggravated siege mentality that suspends the moral principles of the religion in pursuit of the vindications of political power, and the symbolic displays of domination as well.[35] In this siege mentality, there is no room for analytical or critical thought, and there is no room for seriously engaging the Islamic intellectual heritage. There is only room for bombastic dogma, and for a stark functionalism that ultimately impoverishes the Islamic heritage. One of the most salient characteristics of this orientation is a rabidly aggressive form of patriarchy that responds to feelings of political and social defeatism by engaging in symbolic displays of power that are systematically degrading of women. In my view, for example, the girls that died in Mecca were the direct victims of the sense of frustration and disempowerment felt by puritan men over the humiliations experienced in Afghanistan and Palestine. Of course, this is one of those associations that are virtually impossible to prove empirically, but, in my experience in studying puritan orientations in modern Islam, I find that women are not targeted and degraded simply because of textual commitments or determinations.[36] Rather, there is a certain undeniable vehemence and angst in the treatment of women, as if the more women are made to suffer, the more the political future of Islam is made secure. Puritan orientations do not hesitate to treat all theological arguments aimed at honoring women, by augmenting their autonomy and social mobility, as if a part of the Western conspiracy was designed to destroy Islam. This is also manifested in the puritans' tendency to look at Muslim women as a consistent source of danger, and vulnerability for Islam, and to go as far as branding women as the main source of social corruption and evil.[37]

Although it would be rather disingenuous to suggest that demeaning attitudes towards women were invented or exclusively adopted only by modern puritan orientations, it is important to understand the uniqueness and distinctiveness of the current puritan challenge in this specific historical juncture of Islamic history. What makes the puritan challenge today particularly compelling and singularly threatening to the humanistic tradition in Islam is the deconstruction of the institutions of religious authority in the age of modernity. Historically, these institutions played the primary role in undermining and marginalizing the supremacist and puritanical movements of the past. In addition, not only does the primacy of apologetic intellectual orientations within contemporary Islam not bode well for the ability of Muslims to overcome these supremacist and puritanical movements, but, even more, such apologetics are the main undercurrent feeding into such movements. The apologetic orientation consisted of an effort by a large number of commentators to defend and salvage the Islamic system of belief and tradition from the onslaught of orientalism, Westernization, and modernity by simultaneously emphasizing both the compatibility and also the supremacy of Islam. Apologists responded to the intellectual challenges of modernity by adopting pietistic fictions about the Islamic traditions, but such fictions eschewed any critical evaluation of Islamic doctrines, and celebrated the presumed perfection of Islam.[38] A common heuristic device of apologetics was to argue that any meritorious or worthwhile modern institutions were first invented and realized by Muslims. Therefore, according to the apologists, Islam liberated women, created a democracy, endorsed pluralism, protected human rights, and guaranteed social security long before these institutions ever existed in the West. Nonetheless, these concepts were not asserted out of critical understanding or genuine ideological commitment, but primarily as a means of resisting the deconstructive effects of modernity, affirming self-worth, and attaining a measure of emotional empowerment. The main effect of apologetics, however, was to contribute to a sense of intellectual self-sufficiency that often descended into moral arrogance. To the extent that apologetics were habit forming, they produced a culture that eschewed self-critical and introspective insight, and embraced the projection of blame and a fantasy-like level of confidence and arrogance. Effectively, apologists got into the habit of paying homage to the presumed superiority of the Islamic tradition, but marginalized the Islamic intellectual heritage in everyday life. While apologists revered Islam in the abstract, they failed to engage the Islamic tradition as a dynamic and viable living tradition. To a large extent, apologists turned Islam into an untouchable, but also entirely ineffective, beauty queen, simply to be admired and showcased as a symbol, but not to be critically engaged in its full nuance and complexity.[39] In many ways, apologists ended up reproducing the legacy of orientalism – a legacy of which they were very critical. Orientalists dealt with the Islamic tradition as a static and, perhaps, even mummified heritage that is represented by a set of self-contained intellectual paradigms, and that is incapable of adapting to the demands of modernity without becoming thoroughly deconstructed and collapsing into itself. In essence, orientalists, who worked in the service of colonialism, paid nothing more than lip service to Islam, but otherwise negated the practical value of Islamic culture. The most typical strategy was for orientalists to insist that the Islamic tradition, while generally decent, lacked essential features necessary for rational modernization. As such, it is not so much that orientalists deprecated Islam, as a religion, rather, they cast serious doubts on the ability of what might be called "active" or "dynamic" Islam to deal with rational modernity.[40] Ironically, Muslim apologists ended up with the same basic construct. They paid lip service to the Islamic tradition, by, among other things, insisting that not only was Islam compatible with modernity, but, in fact, it had already achieved "rational modernization" fourteen hundred years ago. Effectively, apologists treated the Islamic tradition as if it was fossilized at the time of the Prophet and the Rightly Guided Companions, and, thus, rendered this tradition non-dynamic and un-living.[41]

Not only was the practice of apologetics unhelpful in dealing with the challenges of modernity, but also it significantly contributed to the sense of intellectual dissonance felt in many parts of the Muslim world. The problems posed by this response to modernity were only aggravated by the fact that Islam was, and continues to this day, to live through a major paradigm shift the likes of which it had not experienced in the past. There is a profound vacuum in religious authority, where it is not clear who speaks for the religion and how. Traditionally, the institutions of Islamic law were de-centralized, and Islamic epistemology tolerated and even celebrated differences of opinions and a variety of schools of thought. Islamic law was not state centered or state generated, but was developed by judges and jurists through a slow, creative, indeterminate, and dialectical process, somewhat similar to the common law system.[42] Classical Islam did develop semi-autonomous institutions of law and theology that trained and qualified jurists, who then provided a class of individuals who authoritatively spoke for, and most often disagreed about, the Divine law. The institutions of religion and law were supported by a complex system of private endowments (*awqaf*), which enabled Muslim scholars to generate a remarkably rich intellectual tradition.[43] The guardians of this were the *fuqaha*, whose legitimacy to a large extent rested in their semi-independence from the political system, which was already fairly de-centralized, and in their dual function of representing the interests of the state to the laity and the interests of the laity to the state.[44] Importantly, however, much of this drastically changed in the modern age. The traditional institutions that once sustained the juristic discourse have all but vanished. Furthermore, the normative categories and moral foundations that once mapped out Islamic law and theology have disintegrated, leaving an unsettling epistemological vacuum. Colonialism formally dismantled the traditional institutions of civil society, and Muslims witnessed the emergence of highly centralized and despotic, and often corrupt, governments that nationalized the institutions of religious learning and brought the *awqaf* under state control. This contributed to the undermining of the mediating role of jurists in Muslim societies.[45] The fact that nearly all charitable religious endowments became state controlled entities, and that Muslim jurists in most Muslim nations became salaried state employees, de-legitimated the traditional clergy and effectively transformed them into what may be called "court priests."[46] In addition, Western cultural symbols, modes of production, and normative social values aggressively penetrated the Muslim world, seriously challenging inherited normative categories and practices, and adding to a profound sense of socio-cultural alienation and dissonance.

Most Muslim nations experienced the wholesale borrowing of civil law concepts. Instead of the dialectical and indeterminate methodology of traditional Islamic jurisprudence, Muslim nations opted for more centralized, determinative, and often code based systems of law.[47] These developments only contributed to the power of the state, which had become extremely meddlesome, and which was now capable of a level of centralization that was inconceivable just two centuries ago. Even Muslim modernists who attempted to reform Islamic jurisprudence were heavily influenced by the civil law system, and thus sought to resist the indeterminate fluidity of Islamic law and increase its unitary and centralized character. Not only were the concepts of law heavily influenced by the European legal tradition, but even the ideologies of resistance employed by Muslims were laden with Third World notions of national liberation and self determination. For instance, modern nationalistic thought exercised a greater influence on the resistance ideologies of Muslim and Arab national liberation movements than anything in the Islamic tradition. The Islamic tradition was reconstructed to fit Third World nationalistic ideologies of anti-colonialism and anti-imperialism, rather than the other way around.

The disintegration of the traditional institutions of Islamic learning and authority meant a descent into a condition of virtual anarchy, particularly with respect to the mechanisms of defining Islamic authenticity. It was not so much that no one could authoritatively speak for Islam, but that virtually every Muslim was suddenly considered to possess the requisite qualifications to become a representative and spokesperson for the Islamic tradition, and even *Shari'ah* law.[48] This was primarily because the standards were set so low that a person who had a modest degree of knowledge of the Qur'an and the traditions of the Prophet was considered sufficiently qualified to authoritatively represent the Shari'ah, even if such a person was not familiar with the precedents and discourses of the interpretive communities of the past.[49] Consequently, persons, mostly engineers, medical doctors, and physical scientists, who were primarily self-taught and whose knowledge of Islamic text and history was quite superficial were able to position themselves as authorities on Islamic law and theology. Islamic law and theology became the extracurricular hobby of pamphlet readers and writers. As such, Islamic intellectual culture witnessed an unprecedented level of deterioration, as self-proclaimed and self-taught experts reduced the Islamic heritage to the least common denominator, which often amounted to engaging in crass generalizations about the nature of Islam, and the nature of the non-Muslim "other."[50] Clinging to vulgar apologetics, the point of the self-proclaimed experts was to increase the Islamic tradition's mass appeal by transforming it into a vehicle for displays of power symbolisms. These power symbolisms were motivated by the desire to overcome a pervasive sense of powerlessness and to express resistance to Western hegemony in the contemporary age, as well as a means of voicing national aspirations for political, social, and cultural independence. The irony, however, was that these self-proclaimed experts, being primarily medical doctors, engineers, or computer scientists, were trained only in Western scientific methods and according to Western invented educational curricula, and therefore, methodologically and epistemologically, they were effectively a part of Western culture. Although defiant and rebellious, in every way, they were the children of the West, despite the power symbolisms of resistance in which they engaged.[51] Most significantly, as they searched Islam for black-and-white and definitive answers to all their socio-political problems, these Muslim activists superimposed the logic of empirical precision and the determinism of Western scientific methods upon the Islamic intellectual, and particularly the juristic, tradition.[52]

With the deconstruction of the traditional institutions of religious authority emerged organizations such as the Jihad, Tanzim, al-Qaeda, and the Taliban, who were influenced by the resistance paradigms of national liberation and anti-colonialist ideologies, but who also anchored themselves in a religious orientation that is distinctively puritan, supremacist, and thoroughly opportunistic in nature. This theology is the byproduct of the emergence and eventual primacy of a synchronistic orientation that unites Wahhabism and Salafism in modern Islam. Puritan orientations, such as Wahhabism, imagine that God's perfection and immutability are fully attainable by human beings in this lifetime. It is as if God's perfection had been deposited in the Divine law, and by giving effect to this law, it is possible to create a social order that mirrors the Divine Truth. But by associating themselves with the Supreme Being in this fashion, puritan groups are able to claim a self-righteous perfectionism that easily slips into a pretense of supremacy. The existence of this puritan orientation in Islam is hardly surprising. All religious systems have suffered at one time or another from absolutist extremism, and Islam is not an exception. Within the first century of Islam, religious extremists known as the Khawarij (literally, the secessionists) slaughtered a large number of Muslims and non-Muslims, and were even responsible for the assassination of the Prophet's cousin and Companion the Caliph 'Ali b. Abi Talib. The descendants of the Khawarij exist today in Oman and Algeria, but after centuries of bloodshed, they have become moderates, if not pacifists. Other than the Khawarij, there were other extremists such as the Qaramitah and Assassins, whose terror became the *raison d'être* for their very existence, and who earned unmitigated infamy in the writings of Muslim historians, theologians, and jurists. Again, after centuries of bloodshed, these two groups learned moderation, and they continue to exist in small numbers in North Africa and Iraq. The essential lesson taught by Islamic history is that extremist groups, such as those mentioned above and others, are ejected from the mainstream of Islam; they are marginalized, and they eventually come to be treated as a heretical aberration from the Islamic message. The problem, however, as noted earlier, is that the traditional institutions of Islam that historically acted to marginalize extremist creeds no longer exist. This is what makes this period of Islamic history far more troublesome than any other, and this is also what makes modern puritan orientations far more threatening to the integrity of the morality and values of Islam than any of the previous extremist movements. Extreme acts of ugliness today represent the culmination of a process that has been in the making for the past two centuries. In the same fashion, the culmination of Salafism, Wahhabism, apologetics, and Islamic nationalisms has become a synchronism that could be called Salafabism.

WAHHABIS, SALAFIS, AND SALAFABIS

The story of modern puritanical Islam must start with the Saudi movement known as Wahhabism. It is impossible to quantify the exact amount of influence that Wahhabism has had on modern Muslim thinking. However, it is notable that Islamist groups, such as the Taliban and al-Qaeda, that have achieved a degree of international infamy, usually, have been heavily influenced by Wahhabi thought. Particularly on the issue of women, Wahhabis tend to espouse some of the most patriarchical and exclusionary orientations within contemporary Islam. Furthermore, in countries that have attempted to implement Islamic law, one notices that such efforts at implementation tend to be heavily influenced by Wahhabi paradigms and systems of thought. This is so, even in countries that are predominately Hanafi, such as Pakistan, or predominately Maliki, such as Nigeria. Finally, many of the theological paradigms of Wahhabism, such as anti-rationalism, the rejection of the doctrine of intercession, the reliance on isolated *hadith* in the deduction of laws, the prohibition of music, or the mechanics of prayer have become part of the pervasive system of belief adopted by a wide variety of Sunni Islamic movements. One even finds that the pedantic doctrines adopted by Wahhabis, such as whether it is permissible to use prayer beads, whether one may wipe one's neck during the ablutions before prayer, or whether women may attend funeral services, have become widespread in various parts of the Muslim world. Part of what accounts for the Wahhabi influence in the Muslim world is Saudi Arabia's unique position as the guardian of the two holy sites of Mecca and Medina. Through the regulation of orthodoxy at pilgrimage, Wahhabis have an opportunity to influence the way Islam is practiced around the world. In addition, Wahhabism is supported by the substantial financial resources of the Saudi government.

The foundations of Wahhabi theology were set into place by the eighteenth-century evangelist Muhammad b. 'Abd al-Wahhab (d. 1206/1792). With a puritanical zeal, 'Abd al-Wahhab sought to rid Islam of all the corruptions that he believed had crept into the religion – corruptions that included mysticism, including the doctrine of intercession, and rationalism. Wahhabism resisted the indeterminacy of the modern age by escaping to a strict literalism in which the text became the sole source of legitimacy. Wahhabism exhibited extreme hostility to all forms of intellectualism, mysticism, and any sectarianism within Islam, considering all of these to be corrupt innovations that had crept into the religion because of un-Islamic influences. The Wahhabi creed also considered any form of moral thought that was not entirely dependent on the text as a form of self-idolatry, and treated humanistic fields of knowledge, especially philosophy, as "the sciences of the devil."[53] According to the Wahhabi creed, it was imperative to return to a presumed pristine, simple, and straightforward Islam, which was believed to be entirely reclaimable by a literal implementation of the commands and precedents of the Prophet, and by a strict adherence to correct ritual practice. Wahhabism also rejected any attempt to interpret the Divine law from a historical, contextual perspective, and, in fact, treated the vast majority of Islamic history as a corruption or aberration from the true and authentic Islam.[54] The dialectical and indeterminate hermeneutics of the classical jurisprudential tradition were considered corruptions of the purity of the faith and law. Furthermore, Wahhabism became very intolerant of the long-established Islamic practice of considering a variety of schools of thought to be equally orthodox, and attempted to narrow considerably the range of issues upon which Muslims may legitimately disagree. Orthodoxy was narrowly defined, and 'Abd al-Wahhab, himself, was fond of creating long lists of beliefs and acts that he considered hypocritical and the adoption or commission of which would immediately render a Muslim an unbeliever.[55] 'Abd al-Wahhab had a near obsessive concern with the doctrine of *shirk* (associating partners with God). For him, a practicing Muslim could commit particular acts that would expose the impurity of his belief in God and Islam. Such acts, according to 'Abd al-Wahhab, betray a willingness to engage in *shirk*, and thus would result in taking a person out of the fold of Islam. In his writings, he consistently emphasized that there is no middle of the road for a Muslim – either a Muslim was a true believer or not, and if a Muslim was not a true believer 'Abd al-Wahhab had no qualms about declaring a Muslim to be an infidel and treating him or her as such.[56] But other than the practice of *takfir* (accusing Muslims of heresy and of being infidels), perhaps the most stultifying, and even deadly, characteristic of Wahhabism was its hostility to any human practice that would excite the imagination or bolster creativity. According to the Wahhabis, only frivolous people would be fond of the arts, such as music or poetry. In fact, according to them, any act that excites the imagination or augments individual creativity constitutes a step towards *kufr* (becoming an infidel) because it is bound to lead to heretical thoughts.[57] Therefore, even poetry written in praise of the Prophet is reprehensible if it indulges in exaggerations and excessive imagery.[58]

'Abd al-Wahhab was rabidly hostile towards non-Muslims as well, insisting that a Muslim should adopt none of the customs of non-Muslims, and should not befriend them either. He argued that it was entirely immaterial what a non-Muslim might think about Muslim practices, and in fact it was a sign of spiritual weakness to care about whether non-Muslims were impressed by Muslim behavior or not.[59] Effectively, 'Abd al-Wahhab espoused a self-sufficient and closed system of belief that has no reason to engage or interact with the other, except from a position of dominance. Rather tellingly, 'Abd al-Wahhab's orientation does not materially differ from the approach adopted by later Muslim groups concerning the irrelevance of universal moral values to the Islamic mission. This insularism and moral isolationism, clearly manifested in the writings of 'Abd al-Wahhab, was powerfully reproduced by ideologues of subsequent Islamic movements.[60] However, 'Abd al-Wahhab's primary concern was not with non-Muslims, but with purportedly corrupt Muslims, among which he included the Ottoman Turks. In this sense, as in later puritan movements, there was a strong political and nationalistic component to 'Abd al-Wahhab's thought. He described the Turks as the moral equivalents of the Mongols who invaded Muslim territories and then converted to Islam in name only. Therefore, the Ottoman Turks were treated as the primary enemy of Islam because, according to 'Abd al-Wahhab, they exercised a corrupting influence upon the religion.[61] Importantly, 'Abd al-Wahhab argued that Muslims who engage in acts of *shirk* must be fought and killed, and interpreted precedents set by the first Rightly Guided Caliph, Abu Bakr, in support of the argument that although people might hold themselves as Muslims, they could, and should, be killed as hypocrites.[62] In addition, 'Abd al-Wahhab, and his followers, engaged in rhetorical tirades against prominent medieval and contemporaneous jurists who they considered heretical, and even ordered the execution or assassination of a large number of jurists with whom they disagreed.[63] According to 'Abd al-Wahhab, and his followers, the juristic tradition, save a few jurists such as Ibn Taymiyya whom they held in high esteem, was largely corrupt, and deference to the well-established schools of jurisprudential thought or even to contemporaneous jurists was an act of heresy.[64] Among the medieval jurists that the Wahhabis explicitly condemned as *kuffar* (infidels) were prominent scholars such as Fakhr al-Din al-Razi (d. 606/1210), Abu Sa'id al-Baydawi (d. 710/1310), Abu Hayyan al-Gharnati (d. 745/1344), al-Khazin (d. 741/1341), Muhammad al-Balkhi (d. 830/1426), Shihab al-Din al-Qastalani (d. 923/1517), Abu Sa'ud al-'Imadi, (d. 982/1574), and many others. The characteristic common to these jurists was that, as far as textual interpretation was concerned, they were not strict literalists. In addition, some of these scholars were suspected of harboring Shi'i sympathies, or had integrated rationalist methods of analysis into their interpretive approaches.[65]

Given the dismissive attitude of the Wahhabis towards Islamic history and law, the movement came under severe criticism from a considerable number of contemporaneous scholars, most notably 'Abd al-Wahhab's own brother, Sulayman, and reportedly his father as well.[66] The main criticism leveled against 'Abd al-Wahhab and his followers was that they exhibited very little regard for Islamic history, historical monuments, the Islamic intellectual tradition, or the sanctity of Muslim life.[67] 'Abd al-Wahhab's brother, as well as other critics, claimed that 'Abd al-Wahhab, himself, was an ill-educated, intolerant man, who was ignorantly and arrogantly dismissive of any thoughts or individuals that disagreed with him.[68] Sulayman complained that, except among the most extreme and fringe fanatical elements, his brother's views were without precedent in Islamic history.[69] Muhammad b. 'Abd al-Wahhab, according to his brother, did not concern himself with reading or understanding the works of the juristic predecessors, but at the same time he treated the words of some, such as Hanbali jurist Ibn Taymiyya (d. 728/1328), as if they were Divinely revealed, not to be questioned or debated. But, even then, Muhammad b. 'Abd al-Wahhab was very selective with the works of Ibn Taymiyya, citing only what he liked and ignoring the rest.[70] Sulayman, and other scholars, noted the irony in fact that Muhammad b. 'Abd al-Wahhab and his followers, while prohibiting *taqlid* (imitation or following the precedents of jurists), ended up affirming and even mandating it, but in a different form. They prohibited the practice of *taqlid* as far as it related to jurists whom they did not like, but demanded that Muslims imitate them blindly and unthinkingly. Sulayman complained that the Wahhabi methodology was based on a profound sense of despotism, where the whole of the Islamic intellectual tradition was dismissed off hand, and Muslims were given the choice of either accepting the idiosyncratic Wahhabi interpretations of Islam or being declared *kafirs* (infidels) and killed. Effectively, Sulayman argued, the Wahhabis behaved as if they alone, after several hundred years of history, had discovered the truth about Islam, and they considered themselves as if infallible.[71] Therefore, in the Wahhabi paradigm, the only actual measure of commitment to Islam is to follow and obey them. If a Muslim disagrees with them then, by definition, that Muslim is a heretic.[72] According to Sulayman, declaring Muslims infidels is considered a grave sin in Islam, and even Ibn Taymiyya prohibited the practice of *takfir* (branding Muslims as infidels).[73] In order to prove his point, Sulayman concluded his treatise by quoting fifty-two traditions, attributed to the Prophet and some of the Companions, on the sin of accusing a Muslim of being an unbeliever or heretic.[74]

The simplicity, decisiveness, and incorruptibility of the religious thought of 'Abd al-Wahhab made it attractive to the desert tribes, especially in the area of Najd. Ultimately, however, his ideas were too radical and extreme to have widespread influence on the Arab world, let alone the Muslim world. It is quite likely that 'Abd al-Wahhab's ideas would not have spread even in Arabia had it not been for the fact that in the late eighteenth century the Al Saud family united itself with the Wahhabi movement, and rebelled against Ottoman rule in Arabia.[75] Armed with religious zeal and a strong sense of Arab nationalism, the rebellion was considerable, at one point reaching as far as Damascus in the north and Oman in the south. Egyptian forces under the leadership of Muhammad Ali in 1818, however, after several failed expeditions, quashed the rebellion, and Wahhabism, like other extremist movements in Islamic history, seemed to be on its way to extinction.[76] Nevertheless, Wahhabi ideology was resuscitated once again in the early twentieth century under the leadership of 'Abd al-'Aziz b. Al Sa'ud (r. 1319–73/1902–53), who adopted the puritanical theology of the Wahhabis and allied himself with the tribes of Najd, thereby establishing the nascent beginnings of what would become Saudi Arabia. The various Wahhabi rebellions in the nineteenth and twentieth centuries were very bloody as the Wahhabis indiscriminately slaughtered Muslims, especially those belonging to the Sufi orders and the Shi'i sect. In 1802, for example, the Wahhabi forces massacred the Shi'i inhabitants of Karbala, and in 1803, 1804, and 1806 the Wahhabis executed a large number of Sunnis in Mecca and Medina whom they considered heretical.[77] This led several mainstream jurists writing during this time period, such as the Hanafi jurist Ibn 'Abidin (d. 1253/1837) and the Maliki jurist al-Sawi (d. 1241/1825), to condemn Wahhabis as a fanatic fringe group, and label them the "modern day Khawarij of Islam."[78] In the areas that fell under their control, the Wahhabis introduced practices that considerably expanded the intrusive powers of the state by making the state into the enforcer of a narrowly defined code of behavior, which, in their view, was the only correct Islam. For instance, the Wahhabis regularly flogged the residents of their territories for listening to music, shaving their beards, wearing silk or gold,[79] smoking, playing backgammon, chess, or cards, or for failing to observe strict rules of sex segregation, and they destroyed all the shrines and most of the Muslim historical monuments found in Arabia.[80] They also introduced the first reported precedent of taking rollcall at prayers. The Wahhabis prepared lists of the inhabitants of a city, and called off the names during the five daily prayers in the mosque, and anyone absent without a sufficient excuse was flogged. Being the caretakers of Mecca and Medina, the Wahhabis were uniquely positioned to enforce their version of orthodoxy upon Muslim pilgrims from around the world. As an indication of the limited popularity of the Wahhabi creed, at that stage of their development, the uncompromisingly austere practices of the Wahhabis during pilgrimage led to several clashes with pilgrims coming from Africa and Southeast Asia.[81] In 1926, for example, the Wahhabi hostility to all forms of musical instruments led to a crisis between Egypt and Saudi Arabia, when Egyptian soldiers carrying the ceremonial palanquin to the sound of bugles during pilgrimage were attacked and beaten, and had their musical instruments destroyed. The Wahhabis also criminalized all forms of Sufi chants and dances in Mecca and Medina, and eventually in all of Saudi Arabia.[82]

There were four main factors that contributed to the survival and, in fact, the thriving of Wahhabism in contemporary Islam. (1) by rebelling against the Ottomans, Wahhabism appealed to the emerging ideologies of Arab nationalism in the eighteenth century. By treating Muslim Ottoman rule as a foreign occupying power, Wahhabism set a powerful precedent for notions of Arab self-determination and autonomy. (2) as noted above, Wahhabism advocated the return to the pristine and pure origins of Islam. Accordingly, Wahhabism rejected the cumulative weight of historical baggage, and insisted upon a return to the precedents of the "rightly guided" early generations (*al-salaf al-salih*). This idea was intuitively liberating for Muslim reformers, since it meant the re-birth of *ijtihad*, or the return to *de novo* examination and determination of legal issues unencumbered by the accretions of precedents and inherited doctrines. (3) by controlling Mecca and Medina, Saudi Arabia became naturally positioned to exercise a considerable influence on Muslim culture and thinking. The holy cities of Mecca and Medina are the symbolic heart of Islam, and are the sites where millions of Muslims perform pilgrimage each year. Therefore, by regulating what might be considered orthodox belief and practice while at pilgrimage, Saudi Arabia became uniquely positioned to influence greatly the belief systems of Islam itself. For instance, for purely symbolic purposes, the King of Saudi Arabia adopted the lowly title of the custodian and servant of the two Holy Sites. (4) and most importantly, the discovery and exploitation of oil provided Saudi Arabia with high liquidity. Especially post-1975, with the sharp rise in oil prices, Saudi Arabia aggressively promoted Wahhabi thought around the Muslim world. Even a cursory examination of the predominant ideas and practices would reveal the widespread influence of Wahhabi thought on the Muslim world today. Part of the reason for Saudi Arabia aggressively promulgating its creed is related to the third element mentioned above. It would have been politically awkward for Saudi Arabia to be the custodian of the two Holy Sites, but at the same time adopt a system of belief that is at odds with the rest of the Muslim world. To say the least, custodianship of the Holy Sites is a sensitive position in the Muslim world, and the Saudi exclusive claim to sovereignty over these cities remained problematic from the 1920s through the 1960s, especially because of the Wahhabis' intolerant attitude towards ritualistic practices that they deem unorthodox. In the 1950s and 1960s, Saudi Arabia was coming under considerable pressure from republican and Arab nationalist regimes who tended to consider the Saudi system archaic and reactionary. In the 1970s, Saudi Arabia finally possessed the financial means to address its legitimacy concerns. The Wahhabis either had to alter their own system of belief to make it more consistent with the convictions of other Muslims, or they had to aggressively spread their convictions to the rest of the Muslim world. The first would have required the Saudi regime to re-invent itself, but, in many ways, it was easier to attempt to re-invent the Muslim world, and that is the option they chose.

Wahhabism, however, did not spread in the modern Muslim world under its own banner. Given the marginal origins of the Wahhabi creed, this would have been quite difficult to accomplish. Wahhabism spread in the Muslim world under the banner of Salafism. It is important to note that even the term "Wahhabism" is considered derogatory to the followers of Ibn 'Abd-al-Wahhab, since Wahhabis prefer to see themselves as the representatives of Islamic orthodoxy. According to its adherents, Wahhabism is not a school of thought within Islam, but is Islam itself, and it is the only possible Islam. The fact that Wahhabism rejected the use of a school label gave it a rather diffuse quality and made many of its doctrines and methodologies immanently transferable. Salafism, unlike Wahhabism, was a far more credible paradigm in Islam, and in many ways an ideal vehicle for Wahhabism. Therefore, in their literature,

Wahhabi clerics have consistently described themselves as Salafis (adherents of Salafism), and not Wahhabis.

Salafism is a creed founded in the late nineteenth century by Muslim reformers such as Muhammad 'Abduh (d. 1323/1905), Jamal al-Din al-Afghani (d. 1314/1897), Muhammad Rashid Rida (d. 1354/1935), Muhammad al-Shawkani (d. 1250/1834), and al-Jalal al-San'ani (d. 1225/1810). Salafism appealed to a very basic and fundamental concept in Islam – that Muslims ought to follow the precedent of the Prophet and his Rightly Guided Companions (*al-salaf al-salih*). Methodologically, Salafism was nearly identical to Wahhabism except that Wahhabism is far less tolerant of diversity and differences of opinions. In many ways, Salafism was intuitively undeniable, partly because of its epistemological promise. The founders of Salafism maintained that on all issues Muslims ought to return to the original textual sources of the Qur'an and the *Sunnah* (precedent) of the Prophet. In doing so, Muslims ought to re-interpret the original sources in light of modern needs and demands without being slavishly bound to the interpretive precedents of earlier Muslim generations. As originally conceived, Salafism was not necessarily anti-intellectual, but, like Wahhabism, it did tend to be uninterested in history. By emphasizing a presumed golden age in Islam, the adherents of Salafism idealized the time of the Prophet and his Companions, and ignored or demonized the balance of Islamic history. Furthermore, by rejecting juristic precedents and undervaluing tradition as a source of authoritativeness, Salafism adopted a form of egalitarianism that deconstructed traditional notions of established authority within Islam. According to Salafism, effectively, anyone was considered qualified to return to the original sources and speak for the Divine Will. By liberating Muslims from the burdens of the technocratic tradition of the jurists, Salafism contributed to a real vacuum of authority in contemporary Islam. However, unlike Wahhabism, Salafism was not hostile to the juristic tradition or the practice of various competing schools of thought. In addition, Salafism was not hostile to mysticism or Sufism. The proponents of Salafism were eager to throw off the shackles of tradition, and to engage in the rethinking of Islamic solutions in light of modern demands. As far as the juristic tradition was concerned, Salafi scholars were synchronizers; they tended to engage in a practice known as *talfiq*, in which they mixed and matched various opinions from the past in order to emerge with novel approaches to problems. Importantly, for the most part, Salafism was founded by Muslim nationalists who were eager to read the values of modernism into the original sources of Islam. Hence, Salafism was not necessarily anti-Western. In fact, its founders strove to project contemporary institutions such as democracy, constitutionalism, or socialism onto the foundational texts, and to justify the paradigm of the modern nation-state within Islam. In this sense, Salafism, as originally conceived, betrayed a degree of opportunism. Its proponents tended to be more interested in the end results than in maintaining the integrity or coherence of the juristic method. Salafism was marked by an anxiety to reach results that would render Islam compatible with modernity, far more than by a desire to critically understand either modernity or the Islamic tradition itself. For instance, the Salafis of the nineteenth and early twentieth centuries heavily emphasized the predominance of the concept of *maslaha* (public interest) in the formulation of Islamic law. Accordingly, it was consistently emphasized that whatever would fulfill the public interest ought to be deemed a part of Islamic law.[83]

Although Muhammad 'Abduh and al-Afghani are usually credited with being the founders of Salafism, and some people even attribute the creed to Ibn Taymiyya (d. 728/1328) and his student Ibn Qayyim al-Jawziyya (d. 751/1350), it was Rashid Rida who best exemplified the ideas, and contradictions, of Salafism, and its elusive relationship with Wahhabism. Rashid Rida, a prominent Syrian reformer who trained in the Azhar seminary, and lived in Egypt, was one of the most influential jurists of the early twentieth century.[84] He is today, however, demonized by Wahhabis for his rationalist and humanitarian approaches to Islam, and his jurisprudential works are banned, and frequently attacked, in Saudi Arabia, and outside of Arabia, by various puritan Salafi groups. This is quite ironic because Rida was a staunch defender of the Wahhabi movement against the criticisms of various Azhari jurists, most notably the Maliki jurist al-Dijawi (d. 1365/1946),[85] and even a friend of King 'Abd al-Aziz of Saudi Arabia.[86] Even conceding that the founder of the creed, 'Abd al-Wahhab, was intolerant towards others, and that the Wahhabis of his time engaged in fanatic behavior, Rida still insisted that the Wahhabis deserved the support of Muslims, as a Salafi movement.[87] In many respects, this claim was incongruous because, contrary to the Wahhabis, Rida advocated a critical approach to the evaluation of the authenticity of Prophetic traditions (*hadith*), and also advocated the use of rationalist methods in the practice of Islamic law.[88] Rida consistently argued that in response to modernity, Islamic law must be interpreted in such a way that human rights and public interests are adequately respected, and supported the study of philosophy, and the practice of parliamentary democracy, both of which were an anathema to the Wahhabis.[89] In addition, quite unlike the Wahhabis, Rida, who was a classically trained jurist himself, was strongly supportive of the juristic tradition, and the status and role of the classically trained jurists in modern Islam.[90] There were certain commonalities between Rida, as a Salafi, and the Wahhabis.[91] Rida was critical of the practices and theology of Sufi orders, particularly the doctrine of intercession and saint worship,[92] and he was also critical of the doctrine of *taqlid* (imitation) and a strong advocate of renewed *ijtihad*, although his position was considerably more subtle and nuanced than the Wahhabis'.[93] The commonalities, however, were not sufficiently compelling to explain Rida's willingness to overlook the intolerant and frequently violent practices of the Wahhabis.[94] Nonetheless, Rida defended the Wahhabis because of politics – Rida was an Arab nationalist who was also increasingly anti-Ottoman. It is clear from his own writings that Rida welcomed the Wahhabi rebellion against the Ottomans, as an Arab revolution being waged against their Turkish masters.[95] This, however, exemplified a problem that came to plague Salafi thought throughout the twentieth century, and that is its political opportunism. Salafism, which initially promised a liberal type of renaissance in the Islamic world, persistently compromised theological principle to power dynamics and political expedience. Confronted by the challenge of nationalism, Salafis, often invoking the logic of public interest and necessity,[96] consistently transformed Islam into a politically reactive force engaged in a mundane struggle for identity and self-determination. As a result, Salafism became a highly diluted and unprincipled moral force, constantly re-structuring and re-defining itself to respond to a never ending and constantly shifting power dynamic. In the end, no one could be entirely sure about the ethical and moral principles that Salafism represented, other than a stark form of functionalism that constantly shifted in response to the political demands of the day.[97]

By the mid twentieth century, it had become clear that Salafism had drifted into stifling apologetics. The incipient opportunism in Salafi approaches had degenerated into an intellectual carelessness and even whimsicalness that had all but destroyed any efforts at systematic and rigorous analysis. By the 1960s the initial optimistic liberalism of Salafism had dissipated, and what remained of this liberal bent had become largely apologetic. Through a complex socio-political process, Wahhabism was able to rid itself of some of its extreme forms of intolerance, and proceeded to co-opt the language and symbolisms of Salafism in the 1970s until the two had become practically indistinguishable.[98] Both Wahhabism and Salafism imagined a golden age within Islam; this entailed a belief in a near historical utopia that is entirely retrievable and reproducible in contemporary Islam. Both remained uninterested in critical historical inquiry and responded to the challenge of modernity by escaping to the secure haven of the text. And both advocated a form of egalitarianism and anti-elitism to the point that they came to consider intellectualism and rational moral insight to be inaccessible, and thus corruptions of the purity of the Islamic message.[99] These similarities between the two facilitated the Wahhabi co-optation of Salafism. Wahhabism, from its very inception, and Salafism, especially after it entered into the apologetic phase, were infested with a kind of supremacist thinking that still prevails until today. The level of intellectual sophistication found in the writings of Rashid Rida, for example, became increasingly rare, and increasingly the texts written by Salafis became indistinguishable from those written by Wahhabis. To simplify matters, I will call this unity of Wahhabism with the worst that is in Salafism, "Salafabism."

Salafabism took things to their logical extreme. The bonding of the theologies of Wahhabism and Salafism produced a contemporary orientation that is anchored in profound feelings of defeatism, alienation, and frustration. The synchronistic product of these two theologies is one of profound alienation, not only from the institutions of power of the modern world, but also from the Islamic heritage and tradition. Neither Wahhabism nor Salafism, nor the synchronistic Salafabism, is represented by formal institutions; these are theological orientations and not structured schools of thought. Therefore, one finds a broad range of ideological variations and tendencies within each orientation. But the consistent characteristic of Salafabism is a supremacist puritanism that compensates for feelings of defeatism, disempowerment, and alienation with a distinct sense of self-righteous arrogance *vis-à-vis* the nondescript "other" – whether the "other" is the West, non-believers in general, or even Muslim women. In this sense, it is accurate to describe the Salafabist orientation as supremacist, for it sees the world from the perspective of stations of merit and extreme polarization. It is important to note, however, that this trend de-values the moral worth not only of non-Muslims, but also those that it considers inferior or of a lesser station, such as women or heretical Muslims. Instead of simple apologetics, Salafabism responds to the feelings of powerlessness and defeat with uncompromising and arrogant symbolic displays of power, not only against non-Muslims, but even more so against fellow Muslims.

Salafabism has anchored itself in the confident security of texts. But in my view, far from being respectful towards the integrity of the text, Salafabism is abusive. As a hermeneutic orientation, it empowers its adherents to project their socio-political frustrations and insecurities upon the text. Elsewhere, I have described the dynamics of Salafabism *vis-à-vis* the text as thoroughly despotic and authoritarian. Consistently, religious texts became like whips to be exploited by a select class of readers in order to affirm reactionary power dynamics in society.[100] The adherents of Salafabism, unlike the apologists, no longer concerned themselves with co-opting or claiming Western institutions as their own. Under the guise of reclaiming the true and real Islam, they proceeded to define Islam as the exact antithesis of the West. Apologetic attempts at proving Islam's compatibility with the West were dismissed as inherently defeatist. Salafabists argued that colonialism had ingrained into Muslims a lack of self-pride or dignity, and convinced Muslims of the inferiority of their religion. This has trapped Muslims into an endless and futile race to appease the West by proving Islam's worthiness. According to this model, in reality, there are only two paths in life – the path of God or the straight path, and the path of Satan or the crooked path. By attempting to integrate and co-opt Western ideas such as feminism, democracy, or human rights, Muslims have fallen prey to the temptations of Satan by accepting ungodly innovations (*bida*', sing. *bid'a*). They believe that Islam is the only straight path in life, and such a way must be pursued regardless of what others think and regardless of how it impacts the rights and well being of others. Importantly, the straight path (*al-sirat al-mustaqim*) is firmly anchored in a system of Divine laws that trump any considerations of morality or ethical normative values. God is manifested through a set of determinable legal commands that cover nearly all aspects of life, and the sole purpose of human beings is to realize the Divine manifestation by dutifully and faithfully implementing the Divine law. Salafabists insist that only the mechanics and technicalities of Islamic law define morality – there are no moral considerations that can be found outside the technical law. This technical and legalistic way of life is considered inherently superior to all others, and the followers of any other way are considered either infidels (*kuffar*), hypocrites (*munafiqun*), or iniquitous (*fasiqun*). Anchored in the security and assuredness of a determinable law, it becomes fairly easy to differentiate between the rightly guided and the misguided. The rightly guided obey the law; the misguided either deny, attempt to dilute, or argue about the law. Any method of thought or process that would lead to indeterminate results such as social theory, philosophy, or any speculative thought is part of the crooked path of Satan. According to the Salafabists, lives that are lived outside the Divine law are inherently unlawful, and therefore an offense against God that must be actively fought or punished.

Whether Salafabism contributed, or could contribute, to honoring God's Kingdom on this earth is a question I am not prepared to engage here. But in my view, it is clear that the impact of Salafabism on the Islamic intellectual heritage and the humanistic and universalistic orientations within Islam has been devastating. Two of the main problematics that distinguish Salafabists from others are: (1) whether the religious text is intended to regulate most aspects of life, and (2) Whether aesthetics or an innate human capacity to reflect upon and realize the good is possible. Not surprisingly, Salafabists exaggerate the role of the text, and minimize the role of the human agent who interprets the religious text. According to Salafabists, not only does the text regulate most aspects of human life, but also the author of the text determines the meaning of the text, while the reader's job in engaging the text is simply to understand and implement. In the Salafabist paradigm, the subjectivities of the interpreting agent are irrelevant to the realization and implementation of the Divine command, which is fully and comprehensively contained in the text. Therefore, the aesthetics and moral insights or experiences of the interpreting agent are considered irrelevant and superfluous. According to Salafabists, public interests, such as the interest in protecting society from the sexual lures of women, can be empirically verified.[101] However, in contrast, moral or ethical values and aesthetic judgments about what is necessary or compelling cannot be empirically quantified, and therefore must be ignored. So values like human dignity, love, mercy, and compassion are not subject to quantification, and therefore they cannot be integrated into legal determinations. Importantly, because Salafabists are dismissive towards the subjectivities of the interpreting agent, and aesthetic judgments are considered anathema, they largely ignore the intellectual products of the interpretive communities of past generations, and contribute to a sense of disoriented rootlessness among modern Muslims. Their approach to Islamic texts is very reminiscent of the pedantic literalism of the *Ahl al-Hadith* in the pre-modern period, who opposed every rationalist orientation in Islam.[102]

One event that is aptly demonstrative of the impact of the Salafabists, and the marked ambivalence that plagues current attitudes towards the Islamic intellectual heritage, is the controversy that surrounded the late Muslim scholar Muhammad al-Ghazali (d. 1410/1989). Al-Ghazali, a prolific Azhari jurist who, like Rashid Rida, described himself as a Salafi, grew increasingly weary of the anti-rationalism and amoralism of those who described themselves as Salafis, and those whom I have called Salafabists. Cognizant of the influence of Wahhabis in contemporary Islam, al-Ghazali did not dare criticize the Wahhabis explicitly or directly. In fact, some Muslim thinkers who were known for their liberalism and rationalism had written books defending Muhammad b. 'Abd al-Wahhab and Wahhabism – portraying it as a movement most capable of confronting the challenges of modernity.[103] Instead of criticizing the Wahhabis, al-Ghazali wrote a book severely criticizing what he called the modern-day *Ahl al-Hadith* – their literalism, anti-rationalism, and anti-interpretive approaches.[104] Al-Ghazali also blamed the modern *Ahl al-Hadith* for perpetuating acts of fanaticism that have defiled the image of Islam in the world. He contended that the *Ahl al-Hadith* suffer from an isolationist and arrogant attitude that makes them uninterested in what the rest of humanity thinks about Islam or Muslims. In al-Ghazali's view, this arrogant and intolerant attitude has deprecated and impoverished Islamic thinking, and denied Islam its universalism and humanism. Rather tellingly, al-Ghazali claimed that the modern *Ahl al-Hadith* have trapped Islam in an arid, harsh, and Bedouin-like environment in which the earmarks of a humanist civilization were clearly absent. This, of course, was an indirect reference to the Wahhabis and their legacy. In addition, al-Ghazali strongly defended the juristic tradition in Islam, and decried the ambivalence and dismissiveness with which this tradition is treated. Being aware of the confusion that has come to surround the meaning of the word "Salafism," al-Ghazali avoided engaging in an argument about who are the real and genuine Salafis, but he did advocate a return to the methodologies of the scholars, such as Muhammad 'Abduh and Rashid Rida, both of whom were pioneers of the Salafi movement.

The reaction to al-Ghazali's book was very strong, with a large number of Salafabis writing to condemn him, and to question his motives and competence.[105] It is difficult to assess whether the harsh response to al-Ghazali's book was indicative of his own importance and the power of his argument, or whether, in the 1980s, the Wahhabis had grown accustomed to not being criticized by any influential Sunni jurist. As noted earlier, apologetics and the sheer financial power of the Saudis have made critiques of Wahhabism written from within a non-Sufi juristic perspective exceedingly rare.[106] Muhammad al-Ghazali died shortly after suffering through the controversy that surrounded his book. Although my sense is that al-Ghazali's book did not receive the kind of attention and fair hearing it deserved, this book has come to symbolize a cry of protest over the fate of Salafism, and its transformation into Salafabism – a transformation that ultimately undermined much of the efforts of the Muslim reformers writing at the end of the nineteenth and beginning of the twentieth centuries.[107]

In light of the recent attention focused on the issue of terrorism, it is important to note that bin Laden, Ayman al-Zawahiri, and the religious police who caused the death of schoolgirls in Mecca, as well as most extremist Muslims, belong to the orientation that I have called Salafabist. Bin Laden, although raised in a Wahhabi environment, is not, strictly speaking, part of that creed. Wahhabism is distinctively introverted – although focused on power, it primarily asserts power over other Muslims. From that perspective, the religious police involved in the school fire incident are more within the classic Wahhabi paradigm than bin Laden. This is consistent with Wahhabism's classic obsession with orthodoxy and correct ritualistic practice, especially as they pertain to the seclusion of women. Militant puritan groups, however, are both introverted and extroverted – they attempt to assert power against both Muslims and non-Muslims. As populist movements, they are a reaction to the disempowerment most Muslims have suffered in the modern age at the hands of harshly despotic governments, and at the hands of interventionist foreign powers. In many ways, these militant groups compensate for extreme feelings of disempowerment by extreme and vulgar claims to power. Fueled by the supremacist and puritan creed of Salafabism, these groups' symbolic acts of power become uncompromisingly fanatic and violent.

It would be inaccurate to contend that the militant supremacist groups fill the vacuum of authority in contemporary Islam. Militant groups such as al-Qaeda or the Taliban, despite their ability to commit highly visible acts of violence, are a sociological and intellectual marginality in Islam. However, these groups are in fact extreme manifestations of more prevalent intellectual and theological currents in modern Islam. In my view, they are extreme manifestations of the rather widespread theological orientation of Salafabism. While it is true that bin Laden is the quintessential example of a Muslim who was created, shaped, and motivated by the post-colonial experience, he is representative of underlying currents in contemporary Islam. Much of what constitutes Islam today was shaped as a defensive reaction to the post-colonial experience, as the product of either uncritical cheerleading on behalf of what was presumed to be the Islamic tradition, or an obstinate rejectionism against what was presumed to be the Western tradition. As such, the likes of bin Laden are the children of a profound dissonance and dysfunctionalism experienced towards both the Islamic heritage and modernity. In my view, bin Laden, like the whole of the Salafabist movement, is an orphan of modernity, but their claim to an authentic lineage in the Islamic civilization is tenuous at best.

After 9/11 and the bloodletting that followed, and the many extreme acts of ugliness that have become associated with the word "Islam," the question is: now that we have witnessed the sheer amount of senseless destruction that the children of this orientation are capable of producing and the type of world that they are capable of instigating, will Muslims be able to marginalize Salafabism and render it, like many of the arrogant movements that preceded it, a historical curiosity? The burden on Muslim intellectuals today is heavy indeed. There ought to be no question that Islam inspired one of the most humanistic, tolerant, and intellectually rich civilizations, but it would be a grievous mistake to assume any historical inevitabilities – just because Muslims achieved moral greatness once does not necessarily mean that they will do so again. From a Muslim perspective, it is arrogant to assume that regardless of the efforts and behavior of Muslims, God is, somehow, obligated to save Muslims from the consequences of their own deeds.[108] Classical jurists used to repeat that political power is necessary to safeguard the interests of religion, but they also used to warn that political power is fundamentally corrupting of the human conscience and the mandates of justice.[109] This is particularly true of the current Muslim reality. Since the severe sense of disempowerment experienced in the age of colonialism, Muslim intellectual activities have been abysmal. In the recent past, when contemporary Muslim intellectuals have attempted a critical engagement with their tradition and a search for the moral and humanistic aspects of the intellectual heritage, invariably they have been confronted by the specter of post-colonialism; their efforts have been evaluated purely in terms of whether these appease or displease the West, and whether they politically and socially empower Muslims or not, and are accepted or rejected by many Muslims accordingly. Extreme acts of ugliness, perpetrated in the name of Islam, are stark manifestations of a way of thinking that has come to value a superficial sense of independence, control, security, and power, regardless of their moral antecedents or consequences. Since the age of colonialism, Muslims have become politically hyperactive – a hyperactivity that has often led to much infighting, divisiveness, and inter-Muslim persecution – but they have also remained morally lethargic. If Islam is to be reclaimed from colonialism, blind nationalism, political hyperactivism, and Salafabism, this moral lethargy must be transformed. But, in my view, this moral lethargy can only be transformed through an intellectual commitment and activism that honors the Islamic heritage, by honestly and critically engaging it, and that also honors Islam, by honestly and critically confronting any extreme act of ugliness perpetrated in the name of the Islamic religion. In my view, there is no question that colonialism, and its many byproducts, was a violent rupture in Muslim history. Unfortunately, modernity, despite its many scientific advancements, reached Muslims packaged in the ugliness of disempowerment and alienation. This legacy has produced the modern ugly, and it is the modern ugly that Muslims must overcome today, as they go about reclaiming the beautiful in the vast and rich moral tradition of Islam. As argued in this essay, it would be unwise to rely on historical inevitabilities, but it would be most fitting for Muslims to recognize that the history of Islam does establish moral imperatives, the most powerful of which is the imperative of beauty.

ENDNOTES

*I thank my wife Grace and assistant Naheed Fakoor for reading and commenting on this article. I also thank Adel al-Mu'allim and Shorouk Press for supplying me with many rare sources.

1. On the modern origins of the *mutawwa'un*, and their often violent practices, see Michael Cook, "The Expansion of the First Saudi State: The Case of Washm," in C.E. Bosworth et al. (eds.), *Essays in Honor of Bernard Lewis: The Islamic World From Classical to Modern Times* (Princeton: Princeton University Press, 1989), 672–5; Ameen Fares Rihani, *The Maker of Modern Arabia* (New York: Greenwood, 1983), 203. William Gifford Palgrave, *Personal Narrative of Year's Journey through Central and Eastern Arabia* (London: Gregg, 1883), 243–50, 316–18, reports that during the reign of King Faysal b. Turki (r. 1249–54/ 1834–8 and 1259–82/1843–65), in response to a cholera outbreak, twenty-two so-called zealots were selected to combat vice in Mecca and elsewhere. Apparently, this was the beginning of the system of the *mutawwa'un*. Also, see Michael Cook, "On the Origins of Wahhabism," *Journal of the Royal Asiatic Society*, 3(2), 1992.
2. This incident was reported in Saudi newspapers such as the *Saudi Gazette* and *Al-Iqtisadiyya*. In rarely voiced criticism against the religious police, both papers demanded investigations and prosecutions of those responsible. The day after the event, Crown Prince 'Abdullah announced that the government would investigate and punish those responsible. Three days after the event, the Saudi government ordered all newspapers to desist from publishing anything about the tragedy, and, to date, no one has been prosecuted or fired for the death of the girls. The tragedy was reported on extensively in the West, but received very limited coverage in the Muslim world. On the tragedy, its causes, and aftermath, see Eleanor Doumato, "Saudi Sex-Segregation Can be Fatal," March 31, 2002, www.projo.com/opinion/contributors; Tarek Al-Issawi, "Saudi Schoolgirls' Fire Deaths Decried," March 18, 2002, www.washtimes.com/world; Mona Eltahawy, "They Died for Lack of a Head Scarf," *Washington Post*, March 19, 2002, A21; "Muslims Allow Girls to Burn to Death in So-Called Moderate Saudi Arabia," March 18, 2002, www.welchreport.com; "Saudi Police Stopped Fire Rescue," March 15, 2002, http://news.bbc.co.uk.
3. Quoted in A.A. Vasiliev, *History of the Byzantine Empire* (Madison: University of Wisconsin Press, 1952), vol. 1, 216. During that time a large number of Christians adopted the Arabic language without adopting Islam and became known as the *mozarabs* (the Arabized).
4. It is rather telling that the overwhelming majority of Muslim classical jurists were ethnically not Arabs, but they composed their works of jurisprudence in Arabic. In other words, although most Muslim jurists were descended from non-Arab ethnicities such as those of Central and South Asia and North Africa, the vast majority of Islamic law was composed in Arabic. Through the dynamic transformative power of the Arabic language in the pre-modern period, these jurists were Arabized.
5. For excellent studies on the historical misconceptions about Islam prevalent in Europe, see Franco Cardini, *Europe and Islam* (Oxford: Blackwell Press, 2001); Albert Hourani, *Islam in European Thought* (Cambridge: Cambridge University Press, 1991); Maxime Rodinson, *Europe and the Mystique of Islam* (London: I.B. Tauris, 1987); Thierry Hentsch, *L'Orient Imaginaire: La Vision Politique Occidentale de l'Est Mediterraneen* (Paris: Ed. Minuit, 1988); R.W. Southern, *Western Views of Islam in the Middle Ages* (Cambridge: Harvard University Press, 1962). The most comprehensive work on the subject, however, remains: Norman Daniel, *Islam and the West: The Making of an Image* (Edinburgh: Edinburgh University Press, 1960; reprint, Oxford: Oneworld, 2000). Also, see Norman Daniel, *The Arabs and Medieval Europe* (London: Longman, 1975). For a particularly useful and sophisticated collection of studies on the topic, see John Victor Tolan, *Medieval Christian Perceptions of Islam* (London: Routledge, 2000).

6. On binary instincts, their impact, and challenge, see Rush W. Dozier, *Why We Hate: Understanding, Curbing, and Eliminating Hate in Ourselves and Our World* (New York: McGraw Hill, 2002), 39–48.

7. This is evidenced, for instance, by the influence of Muslim thought upon Maimonides, the intellectual movement known as the Averroists in medieval Europe, and the teaching of the medical treatises of Ibn al-Haytham in European universities; see Montgomery Watt, *The Influence of Islam on Medieval Europe* (Edinburgh: Edinburgh University Press, 1972).

8. I am discounting the West's need for Arab oil because it is a mineral extracted by Western technology, often through the use of Western technical expertise, and which benefits Western industries. More importantly, Western dependence on oil does not lead to cross-cultural or intellectual exchanges. All cultural and intellectual influences go one way and that is from West to East.

9. Tragic events such as the Salman Rushdie incident, the treatment of women by the Taliban, and the 9/11 terrorist attacks upon the U.S.A. have fed an extensive amount of vulgar anti-Islamic propaganda. For a partial list of Islamophobic works that were published after 9/11, see: Steven Emerson, *American Jihad: The Terrorists among Us* (New York: Simon & Schuster, 2002); Daniel Pipes, *Militant Islam Reaches America* (New York: W.W. Norton, 2002); Dan Benjamin, *The Age of Sacred Terror: Radical Islam's War against America* (New York: Random House, 2002); Ergun Caner and Emir Caner, *Unveiling Islam: An Insider's Look at Muslim Life and Beliefs* (Grand Rapids, MI: Kregel, 2002); Anthony J. Dennis, *The Rise of the Islamic Empire and the Threat to the West* (New York: Wyndham Hall Press, 2001); Mark A. Gabriel, *Islam and Terrorism: What the Quran Really Teaches about Christianity, Violence, and the Goals of the Islamic Jihad* (New York: Charisma House, 2002); S.F. Fleming, *Islam and New Global Realities: The Roots of Islamic Fundamentalism* (Surprise, AZ: Selah, 2002); George Grant, *The Blood of the Moon: Understanding the Historic Struggle between Islam and Western Civilization* (New York: Thomas Nelson Press, 2001); David Earle Johnson, *Conspiracy in Mecca: What You Need to Know about the Islamic Threat* (New York: David Johnson, 2002); Sumrall Lester, *Jihad – The Holy War: Time Bomb in the Middle East* (New York: Sumrall, 2002); John F. MacArthur, *Terrorism, Jihad, and the Bible* (New York: W, 2001); John F. Murphy, Jr, *The Sword of Islam: Muslim Extremism from the Arab Conquests to the Attack on America* (New York: Prometheus, 2002); Adam Parfrey (ed.), *Extreme Islam: Anti-American Propaganda of Muslim Fundamentalism* (New York: Feral House, 2002); Robert Spencer, *Islam Unveiled: Disturbing Questions about the World's Fastest Growing Faith* (New York: Encounter, 2002); Larry Spargimino, *Religion of Peace or Refuge for Terror?* (New York: Hearthstone: 2002); Marvin Yakos, *Jesus vs. Jihad* (New York: Creation House, 2001). For blatantly anti-Islamic and, by all measures, Islam-hating works that were published pre-9/11 but that have found new popularity in current times, see Paul Fregosi, *Jihad in the West: Muslim Conquests from the 7th to the 21st Centuries* (New York: Prometheus, 1998); Ibn Warraq, *Why I Am Not a Muslim* (New York: Prometheus, 1995); Norman L. Geisler and Abdul Saleeb, *Answering Islam: The Crescent in Light of the Cross* (New York: Dimensions, 1994); Victor Mordecai, *Is Fanatic Islam a Global Threat?* (Taylor, SC: n.p., 1997); Robert A. Morey, *The Islamic Invasion: Confronting the World's Fastest Growing Religion* (New York: Harvest House, 1992); Anis A. Shorrosh, *Islam Revealed: A Christian Arab's View of Islam* (New York: Thomas Nelson, 1988).

10. There has been an extensive debate about what is called the paradigm of the Clash of Civilizations. The proponents of this paradigm believe that there are values that are distinctly Islamic, and which are fundamentally at odds with the values of the Judeo-Christian West. As many of the critics of this paradigm have pointed out, it is doubtful that there is such a thing as distinctly Judeo-Christian values. Most moral values have a mixed lineage that was heavily shaped by the Islamic heritage. Furthermore, it is not coincidental that the proponents of the Clash of Civilizations invariably ascribe to Islam values that are contrary to democracy, human rights, and liberties. On the debate of Clash of Civilizations, see: Samuel P. Huntington, *The Clash of Civilizations: Remaking of World Order* (New York: Touchstone Press, 1996); Colin Chapman, *Islam and the West: Conflict,*

Co-existence or Conversion? (Carlisle, U.K.: Paternoster Press, 1998); John Esposito, *The Islamic Threat: Myth or Reality?* (Oxford: Oxford University Press, 1995); John Esposito and Zafar Ishaq Ansari (eds.), *Muslims and the West: Encounter and Dialogue* (Islamabad: Islamic Research Institute, 2001); Fred Halliday, *Islam and the Myth of Confrontation* (London: I.B. Tauris, 1995); Shireen T. Hunter, *The Future of Islam and the West: Clash of Civilizations or Peaceful Coexistence?* (Westport, CT: Praeger Press, 1998); Karim H. Karim, *The Islamic Peril: Media and Global Violence* (Montreal: Black Rose, 2000); Jorgen S. Nielsen (ed.), *The Christian–Muslim Frontier: Chaos, Clash or Dialogue?* (London: I.B. Tauris, 1998); Dieter Senghaas, *The Clash within Civilizations: Coming to Terms with Cultural Conflicts* (London: Routledge, 1998). Not surprisingly, writers who clearly do not like Muslims very much have exploited Huntington's thesis. For an example of paranoid Islamophobia, a work that was unfortunately highly praised by various American politicians, see Anthony J. Dennis, *The Rise of the Islamic Empire and the Threat to the West* (Bristol, IN: Wyndham Hall Press, 1996). For another example of a work, written from the perspective of a Christian fundamentalist, that exploits Huntington's argument and that is hostile to Islam, see George Grant, *The Blood of the Moon: Understanding the Historic Struggle between Islam and Western Civilization* (New York: Thomas Nelson Press, 2001). Typically, in this genre of literature, Christianity, Judaism, and Western culture are, rather jovially, all bundled up in a single unitary mass, placed in a corner, and then pitted against the fantasized concept of: THE ISLAM.

11. The expression "vulgarization of Islam" was inspired by an essay written by Robert Scott Appleby in Khaled Abou El Fadl (ed.), *The Place of Tolerance in Islam* (New York: Beacon Press, forthcoming).

12. On the doctrine of necessity (*darura*) see Subhi Mahmassani, *The Philosophy of Jurisprudence in Islam*, trans. Farhat Ziadeh (Leiden: E.J. Brill, 1961), 152–9; Mohammad Hashim Kamali, *Principles of Islamic Jurisprudence* (Cambridge: Islamic Texts Society, 1991), 267–81. The well-established Islamic legal maxim provides: necessities will render the forbidden permissible (*al-darurat tubih al-mahzurat*), and the preservation of human life is considered in Islamic jurisprudence to be the most basic and fundamental necessity of all. Preservation of human life, in the order of Islamic values, is a greater priority than the safeguarding of God's rights (*huquq Allah*). See, on the subject, Khaled Abou El Fadl, *Speaking in God's Name: Islamic Law, Authority and Women* (Oxford: Oneworld Press, 2001), 196–7; Khaled Abou El Fadl, "Constitutionalism and the Islamic Sunni Legacy," *UCLA Journal of Islamic and Near Eastern Law*, 1(1), 2001–2, 86–92.

13. Qur'an 33:59.

14. Not even the puritanical Saudi religious police believe that men are commanded to cover the hair on their head. The custom of Saudi men, including the religious police, however, is to wear a piece of cloth that covers a part of their head.

15. Geoff Simons, *Saudi Arabia: The Shape of Client Feudalism* (London: St Martin's Press, 1998), 48. For other wide-scale human rights abuses committed in Saudi Arabia in the name of Islam, see pp. 3–68. I worked on this case very closely with Human Rights Watch in a vain attempt to save al-Naqshabandi's life, who for three years after his arrest, and despite being tortured, continued to profess his innocence, re-affirm his Muslim faith, and state that he had never believed in or practiced witchcraft until the very end. Citing the works of Ibn Taymiyya, al-Naqshabandi wrote several long letters to the judge in charge of his case, arguing that no authority in Islamic law ever held that the punishment for possession of an amulet was death, and insisted that he was a believing and practicing Muslim. He also asserted that his employer framed him, and that he was never allowed to consult a lawyer after his arrest, and that the court had refused to call any of the twenty-two witnesses who would testify to his innocence. The Committee for the Promotion of Virtue and Prevention of Vice, and the Saudi Ministry of Interior justified the execution by charging that al-Naqshabandi "undertook the practice of works of magic and spells and possession of a collection of polytheistic and superstitious books... In view of what magic and witchcraft produce in the way of serious damage to the individual and society with

respect to religion, the soul, money, and intellect, and considering that what the defendant did has the potential of producing great harm, his acts are worthy of severe punishment so that his evil will be terminated and others will be deterred. Therefore, it was decided that he be sentenced to the discretionary punishment of death." According to the Ministry of Interior, the death sentence was reviewed and affirmed by the Saudi Appeals Committee (*hay'at al-tamyiz*) and the Higher Judicial Council. Having worked on the case, and after reviewing all evidence and legal material, I am thoroughly convinced that this man was unjustly murdered, and even if he was guilty as charged, his execution was a flagrant violation of Islamic law and ethics. For the details of the case, see Clarisa Bencomo, "Flawed Justice: The Execution of 'Abd al-Karim Mara'i al-Naqshabandi," a report of Human Rights Watch / Middle East Division (New York, 1997).

16. Qur'an 9:39; 11:57; 47:38.
17. Qur'an 9:67; 59:19.
18. For a detailed study on the role of authorial enterprise, communities of interpretation, and Islamic law, see Khaled Abou El Fadl, *Speaking in God's Name: Authority, Islamic Law, and Women* (Oxford: Oneworld, 2001).
19. For a valuable study on the duty to enjoin the good and forbid the evil in the Islamic tradition, see Michael Cook, *Commanding Right and Forbidding Wrong in Islamic Thought* (Cambridge: Cambridge University Press, 2000).
20. Qur'an 2:143; 3:110.
21. Qur'an 4:135; 5:8.
22. Interestingly, the expression "false universalisms" was used by Samuel Huntington in arguing that the Western belief in the universality of their values is both immoral and dangerous, Samuel Huntington, *The Clash of Civilizations: Remaking of World Order* (New York: Touchstone Press, 1996), 310.
23. For examples of such accusations, see the essay critiquing my work by Abid Ullah Jan, in Abou El Fadl, *The Place of Tolerance in Islam*.
24. Ironically, this is the gist of Huntington's argument about the wrongfulness of believing in universal Western values, Huntington, *The Clash of Civilizations*, 308–12. This is also Lawrence Rosen's argument in his *The Justice of Islam: Comparative Perspectives on Islamic Law and Society* (Oxford: Oxford University Press, 2000), 153–75, where he contends that what Westerners would consider despotic and oppressive is entirely acceptable for Muslims because of their own conceptions of justice and reality. See my critique of this book in Abou El Fadl, "Islamic Law and Ambivalent Scholarship," *Michigan Law Review*, vol. 100, no. 6, May 2002, 1421–43. For the utilization of the relativism argument in the international human rights field and a critique of this position, see Ann Mayer, *Islam and Human Rights: Tradition and Politics* (Boulder: Westview Press, 1999). Also see Khaled Abou El Fadl, "Soul Searching and the Spirit of Shari'a," *Washington University Global Studies Law Review*, vol. 1, nos. 1–2, Winter/Summer 2002, 553–72.
25. On this subject, see Khaled Abou El Fadl, *And God Knows the Soldiers: The Authoritative and Authoritarian in Islamic Discourses* (Lanham, MD: University Press of America, 2001), 138–56.
26. For instance, see the following valuable studies on the usage of ethical terms in the Qur'an: Toshihiko Izutsu, *The Structure of Ethical Terms in the Quran* (Chicago: ABC, 2000); Toshihiko Izutsu, *Ethico-religious Concepts in the Quran* (Montreal: McGill University Press, 1966).
27. On this subject, see Khaled Abou El Fadl, *Reasoning With God: Rationality and Thought in Islam* (Oxford: Oneworld, forthcoming). Also see George F. Hourani, *Reason and Tradition in Islamic Ethics* (Cambridge: Cambridge University Press, 1985).
28. See my essays in Abou El Fadl, *The Place of Tolerance in Islam*.
29. Qur'an 38:87. The Qur'an states, for instance, "And God does not desire for human beings to suffer injustice." (3:108) A statement such as this generates layers of meaning, but it is reasonable to conclude that the Qur'an recognizes certain ethical principles as universally applicable and pertinent.

30. "Westoxification" is a derogatory expression used to describe self-hating Muslims who are in awe of everything Western to the point that they seem to be intoxicated on the West.
31. Some scholars have argued that most of Muslim society in the modern age is characterized by a cultural schizophrenia in which there are profound distortions in the self-consciousness of Muslims. See Daryush Shayegan, *Cultural Schizophrenia: Islamic Societies Confronting the West*, trans. John Howe (London: Saqi, 1989). Also see Louay M. Safi, *The Challenge of Modernity: The Quest for Authenticity in the Arab World* (Lanham, MD: University Press of America, 1994), esp. pp. 153–93.
32. There are many works that document the influence of Islamic culture and thought on Europe. Two impressive works are: George Makdisi, *The Rise of Humanism in Classical Islam and the Christian West* (Edinburgh: Edinburgh University Press, 1990); Mourad Wahba and Mona Abousenna (eds), *Averroes and the Enlightenment* (New York: Prometheus, 1996). Even when preserving the Greek philosophical tradition, Muslim scholars did not act as mere transmitters, but substantially developed and built upon Greek philosophy. In a fascinating text that demonstrates the level of penetration that Islamic thought achieved in Europe, Thomas Aquinas, in an attempt to refute Ibn Rushd (aka Averroes), whom he labels as a "perverter of Peripatetic philosophy" and Ibn Sina (Avicenna), ends up quoting Abu Hamid al-Ghazali in support of his arguments against Ibn Rushd's. Both al-Ghazali and Ibn Rushd were medieval Muslim philosophers and jurists. Thomas Aquinas, *On the Unity of the Intellect against the Averroists*, trans. Beatrice Zedler (Milwaukee: Marquette University Press, 1968), 46–7. For a collection of articles that demonstrate cross-intellectual influences, see John Inglis, *Medieval Philosophy and the Classical Tradition: In Islam, Judaism, and Christianity* (Richmond, U.K.: Curzon Press, 2002). For an awe-inspiring example of the contributions of medieval Muslim scholars to Greek philosophy, see Kwame Gyekye, *Arabic Logic: Ibn al-Tayyib's Commentary on Porphyry's Eisagoge* (Albany: State University of New York Press, 1979).
33. Khaled Abou El Fadl, "Islam and the Theology of Power Islam," 221 *Middle East Report*, Winter 2001, 28–33.
34. On the hegemony of the United States and the West, and Muslim reaction, see Simon W. Murden, *Islam, the Middle East and the New Global Hegemony* (Boulder: Lynne Rienner, 2002), esp. 43–128.
35. For a study on Muslims, the West, and the prevalence of siege mentalities, see Graham E. Fuller and Ian O. Lesser, *A Sense of Siege: The Geopolitics of Islam and the West* (Boulder: Westview Press, 1995).
36. Among the practices of Muslim puritans is to collect, publish, and disperse traditions, attributed to the Prophet or the Companions, that are demeaning to women. Such collections then act as a foundation for issuing deprecating determinations in regard to women. Muhammad b. 'Abd al-Wahhab, himself, under the subheading of "living with women," collected a group of these women-deprecating traditions; see Muhammad b. 'Abd al-Wahhab, *Mu'allafat al-Shaykh al-Imam Muhammad bin 'Abd al-Wahhab: Qism al-Hadith* (Riyadh: Jami'at al-Imam Muhammad bin Sa'ud al-Islamiyya, n.d.), part 4, 141–51.
37. This is often expressed in terms of describing women as the worst *fitnah*, and claiming that women will constitute the vast majority of the residents of hell-fire, and that most men in hell will be there because of women. For a systematic analysis of this issue, see Abou El Fadl, *Speaking in God's Name*, 170–249.
38. The claim of the perfect religion is incomprehensible because it ignores human agency in the determination of the meaning of religion. Islam, as submission to God, could be a perfect act, and God could conceive of the prerequisites and conditions for submission in a perfect way. This, however, does not mean that Muslims have submitted perfectly, or that they perfectly understand the prerequisites and conditions of submission. Islam is perfect as a metaphysical reality in God's mind, but this does not mean that there could be a perfect realization of God's mind by the human mind.
39. For a critical, and similarly grim, assessment by a Muslim of the state of intellectual thought in the Islamic world, see Tariq Ramadan, *Islam, the West and the Challenges of*

Modernity, trans. Said Amghar (Markefield, U.K.: Islamic Foundation, 2001), 286–90. For an insightful analysis of the role of apologetics in modern Islam, see Wilfred Cantwell Smith, *Islam in Modern History* (Princeton: Princeton University Press, 1977).

40. The classic studies on orientalism and its effects remain those of Edward Said: *Orientalism* (New York: Random House, 1979) and *Culture and Imperialism* (New York: Vintage, 1994). For a probing survey of orientalism and its practices, see Bryan S. Turner, *Orientalism, Postmodernism and Globalism* (London: Routledge Press, 1994), 3–114. Also see Asaf Hussain, Robert Olson, and Jamil Qureshi (eds), *Orientalism, Islam, and Islamists* (Brattleboro, VT: Amana, 1984). For an informative survey of orientalism and its practices, see A.L. Macfie, *Orientalism* (London: Pearson Education, 2002). Roxanne L. Euben, *Enemy in the Mirror: Islamic Fundamentalism and the Limits of Modern Rationalism* (Princeton: Princeton University Press, 1999), argues, somewhat persuasively, that Islamic fundamentalism is a form of critique or protest against rationalist modernism.

41. One way to conceptualize this is to understand that if Islam had figured out all the major answers to the challenge of modernity at the time of the Prophet and his Companions, there would be no incentive to engage in any further thinking or analysis about the Islamic tradition or to engage Islam creatively and innovatively, save on the most marginal issues. It is no coincidence that puritans took this apologetic point to its logical extreme and constructed a discourse that is markedly hostile to innovations, or creative thinking (referred to as *bid'ah*, sing., and *bida'*, pl.).

42. On the epistemology of Islamic law, see Wael Hallaq, *Authority, Continuity and Change in Islamic Law* (Cambridge: Cambridge University Press, 2001); Wael Hallaq, *A History of Islamic Legal Theories* (Cambridge: Cambridge University Press, 1997).

43. On this subject, see George Makdisi, *The Rise of Colleges in Islam* (Edinburgh: Edinburgh University Press, 1981).

44. Afaf Lutfi al-Sayyid Marsot, "The Ulama of Cairo in the Eighteenth and Nineteenth Century," in *Scholars, Saints, and Sufis*, ed. Nikki Keddi (Berkeley: University of California Press, 1972), 149–65, esp. 162–3.

45. Allan Christelow, *Muslim Law Courts and the French Colonial State in Algeria* (Princeton: Princeton University Press, 1985); J.N.D. Anderson, "Modern Trends in Islam: Legal Reform and Modernisation in the Middle East," *International and Comparative Law Quarterly*, 20, 1971, 1–21, reprinted in *Islamic Law and Legal Theory*, ed. Ian Edge (New York: New York University Press, 1996), 547–67; William L. Cleveland, *A History of the Modern Middle East* (Boulder: Westview Press, 2000), 61–98; Jasper Yeates Brinton, *The Mixed Courts of Egypt*, rev. edn (New Haven: Yale University Press, 1968); Ruth Mitchell, "Family Law in Algeria before and after the 1404/1984 Family Code," in *Islamic Law: Theory and Practice*, ed. R. Gleave and E. Kermeli (London: I.B. Tauris, 1997), 194–204, esp. 194–6. Of course, at times, colonial powers took over the implementation of Islamic law, as in the case of the Anglo-Muhammadan law experience in India. Syed Ameer Ali, *Muhammadan Law* (New Delhi: Kitab Bhavan, 1986), 1–4; Joseph Schacht, *An Introduction to Islamic Law* (London: Oxford University Press, 1964; reprinted, Oxford: Clarendon Press, 1993), 94–7; N.J. Coulson, *A History of Islamic Law* (Edinburgh: Edinburgh University Press, 1964), 164–72. On the impact of colonialism on the institutions of Islamic law in India, see Radhika Singha, *A Despotism of Law: Crime & Justice in Early Colonial India* (Delhi: Oxford University Press, 1998), 52–3, 60–70, 294–6, 300.

46. For an example of this in Muhammad Ali's (r. 1805–48) Egypt, see Afaf Lutfi al-Sayyid Marsot, *Women and Men in Late Eighteenth-Century Egypt* (Austin: University of Texas Press, 1995), 136, 141–2.

47. See, J.N.D. Anderson, *Islamic Law in the Modern World* (New York: New York University Press, 1959); J.N.D. Anderson, *Law Reform in the Muslim World* (London: Athlone Press, 1976); Wael Hallaq, *A History of Islamic Legal Theories*, 207–11.

48. This byproduct of the colonial experience made Islamic law lose credibility as a sophisticated and technical field. Interestingly, even non-Muslim Westerners internalized the attitude of Muslim apologists towards Islamic law, as a field ripe for pietistic fictions,

rather than a technical tradition of complex linguistic practices and sophisticated methodologies of social and textual analysis. For instance, it became rather common to hear Westerners repeat the pietistic fiction that Islamic jurisprudence is largely based on the Qur'an. Furthermore, especially in American law schools, being a Muslim activist was deemed sufficient to qualify a person to teach Islamic law.

49. This was often justified by the argument that *taqlid* (imitation or following precedent) is reprehensible, and that adherence to the classical schools of thought in jurisprudence was unjustified. On *taqlid*, see N.J. Coulson, *A History of Islamic Law* (Edinburgh: Edinburgh University Press, 1964), 182–201. In the late nineteenth and early twentieth centuries, motivated by a desire to break out of the shackles of outmoded traditions, a large number of scholars emphasized the importance of *ijtihad* (innovative and creative determinations), and severely criticized the practice of *taqlid*. Because of the influence of puritans upon the development of Muslim contemporary thought, this amounted to the deconstruction of the interpretive communities of the past, and their replacement with the determinations of the new, but intellectually inferior, interpretive communities of the modern age. See Muhammad 'Ali al-Shawkani, *al-Qawl al-Mufid fi Adillat al-Ijtihad wa al-Taqlid*, ed. Abu Mus'ab al-Badri (Cairo: Dar al-Kitab al-Misri, 1991); Abu al-Nasr Hasan Khan al-Qanuji, *al-Qawl al-Sadid fi Adillat al-Ijtihad wa al-Taqlid*, ed. Abu 'Abd al-Rahman Mi'shasha (Beirut: Dar Ibn Hazm, 2000). For a 1935 critique of this orientation, and an attempt to reclaim the importance of honoring and, at times, deferring to the interpretations of the past, see Yusuf bin Ahmad al-Dijawi, "Jawaz al-taqlid wa al-radd 'ala mann yuharrimahu," Nurr al-Islam (aka *Majallat al-Azhar* [*Azhar University Journal*]), 10(5), 1935, 669–79.

50. In 1933, the prominent Azharite Maliki jurist Yusuf al-Dijawi (d. 1365/1946) noted, with great concern, that puritan orientations, such as the Wahhabis, were deprecating the Islamic tradition by enabling people with a very limited education in Islamic sciences to become self-proclaimed experts in *Shari'ah*. See Yusuf bin Ahmad al-Dijawi, "al-hukm 'ala al-muslimin bi'l kufr," *Nurr al-Islam*, 1(4), 1933, 173–4.

51. Arnold Toynbee, the well-known British historian, had already noted the fact that many Muslims in the early twentieth century had hoped to import Western scientific methods, especially the military sciences, while insulating themselves from the rest of Western culture. This proved to be much harder to achieve in practice than in theory. See Arnold Toynbee, *Civilization on Trial* (Oxford: Oxford University Press, 1948), 184–212; Arnold Toynbee, *The World and the West* (Oxford: Oxford University Press, 1953), 18–33. Today, many Muslim puritans come to the West to learn the Western physical sciences, while hoping to insulate themselves from the influence of Western culture by, for example, refusing to study the humanities or social sciences.

52. This is clear, for instance, in very popular slogans such as "Islam is the solution" and "The Qur'an is our constitution." If considered from a historical perspective, both of these slogans would be anachronisms.

53. Muhammad b. 'Abd al-Wahhab, "Kashf al-Shubuhat: al-Risalah al-Thalitha," in *Majmu'at al-Tawhid* (Damascus: al-Maktab al-Islami, 1962), 106; 'Abd al-Rahman b. Muhammad b. 'Abd al-Wahhab, "Bayan al-Mahajja fi al-Radd 'ala al-Lujja: al-Risala al-Thalitha 'Ashra," in *Majmu'at al-Tawhid* (Damascus: al-Maktab al-Islami, 1962), 459, 534. Part of the puritan approach on this issue is to cite and emphasize traditions, attributed to the Prophet or Companions, that seem to condemn debate, argumentativeness, excessive eloquence, or sophistry; see Muhammad b. 'Abd al-Wahhab, *Mu'allafat al-Shaykh al-Imam Muhammad bin 'Abd al-Wahhab: Qism al-'Aqidah wa al-Adab al-Islamiyya* (Riyadh: Jami'at al-Imam Muhammad bin Sa'ud al-Islamiyya, n.d.), part 1, 13–14. For a work by a Wahhabi author attacking all rationalist orientations within Islam, see al-Amin al-Sadiq al-Amin, *Mawqif al-Madrasah al-'Aqliyya min al-Sunna al-Nabawiyya* (Riyadh: Maktabat al-Rushd, 1998), 2 vols. Another Wahhabi author wrote a multi-volume work listing a number of presumably heretical books that Muslims should not read. The list includes a large number of books advocating rationalist approaches to the study of Islam; see Abu 'Ubaydah Mashhur b. Hasan Al Salman, *Kutub Hadhdhar minha al-'Ulama'* (Riyadh: Dar Ibn Hazm,

1995). The author also includes all the books that criticized the Wahhabis, or the founder of their movement; see vol. 1, 250–87.

54. According to 'Abd al-Wahhab's son, only the first three centuries of Islam could be said to have been authentically Islamic to any extent, at all. After these centuries, Islamic history ceased to be Islamic, as the religion was overcome by heretical innovations and corruptions; see 'Abd al-Rahman b. 'Abd al-Wahhab, "Bayan al-Mahajja: al-Risala al-Thalitha 'Ashra," in *Majmu'at al-Tawhid*, 494–5.

55. For an example of a list containing acts the commission of which would make a Muslim an infidel, see 'Abd al-Wahhab, "Bayan al-Najah wa al-Fakak min Muwalat al-Murtaddin wa Ahl al-Shirk: al-Risala al-Thaniya 'Ashra," collected by Hamad b. 'Atiq al-Najdi, in *Majmu'at al-Tawhid*, 413–16. In this treatise, the author contends that anyone who fails to obey the literal commands of God is an infidel. For instance, if a Muslim asserts that the consumption of bread or meat is unlawful in Islam then he has become an infidel because it is clear that bread and meat are lawful in Islamic law.

56. Muhammad b. 'Abd al-Wahhab, "al-Risalah al-Ula," in *Majmu'at al-Tawhid*, 37–9, 50–2; Muhammad b. 'Abd al-Wahhab, "Kashf al-Shubuhat: al-Risalah al-Thalitha," in *Majmu'at al-Tawhid*, 100–3, 114; Muhammad b. 'Abd al-Wahhab, "Asbab Najat al-Sul min al-Sayf al-Maslul: al-Risalah Thamina," in *Majmu'at al-Tawhid*, 205; 'Abd al-Wahhab, "Bayan al-Najah wa al-Fakak: al-Risala al-Thaniya 'Ashra," collected by Hamad al-Najdi, in *Majmu'at al-Tawhid*, 401.

57. Taqi al-Din Abu al-'Abbas 'Abd al-Halim, "'Ubudiyya: al-Risala al-Rabi'a 'Ashra," in *Majmu'at al-Tawhid*, 569. Of course, the lawfulness of music was a hotly contested issue in Islamic law, but what is unique about the Wahhabi discourse on this matter is its explicit reference to the evils of individual creativity, as a general matter, and its unequivocal condemnation of imaginative thinking.

58. 'Abd al-Wahhab's son wrote a long treatise attacking a poet for writing a poem praising the Prophet. In this treatise, he emphasizes, time and again, that poetical imagery, if it is not based on physical facts, is sinful because it exaggerates the truth. Furthermore, he asserts that any poetry that appears to sanctify the Prophet and give him super-human qualities is heretical. See 'Abd al-Rahman b. Muhammad b. 'Abd al-Wahhab, "Bayan al-Mahajja: al-Risala al-Thalitha 'Ashra," in *Majmu'at al-Tawhid*, 436–42, 465–7, 480–1.

59. 'Abd al-Wahhab argued that Muslims must show enmity and hostility to unbelievers (*mushrikun*). This enmity and hostility must be visible and unequivocal. Importantly, among those designated as unbelievers were Muslims who, in 'Abd al-Wahhab's view, became infidels because of their beliefs or actions; see 'Abd al-Wahhab, "al-Risalah al-Ula," in *Majmu'at al-Tawhid*, 30–1, 68; 'Abd al-Wahhab, "Bayan al-Najah wa al-Fakak: al-Risala al-Thaniya 'Ashra," collected by Hamad al-Najdi, in *Majmu'at al-Tawhid*, 394, 400, 421–3, 433.

60. This was, for instance, reproduced in Sayyid Qutb's notion that the world, including the Muslim world, is living in *jahiliya* (darkness and ignorance associated with the pre-Islamic era). See Sayyid Qutb, *Milestones on the Road* (Indianapolis: American Trust Publications, 1990); Ahmad S. Mousalli, *Radical Islamic Fundamentalism: The Ideological and Political Discourse of Sayyid Qutb* (Syracuse: Syracuse University Press, 1993). This intellectual and moral isolationism was resisted, perhaps not very successfully, by a variety of jurists in the first half of the twentieth century. For instance, many of the articles published in the Azhar journal *Nurr al-Islam* in the 1930s and 1940s attempted to engage, interact, and discourse with world thought. It is clear that many Muslim scholars, at that time, tried to stay informed about the latest in European thought, and attempted to discuss how the latest ideas in philosophy and sociology would impact upon Muslim culture.

61. 'Abd al-Wahhab, "Bayan al-Najah wa al-Fakak: al-Risala al-Thaniya 'Ashra," collected by Hamad al-Najdi, in *Majmu'at al-Tawhid*, 358–68, 375, 412. In this treatise, the Ottoman Caliphate is described as a heretical nation (*al-dawlah al-kufriyya*). The author contends that supporting or allying oneself with the Ottomans is as bad a sin as supporting or allying oneself with Christians or Jews.

62. 'Abd al-Wahhab claimed that Abu Bakr fought and killed many so-called hypocrites, despite the fact that they practiced the five pillars or Islam. Arguing that his followers are justified in killing their opponents, he was also fond of citing a precedent in which Abu Bakr reportedly burned hypocrites to death. The Abu Bakr precedent cited by 'Abd al-Wahhab was most certainly apocryphal. See 'Abd al-Wahhab, "al-Risalah al-Ula," in *Majmu'at al-Tawhid*, 36, 70–2; 'Abd al-Wahhab, "Kashf al-Shubuhat: al-Risalah al-Thalitha," in *Majmu'at al-Tawhid*, 117–18; 'Abd al-Wahhab, "Bayan al-Najah wa al-Fakak: al-Risala al-Thaniya 'Ashra," collected by Hamad al-Najdi, in *Majmu'at al-Tawhid*, 403–9.

63. 'Abd al-Wahhab frequently referred to jurists as "devils" or the "spawn of Satan" (*shayatin* and *a'wan al-shayatin*); 'Abd al-Wahhab, "al-Risalah al-Ula," in *Majmu'at al-Tawhid*, 34–5; 'Abd al-Wahhab, "Kashf al-Shubuhat: al-Risalah al-Thalitha," in *Majmu'at al-Tawhid*, 104; also see 'Abd al-Wahhab, "Bayan al-Najah wa al-Fakak: al-Risala al-Thaniya 'Ashra," collected by Hamad al-Najdi, in *Majmu'at al-Tawhid*, 356–7.

64. 'Abd al-Wahhab, "al-Risalah al-Thaniya," in *Majmu'at al-Tawhid*, 4–6; 'Abd al-Wahhab, "Asbab Najat al-Sul: al-Risalah Thamina," in *Majmu'at al-Tawhid*, 208–12; 'Abd al-Wahhab, "Bayan al-Najah wa al-Fakak: al-Risala al-Thaniya 'Ashra," collected by Hamad al-Najdi, in *Majmu'at al-Tawhid*, 382–3; 'Abd al-Rahman b. 'Abd al-Wahhab, "Bayan al-Mahajja: al-Risala al-Thalitha 'Ashra," in *Majmu'at al-Tawhid*, 453.

65. See the treatise written by Muhammad b. 'Abd al-Wahhab's son, who was a devout follower of his father: 'Abd al-Rahman b. 'Abd al-Wahhab, "Bayan al-Mahajja: al-Risala al-Thalitha 'Ashra," in *Majmu'at al-Tawhid*, 466–93.

66. The *mufti* of the Hanbalis in Mecca, Ibn Humaydi (d. 1295/1878), reported that 'Abd al-Wahhab's father was upset with him because 'Abd al-Wahhab was not a good student of Islamic jurisprudence, and was arrogantly defiant towards his teachers. Reportedly, he refused to complete his *Shari'ah* studies. Ibn al-Humaydi claimed that, fearing the wrath of his father, 'Abd al-Wahhab did not dare to start preaching his puritan message until after his father's death. Muhammad b. 'Abd Allah b. Humaydi al-Najdi, *al-Suhub al-Wabila 'ala Dara'ih al-Hanabila* (Beirut: Maktabat al-Imam Ahmad, 1989), 275. Muhammad b. 'Abd al-Wahhab's older brother, Sulayman, wrote a scathing critique of what he called the Najdi Wahhabi creed. Sulayman b. 'Abd al-Wahhab, *al-Sawa'iq al-Ilahiyya fi al-Radd 'ala al-Wahhabiyya* (Damascus: Maktabat Harra', 1997). Although Sulayman does accuse his brother of being ignorant and intolerant, he does not mention the reported friction between Muhammad and his father.

67. Sulayman b. 'Abd al-Wahhab, *al-Sawa'iq al-Ilahiyya fi al-Radd 'ala al-Wahhabiyya*, (Damascus: Maktabat Harra', 1997), 60–1, 120. Ibn Humaydi reports the stories of some jurists who were assassinated by the followers of 'Abd al-Wahhab; see Ibn al-Humaydi, *al-Suhub al-Wabila*, 276–80, 402, 405.

68. Sulayman b. 'Abd al-Wahhab, *al-Sawa'iq al-Ilahiyya*, 9, 34–5. On Muhammad b. 'Abd al-Wahhab's education; see Michael Cook, "On the Origins of Wahhabism," *Journal of the Royal Asiatic Society*, 3(2), 1992, 191–202.

69. In support of his argument that 'Abd al-Wahhab's behavior was unprecedented, Sulayman contended that the majority of the scholars of Islam refrained from accusing the rationalists and mystics of heresy, and instead tried to debate with them peacefully. Sulayman b. 'Abd al-Wahhab, *al-Sawa'iq al-Ilahiyya*, 21, 25, 30–2, 38.

70. Sulayman b. 'Abd al-Wahhab, *al-Sawa'iq al-Ilahiyya*, 16, 72. The Maliki jurist Ibn al-Humaydi, who was an admirer of Ibn Taymiyya as well, makes the same claim about 'Abd al-Wahhab; see Ibn al-Humaydi, *al-Suhub al-Wabila*, 275.

71. Sulayman asserts that, according to the Wahhabis, Islam has been in error for seven hundred years. In addition, the Wahhabis did not hesitate to call even the inhabitants of Mecca infidels. Sulayman contends that, from a theological point of view, this claim is very troublesome. It is impossible, Sulayman argues, for Muslims, especially the inhabitants of the Prophet's city, Mecca, to have been deluded and mistaken in understanding and practicing their religion for so long. Sulayman bin 'Abd al-Wahhab, *al-Sawa'iq al-Ilahiyya*,

17–19, 62–4, 70–1, 74–5, 80–2, 92, 100–2, 110–12. For Rashid Rida's view on the merit of the first three centuries of Islam, see Muhammad Rashid Rida, *Majallat al-Manar* (Mansura, Egypt: Dar al-Wafa', 1327), 28:502–4. (Hereinafter Rida, *al-Manar*).

72. Addressing the Wahhabis, Sulayman states, "wa taj'alun mizan kufr al-nass mukhalafatakum wa mizan al-Islam muwafaqatakum." Sulayman b. 'Abd al-Wahhab, *al-Sawa'iq al-Ilahiyya*, 54, also see pp. 14, 42.

73. Sulayman b. 'Abd al-Wahhab, *al-Sawa'iq al-Ilahiyya*, 48–9.

74. Sulayman b. 'Abd al-Wahhab, *al-Sawa'iq al-Ilahiyya*, 121–42.

75. Ahmad Dallal has already established the relative marginality of Wahhabi extremist thought in the eighteenth and nineteenth centuries. Dallal has also shown that the thought of Salafi revivalists such as Muhammad al-Shawkani (d. 1250/1834) and al-Jalal al-San'ani (d. 1225/1810) were quite dissimilar to Wahhabi thinking, and far more influential at that time. Ahmad Dallal, "The Origins and Objectives of Islamic Revivalist Thought, 1750–1850," *Journal of the American Oriental Society*, 113(3), 1993, 341–59.

76. Egyptian and Turkish forces destroyed the city of Dhar'iyya, the hometown of the first Saudi kingdom, and massacred its inhabitants. D. Van der Meulen, *The Wells of Ibn Sa'ud* (London: Kegan Paul, 2000), 35–6.

77. Van der Meulen, *The Wells of Ibn Sa'ud*, 33–4; Simons, *Saudi Arabia*, 151–73. For good historical surveys on these and subsequent events, see Joseph Kostiner, *The Making of Saudi Arabia: From Chieftaincy to Monarchical State* (Oxford: Oxford University Press, 1993), 62–70, 100–17; Joseph A. Kechichian, *Succession in Saudi Arabia* (New York: Palgrave Press, 2001), 161–8; Madawi Al-Rasheed, *A History of Saudi Arabia* (Cambridge: Cambridge University Press, 2002), 22. The Shi'i jurist known as al-'Assar strongly protested the massacres that took place in Karbala, in the context of his critique of the Wahhabi creed; see Muhammad b. al-Layasani (aka al-'Assar), *Risala fi Radd Madhhab al-Wahhabiyya*, ed. Nu'man al-Nassari (n.p., 1999), 23.

78. Muhammad Amin Ibn 'Abidin, *Hashiyat Radd al-Muhtar* (Cairo: Mustafa al-Babi, 1966), 6:413; Ahmad al-Sawi, *Hashiyat al-'Allamah al-Sawi 'ala Tafsir al-Jalalayn* (Beirut: Dar Ihya' al-Turath al-'Arabi, n.d.), 3:307–8. See also, Ahmad Dallal, "The Origins and Objectives of Islamic Revivalist Thought, 1750–1850," *Journal of the American Oriental Society*, 113(3), 1993, 341–59. The same accusation of being the Khawarij of modern Islam is made in Sulayman b. 'Abd al-Wahhab, *al-Sawa'iq al-Ilahiyya*, 10, 28, 50–1; Yusuf b. Ahmad al-Dijawi, "Tawhid al-Uluhiyya wa Tawhid al-Rububiyya," *Nurr al-Islam*, 1(4), 1933, 320, 329. The Shi'i jurist known as al-'Assar noted that the creeds of the Wahhabis and Khawarij were, in many respects, substantially the same; see al-Layasani (aka al-'Assar), *Risala fi Radd Madhhab al-Wahhabiyya*, 135.

79. Wearing silk or gold is prohibited for men only. For a report in which the *mutawwa'un* punished a young boy for wearing a wristwatch in the 1940s, see Al-Rasheed, *A History of Saudi Arabia*, 53. Apparently, the *mutawwa'un* considered the wearing of a wristwatch an innovation (*bid'a*), but a pocket watch was considered acceptable.

80. Simons, *Saudi Arabia*, 152–9; Kostiner, *The Making of Saudi Arabia*, 119; Van der Meulen, *The Wells of Ibn Sa'ud*, 62–113. One scholar commented that the *mutawwa'un* operated a system of terror against the inhabitants of lands they controlled; see Al-Rasheed, *A History of Saudi Arabia*, 62–3.

81. In 1912, King 'Abd al-Aziz formed a fighting force known as the Ikhwan, which was constituted of Najdi religious zealots, strongly committed to the thought of 'Abd al-Wahhab. The Ikhwan played an effective role in establishing and expanding 'Abd al-Aziz's control, but they eventually became dissatisfied with what they saw as 'Abd al-Aziz's liberalism, and willingness to cooperate with non-Muslims. 'Abd al-Aziz tried to prevent the Ikhwan from raiding neighboring territories under British control, and also tried to restrain the Ikhwan from interfering with pilgrims coming to Mecca from outside of Arabia, whom the Ikhwan had a habit of attacking and punishing for engaging in un-Islamic practices. The Ikhwan rebelled against the King in 1929, but with the assistance of the British, who used airpower to massacre them, he crushed and disbanded their forces.

Van der Meulen, *The Wells of Ibn Sa'ud*, 65–8; Kostiner, *The Making of Saudi Arabia*, 117–40; Al-Rasheed, *A History of Saudi Arabia*, 62–71.

82. See, on these events and others, Michael Cook, *Commanding Right and Forbidding Wrong*, 180–91; Van der Meulen, *The Wells of Ibn Sa'ud*, 104–13. Reportedly, the Egyptian media severely criticized the Wahhabis over this incident; see Rida, *al-Manar*, 27:463–8.

83. On this process, and the use of *talfiq* and *maslaha* in modern Islam, see Coulson, *A History of Islamic Law*, 197–217. Also see Rida, *al-Manar*, 17:372–84.

84. Rashid Rida's main work was a monthly journal, titled *Majallat al-Manar*, which he issued from 1315/1897 to 1354/1935. Rida wrote most of the articles of the journal himself. Eventually, the issues of the journal were collected and published in a multi-volume work. Below I cite the Dar al-Wafa' edition of the multi-volume work, which contains all the issues of the *Manar*, save the Qur'anic commentary, which was published separately.

85. Rida severely criticizes al-Dijawi for attacking the Wahhabis; see Rida, *al-Manar*, 31:745–50. Rida also chronicles his disagreements with a number of jurists from the Azhar, and the attempts made to bring reconciliation to their disagreements, which included the contentious issue of the merit, or lack thereof, of the Wahhabis; see 32:673–04. However, it is clear that the rift between Rida, on the one hand, and al-Dijawi and several other Azhari jurists, on the other, continued until 1933, the last year in which the *Manar* was published; see 33:34–1, 118–9 373–82, 682–3. During this era, one of the most poignant critiques of Wahhabism was written by an influential Shi'i jurist, known as al-'Assar (d. 1356/1937), who had lived and studied for a period of time in Mecca and Medina. Although a Shi'i-trained cleric from Iran, al-'Assar had studied Sunni law with Hanafi and Shafi'i jurists. In 1343/1924, relying primarily on Sunni sources, he wrote a comprehensive and systematic refutation of the Wahhabi creed in which he strongly condemned their practice of *takfir* and fanaticism. Al-'Assar argued that the Wahhabis were an aberration in Sunni history, and condemned the many injustices they committed in the name of Islam. Al-'Assar's text is intellectually impressive, but it does not seem to have been widely disseminated in the Arabic speaking Muslim world, and, apparently, Rida was not aware of the text. See al-Layasani (aka al-'Assar), *Risala fi Radd Madhhab al-Wahhabiyya*, esp. 110–37, 152–74.

86. For Rida's defense of his relationship with King 'Abd al-'Aziz, see Rida, *al-Manar*, 27:548–55. For his defense of his support of the Wahhabis, see 29:531–8, 604–7.

87. Rida, *al-Manar*, 12:389–96; 16:776; 24:584–92.

88. Rida, *al-Manar*, 12:371–87, 525–8; 19–20:342–52; 29:40–51.

89. On philosophy, see Rida, *al-Manar*, 5:727–70. For his condemnation of political despotism and advocacy of democratic government, see Rida, *al-Manar*, 4:809–13, 7:899–912; 23:751; 27:357–9. For an article written on the same subject by al-Afghani, see, in the same source, 3:577–82, 602–7.

90. Although supportive of the juristic class and their tradition, Rida was also critical of overly conservative jurists who resisted the reformation of Islamic law; see Rida, *al-Manar*, 1:462–6, 696–704, 822–6; 4:401–11, 441–8. This issue was one of the causes for the rift between him and the Azhar seminary in the early 1930s; see 33:33–49, 113–20, 130–3, 290–304. However, Rida was also concerned about the turmoil and divisiveness that could result from a too rigid adherence to the established schools of thought in jurisprudence; see 14:775–81; 28:423–32.

91. On Rida and his views regarding Salafism and Hanbalism, see Rida, *al-Manar*, 8:614–20, 649–55; 29:185–96. Also, see the excerpt on Ibn Taymiyya; 24:473–8.

92. Rida was particularly critical of the fact that in Sufi orders a disciple surrenders his free agency to a master, and is expected to follow the rules set by the master blindly. He was also critical of the superstitious beliefs of some Sufi orders, and their practice of miracles. But Rida did not condemn the Sufi as heretics, or *kafirs*. For his criticism of Sufi orders, but his opposition to *takfir*, see Rida, *al-Manar*, 1:404–16, 447–54, 598–601, 722–30; 2:401–6, 449–54, 481–8, 545–52; 3:617–23; 4:318–20; 6:12–20, 41–62, 109–15, 184–95,

255–9, 286–93, 369–73, 406–12; 11:504–27, 911–17; 23:345–60; 27:556–8. On Shi'ism and worshipping at gravesites, see 28:350–67, 429–49, 516–33, 593–601, 684–92, 776–81.

93. Among other things, Rida wrote a fascinating fictitious debate between a reformer and a conservative traditionalist. In this debate and in other articles, he acknowledges that adherence to juristic precedent is, in many cases, appropriate and even important. But he insists upon the necessity of rethinking certain classical law positions in response to the new challenges confronting Muslims in the modern age. Rida also argues for the importance of Muslims mastering history and philosophy in responding to the challenges of modernity; see Rida, *al-Manar*, 3:635–40, 676–83, 715–25, 796–804; 4:51–60, 161–70, 205–17, 280–97, 521–9, 692–702, 852–66; 5:522–45, 570–8; 6:500–6, 539–44, 594–8, 766–70, 820–2, 696–9, 768–71, 853–6, 939–43; 7:121–33, 222–5, 253–8, 409–12, 449–53, 491–5; 12:615–21; 13:105–8, 529–38, 569–71, 665–80, 779–82; 14:137–8, 510–15, 743–50; 17:501–3. On closing the doors of *ijtihad*, see 7:374–80; 15:183–7. For an excerpt by Jamal al-Din al-Qasmi opposing the practice of *takfir* and criticizing the Ahl al-Hadith for attacking innovative jurists; see 15:857–74, 912–20; also see the excerpt in 17:41–53.

94. Rida, apologetically, defended the Wahhabis despite their insistence on *takfir*, destruction of Islamic monuments, attacking pilgrims to Mecca, and killing of innocents; see Rida, *al-Manar*, 21:226–49, 281–4; 26:200–5, 320, 454–77; 29:162–80; 33:544–7. Rida argued that, even if the Wahhabis committed some excesses, their opponent, the Hashmite Sharif Husayn, did much worse; see 26:462–3. Rida critically noted that some of his contemporaries praised Muhammad Ali, Egypt's ruler, for defeating the Wahhabis; see Rida, *al-Manar*, 5:183. Rida strongly defended the Wahhabis over the Egyptian *mahmal* incident in 1926; 27:463–8. Also see his *fatwa* in favor of the Wahhabi Ibn Al Saud, and against King Husayn b. Ali, who seized control of Mecca in 1916; 24:593–618; 25:713–18. On the refusal of King Husayn to accept the Egyptian medical mission to Mecca, see 24:625–9. For a *fatwa* on whether King 'Abd al-'Aziz could declare a national holiday on the occasion of his becoming King of Arabia, see 30:521–3.

95. Rida, *al-Manar*, 12:818–32, 913–32; 14:849–53; 16:773–6; 19–20:129–69, 433–43, 278–88; 25:540–60, 604–21, 761–9. Rather tellingly, in 1928, Rida finally acknowledged that some Salafis and Wahhabis had nothing but disdain for jurists, like himself; see 29:618. This was indicative of the contradictions between his theology and nationalism – contradictions that Rida did not seem willing to confront openly.

96. On public interest (*maslaha*) and Islamic law in Rida's thought, see Rida, *al-Manar*, 9:721–70.

97. Admittedly, however, Rida argued that one of the reasons that he supported the Wahhabis was because the Bedouins of Arabia and the Ottomans had become areligious in many of their practices, and cared little for what Islamic law had to say about anything. In contrast, the Wahhabis were religiously committed, and, in principle, put Islamic law before social customs or politics. See Rida, *al-Manar*, 21:226–49. While Rida probably did believe this to be true, the vast majority of his writings focused on nationalistic considerations such as anti-colonialism and pro-Arab nationalism. For instance, Rida urged Muslims to support the Turkish Kemalists against the British colonialists; see 23:713–20. But when it became clear that Kemal Ataturk was pro-Western and anti-Islamic, Rida wrote opposing him; see 25:273–92; 27:356.

98. In the early twentieth century, Wahhabis referred to themselves as Salafis. The word *salaf* means "predecessors," and in the Islamic context it usually refers to the period of the Companions of the Prophet and his successors. The term *salafi* has a natural appeal because it connotes authenticity and legitimacy. As a term, it is exploitable by any movement that wants to claim that it is grounded in Islamic authenticity. Although the Wahhabis referred to themselves as Salafis, the term did not become associated with the Wahhabi creed until the 1970s.

99. The Wahhabi notion of egalitarianism reached the point of prohibiting labels of respect intended to honor human beings, such as "Doctor," "Mister," or "sir." Muhammad bin 'Abd al-Wahhab argued that such prefixes were a form of associating partners with God

(i.e. *shirk*), and also were condemnable because they constituted an imitation of the Western unbelievers. Muhammad b. 'Abd al-Wahhab, "Awthaq al-'Ura: al-Risalah al-Sadisa," in *Majmu'at al-Tawhid* (Damascus: al-Maktab al-Islami, 1962), 171.

100. My two books *And God Knows the Soldiers* and *Speaking in God's Name* are primarily concerned with this phenomenon.

101. I recall one incident that, to me, represented the profound contradictions of the Salafabists, especially as regards women. A few years ago, I was lecturing in an Islamic center in Ohio when a Saudi leader of the community strongly protested that some of the women attending the lecture were sitting in the front row and were not hidden from the sight of men. The Saudi leader insisted that the women must promptly relocate to seats placed behind a curtain so that men could not see them. He insisted that the women sitting in the front row created the potential of *fitna* for others. Later on, I discovered that this man was a practicing gynecologist in Ohio, who treated the same women that he insisted should sit behind a curtain. The Salafabist obsession with excluding women from public life was the subject of my book *Speaking in God's Name*. But as further evidence of this pervasive phenomenon, one should read the three-volume work written on the merits and importance of secluding women in Islam: Muhammad Ahmad al-Muqaddim, *'Awdat al-Hijab* (Riyadh: Dar Tayba, 1996). There is a highly accessible and remarkably misogynist literature that floods the Arab–Muslim book market, reproducing what is supposed to be the Islamic position on women, but which is also extremely deprecating to women. For instance, I recently picked up a short book published in Lebanon, authoritatively titled a *responsa* (*fatawa*) for women by a Ph.D.-carrying Salafabist scholar: al-Sadiq 'Abd al-Rahman al-Ghiryani, *Fatawa min Hayat al-Mar'ah al-Muslimah* (Beirut: Dar al-Rayyan, 2001). The author's *responsa* reproduces the same misogynist determinations that have become commonplace in contemporary Muslim culture. For example, according to the author, a Muslim wife may not worship God by fasting without the permission of her husband because her husband may want to have sex with her during the day (p. 47); a woman may not speak with her fiancé over the telephone because she may seduce him (pp. 59–60); a woman engaged to a man may not go out with him in public because she may seduce him (p. 62); a bride riding with her groom in a car driven by a relative must make sure not to wear perfume because she may seduce the driver, who is not her husband (p. 63); a woman who wishes to go to the mosque to learn the Qur'an must obey her father if he forbids her from going, and the father need not express any reason for his opposition (p. 77); a man who marries a woman with the intention of divorcing her after having his pleasure with her but fails to inform her of his intention does not commit a sin, and the marriage is valid (pp. 82–3); a woman may not refuse her husband sex, except if she is ill, and refusing a husband sex without compelling justification is a grave sin (*kabira*). On the other hand, a husband may refuse his wife sex for a reason or no reason at all (pp. 86–7); as a legal matter, the voice of a woman is not an *'awrah* (a privacy that must be concealed from all except a *mahram*), but nonetheless because of its seductive powers the voice of a women should not be heard in public, or in a private setting where it might cause sexual enticement (pp. 111–12); women should not mix with men even in public ways and even if women are wearing the *hijab*, and women should not travel unaccompanied by a male *mahram* (pp. 116–17); a woman may not chew gum because it is seductive (p. 122); women may not dance in front of other women in a wedding even if there are no men around because it might be sexually arousing (p. 130); women may not shorten their head hair because doing so is considered imitating men. However, women *must* remove any facial hair, such as a beard or moustache, because it is more feminine to do so, and because a woman must be sexually appealing to her husband (i.e. facial hair on a woman is not sexually appealing) (pp. 137–8, 146); women should not attend funerals or gravesites or convey their condolences to foreign men, so as to avoid sexual enticement (p. 149). I have dealt with very similar determinations in *Speaking in God's Name*, and attempted to prove that such determinations are not objectively mandated by Islamic sources. In fact, these

determinations engage in what I called textual authoritarianism by abusing the integrity of the text.

102. *"Ahl al-Hadith"* is a broad term that refers to a literalist movement that claimed to adhere to the traditions of the Prophet faithfully, and without the corrupting influence of human interpretations. In the fourth/tenth century, there was an affinity between the followers of Ahmad Ibn Hanbal, the founder of the Hanbali school of thought, and the Ahl al-Hadith – although the Ahl al-Hadith claimed not to follow any of the established schools of thought, and to simply be the adherents of the truth. On the Ahl al-Hadith, see Abou El Fadl, *Speaking in God's Name*, 114; Abou El Fadl, *And God Knows the Soldiers*, 48, 78.

103. Of course, I will not speculate about what induced these liberal thinkers to defend Wahhabism, but the least one can say about their writing on this topic is that it is very selective and full of historical inaccuracies. For examples of such works, see Muhammad Fathy Osman, *al-Salafiyya fi al-Mujtama'at al-Mu'asira* [*Salafis in Modern Societies*] (Kuwait: Dar al-Qalam, 1981). The author equates the Wahhabis and the Salafis, and also engages in lengthy and unequivocal praise of 'Abd al-Wahhab and his movement; see especially pp. 31–87. Interestingly, the author was a professor in Saudi Arabia when he wrote the book. Another unabashed defense of the Wahhabi movement by a liberal scholar is: Muhammad Jalal Kishk, *al-Sa'udiyyun wa al-Hall al-Islami* [*The Saudis and the Islamic Solution*], (West Hanover, MA: Halliday Lithograph, 1981). This book, however, is a bit more balanced than Osman's work. Interestingly, Kishk became the recipient of the influential King Faysal Award.

104. Muhammad al-Ghazali, *al-Sunnah al-Nabawiyya Bayn Ahl al-Fiqh wa Ahl al-Hadith* (Cairo: Dar al-Shuruq, 1989).

105. Several major conferences were held in Egypt and Saudi Arabia to criticize the book, and the Saudi newspaper *al-Sharq al-Awsat* published several long articles responding to al-Ghazali in 1989. Notably, perhaps as an indication of Saudi influence and contrary to what one would expect, most of the books written against al-Ghazali were published in Egypt, and not Saudi Arabia. The following is a partial list of attacks on al-Ghazali's books: Muhammad Jalal Kishk, *Al-Shaykh al-Ghazali bayn al-Naqd al-'Atib wa al-Madh al-Shamit* (Cairo: Maktabat al-Turath Islami, 1990); Ashraf b. Ibn al-Maqsud b. 'Abd al-Rahim, *Jinayat al-Shaykh al-Ghazali 'ala al-Hadith wa Ahlihi* (al-Isma'iliyya, Egypt: Maktabat al-Bukhari, 1989); Jamal Sultan, *Azmat al-Hiwar al-Dini: Naqd Kitab al-Sunnah al-Nabawiyya bayn Ahl al-Fiqh wa Ahl al-Hadith* (Cairo: Dar al-Safa, 1990); Salman b. Fahd 'Uwda, *Fi Hiwar Hadi' ma 'a Muhammad al-Ghazali* (Riyadh: n.p., 1989); Rabi' b. Hadi Madkhali, *Kashf Mawqif al-Ghazali min al-Sunna wa Ahliha wa Naqd Ba'd Ara'ihi* (Cairo: Maktabat al-Sunna, 1410). Also see Abu 'Ubaydah, *Kutub Hadhdhar minha al-'Ulama'*, 1:214–28, 327–9. At the time of the controversy, the influential Egyptian jurist Yusuf al-Qaradawi remained conspicuously silent, but a few years after al-Ghazali died, he wrote two books; one about al-Ghazali's life and the other about the controversy. In both books, he defended al-Ghazali's piety and knowledge, but he stopped short of criticizing the Wahhabis; see Yusuf al-Qaradawi, *al-Imam al-Ghazali bayn Madihih wa Naqidih* (Beirut: Mu'assasat al-Risalah, 1994); Yusuf al-Qaradawi, *al-Shaykh al-Ghazali kama 'Araftuh: Rihlat Nisf Qarn* (Cairo: Dar al-Shuruq, 1994).

106. By the 1990s, the only Islamic critics of the Wahhabis were Sufis and Shi'is, but even Sufi scholars had become heavily influenced by the Salafabi methodology. It was not unusual to find Sufi scholars engage in the same literalist and myopic adherence to *hadith* as the Wahhabis. The main issues of contention between Sufis and Wahhabis, however, remained the validity of the doctrine of intercession and the lawfulness of showing reverence for saints. For a Sufi response to many of the doctrines of Wahhabism, see Muhammad Hisham al-Kabbani, *Encyclopedia of Islamic Doctrine* (Mountain View, CA: As-Sunna Foundation of America, 1998), 7 vols; for a response to Wahhabism by a Shi'i scholar who does not cite Shi'i sources but only Sunni sources, see Najm al-Din al-Tabasi, *al-Wahabiyya Da'awi wa Rudud* (Matba'at al-Hadi, 1420/1999).

107. This period has been described by some scholars as the liberal age of modern Islam; see Albert Hourani, *Arabic Thought in the Liberal Age: 1798–1939* (Cambridge: Cambridge University Press, 1983); Leonard Binder, *Islamic Liberalism: A Critique of Development Ideologies* (Chicago: Chicago University Press, 1988). For excerpts from the works of Muslim liberals, see Charles Kurzman (ed.), *Liberal Islam: A Sourcebook* (Oxford: Oxford University Press, 1998). Also see Huseyn Hilmi Isik, *The Religion Reformers in Islam*, 3rd edn (Istanbul: Wakf Ikhlas, 1978), and Daniel Brown, *Rethinking Tradition in Modern Islamic Thought* (Cambridge: Cambridge University Press, 1996).

108. The Qur'an proclaims that God does not change the fortunes of people until they first change themselves. Qur'an 13:11.

109. See Abou El Fadl, "Constitutionalism and Islamic Sunni Legacy," 94–6.

ב

IN SEARCH OF PROGRESSIVE ISLAM
BEYOND 9/11

Farid Esack

It is not sufficient to say that we must return to Islam.
We must specify which Islam: That of Abu Dharr or that of Marwan,
the ruler ... One is the Islam of Caliphate, of the palace, and of rulers.
The other is the Islam of the people, of the exploited, and of the poor.[1]

They may prefer to burn the temple down, rather than succumb to
the worship of a foreign god.[2]

DEFINING PROGRESSIVE ISLAM

In some ways all attempts at definitions are authoritarian. Like any social
movement, progressive Islam has a contingent nature and is likely to be
interpreted in a variety of different ways. What H. Moghissi said about Islamic
feminism is equally applicable to progressive Islam: "There is no coherent, self-
identified and or easily identifiable Islamic feminist ideology and movement
operating within the boundaries of Islamic societies."[3] While there is – or ought
to be – a dynamism in any phenomenon described as "progressive," there may be
certain parameters beyond which one cannot stretch the application of the term
and still make any claims to coherence. As Terry Eagleton has pointed out, "any
term which tries to cover everything would end up meaning nothing in
particular, since signs work by virtue of their differences."[4] The *Shorter Oxford
Dictionary* defines "progressive" as "moving forward, advocating progress or
reform." In a political or ideological context the term has decidedly leftist
overtones and is usually contraposed to "reactionary," i.e. being wedded to the
status quo or to conservative political ideas. In critical discourse the term

"progressive" also denotes an affinity with some form of communitarianism, as opposed to liberalism, which espouses greater individualism.[5] Many leftists use the terms exclusively in relation to them as an ideological group engaging in a radical critique of society and challenging the structural basis of various injustices such as class and gender rather than opting for simple reformism that leaves the structural basis of such injustices intact. While others would, for example, be content with asking why men cannot create more social space for women or present systematic charity such as *zakah* as a response to poverty, progressives attempt to go beyond this and challenge the patriarchal nature of social reality and an economic system that, in their reasoning, must lead to a society where the poor will forever be dependent on the rich. The term is also used in opposition to liberalism with its emphasis on individual liberties within a societal framework in which all have equal opportunity regardless of the starting points of various classes within a society. While liberals would advocate social change, progressives would additionally interrogate the nature of change and ask which socio-economic class stands to benefit from these changes. Within the broader socio-economic context, liberalism with its commitment to minimalist universal ethics (and minimum state intervention in the market) is often seen as merely a set of ideas advocating greater individual liberties while it is actually inextricably interwoven with the free market ideology. Progressive ideologues have, in fact, argued that the North[6] – or the developed countries – with its stress on an individualistic competitive system causes social dislocation and injustice and that while it has the outward forms of freedom and human rights, in reality there are subtle forms of violation which are even more repressive and unjust. An example of this would be the emphasis on the right to complain about unemployment while structuring one's economy in such a way that there will always be unemployment.

In Muslim discourse the term "Progressive" is usually used in a variety of contexts and for many it often represents simply an anti-authoritarian or anti-conservative Muslim discourse. The expression "progressive Islam" was first popularized by Suroosh Irfani with his *Revolutionary Islam in Iran – Popular Liberation or Religious Dictatorship?*, published in 1983.[7] Prior to that the term had a few sporadic appearances in some articles where it was really employed as a synonym for modernist or liberal Islam. Irfani's work was the first to employ the term in the way that it was used in leftist ideological circles although his broad sweep minimizes differences between earlier Muslim reformers such as the decidedly pro-British Indian scholar Sir Sayyid Ahmad Khan (1817–98) and Sayyid Jamal al-Din Al-Afghani (1838–97) – the quintessential representatives of early expressions of liberal and progressive Islam, respectively. Irfani utilized the life and ideas of Dr 'Ali Shari'ati (1933–77) and the tendency in activist Islam, then represented by the Mujahidin-i Khalq in Iran,[8] to both elaborate on and support the notion of progressive Islam.

[the] progressive Islamic movement is anti-imperialist, and in the economic domain, its opposition to capitalism and the exploitative system on which capitalism rests is unequivocal. It believes that Islam as an ideology can mobilize the Muslim masses by its appeal to social justice and the challenge it poses to the status quo.[9]

A DEFINITION AND DECLARATION

The only systematic attempt to define progressive Islam hitherto was the initiative undertaken by the Progressive Muslim Network (hereinafter "PMN") late in 1998 on the internet by a number of activists and scholars, including the present author, from various parts of the Muslim world. After several drafts consensus was reached on a final document titled "Progressive Islam – A Definition and Declaration." This declaration (hereinafter "the Declaration") continues to form the basis of membership in the PMN and is the framework against which I want to reflect on liberal Muslim responses to the events of September 11, 2001 and offer an alternative progressive Muslim view. The following definition is offered in this Declaration:

> Progressive Islam is that understanding of Islam and its sources which comes from and is shaped within a commitment to transform society from an unjust one where people are mere objects of exploitation by governments, socio-economic institutions and unequal relationships. The new society will be a just one where people are the subjects of history, the shapers of their own destiny in the full awareness that all of humankind is in a state of returning to God and that the universe was created as a sign of God's presence.[10]

There are several pertinent issues here that frame my discussion on a progressive Muslim perspective of the events of September 11, 2001. Some of these are specifically outlined in the document when it elaborates on the definition:

- First, while there is a commitment to "understanding," the locus of progressive Islam is the terrain of the struggle for justice – or praxis – rather than the arenas of critical thinking for its own sake. Understanding is viewed as the product of engagement for justice combined with reflection rather than the product of a disemboweled critical enquiry. In the words of Rebecca S. Chopp, who has done much to examine the tensions between modernist and liberation theology, the "turn to praxis [is] a way of making theology less a false theology, less an academic illusion and less an incoherent abstraction."[11] "Understanding" or "critical enquiry" is thus secondary to the task of working for justice and an extension of "an expression of Islam that places socio-economic, gender and environmental justice at its core."[12]

- Second, the concerns of the privileged or the dominant classes are not the primary subject of progressive Islam; its focus is on those who have become "objects of exploitation by governments, socio-economic institutions and unequal relationships"; in the words of the Qur'an, those who had been marginalized (*aradhil*, Q. 11:27; 26:70; 22:5) or downtrodden in the earth (*mustad'afun fi'l-ard*, Q. 4:97; 8:26). The Declaration describes the *mustad'afun fi'l-ard* as "those individuals and groups who, for no willful reason of their own, find themselves pushed to the edges of society to live in conditions of social, political and economic oppression."

- Third, humankind is located within the dual position of being simultaneously autonomous beings with full agency and of returning to God. Agency implies power over one's life and one's status as returning to God implies both a sacredness beyond one's commodity value as well as defining the limits of that agency. "In other words, our struggle to experience a personally and socially meaningful Islam is rooted in praxis geared towards creating a more humane society as part of a sustainable eco-system in the service of the Transcendent."[13]

- Fourth, there is an "intolerance" toward those who are viewed as responsible for exploitation; the document covers three elements that may be "blameworthy": governments, socio-economic institutions, and unequal (personal?) relationships. This seems to be an attempt to reflect comprehensively on how, not only governments or obviously political institutions, but also those who play more covert political roles, such as large corporations and the international monetary institutions, as well personal relationships can militate against human dignity. In opposition to the *mustad'afun fi'l ard*, the Qur'an does present – and demonizes – the *mustakbirun* (those who exalt themselves above others; Q. 16:22).

Finally, the Declaration significantly omits any mention of "peace" or "tolerance" and outlines the following as tendencies that must be opposed:

- The projection of an inevitable of *Pax Americana* and the unfettered march of globalization in the service of the market.
- The relentless promotion of corporate culture and consumerism which results in the exploitation of our natural environment, deforestation, the destruction of local communities and the eco-system, and cruelty to animals.
- Racism, sexism, homophobia, and all other forms of socio-economic injustices, both within and outside of Muslim societies and communities. "These injustices," the Declaration says, "detract from the sacredness of all humankind imbued when God blew of His own spirit into the first created person."

- Intolerance and fascist tendencies that insist on and seek to enforce a single and absolute appreciation of truth in all religious and cultural communities, including Islam.

FROM THE "MAJOR JIHAD" TO THE "SUPERIOR JIHAD" – LIBERAL ISLAM'S RESPONSE TO 9/11

In the media frenzy that followed September 11, 2001 numerous Muslims were interviewed in the media and a large number offered editorial pieces or had their own thoughts circulated on the internet. While it was a time for conservatives to go into hiding or re-invent themselves as liberal apologists for the faith and for the fundamentalists to quietly vent their glee as they dispersed in order to regroup for another battle at a later stage,[14] the more authentic liberals dominated the media as spokespersons for the Muslim community. Large sectors of the media wanted to allay the fears of the Western public that the "majority of Muslims, unlike those Afghanistan-based barbarians or the fanatical Wahhabis, are really decent folk with whom we can do business." "It's a bad analogy," said Emran Qureshi, an independent scholar and software designer who lives in Ottawa, "but I feel like I can come out of the closet and criticize these guys" (*New York Times*, October 28, 2001). Several of these liberal Muslims, as Qureshi's response suggests, were also the victims of past or ongoing persecution by the conservative or fundamentalist elements in the Muslim communities and the ravages of those injuries clearly showed in their responses. It was one of the rare opportunities when liberals emerged as – even if grudgingly – publicly recognized saviors by and of the Muslim community.

From a perusal of more than a hundred articles circulated on the internet the following salient features may describe the liberal Muslim response.

First, there was the widespread acknowledgement that Muslims and or certain tendencies in Islam are "the problem." Tendencies singled out for criticism or condemnation included intra-Muslim intolerance, Wahhabism, Muslim fundamentalism, stagnation in Islamic jurisprudence, and a refusal to recognize the religious legitimacy of Christians and Jews. While most commentators dealt at length and exclusively with these, a few suggested that attention also needs to be paid to other broader political or ideological concerns that either breed fundamentalism or are invoked to fire it among Muslims.[15]

Second, liberal Muslims responded from the premise that "fundamentalism" was perhaps the single most important issue facing the world, and the events of September 11 the single-most important event that required a radical shift in Muslim responses to modernity and being in the world. "I am a Muslim," wrote Mona Eltahawy. "The terrorist attacks on Sept. 11 shook my faith to its foundation. I am angry and ashamed that Muslims will forever be remembered for such horror."[16] While the way the North, particularly the U.S.A., responded to those events ensured that it was going to be a decisive moment in world history, liberal Muslims did nothing to challenge the idea that this was inevitable and that the U.S.A.'s pain was not or should not be – the axis around which the earth rotates. With few exceptions, the frightening and calculated short-termism of the U.S.A. was embraced with a fury. The death of millions of people through lack of access to clean water, or from HIV/AIDS and the insistence of the pharmaceutical industry on placing patent rights ahead of the lives of patients, the thousands killed by a Christian equivalent of the Taliban – the Lord's Army – in northern Uganda, and environmental degradation did not count for much in liberal responses to September 11. One has no desire to engage in maleficent calculus but one must challenge the implicit assumption that everyone must re-define their existence and struggles in terms of the demands of the U.S.A. The head of the empire was bleeding and all efforts concentrated on those wounds – even as the wounded Goliath, "armed to the teeth, adored by the polls, unfettered by law, [and] answering to no-one"[17] was readying itself to inflict collateral damage on greater numbers of innocent civilian Afghanis than those who perished in the attacks of September 11.[18]

Third, there was desperation to distance Islam from "terrorism" and while some attempted to reflect on the underlying causes of terrorism there was little or no attempt at defining it.[19] When it was discussed at all, it was presented as "the result of long-standing and cumulative cultural and rhetorical dynamics" rather than concrete historical conditions of political marginalization or dispossession.[20] Demands for clarity were usually dismissed as "fudging the issue" or unhelpful in the attempt to prove that Islam is a peaceful religion. In this desperation, the *hadith* of the Prophet Muhammad – acknowledged by all *hadith* scholars as "weak" – that armed combat was a lesser (*asghar*) jihad compared with the greater (*akbar*) jihad against one's lower self was elevated to canonical status and one liberal commentator even rendered *asghar* as "inferior" and *akbar* as "superior."[21] While jihad was critiqued and repackaged as entirely non-threatening, an uncritiqued "peace" was presented as an absolute pillar of faith. Islam was persistently and erroneously declared to mean "peace."[22]

Fourth, most Muslim liberal commentators presented themselves as the "authentic" interpreters of Islam and engaged in the decidedly non-liberal tendency to essentialize Islam; "Osama bin Ladin was not a Muslim"; "Wahhabism and fundamentalism have nothing to do with 'true Islam.'" "True Islam" was presented as a concrete immutable set of ideas and beliefs, while others became the "inauthentic usurpers" of this set of beliefs: "Why have we allowed the sacred terms of Islam, such as fatwa and jihad, to be hijacked by obscurantist, fanatic extremists?" asked Ziauddin Sardar.[23]

Finally, none of the liberal Muslim responses suggested any awareness of the larger context wherein the tragedy of September 11 was unfolding. It sadly appeared as if issues of globalization, the rise of the new empire and corporate power, the unbridled exploitation of the earth's limited resources, global warming, consumerism and its twin sister, poverty, as well as HIV/AIDS belonged to another planet. Flushed away were all memories of the cooperative relationship between the Taliban and the U.S. administration and oil industry nexus.[24] While progressive intellectuals such as Edward Said and Noam Chomsky and journalists such as Robert Fisk remained useful sources to invoke in a limited anti-Isreal and anti-Zionist rhetoric, their broader critique of power and powerlessness escaped liberal Islam.

A PROGRESSIVE CRITIQUE OF LIBERAL ISLAM

The most important underlying distinction between the progressive and liberal responses concerns the primary subject of discourse. In owning the obsession of the powerful as theirs, liberal Muslims made the powerful their own primary subject and issues of authenticity and meaning the central crisis for their understanding of Islam. Progressive Muslims insisted that the primary subject and focus of their Islam were the "non-subjects of history." In effect, liberal Islam has functioned as an ideology of and for the bourgeois, struggling to secure freedom as individual and ahistorical. Elsewhere I have argued that there is no objective theory unaffected by each person's socio-historical particularity and for Islam to be self-consciously grounded in praxis.[25] When scholars or commentators deny their social location or base their responses entirely on personal negative encounters with their communities they end up effectively being extensions of the structures of the powerful. The current "Islam means peace" and "The basic message of the Qur'an is really identical to the U.S. constitution" discourse, within the context of the rise of the new empire and all the concomitant injustices, is really the beginnings of what the Kairos theologians operating in the South African context described as a "theology of accommodation." In this theology religion is used to buttress the often unstated ideological assumptions of the dominant classes and corporate interest on the one hand and to placate those who are marginalized by siphoning of "any critical energy through charitable goodwill" on the other.[26]

While progressive Muslims shared the revulsion of others at the death of innocents, they display a much more cynical attitude towards an uncritiqued peace discourse. For progressive Muslims, "real peace" seems to be one that follows the creation of a just world. In contrast, a seemingly ideology-less peace that, uncritiqued, translates into acquiescence to a new corporate dominated world – most starkly represented by the United States of America – is one to be not only avoided but also opposed. Dominant empires develop an ideological rooted interest in peace which reinforces a *status quo* that may very well be an unjust one, as Paul Salem points out: "Conflict and bellicosity is useful – indeed essential – in building empires, but an ideology of peace and conflict resolution is clearly more appropriate for its maintenance."[27] When we fail to raise critical questions about the *status quo* that requires peace then we run the risk of becoming a part of the problem.

In a more local context, this was certainly true for all the progressive forces in South Africa, where "making the state ungovernable" was a necessary first step towards the creation of a just society. South Africa had for long been a deeply conflict-ridden society. This conflict assumed a structural nature under colonialism with more pronounced racial undertones during apartheid. The apartheid regime, attempting to obscure its own violent nature, consistently presented any opposition to it as an affront to peace and stability. A series of laws criminalizing opposition to apartheid were presented as peace-keeping and stability-ensuring measures. As in most totalitarian states in the world, "law and order" were the watchwords. When peace comes to mean the absence of conflict on the one hand, and when conflict with an unjust and racist political order is a moral imperative on the other, then it is not difficult to understand that the better class of human beings are, in fact, deeply committed to disturbing the peace and creating conflict. Along with other progressive forces in South Africa, I affirmed the value of revolutionary insurrection against the apartheid state and conflict as a means to disturbing an unjust peace and a path to just peace. In other words, peace, law, and order were of no substantive consequence to us; the fundamental question was "Stability and peace to what end?" Our response to the regime's call for peace and stability was to call on people to wage a jihad against the apartheid state.

A PROGRESSIVE MUSLIM RESPONSE TO 9/11

In the immediate aftermath of 9/11 and the "war against terrorism" the progressive Islam response was perhaps best captured in a *khutbah* (sermon) delivered in Johannesburg by Naeem Jeenah, a leading figure among progressive Muslims. Jeenah dealt with the crisis at two levels of responsibilities – that of the U.S.A. and that of Muslims. He described the "war against terrorism" as "what Allah calls *istikbar* (arrogance)" – which is most evident in Bush's "dead or alive" statement and his assertion that "you are either with us or with the terrorists."

> So without asking the world where it stands or what its options are, Bush has made the decision for us. There is really no need for us to even think about it; he has decided: you either shout "Viva America" or you are a terrorist! It is the kind of pharaonic arrogance that has seen the downfall of dictators all through time. Because, all through time, the arrogant – *mustakbirin* – have been opposed by the oppressed – *mustad'afin.* It is the *Sunnah* of history.

Unlike most traditional and liberal Muslims, Jeenah locates the "problem with the U.S.A." beyond the Middle East and "our suffering Muslim brothers in Palestine/Kashmir/Chechnya/Azerbaijan":

In their arrogance and their cynicism the U.S. has forgotten the most crucial response to September 11. They have forgotten to ask "Why?" Why did such an attack against the symbols of American economy and military happen? Why is the U.S. so hated that such a heinous act is not only contemplated but actually executed? The Americans seem keen not to learn! They should have learnt some lesson after Vietnam; they should have learnt some lesson after the Gulf Massacre; they should have asked how endearing they have made themselves to people of the Third World. It seems the only thing they are willing to learn is that they are able to attack and massacre foreign populations with impunity; and they will do it repeatedly – with no regard for the consequences. If Americans were serious about the "why?" question they could easily find the answers. The answers are in the occupation and dispossession in Palestine; in the murder of one million Iraqi children; in the blockade of Cuba; in the carpet bombing of Colombia; in the assassination of Patrice Lumumba; in the terrorist dictatorships supported by the U.S. government: Saddam Hussein, Manuel Noriega, Mobutu Sese Seko, the Shah of Iran, Suharto, successive apartheid governments in South Africa and Israel. All of these, too, are acts of terrorism.

Jeenah looks beyond the drama of TV and the grand events of the moment:

The World Trade Center slaughter was despicable. We can say it a million times. But on that same day (and every day recently), 35000 children in the Third World starved to death because of a global capitalist system that comforts the rich and causes misery for the poor and dispossessed. These children did not (do not) get minutes of silence, lowering of flags or thousands of action replays on TV.

The Islamic religious inspiration of the terrorists of September 11 was acknowledged as well as their culpability. Furthermore, the painful reality of people rejoicing at the collapse of the Twin Towers and the Pentagon, as well as widespread support for Osama bin Laden in perhaps two-thirds of the world, particularly the South,[28] was acknowledged and challenged:

Then there are those of us who have suddenly become pro-Osama and pro-Taliban without necessarily understanding what that means. We extend our support to those who deserve it. In this case we extend our unqualified support to the Afghan people who have been victimized for more than two decades. But the Taliban? ... whose intolerance against people of other faiths is legend and whose intolerance against other Muslims is often violent? ... if the Taliban or their local supporters were ruling this country, I probably wouldn't be allowed to deliver this sermon in English (if I would be allowed to deliver it at all), the women upstairs would not be allowed to attend the mosque, we probably would know very little of what's happening in Afghanistan because our TVs would be smashed and our access to information restricted.

THE CLASH OF TWIN FUNDAMENTALISMS[29]

In the wake of the terrorist attack several observers began commenting on the similarity between the style and rhetoric of Osama bin Laden and the U.S. President, George W. Bush. Indeed, at times it appeared as if they were in competition to out-evil each other, each referring to the other as the "head of a snake."[30] This self as other, captured on the cover of Tariq Ali's *Clash of Fundamentalisms* where Bush appears fully bearded and wearing a turban, was also reflected in the comments of several leftist writers.[31] Arundhati Roy wrote,

> Both invoke God and use the loose millenarian currency of good and evil as their terms of reference. Both are engaged in unequivocal political crimes. Both are dangerously armed – one with the nuclear arsenal of the obscenely powerful, the other with the incandescent, destructive power of the utterly hopeless. The fireball and the ice pick. The bludgeon and the axe. The important thing to keep in mind is that neither is an acceptable alternative to the other.[32]

Both bin Laden and Bush were being singled out as the "bad king" by some and the "good king" by others, and vice versa, all of this in some ways reflecting a very inadequate view of how history unfolds. Individuals certainly contribute immensely to the shaping of history. However, reducing the problem to a "bad king versus good king" ignores the fundamental tensions in the world, the class and gender interests of some, and the way these are represented only by "good kings" and "bad kings."[33] The liberal rhetoric of "if only we get rid of Saddam/ Gaddhafi/Bush/Sharon/Arafat" usually prevents or at least impedes any serious analysis of a problem – and indeed, one sometimes gets the impression that this is intentional. Roy, however, takes the analogy of the terrible twins further to actually embrace issues much wider than the persons of Bush and bin Laden:

> But who is Osama bin Laden really? Let me rephrase that. What is Osama bin Laden? He's America's family secret. He is the American president's dark *doppelgänger*. The savage twin of all that purports to be beautiful and civilized. He has been sculpted from the spare rib of a world laid to waste by America's foreign policy: its gunboat diplomacy, its nuclear arsenal, its vulgarly stated policy of "full-spectrum dominance," its chilling disregard for non-American lives, its barbarous military

interventions, its support for despotic and dictatorial regimes, its merciless economic agenda that has munched through the economies of poor countries like a cloud of locusts, its marauding multinationals who are taking over the air we breathe, the ground we stand on, the water we drink, the thoughts we think.

Now that the family secret has been spilled, the twins are blurring into one another and gradually becoming interchangeable. Their guns, bombs, money and drugs have been going around in the loop for a while. (The Stinger missiles that will greet U.S. helicopters were supplied by the CIA. The heroin used by America's drug addicts comes from Afghanistan. The Bush administration recently gave Afghanistan a $43m subsidy for a "war on drugs.")[34]

The attack on the Twin Towers and the Pentagon represents the collision of two forms of religious fundamentalism; the one only cruder than the other. The fundamentalism of the Market was attacked not by Islam but by a particular manifestation of it – a fierce, angry, and vicious fundamentalism driven by pathological and deluded, but nevertheless religious, individuals. David Loy, the Buddhist thinker, and Harvey Cox, the Harvard-based Christian scholar, have both provided valuable insights into how the Market is becoming "the first truly world religion, binding all corners of the globe into a world-view and set of values whose religious role we overlook only because we insist on seeing them as 'secular.'"[35] Cox writes about his trepidation when he first ventured into reading about economics – deviating from his more familiar theological terrain. He was surprised by the familiarity of all the concepts that he encountered:

> Expecting a terra incognita, I found myself instead in the land of déjà vu. The lexicon of The Wall Street Journal and the business sections of Time and Newsweek turned out to bear a striking resemblance to Genesis, the Epistle to the Romans, and Saint Augustine's City of God. Behind descriptions of market reforms, monetary policy, and the convolutions of the Dow, I gradually made out the pieces of a grand narrative about the inner meaning of human history, why things had gone wrong, and how to put them right. Theologians call these myths of origin, legends of the fall, and doctrines of sin and redemption. But here they were again, and in only thin disguise: chronicles about the creation of wealth, the seductive temptations of statism, captivity to faceless economic cycles, and, ultimately, salvation through the advent of free markets, with a small dose of ascetic belt tightening along the way, especially for the East Asian economies.[36]

Definitions of religion have constantly eluded scholars of religion. In a general sense a Transcendent, usually called "God," or an "Ultimate Concern" is at the core of religion and the focus of the believer's life and physical death is an attempt at moving closer towards that or concretizing that in his or her life. Religions in general have a theology of selfhood and otherness, temples that are abodes where a purer form of that attempt to connect with the Transcendent is expressed. Being religious is a way of being in the world with its unique and often competing symbols, e.g. the cross and the crescent. For many religious believers there is also a paradise or nirvana for the faithful adherents and a hell for those who refuse to join them or who fail to do so because of their "essentially evil nature." The term "fundamentalism" is also used in a variety of different ways. It has a peculiar history in twentieth-century North American Protestantism with its insistence on adherence to the literal inerrancy of the Bible, and many have argued that its imposition by journalism onto Islam and Muslims is an unfair one that does little to advance any understanding of contemporary developments in the Muslim world. Whatever its origins, fundamentalism is today widely regarded as a combination of several attitudes:

- An obsession with a single truth as understood by the believer or the believer's group.
- A sense of chosenness tied to the demonizing or damnation of all others who refuse to get behind this "truth."
- The willingness to destroy those who offer alternatives in a "holy war" where innocent victims are referred to as "collaterals."
- The conflation of ideals with one's personal being: "Islam is a perfect religion, therefore I am beyond questioning"; "The American Dream is perfect, therefore trust me."

While the Taliban and Al-Qaeda represented the worst of Muslim fundamentalism, in the larger scheme of things their reach was and remains rather limited. This is particularly true if one does not embrace the growing tendency of many states to utilize the new anti-terrorist orthodoxy as a way of dealing with all forms of internal dissent and resistance to foreign occupation, ranging from the Uighur Chinese, to the Tibetans and Chechens. Far more extensive in its actual – as opposed to perceived reach – is the fundamentalism of the Market. As David Loy argues, because we have failed to recognize Market Capitalism as a religion, let alone a fundamentalist one, we have failed to offer "what is most needed, a meaningful challenge to the aggressive proselytizing of market capitalism, which has already become the most successful religion of all time, winning more converts more quickly than any previous belief system in human history."[37]

Harvey Cox has detailed the remarkable similarities between the description of God and the Market as omnipotent, omniscient, and omnipresent. Here I want to briefly deal with the way we relate to the Market as God and to Market Capitalism as religion. Adherents of the Free Market see their lives driven to the worship of the One All-Powerful and Jealous God: Capital. Underpinned by its theology – economics – it has numerous huge temples in the form of shopping malls to which people are increasingly being drawn by deeply unfilled inner needs, for which the temple, church, or mosque are now perceived as inadequate. ("I shop to feel good"; "I go to the mall to hang out"). The connectedness with both God and community provided by the temple has now been supplanted by the highly individualized and anonymous encounters between cashier and consumer. These temples of consumerism often display a determination to drive out all the smaller little corner churches propounding insignificant little heresies such as "the humanness of chatting to your own friendly butcher." The major symbol of this religion, the "Golden Arches" of McDonalds, has driven out that other symbol of a now old-fashioned religion, the crucifix of Christianity, as the most widely recognized symbol in the world. The arches are telling the crucifix "The Lord, your God is One; you shall have none others in my presence."

Many who have remained nominal religionists find their lives rotating around the worship of Capital and like suicide bombers drive themselves to death as sacrificial lambs (or martyrs) at the altar of "success" in its service. "Shop till you drop" is a basic creed of faith. It is difficult to leave one's home or switch on one's TV without being confronted by its missionaries or having a pamphlet thrust in one's hand. ("Convert Now Or You Will Lose Out!" "Buy Now – The Sale Ends Today!") So successful have these missionary activities been that no one seems to be annoyed by their intrusion, unlike the response given to missionaries such as the Jehovah's Witnesses. The religion of the Market also has an eschatology, even a theory of the "End of History"; paradise awaits those who believe and hell those who reject or who fail – or have failure written in their destiny. ("The unemployed are just lazy"; "The poor shall always be with us.") Images of the ideal of "the glorious lounge," "the perfect toilet for you," "the BMW accompanied by your very own sex-bomb" correspond to images of paradise presented by other religions that sometimes have their own sex-bombs, houris thrown in as an added incentive for martyrdom. While very few can ever hope to possess the "houri" accompanying the picture of the BMW, hope springs eternal.

The struggle against countries that choose an independent economic path is unashamedly described as a "crusade" with collateral damage. ("There are no innocent victims in our crusade against Cuba. Their children dying under our sanctions are either the offspring of infidels so who cares. We are doing it for the greater good.") Damnation awaits those who do not share the beliefs of this religion's adherents. Belief is important; for believers will always fall short as practitioners. The vast majority of believers in the Market are destined to be failures simply because in the market economy success can only come to a minority. Its paradise, after all, is founded on an earth that has limited resources. This fundamentalism of the Market seeks to convert all other cultures in its image, utilizing them for consolidating the system. In the aftermath of

September 11, several spokespersons for the U.S.A., including Colin Powell, have linked "anti-terrorism" to the adoption of "free trade" policies as the dual requirements of allies in the "you're either with us or against us" doctrine of the Bush administration. The Market is thus being openly presented as the only way with the assertion that outside its pale there is no salvation for the world, only the hell-fire of destruction, or the limbo of "primitivism."

Beyond the public drama of religious fundamentalism and more covert forms of religiously justified political violence are realities that impact on a much larger number of people and on the only home of humankind, the earth. The obsession with Muslim fundamentalism may, in fact, serve to detract from this (regardless of whether there is a causal relationship between Muslim fundamentalism and these realities).[38] There may indeed be a relationship between the war on terrorism and the decision of the Bush administration to open the Alaskan wilderness to oil-drilling exploration. The United Nations Development Program's statistics indicate that in 1960 the countries of the North were about twenty times richer than those of the South. By 1990 Northern countries had become fifty times richer. The richest twenty percent of the world's population now have an income about 150 times than that of the poorest twenty percent, a gap that has continued to grow. According to the UN Development Report for 1996, the world's 358 billionaires are wealthier than the combined annual income of countries with forty-five percent of the world's people. As a result, a quarter million children die of malnutrition or infection every week, while hundreds of millions more survive in a limbo of hunger and deteriorating health. For the *mustad'afun fil'ard* bin Laden is a distant figure or, sadly, a hope, as some demonstrators at the World Summit on Sustainable Development in Johannesburg seemed to think with their T-shirts displaying his smiling face. For those 2.8 billion who live on less than U.S.$2 a day and who confront death by starvation or half an existence under foreign occupation the realities cited above may well be the terrorism of our age. When Muslim liberals suggested any relationship between September 11 and political grievances, it was confined to U.S. foreign policy in the Middle East. One searches in vain for any critique on the problems of domestic wealth, domestic consumption, domestic corporate greed, domestic homelessness, and domestic racism – all issues that drive foreign policy considerations. It's as if the only tragedy was one of exclusion from the table of the new empire, leading to sadly misguided yearnings of "if only our lobby could be as powerful as the Jewish lobby." A progressive rereading of our theological heritage does not take its point of departure from the concerns of dominant and dominating classes nor from yearnings to join "the club" but "in a perception of the real situation of the poor, and, with new eyes, bestowed by this experience, it rereads the foundational texts of the faith."[39] The location of the progressive Muslims among the marginalized of the world is the *Sunnah* (precedent) of the all the Prophets of God and the choice that God himself exercises (Q. 7:136–7; 34:31–33).[40]

CONCLUSION

There is nothing in this clash of fundamentalisms that is intrinsically Islamic, in the same way that there is nothing intrinsically Christian about the religion of the Market or of the ideology of apartheid. That the Muslims responsible for this attack may have been inspired by Islam is plausible; that they used Islam as justification for their deeds is apparent, for the Qur'an is as open to diverse readings as any other text. There is thus some responsibility on the part of Muslim thinkers to expose and oppose the theological and textual basis of their arguments. To confine oneself to combat with those tendencies, however, is inadequate from both a Southern perspective as well as an Islamic one. To do so also risks being co-opted in an uncritical peace discourse that has a name: *Pax Americana*; peace on the terms of the United States and with an ideology incompatible with social, economic, political, and environmental justice.

A progressive commitment to destabilizing the current world order – and destabilization is not to be conflated with political violence, as numerous activists in the global justice movement are increasingly demonstrating – is not to be undertaken out of blind hatred for the advocates of the religion of the Market. Rather, unlike the Market fundamentalists, we progressive Muslims actually believe that an alternative vision of the world and being in it is possible. Humankind, as the Progressive Muslim Network Declaration affirms, are not only consumers or the objects of greed; we are in a state of returning to God. Islam is, indeed, a religion of peace, but not exclusively that. It also calls upon people to destabilize the peace when it hides the demons of injustice. In addition to confronting the fundamentalism of the Market and the havoc that it has bought forth, we also have to deal with the problem of Muslim brokenness, fragile egos, and delusions of grandeur involving our power and control over a world governed by the *Shari'ah*. The problem with Muslim fundamentalism is that it is as totalitarian and exclusive as the order that it seeks to displace. It seeks to create an order wherein its proponents are the sole spokespersons for a rather vengeful, patriarchal, and chauvinistic God – a God that incidentally resembles that of George W. Bush and his fellow travelers in the religious right wing. The Taliban represent the logical consequence of a literalist and misogynistic reading of our earlier Islamic heritage. Their reading is not so much an aberration of Islam as a carrying out to an illogical conclusion previous extremist stands of interpretation. They have, for example, always insisted that women will also have access to medical treatment if the government can afford it. How different is this from the Wahhabi Saudi regime, where gender segregation is enforced because they have the financial resources to do so. When we see Osama sitting cross-legged surrounded by hundreds of books on Islamic jurisprudence and theology, we are seeing one of the strands in the Islamic. Arguing that the Taliban and the Wahhabis do not "really" represent Islam is unhelpful, for we fall into the trap of setting ourselves up as the sole authentic spokespersons – the same weapon that is being used against liberal and progressive Muslims. We can insist on asking, along with 'Ali Shari'ati, "Whose Islam? Whose lives and interest are being advanced by our understanding and interpretation of Islam?"

> Which Islam is it that the Shah refers to? Is it the Islam of imperialism? An Islam which is made for the next world and says nothing about this world. The imperialist brand of Islam dictates that Islamic nations be their colonies and allows them to loot the wealth, resources and productivity of Muslim lands.[41]

People concerned about other people and aware that the earth is our only home and has finite resources need to find each other and collectively work for socioeconomic alternatives before these fanatics – led by corporate America under the McDonalds Golden Arches and Bush as its spokesperson or Al-Qaeda under the crescent with Osama bin Ladin as its spokesperson – destroy all of us.

ENDNOTES

1. 'Ali Shari'ati, cited in E. Abrahimian, "'Ali Shari'ati: Ideologue of the Iranian Revolution," *MERIP Reports*, January 1982, 14–15.
2. Paul Salem, "A Critique of Western Conflict Resolution from a Non-Western Perspective," *Negotiation Journal*, 9(4), 1993, 364.
3. Haideh Moghissi, *Feminism and Islamic Fundamentalism: The Limits of Postmodern Analysis* (London: Zed, 1999), 126.
4. Terry Eagleton, *The Illusions of Postmodernism* (Oxford: Blackwell, 1996), 103.
5. For a contemporary discussion on the philosophical bases of liberalism and communitarianism in these debates see Stephen Mulhall and Adam Swift, *Liberals and Communitarians* (Oxford: Blackwell, 1996).
6. While I use the term "North" (juxtaposed against the "South) to refer to the economically developed countries, I believe that one needs to be careful not to view these societies as homogeneous. There are significant variations of class, race, and gender and a lack of awareness of these can obscure the value of the progressive tendencies within these societies.
7. Sorush Irfani, *Revolutionary Islam in Iran – Popular Liberation or Religious Dictatorship?* (London: Zed, 1983).
8. Other than Iran, another area where the term gained relatively wide coverage as a reflection of trends within Islam was among a section of the Islamists in South Africa during the struggle against apartheid in the 1980s, when both the Muslim Youth Movement and the Call of Islam used it to characterize their understanding of an Islam opposed to racism, sexism, and the degradation of the environment. See Esack, *Qur'an, Liberation, and Pluralism* (Oxford: Oneworld, 1997).
9. Irfani, *Revolutionary Islam in Iran*, 33.
10. From the Progressive Muslim Network website: http://www.progressivemuslims.com/index2.html.
11. Rebecca S. Chopp, *The Praxis of Suffering: An Interpretation of Liberation and Political Theologies* (New York: Orbis, 1989), 38.
12. From the Progressive Muslim Network website: http://www.progressivemuslims.com/index2.html.
13. Ibid.

14. The rejoicing was quite widespread in the Muslim world and was roundly condemned by liberal Muslim commentators. The limited base of their perspectives was however evident from the fact that Muslim responses were treated in isolation, as if only these responses required a moralistic condemnation. There was no reference in their comments to the broader rejoicing that occurred in other parts of the South, such as Brazil and China. When there was any suggestion that the rejoicing might have some explanation, although not justification, such explanations were confined to U.S. foreign policy in the Middle East. They displayed no awareness of the way foreign policy is driven by domestic imperatives related to consumerism, corporate interest, and the commodification of people.

15. Writing in *The Independent*, Yasmine Alibhai-Brown argued that "Enlightened Muslims have an almost impossible role, but it is one which must be taken up. We must continue to rebut the foolish claims of fundamentalist liberals and remind them of the distressed, atomized and utterly lonely society which they have created through aggressive individualism, where the habits of obligation and duty have been obliterated. But whatever our feelings about this and the failures of the West in Afghanistan, Iraq, Palestine, or colonialism and the unbearable U.S. hypocrisy and hubris, we must act to stop the rot within." See Alibhai-Brown, "Don't Tell Me How I Should Worship," *The Independent* (London), October 15, 2001.

16. Mona Eltahtawy, *Washington Post*, January 3, 2002, 17.

17. Richard Neville, "Beyond Good and Evil," April 15, 2002, 3. The article can be accessed at http://www.theage.com.au/articles/2002/04/15/1018333477336.html.

18. Scholarly estimates suggest U.S. bombs killed at least 3767 civilians by the middle of December 2001. The price in blood was paid by ordinary Afghans who had nothing to do with the atrocities, did not elect the Taliban who ruled over them, and had no say in the decision to offer hospitality to Osama bin Laden and Al-Qaeda. See Seumas Milne, "The Innocent Dead in a Coward's War" *The Guardian*, December 20, 2001, p. 7. Marc Herold, an economics professor from the University of New Hampshire, who conducted the research that led to this figure told ABC Radio that "a much more realistic" estimate of civilian deaths is five thousand in the period October 7 to December 10, 2001. See Marc Herold, "Counting the Dead – Attempts to Hide the Number of Afghan Civilians Killed by U.S. Bombs Are an Affront to Justice," *The Guardian*, August 8, 2002.

19. The reality, as John Whitbeck has argued, "is that most acts to which the word 'terrorism' is applied are tactics of the weak, usually (although not always) against the strong." Whitbeck argues that "such acts are not a tactic of choice but of last resort ... the Palestinians would certainly prefer to be able to fight for their freedom from a never-ending occupation by 'respectable' means, using F-16's, Apache attack helicopters and laser-guided missiles such as those the United States provides to Israel. If the United States provided such weapons to Palestine as well, the problem of suicide bombers would be solved. Until it does, or at least until the Palestinians can see some genuine and credible hope for a decent future, no one should be surprised or shocked that Palestinians use the 'delivery systems' available to them – their own bodies. In this regard, it is worth noting that the poor, the weak and the oppressed rarely complain about 'terrorism.' The rich, the strong and the oppressors constantly do. While most of mankind has more reason to fear the high-technology violence of the strong than the low-technology violence of the weak, the fundamental mind-trick employed by the abusers of the epithet 'terrorism' (no doubt, in some cases, unconsciously) is essentially this: The low-technology violence of the weak is such an abomination that there are no limits on the high-technology violence of the strong which can be deployed against it." See John Whitbeck, "'Terrorism': The Word Itself Is Dangerous", *Al-Ahram Weekly Online*, 564, 2001, www.ahram.org.eg/weekly/2001/564/op10.htm

20. Khaled Abou El-Fadl was one of the few Muslim liberal commentators who attempted to place "terrorism" within some social framework. He wrote "The extreme political violence we call terrorism is not a simple aberration unrelated to the political dynamics of a society. Generally, terrorism is the quintessential crime of those who feel powerless seeking to

undermine the perceived power of a targeted group. Like many crimes of power, terrorism is also a hate crime, for it relies on a polarized rhetoric of belligerence toward a particular group that is demonized to the point of being denied any moral worth. To recruit and communicate effectively, this rhetoric of belligerence needs to tap into and exploit an already radicalized discourse with the expectation of resonating with the social and political frustrations of a people. If acts of terrorism find little resonance within a society, such acts and their ideological defenders are marginalized. But if these acts do find a degree of resonance, terrorism becomes incrementally more acute and severe, and its ideological justifications become progressively more radical." See Abou El Fadl, "Islam and the Theology of Power," *Middle East Report*, 221, 2001, p. 2.

21. Cf. M.A. Khan, "Memo to Muslims," http://www.ijtihad.org/memo.html.
22. "Islam" literally means "submission," i.e., submission to the will of God. While the *root* of the word is *s-l-m*, which is the same root as *salam* (peace), the structure of Arabic words allows a large variety of words to come from the same root. It is misleading – or ignorance – to suggest that identical roots lead to identical meanings. If violence to the text were real then some of these commentators really got away with murder; in a widely circulated "Memo to Muslims," Muqtedar Khan offered numerous Qur'anic references in support of his arguments, very few of them having any relation to the point that he makes. For example, he writes, "While encouraging Muslims to struggle against injustice (Al Quran 4:135) He (God) also encourages Muslims to forgive Jews and Christians if they have committed injustices against us (Al Quran 2:109, 3:159, 5:85)." A casual perusal of these verses indicates that none bears a remote resemblance to his assertion about God encouraging Muslims to "forgive Jews and Christians." Liberal Muslims were not the only ones culpable of this violence towards the text. Hamza Yusuf, a prominent traditional scholar, wrote, "We have seen images since of American flags burning to further arouse the wrath of a nation filled with grief, confusion and anger. Again, Islam prohibits the burning of flags according to the explicit verse, Do not curse [the idols] of those who call on other than Allah, thus causing them to curse Allah out of animosity [toward you] and without knowledge." In Yusuf's apologetic the U.S. flag becomes an idol worthy of respect in one neat stroke and the verse is presented as "explicit." Hamza Yusuf, "A Time for Introspection," http://www.islamfortoday.com/hamza01.htm.
23. Ziauddin Sardar, *The Observer*, September 23, 2001.
24. In 1997 senior Taliban figures were entertained at George Bush (Sr)'s home in Texas, where they enjoyed halal barbeque with the Vice-President of the oil giant Unocal. Unocal produced billions of barrels of oil from Turkmenistan, and wanted to pump it across landlocked Afghanistan, through Pakistan to the Arabian Sea. The talks broke down in 1998 but resumed immediately after the current administration took office. It is worth noting that both Hamid Karzai, the current Afghan leader, and Zalmay Khalilzad, the U.S. special envoy to Kabul, are "former" consultants to Unocal.
25. Farid Esack, *Qur'an, Liberation, and Pluralism* (Oxford: Oneworld, 1997).
26. Rebecca Chopp, *The Praxis of Suffering*, 34.
27. In a challenging essay, Paul Salem challenges conventional notions of Western approaches to conflict resolution and points out that its "theorists and practitioners operate within a macro-political context that they may overlook, but which colors their attitudes and values. This seems remarkably striking from an outsider's point of view and is largely related to the West's dominant position in the world. All successful 'empires' develop an inherent interest in peace. The ideology of peace reinforces a status quo that is favorable to the dominant power. The Romans, for example, preached a *Pax Romana*, the British favored a *Pax Britannica*, and the Americans today pursue – consciously or not – a *Pax Americana*. Conflict and bellicosity is useful – indeed essential – in building empires, but an ideology of peace and conflict resolution is clearly more appropriate for its maintenance." See Paul Salem, "A Critique of Western Conflict Resolution," 362–4.
28. For distinctions between the "North" and the "South" in terms of unequal distribution of wealth, resources, and consumption, see note 6 in this essay.

29. This was the title of an op-ed piece that I wrote for the *Financial Mail* (Johannesburg), September 21, 2001.

30. The similarities between the current rhetoric of Muslim and Christian fundamentalism are also evident from the following statement made by (then Senator) John Ashcroft upon receiving an honorary degree from Bob Jones University in 1999: "Unique among the nations, America recognized the source of our character as being Godly and eternal, not being civic and temporal. And because we have understood that our source is eternal, America has been different. We have no king but Jesus." Regrettably, this is the tendency that the mainstream American Muslim organizations, ranging from the Islamic Society of North America to the Washington, DC based International Institute for Islamic Thought, embraced prior to the Presidential elections. While there is now great regret about this, the reasons for this shift are dubious, given the way the Bush administration has embraced Israeli policies in Palestine.

31. Tariq Ali, *Clash of Fundamentalisms* (London: Verso, 2002).

32. Arundhati Roy, "The Algebra of Infinite Justice," *The Guardian*, September 29, 2001, http://www.guardian.co.uk/Archive/Article/0,4273,4266289,00.html.

33. Some U.S.-based scholars of Islamic law attempted to indict bin Laden under the laws of the *Shari'ah* in addition to any indictments that he may face under international law. (Alan Cooper, "Scholars Plan to Show How Attacks Violated Islamic Law," *Washington Post*, January 20, 2002, A 15.) Holding individual alleged criminals against humanity accountable for atrocities is obviously an important measure of our commitment to human rights. While an insistence that this also be uniformly applied to all such alleged criminals, whether they are named Henry Kissinger or Osama bin Laden, is even more important, my criticism is about the reduction of problems and solutions to "evil" or "good" individuals.

34. Arundhati Roy, "The Algebra of Infinite Justice."

35. David Loy, "Religion of the Market," http://www.just-international.org/comm-30.htm.

36. Harvey Cox, "The Market as God," www.theatlantic.com/issues/99mar/marketgod.htm.

37. David Loy, "Religion of the Market."

38. Many scholars have argued that there is a direct relationship between the rise of religious extremism and the socio-political conditions of political repression and poverty. Dario Fo, the Italian playwright and satirist who won the Nobel Prize for literature in 1997, said rather bluntly in a widely circulated email, "The great speculators wallow in an economy that every year kills tens of millions of people with poverty – so what is 20,000 dead in New York? Regardless of who carried out the massacre, this violence is the legitimate daughter of the culture of violence, hunger and inhumane exploitation." While this may well be the case it offers a rather inadequate explanation of why this expression of righteous rage is much more characteristic of Muslim countries than others. Cited in Steven Erlanger, "In Europe, Some Say the Attacks Stemmed from American Failings," *The Guardian*, September 22, 2001.

39. Leonardo Boff and Clodovis Boff, *Salvation and Liberation – In Search of a Balance between Faith and Politics* (New York: Orbis, 1985), 25–6.

40. According to the Qur'an, virtually all the Prophets, including Muhammad, came from peasant or working class backgrounds and the option for the marginalized seems to be implicit in their very origins. All the Abrahamic Prophets mentioned in the Qur'an had their origins among the peasants and were generally shepherds in their formative years. The singular exception, Moses, was destined to sojourn in the desert of Madyan, where he was employed as a shepherd for eight or ten years (Q. 28:27). One may describe this as a process of "deschooling" in the ways of the powerful, in anticipation of his mission as a Prophet of God unto them and as a liberator of his people. Opposition invariably came from the ruling and dominant classes that the Qur'an describes as the *mala'* rulers or aristocracy (Q. 11:27, 38; 23:24, 33; 26:34), the *mutrafun* (ostentatious) (Q. 34:34; 43:23), and the *mustakbirun* (arrogant) (e.g. Q. 16:22; 23:67; 31:7). Support for the Prophets was usually forthcoming from the *aradhil* (lower classes), the *fuqara* (poor), and the *masakin*

(indigent). In fact, the disdain of the aristocracy for social intercourse with slaves, serfs, and workers was a significant factor blocking their own entry into Islam. In Muhammad's latter years in Mecca, the aristocracy indicated their willingness to enter Islam if he got rid of the riff-raff surrounding him. The Qur'an condemned such offers and warned Muhammad against considering them (Q. 18:28, cf. 6:52–4).

41. 'Ali Shari'ati, cited in Arabimian, *op. cit.*

3

ISLAM: A CIVILIZATIONAL PROJECT IN PROGRESS

Ahmet Karamustafa

WHAT IS ISLAM?

One of the most difficult challenges awaiting anyone – Muslim or non-Muslim – who would like to observe, study, or understand Islam is to define and identify it. What is Islam, after all? To many, it will come as a surprise that such an innocent question does not have a simple answer. Wouldn't most people – again, Muslim or non-Muslim – agree in calling Islam a religion, for instance? Aren't there Islamic cultures? Isn't Islam a civilization? Each of the statements implicit in these questions ("Islam is a religion," "Islam is a culture or a set of cultures," and "Islam is a civilization") may look simple and straightforward, but in reality each is a mask that serves to cover up interminable difficulties.

ISLAM AS RELIGION

Let us first examine the assertion "Islam is a religion." What exactly does this statement tell us? Not much, unless we agree on a definition of religion first. It turns out, however, that there is no universally accepted definition of religion. Even though scholars of all stripes, over the course of the past century or so, have made valiant attempts to fashion a universally applicable definition, it is fair to say that their attempts have not led to any meaningful consensus. The one candidate for a commonly accepted definition – that religion is belief in supernatural beings – has proven to be riddled with problems. Foremost among these is the indisputable fact that some major faith traditions like Buddhism lack beliefs in supernatural beings of a kind comparable to the one God of Western monotheisms! Further, there is the problem of determining the exact referents of the term "supernatural," which has proven to be a frustratingly elusive enterprise. The lack of consensus and the spread of confusion over the subject matter of religion have in fact led to powerful calls recently to abandon the concept of religion altogether for scholarly purposes on the grounds that it is an analytically obscure and methodologically unhelpful category.

The woes of scholarship are also reflected in popular usage, where the term "religion" is often passed over in favor of more appealing terms like "myth" and "spirituality" in reference to originally Asian, African, or Native American beliefs and practices, while observers as well as practitioners of Western monotheisms (Islam, Judaism, and Christianity) frequently have difficulty in fitting these faith traditions into the concept of religion. Perhaps the most notorious instance of this difficulty is the oft-repeated adage that "Islam is not simply a religion but a way of life." When used by outsiders, this maxim normally carries an air of opprobrium around it, with the implication that Islam should not, of course, be more than a religion, while insiders tend to repeat it with a special relish that also betrays a degree of astonishment ("How could anyone possibly have thought of reducing Islam to the level of being a mere religion?") When we probe this issue further, however, it emerges that Orthodox and Catholic Christianity as well as Conservative and Orthodox Judaism are also viewed by most parties – both insiders and outsiders, scholars and observers – as "ways of life." After all, who could say, in good conscience, that there is no such thing as "leading the life of an Orthodox Jew or of a devout Catholic?" To put it slightly differently, for most people there would be something amiss about any attempt to reduce Catholicism or traditional Judaism to a limited set of beliefs and practices called religion which is completely cut off from other aspects of human life. What, one wonders, is this thing called religion if Western monotheisms and non-Western beliefs and practices are not adequately captured by it?

At this point, many of you will no doubt want to object to this unexpected assertion that the term "religion" does not adequately embrace either Western or non-Western beliefs and practices. You will point to the existence of religious institutions (typically the Church is offered here as the obvious example), or to the widely held opinion that religion is a matter of beliefs about the cardinal questions of human life nourished in individual consciences. Could it not be claimed, you will continue, that "religion," as a descriptive term, denotes particular institutional structures like the Church or, failing that, personal beliefs held by individuals and/or collective doctrines shared by large human groups? The term should have a referent after all!

Unfortunately, this well-intentioned attempt to salvage the term is ill-fated from the start. On closer scrutiny, "religious" institutions do not prove to be significantly different than "non-religious" institutions like the state or the market, so that it proves to be impossible to distinguish one from the other. Worse yet, not all faith traditions seem to have developed complicated institutional structures like the Church. Many, indeed, display relatively low levels of institutionalization. And where institutions do exist, they do not serve to define the boundaries of the faith traditions. As is well known (though not adequately appreciated), there is, for instance, no church in Islam, though religious institutions of various kinds have existed from very early on in Islamic history. And none of those institutions (for instance, the religious college or the mystical association) can be said to stand for the whole of Islam. In short, trying to *fill in* the concept of religion by focusing on institutions is like describing the human body by fixing one's attention only on the bones.

If institutions do not help us define religion, what about the assertion that religion is all about belief and faith? Surely, this assumption at least will withstand scrutiny? Surely, all religious traditions are built around matters of individual conscience? Interestingly, it turns out that only Protestant Christianity fits this particular take on religion. It is true, of course, that concepts of belief, faith, individuality, and individual conscience were not invented by reformed Christianity: they are more or less universally found in the last three millennia of human history. But the suggestion that faith, hence religion, is to be understood primarily, even solely, as a matter of individual conscience is peculiar to Protestant Christianity. Since this form of Christianity was the civil religion of the United States throughout the twentieth century, it should not be surprising that popular conceptions of religion in America were shaped by it. But this view on religion does not serve us well when we turn our gaze to faith traditions other than Protestant Christianity (not to mention evangelical Protestantism, where it also fails). In Islam, for instance, individuality and individual conscience have always been at the core of the tradition, but very few have ever suggested that Islam can be defined using only these concepts.

To summarize our discussion so far: in both scholarly and popular usage, "religion" proves to be a murky concept with an unclear content, and there are serious doubts about its universal applicability. Under these circumstances, trying to define Islam by calling it a religion is, to say the least, singularly unhelpful. To the extent it can give rise to the false impression that Islam is a distinct entity with clearly delineated borders, the statement "Islam is a religion" might even be downright misleading.

But if viewing Islam as a religion is not particularly illuminating, how *should* we view it?

ISLAM AS CULTURE

If, in spite of our popular inclinations, the concept religion proves to be of little use in our attempt to answer the question "What is Islam?" do we perhaps stand a better chance by turning to the concept of culture? Is Islam a culture?

Indeed, there are many who claim or implicitly assume that Islam is completely identical with a particular culture, so much so that they almost see Islam as another name for that culture. This kind of cultural particularism has always been more influential than you might suppose. A version of it, popular among both Muslims and non-Muslims (though more among non-Muslim Westerners), for instance, has been the tendency to establish an equivalence between Islam and Arab culture. In this view, Islam is seen as a divine sanction placed upon certain or even all aspects of Arabian culture after certain undesirable aspects of it (for instance, unlimited polygamy) were removed or reformed through the prophetic mission of the Arabian Prophet Muhammad. Especially prevalent in the first centuries of Islamic history, this view was successfully challenged and eventually displaced both by other cultural particularisms (not surprisingly, non-Arab Muslims too tended to value their own indigenous cultures over those of others) and by other intellectually and culturally more egalitarian approaches to Islam. Yet cultural particularism never completely faded away, and it was given new license in the twentieth century with the emergence of nationalism among Muslims. The new Muslim nationalists, the majority of whom worldwide were non-Arab, claimed Islam for themselves and their own nations. The new nationalisms were on the whole built on secularist foundations, but many nationalist Muslims, Arab and non-Arab, had to build their nationalist ideologies on the cultural particularisms of the pre-modern era, which were intertwined with Islam. This naturalization of Islam by the new national cultures of the second half of the twentieth century, though never built on solid intellectual grounds, has proven to be influential in the formation of the popular cultures of these societies, so that it would be fair to assume that most Muslims on the globe today, as members of nationalistic cultures, associate Islam in the first instance with their own national culture and only secondarily with any other culture. This is not to deny the global dimensions of Islam, but only to observe that the identification of Islam with particular local, regional, and national cultures is the norm among Muslim populations in the world. Cultural particularism is a major force to be reckoned with.

Does this mean that for all practical purposes, we should accept the claim that Islam is to be understood as culture? Not quite. For one thing, it is crucial to remember that particularism of any kind (ethnic, cultural, racial, and, yes, even gender based) has always been challenged, contested, and, more often than not, counterbalanced in Islamic history by universalism (as most definitively demonstrated by the declining fortunes of Arabism after the third Islamic century). In other words, the globalist, universalist, and humanist dimensions of Islam have never been completely submerged by any limited and limiting particularism. Yes, there are many different Islamic cultures on local, regional, and national levels, but identifying Islam with any one of these cultures would be to reduce and to distort it. This is because Islam is primarily a supra-cultural package of values, practices, and resources that Muslims adopt to navigate the stormy waters of human life on earth. We simply cannot ignore this global, universalizing nature of Islam.

Conversely, it would be equally erroneous to identify any particular culture thoroughly with Islam. In the first place, the attempt to identify Islam with only one of the literally innumerable particular cultures that claim to be Islamic is manifestly nonsensical. Also, it is crucial to remember that the fit between Islam and culture is never snug. No matter how we choose to delimit and define any particular culture, we can be certain that it can never be completely identified with Islam, which is simultaneously in and above cultures. This is emphatically the case with Arab culture as well, which was, it is true, the locus of the latest divine intervention in human history that resulted in the two sources of Islam, the Qur'an and the exemplary life story of Muhammad. Contrary to what some rabid Arab Muslim nationalists and their non-Muslim counterparts may believe, however, Muslims have never seen this as a divine command to Arabize humanity. Instead, wherever they are in the world they have always been and likely will always be engaged in an ongoing struggle to bring their own local cultures into concordance with their own understandings of Islam. This engagement is not a restrictive or destructive one, nor is it meant to level the rich cultural diversity of the worldwide Muslim community into a banal cultural uniformity. On the contrary, it is a productive and creative affair whereby believers actively attempt to shape and resculpt their cultures in the light of Islamic precepts. Particular cultures will always be both more and less than Islam, and Islam will forever be both in and outside of particular cultures. It is this creative tension between the two that attracts and fascinates Muslims.

The inevitable conclusion is that Islam cannot be viewed as a culture, nor can it be identified with any particular human culture. Some cultures have longer histories of Islamization than others, but the cultures of all people who self-identify as Muslims are all equally Islamic and cannot be hierarchically organized as being more or less Islamic. This is primarily because Islam is a transethnic, transnational, transracial idiom that people use to craft cultural identities for themselves. Could it be, then, that Islam should be understood as a civilization?

WHAT IS IN A CIVILIZATION?

It is a common practice to view human history as a composite narrative of numerous civilizational stories: ancient Mesopotamian, Egyptian, Greek, Persian, Indian, Chinese, Aztec, Mayan ... the list is a very long one. In this perspective, individual civilizations are self-contained entities that come into being, live their stories, then disappear from view, leaving behind physical and mental traces – some faint, some spectacular – on the stage of history. Civilizations, it would seem, are all but natural entities with distinct characteristics and life-cycles, not much different than the animate and inanimate genera and species that collectively make up our natural habitat. And who can take issue with this popular view? Civilizations indeed existed and continue to exist (though endangered by the onslaught of globalization), and, since none has yet proven to be permanent, they are indeed transient, some would even say fickle, phenomena.

Agreed? Yes, but there is a nagging concern. Granted that civilizations are entities of some kind, where and how do we draw their boundaries? Better yet, do they even have boundaries in the first place? This turns out to be a thornier question than first imagined. And in asking it, we run into a major misconception about civilizations that we need to dismantle in our attempt to identify Islam as a civilization. This misconception can be called the "cocoon theory of civilization." Contrary to this all too pervasive idea that civilizations somehow have protective skins around them that jealously guard their quintessential kernels, close scrutiny of any civilization worthy of the name reveals only highly porous transitional areas instead of continuous and firm borders. Civilizations are entities alright, but they are not self-contained, water-tight units. Their stories often tend to be thoroughly intertwined, even incomprehensible when told in isolation from the stories of other civilizations.

What leads to the prevalence of the cocoon theory is often the temptation to imagine civilizations not only as natural entities of some sort but also, and more specifically, as *biological* entities endowed with life and purpose. The naturalization of the concept of civilization does not stop at the observation that civilizations are similar to natural entities: since a civilization has a beginning and an end and is subject to growth and decay, we naturally assume, it must be alive and must function like any living organism. This is another major misconception about civilizations that we have to clear up, and it can be called the "personification of civilization." Contrary to this view, civilizations are not independent agents on the stage of human history. They are not capable of any kind of action, nor are they alive in any biological sense. A civilization is nothing more than a particular, even unique (though this *singularity* should not be abused), combination of ideas and practices that groups of human actors – who are the real agents of human history – affirm as their own and use to define and develop their own sense of presence and agency in the world. On a radical level, human history is not the cumulative narrative of civilizational stories; it is the story of individual and collective human agency as defined around a fascinating series of core ideas and practices that we call civilizations. Islam, we contend, is best understood as a civilization in this sense.

Before we can identify Islam as a civilization, however, we need to unwrap the layers of misconception woven around the concept of Islamic civilization by proponents of the cocoon and personification theories. You should be forewarned that these misconceptions are held by Muslims and non-Muslims, Westerners and Easterners alike: if no one has a monopoly over the truth, much the same can be said about untruths.

It is often thought that Islamic civilization, built originally on divine foundations (the view of most Muslims) or ideas and practices derivative from Judaism and Christianity (possibly the view of most non-Muslims), took its peculiar shape through a series of complicated, evasive maneuvers that enabled it to preserve its pristine purity. Muslims, it is assumed, rejected cultural influences from the outside and jealously guarded their core values from being contaminated through contact with other civilizations. An influential Muslim view, perhaps the prevalent one, is that whenever and wherever they succeeded in preserving the divine kernel, Muslims flourished; whenever and wherever they succumbed to non-Islamic "contamination," they perished or lost power and became weak, even subjugated. The prevalent non-Muslim view seems to be the exact opposite: Muslims gained power where and when they were willing to temper the rather uncompromising, even rigid dictates of their religion with unabashed borrowing from other civilizations and lost this power where and when they turned a blind eye to the benefits that others had to offer.

Yes, you have guessed it: this is one, perhaps the most prevalent, version of the cocoon theory of Islamic civilization. Islam, it is often observed, came into this world fully grown and, to boot, in full daylight: a holy book, a prophet, a divine law – all introduced into this world from the other world, like a potent drug injected into the body. Exceptionally, however, this drug – which is "true Islam" – does not interact with the body and is only efficacious when it is preserved intact in its pure and pristine state.

Proponents of this view often focus on the interaction between the nascent Islamic civilization and the Hellenistic philosophical traditions of late antiquity to exemplify what can be characterized alternatively as the presumed civilizational/cultural xenophobia (if the proponent is a non-Muslim detractor) or the unsullied purity (if she or he is a Muslim defender) of Islam. According to this reading of Islamic history, Islam had one genuine opportunity to assimilate the admirable qualities of Greek philosophical and scientific traditions (most crucially, its *rationalism*), made a serious venture in this direction (hence the glorious period of Islamic philosophy and science of the ninth and tenth centuries CE prompted by a massive translation movement from Greek into Arabic), but ultimately reverted to its original stock of ideas and practices unaffected by any cultural or civilizational influences (like Greek rationalism) that did not bear the divine stamp of approval.

That this caricature of an account of the encounter and interaction between an emerging Islamic civilization and the pre-existing Hellenistic traditions of learning still appeals to a significant number of Muslim and non-Muslims around the globe is disturbing indeed. What is wrong with this view? Wasn't Islam the product of a revealed message after all? And wasn't the revelation at the very core of the civilization that was fashioned in its image? Even if we answer both of these questions with a resounding "yes!," the cocoon theory of Islam in general and its representation of its encounter with Greek learning in particular still remains indefensible. The divine message may have supplied the impetus for the development of a civilization, may have even been its nucleus, but the civilization undoubtedly drew from many other cultural wellsprings. Heir to the variegated cultural heritage of the Hellenistic Near East of late antiquity (with distinct Greek, Persian, Mesopotamian, Syrian and Egyptian strands, to name only the most prominent), the new civilization proceeded to incorporate many other cultural traditions – North African, Saharan/sub-Saharan African, Iberian, South-east European, Indian, Central Asian, South-east Asian – into its multicolored fabric. Indeed, it would be more proper to talk about an Islamic civilizational sphere with numerous distinct cultural regions instead of a single, uniform Islamic civilization with an unchangeable cultural kernel. Simply put, Islamic civilization went global almost immediately after its formative stage. The cocoon theory either ignores this "global" facet of Islamic civilization or belittles it. It ignores the cultural plurality and diversity of Islamic civilization by placing the Arab Middle East at its cultural center (so that Arab Islam is purported to be "true Islam"). It belittles such diversity by suggesting that Islamic civilization remained forever closed to non-Arab cultures even where significant interaction took place. Islam's Greek heritage (yes, *heritage* and not just a fleeting, traceless flirtation) is just one prominent aspect of the historical development of Islam that is almost thoroughly masked by the cocoonists. Other aspects of Islamic civilization – some weighty and broad, others more subtle – similarly concealed from view by the senseless application of the cocoon theory are so numerous that we cannot hope to list them here. But whether local, regional, or global in nature, all interactions of Islamic civilization with originally non-Islamic cultures and civilizations are equally interesting and important: they all deserve our full attention and complete acknowledgement. Any other approach would be to impoverish and ultimately to desiccate Islam.

But cocoonists are not the only guilty party: there are also those – though they are frequently one and the same as the cocoonists – who talk about Islam as if it were a living organism or even a person. We may call these the "personifiers." They falsely and, alas, perniciously imagine Islam (and other civilizations) to be self-contained *organisms* closed in on themselves and engaged in perpetual strife and competition with others of their kind. Their "proof" of Islamic xenophobia/purity (as the case may be), tirelessly fed especially to Western audiences from many media and pseudo-educational venues, is Islam's supposed intolerance of others and its willingness to overwhelm them through *jihad*. This "proof" is equally as alarming – if not more – as the cocoonists' attempt to erase Islam's Greek heritage. This view too finds high numbers of subscribers, both Muslim and non-Muslim, though its Muslim proponents are an extremely small, yet highly vocal and visible, minority made up largely of discontented urban youth who find themselves in deplorable economic and cultural conditions.

What is wrong with this view? After all, did not Islam break into the world scene through a spectacular series of conquests? Is not jihad often proffered as the sixth pillar of Islam? Isn't there a certain exclusiveness written into the very core of Islam? The answer is straightforward, though it comes from an oblique angle, thus avoiding the deception conjured by talk of jihad: no, Islam is not doomed to such a poisonous exclusivism of the kind imagined by personifiers, since Islam is not an "agent" in any sense of this word. The personifiers are guilty of a chilling, indeed deadly, fallacy, which is the fallacy of denying agency to real human actors (individual and collective) and imputing it instead to phantasmagoric concoctions called religions or civilizations that are seen as the true agents of history. Only Muslims (and of course non-Muslims), and not some imaginary agent named Islam, can determine the historical course of Islamic civilization. Of course, overlaying this fallacy and concealing it from view is another fallacy about jihad that needs to be set aright. This will be to dwell on the obvious, but it bears repetition: no, jihad is not an exclusivistic doctrine of elimination of non-Muslims but an attempt to realize the central mandate of Islam, which is the ceaseless, perpetual attempt to *become* a true believer.

Let us take stock. The cocoon and the personification fallacies, it emerges, are simply instances of that exclusive particularism we have already met under the name "cultural particularism" in our discussion on culture above. They betray the same unfortunate attempt to erect permanent, waterproof boundaries among social entities (cultures, civilizations) that are erroneously projected as the only true yet necessarily aggressive and mutually hostile actors of history. This combination of *exclusive particularism* – call it the grand illusion! – and *misplaced agency* – should we refer to it as the great agency robbery in human history that utterly dehumanizes all history? – this *unholy alliance* is utterly dangerous and should be resisted at all costs. The fundamental assumptions of all who push this envelope, namely, Islam's supposed imperviousness to historical and social change as well as its totally exclusive and, to boot, imperialist particularism, fly in the face of incontrovertible historical and, ultimately, human evidence to the contrary from Islamic history and contemporary Muslim communities. In this connection, it is absolutely crucial to realize that this toxic combination is peddled equally by both Muslims and non-Muslims, Westerners and non-Westerners. The Muslims are, yes, you've guessed it, those "fundamentalists" who crowd all other Muslims out of our screens, while the non-Muslims – from self-appointed voices of Western civilization like Bernard Lewis through Samuel Huntington, to Hindu nationalists and those like V.S. Naipaul who willingly cooperate with their appalling agenda of cleansing India of Muslims, not to mention Christian fundamentalists like Jerry Falwell and Pat Robertson – are those who divide the world into civilizational cocoons and like to transform Islamic civilization into a bogus enemy called the Islamic menace. It is imperative to expose this unholy alliance between Muslim and non-Muslim exclusivists for what it is: a dangerous game of recasting Islam into their own particularistic molds, one that dehumanizes not just Muslims but all humanity.

At this stage, you will no doubt want to point out that our main objective, which was to answer the question "What is Islam?" has yet to be accomplished. We may have dispensed with some misperceptions that plague our understanding of Islam as a civilization, but we have said precious little about what exactly a civilization is and how it furthers our understanding of Islam to identify it as a civilization. This is precisely where we are headed, but there is one more stop on the way before we reach our final destination ...

DEFINING ISLAM

We have been searching for a definition of Islam, and many of you have no doubt been somewhat uneasy about the fact that we have not yet considered any of the common, standard definitions of Islam even though these proliferate in popular venues among both Muslims and non-Muslims worldwide. These standard definitions, you might even assert, are rather straightforward and fairly easy to understand. Why not use them? Why, they may even help us supply the substance for the otherwise hollow concept of religion and steer clear of the problematic concepts of culture and civilization!

Let us take this point seriously and consider these common definitions, encountered in descriptions of Islam provided by scholars and non-scholarly observers and believers alike. The ubiquitous "five pillars" formula is the obvious example, and we will limit our discussion to this definition. According to this formulaic approach, Islam can be defined as honoring the foundational principle of *shahada* (standing witness to the truth of the claims that there is only one God and that Muhammad is His messenger) and performing the four foundational ritualistic acts of *salat* (daily prayer), *zakat* (charity), *sawm* (fasting during Ramadan), and *hajj* (pilgrimage to sites in and around Mecca during a set time period in the Islamic calendar). Does this formula work?

Contrary to the popular view that it works, I would like to argue that it largely fails. In fact, the only part of this formula that stands up to close scrutiny is the *shahada*: it would be fair to say that anyone who does not subscribe to it (of course, after interpreting it in his or her own fashion) cannot be considered a Muslim. But the same cannot be said for the other four pillars, since the ways in which these four performative acts factor into the definition of Islam have always been hotly contested theologically, legally, and culturally. Let me cut to the chase here and announce the main point directly and clearly: the four ritualistic pillars do not form a good and accurate measure of being a Muslim, historically, sociologically, or theologically. To put it in reverse, there have been and continue to be millions of people who wholeheartedly adhere to the *shahada* but who do *not* perform these four particular ritualistic acts in the manner prescribed in legalistic manuals. Not only that: a good percentage of such Muslims would *not* agree that these four rituals are necessary to be considered a Muslim. In other words, these "believers" are not just slackers who know perfectly well that they should perform these rituals but fail to do so for a number of reasons. (Incidentally, it is chastening to remember that there may well be more *negligent* Muslims in the world than *observant* Muslims. The largest Muslim movement on the globe by a wide margin, *Tabligh-i Jama'at* with its headquarters in Pakistan, is out there to win the slackers back to Islam by teaching them the five pillars.) Instead, they are Muslims who consciously and deliberately stay clear of some or all of these rituals and express their allegiance to alternative ritual packages. Examples in history and contemporary societies simply abound. To stick to only the contemporary Middle East, one can name the Alevis in Turkey (fully one-fourth of the population, perhaps even more), the Ahl-i Haqq in Iran, the Alawis in Syria, the Ismailis in both Syria and Iran, the Yezidis and some radical Shi'i communities in Iraq, Syria, and Turkey. To these Muslims who observe the precepts of Islam according to their own, alternative pillars, one should add the millions who choose to emphasize belief over acts and consequently de-value the performance of some or all of the four ritualistic pillars. These are not negligent believers or simply non-believers, but Muslims who choose to prioritize certain beliefs over certain ritualistic acts in accordance with long-standing theological orientations in Islamic history.

Where does all this leave us? Should we do away with the definition of Islam that is based on the five pillars, since it fails to be as comprehensive as it is sometimes made out to be? Or, more to the point perhaps, is this formulaic approach of any value to us in our attempt to identify Islam? In answer to these questions, we can say that there is utility in this formulaic definition, but only if it is embedded in a civilizational framework and used with care and caution. Islam *does* revolve around certain key ideas and practices, but it is imperative to catch the dynamic spirit in which these core ideas and practices are constantly negotiated by Muslims in concrete historical circumstances and not to reify them into a rigid formula that is at once ahistorical and idealistic. Many different formulae made up of the same core stock of ideas and practices that we call Islam have always co-existed in Islamic history, and it would be a mistake to attempt to freeze Islam into only one of these molds by fiat.

ISLAM AS CIVILIZATION

We are now in a position to identify Islam as a sprawling civilizational edifice under continuous construction and renovation in accordance with multiple blueprints (these are the numerous Islamic cultures at local, regional, and national levels encompassing innumerable individual, familial, ethnic, racial, and gender identities) all generated from a nucleus of key ideas and practices ultimately linked to the historical legacy of the Prophet Muhammad. It is vital to realize that nothing about this edifice is ever fixed or frozen in either space or time and that the construction itself is in constant flux. Alternative plans of new construction, renovation, even partial demolition emerge, rise to prominence, are implemented to different degrees, and fade away, while the core ideas and practices themselves, visible only through these very plans, assume different shape and color depending on the blueprint one uses to view them. What ties all this together is the commitment of Muslims to a shared stock of ideals and key ideas along with their willingness to express these in a shared idiom, a common language. In short, Islam is a civilizational project in progress; it is an evolving civilizational tradition constantly churning different cultures in its crucible to generate innumerable, alternative social and cultural blueprints for the conduct of human life on earth.

"But, what," you will ask, "exactly is in that nucleus of ideas and practices lying at the center of this civilizational tradition?" Unfortunately, there is no pithy and definitive answer to this question. There have always been and continues to be a multiplicity of perspectives among Muslims even about what the core ideas and practices of Islam are. Minimally, however, we can assume a set of beliefs (a version each of monotheism, prophecy, genesis, and eschatology) that underwrite a set of values (dignity of human life, individual and collective rights and duties, the necessity of ethical human conduct – in short, a comprehensive moral program), in turn reflected in a set of concrete human acts (ranging from the necessity of greeting others to acts of humility like prayer). It is also necessary to add, though this is an obvious point, that this nucleus is believed to be contained in the fundamental sources of Islam, the Qur'an and the exemplary life story of Muhammad. It is a version of this core that lies at the center of each and every one of the innumerable manifestations of the Islamic civilizational tradition in human history.

We have arrived at our final destination. We now know what Islam is, and, equally important, what it is not. Has the journey been worth it? How useful is it to view Islam as a civilizational tradition, as opposed to seeing it as a religion or a culture? By way of closure, let us enumerate some of the virtues of this perspective on Islam.

- Viewed as a civilizational project, Islam emerges as a dynamic, evolving phenomenon, one that cannot be reified or fixed in any way. This is a healthy reality, one that needs to be acknowledged and celebrated, and not to be concealed from view under the banner of dubious calls issued by some Muslim activists "to establish true Islam" (normally an unmistakable sign of authoritarianism) or "to unify all Muslims" (normally betraying an extremely naive political utopianism).

- When it is understood as an ongoing civilizational construct, it is easier to highlight and to appreciate Islam as a truly global tradition. Not only is Islam not inextricably attached to specific human groups or to specific geographical locales (Judaic, Chinese, and Hindu traditions, for instance, have largely been so attached), but it is genuinely adaptable to most, if not all, human communities anywhere on the globe. To put it in other words, the emphasis on Islam's globality enables us to acknowledge and cherish its transcultural, transethnic, transracial, transnational, in short, its truly *humanistic* dimensions.

- A civilizational tradition, simultaneously in and above specific cultures, is fundamentally interactive with and inclusive of culture. As an ongoing civilizational discourse, Islam is an interactive and inclusive tradition: it interacts with the cultures it comes into contact with and, where it takes root, reshapes and reforms cultures inclusively from within. As a result, there are numerous different Islamic cultures on the globe, and they are all equally Islamic, equal partners in the making and remaking of the Islamic civilizational tradition.

- Finally, identifying Islam as civilization puts it on a par with the other major civilizations on the globe that share all of these same characteristics. While all civilizational traditions are by definition *dynamic*, surprisingly there are only a few traditions other than Islam that are also *global* and *inclusively interactive* in the sense we have discussed: Christianity, Buddhism, and Secular Humanism (which normally goes by the name Western civilization). The history of these civilizations clearly needs to be retold in a comparative and interrelated manner, and the future of all civilizational traditions (some global and interactive, but all dynamic) needs to be considered in the light of this history and in the context of increasing globalization. These are weighty and involved matters that need not, however, detain us from proceeding to our final point: Islam is one of only several truly global and inclusively interactive civilizational projects currently available on our globe, and all signs are that it will remain a major civilizational resource from which all humanity will continue to benefit. Let us all, Muslim and non-Muslim, contribute to the realization of this prospect by acknowledging Islam as a treasure trove of civilizational riches.

4

THE DEBTS AND BURDENS OF CRITICAL ISLAM

Ebrahim Moosa

A great painter does not content himself by affecting us with masterpieces; ultimately, he succeeds in changing the landscape of our minds.[1]

INTRODUCTION

Modern Muslim thinkers are not only challenged to be innovative, but they are also simultaneously required to engage with tradition. And yet, the content of tradition is possibly one of the most complex and contentious issues contemporary Muslims face. In the past two hundred years, tradition has been subject to an extraordinary assault both from within Muslim societies as well as from outside. The advent of colonization brought yet another tradition, namely modernity, into a more forceful encounter with Muslim tradition.

On the one hand there are the pre-modern or traditionalist/"orthodox" accounts of tradition.[2] On the other hand, staunch advocates of Enlightenment rationality within Muslim societies not only challenge the idea of the pre-modern tradition or tradition itself, but propose a version of modernity as a mode of living and thinking for Muslim societies. The poet-philosopher Muhammad Iqbal was extremely perceptive in understanding the challenge with which the modern Muslim intellectual has to grapple. "The task before the modern Muslim is therefore, immense. He has to rethink the whole system of Islam without completely breaking with the past ... The only course open to us is to approach modern knowledge with a respectful but independent attitude and to appreciate the teachings of Islam in the light of that knowledge, even though we may be led to differ from those who have gone before us."[3]

This dilemma to keep past and present in a productive conversation while producing something entirely innovative and fresh has had a fairly schizophrenic outcome, to put it mildly. On the one hand, religious knowledge is regarded as being coterminous with the pre-modern Muslim tradition itself, with the full pedigree of authenticity and legitimacy. That version of tradition continues its passage through the modern period largely by resisting modernity or grudgingly adjusting to modernity, on its own terms. On the other hand, another more contested Muslim tradition that is more euphoric about modernity and dazzled by its rapture develops side-by-side with the pre-modern tradition. This one is relatively smaller, has less popular appeal, and remains the domain of a small elite. In between these two polarities a plethora of traditions emerge that co-exist within Muslim societies and communities globally. Thus, it is preferable to speak of Muslim traditions in the plural. Like all traditions, continuity and discontinuity are essential elements in a dynamic and organic tradition.

The question of innovation and continuity in tradition has never been an unproblematic one in Muslim societies. From Islam's very inception in the seventh century and afterwards, Muslim intellectuals have found themselves embattled by this question. It has its roots in the furious debates about the legitimacy of borrowing knowledge and insights from the Greeks, Indians, Persians, especially Aristotelian philosophy and Neoplatonic mystical knowledge. Intellectuals have found themselves on both sides of the debate. A close examination enables one to see clear battlefield scars on the knowledge handed down the centuries in the multi-dimensional and polyvalent Muslim intellectual tradition. For many scholars, like al-Farabi, al-Baqillani, Ibn Sina, al-Juwayni, al-Ghazali, and many others, there could be no boundaries in matters of knowledge. Knowledge itself could not be tainted by the religion, ethnicity, or beliefs of the producer of knowledge, since we have the tools of independent judgment to evaluate it on its merits. Their attitude was shaped by the belief that "foreign knowledge" was the "lost camel of the believer." Wherever believers find such knowledge, they were the most deserving of it. But these scholars have also had their opponents. Many luminaries in the early intellectual tradition balked at even studying the knowledge of "others," let alone internalizing it and employing such knowledge to illuminate the teachings of Islam. For men like al-Shafi'i, Ibn Hanbal, Ibn Salah, and even more so Ibn Taymiyya, knowledge that had its provenance in other cultures and civilizations had a corrupting influence on the legacy of the pious ancestors of early Islam. For them the teachings of the Qur'an and those of the Arabian Prophet were sufficient and could not be contaminated with the ways of thinking of other cultures.

This is but a very brief and simplified snapshot of the kinds of debates that preceded us. Knowledge produced in those medieval contexts was not uncontested. In fact, what is often hailed as the high point of Islamic civilization and knowledge was also a period of contestation, conflict, and debate not very different from ours. Innovation in knowledge did not come without a price.

Knowledge, like the birth of a new style in the art of miniature portraits, "is the result of years of disagreements, jealousies, rivalries and studies in colors and painting," says one of the characters of the Turkish novelist Orhan Pamuk.[4] While the most gifted of painters, writers, and scholars will beget the innovations, to the rest will fall the "singular duty of perfecting and refining this style through perpetual imitation." Both the innovators as well as the imitators deserve our respect, even though we acknowledge that we may no longer be able to agree with their views today.

How do we both acknowledge the debt we owe to our intellectual predecessors and at the same time also recognize that they are products of their time just as we too are products of our time? To simultaneously acknowledge and respectfully disagree requires humility. The British historian E.P. Thompson offers sobering advice. When reviewing the past, we moderns have a tendency to gravitate towards elitism and vanguardism, especially when our practical experiences do not live up to theoretical hopes we thought the past could offer.[5] Often we may incline to judge the people and the times of the past rather harshly when they do not live up to our expectations. This is what Thompson in his justly famous and endlessly quoted phrase calls that "enormous condescension of posterity" to dismiss all movements and ideas that have not made the grade by today's standards of ideology of achievement.[6] For people who wish to build and innovate in tradition such condescension will be unhelpful, if not serve as an obstacle to any kind of progress.

Another useful approach is offered by the prodigious belletrist (*adib*) and rational thinker 'Amr b. Bahr al-Jahiz (d. 255/868). Jahiz shows complete awareness of the double debt of the Muslim community, both to the hereditary intellectual tradition, as well as to the tradition in the making: the ongoing and unfolding knowledge-making (discursive) tradition. Yet, he notes that one's attitude towards the earliest fathers of the tradition should not be marked by a stultifying reverence, but that it should rather be similar to one's stance towards posterity. "For surely we inherited more edificatory admonition ('*ibra*)," observes Jahiz, "than our predecessors ever found; just as posterity will acquire an even larger amount of edificatory admonitions than we did."[7] Jahiz implies that by means of an unending and continuous process of accumulation, each later generation will have an advantage over its predecessors because they will have a larger body of knowledge at their disposal from which they can derive meaningful insights. His social Darwinism aside, Jahiz does open the door for a continuous revision and engagement with the legacy of the past.

ISLAM/ISLAMS OR SPECIES OF MUSLIMNESS?

Like our predecessors, we too are faced with uncomfortable questions. Whenever we, like those in the past, go about our ordinary practices or when we raise difficult questions, we consciously or unconsciously make assumptions and tenaciously hold on to certain imaginations, about ourselves as well as the worlds that we inhabit. In doing so, each one of us also articulates a version of "Islam." This proposition has led some scholars to say that there is not one, single, monolithic "Islam," but a multiplicity of "Islams." While I may not disagree with the underlying idea in this formulation, it also has the tendency to miscommunicate with lay audiences or tends to deny the idea of Islam as an event in history. What many "Islams" suggest is that there are many discursive traditions through which Muslims imagine themselves. It is through different ways of conceiving knowledge in all its complexity of time and space that people adhering to this faith identify themselves as "Muslim." In other words we can say that there are multiple and diverse forms and articulations of "Muslimness" or "being Muslim." In other words what we really have are multiple representations of being Muslim, embodied by concrete individuals and communities.

To argue whether there is one Islam or many leads to a somewhat fruitless and hypothetical debate as to whether an ideal formulation of Islam existed in the first place. And, if it did exist, where, when, and how did it do so and why did it cease to exist? These questions certainly have the character of being conversation stoppers. For, whatever Islam *is*, the closest we can come to what "it" is or is not, is through its embodiment in concrete forms, practices, beliefs, traditions, values, prejudices, tastes, forms of power that emanate from human beings who profess and claim to be Muslim or profess belonging to a community that calls itself Muslim. Needless to say, in each representation of themselves as being Muslim, they also simultaneously contest the meaning of their Muslimness in relation to others. Their claims inevitably make them assert doctrines and practices that signify some of kind of sectarian, political, and ideological affiliation. In the process, they either de-legitimize, affirm, or are indifferent to each other. Nevertheless, whatever they do, they do so in the matrix of the complexity of their Muslimness. In doing so they may put on display appealing and desirable manifestations of their Muslimness or they could represent ugly and disgusting manifestations of their Muslimness.

Imagine how jarring it might be to the sensibilities of ordinary Muslims, if one were to talk about an ugly Islam and a pretty Islam? For the immediate reflex would be to attribute that goodness or detestability to some founding sacred text, a revered person, or a symbol that believers might tend to regard as sacred and sacrosanct. While the idea of many Islams may make philosophical sense, ordinary discourse is not always very receptive to such presentations. Perhaps ugly and pretty versions of Muslimness may be less offensive or jarring.

But we should also readily admit that all we really know about what we call "Islam" is what humans have ever told us. God never directly spoke to humans, except to Prophets such as Moses and Muhammad through the medium of revelation (*wahi*). Islam is what a mortal, in his authority as Prophet, told us what it is; this is God's revelation, this is the moral conduct that God approves of from you His followers, and this is how we view ourselves *vis-à-vis* other faiths and communities. In the post-revelatory period, Islam is what the Companions, the imams, the scholars, jurists, and authorities said, practiced, and imagined it is. In short, all we know about what Islam is, is and was always the claims made by fellow Muslims, whether they be the Prophet, the Companions, the learned scholars past and present, or the most humble individual Muslims. Each one expresses what Islam is from their experience as a Muslim. In the language of the modern humanities, these claims *about* authoritative and authentic Islam are called "constructions."

Of course there are other Muslims who would forcefully resist such categorization and insist that what they hold out to be Islam is anything but a construction. They would challenge my statement and say that they do not talk *about* Islam; they *talk* Islam or they just purely *do* Islam or they *just Islam*. But I can counter by saying that unless they claim to being God themselves – which surely takes the debate out of the realm of sanity – and therefore claim the right to speak with unmediated authority, then what they claim can be nothing but representations of Islam or plainly "talk" *about* Islam.

Plainly "talking" Islam is a hallmark of Muslims who not only imagine but also practice Islam with a heavy dose of authoritarianism. In other words, religion and Islam are in the final instance about authority: an unquestionable and given (a priori) set of obligations. The discourse of religion in this construction is about such an overwhelming authority that it silences one into submission. Even in this narrowly conceived authoritarian mode, one cannot avoid the reality that it is people in flesh and blood, namely Muslims who embody beliefs and practices, that make the ultimate moral judgments. They have to listen, understand, and then follow that "given" divine authority and live accordingly. It is human beings who are required to mediate this authority. In this entire process, there are as many subjective moments that undermine notions of objectivity: there is proverbially many a slip between the cup and the lip.

No one has seen "Islam" in its transparent glory to really judge it. But what we have seen are Muslims: good Muslims and bad Muslims; ugly Muslims and pretty Muslims; just Muslims and unjust Muslims; Muslims who are oppressors, racists, bigots, misogynists, and criminals as well as Muslims who are compassionate, liberators, seekers of an end to racism and sexism, and those who aspire for global justice and equity. Therefore it is not uncommon to encounter Muslims saying, "You have to separate between Islam and Muslims"; "Islam is great, with every epithet of perfection." The general rhetoric would be: "Islam is a religion of peace, it is Muslims who are bad." But can one ever imagine Islam without Muslims? While the rhetoric that pleads for a separation between "Islam" and "Muslims" implicitly endorses my claim that it is actually Muslims who embody Islam, it is often employed in order to defend "Islam," as if the tradition is in need of protection in the first place. More harmful than being part of an apologetic move, such rhetoric absolves Muslims from responsibility for what they do in the "name" of Islam. For every time Muslims perform an act and claim that it has religious sanction and cite their scriptural authority, one cannot deny them their claim when they insist that what they did was a religiously mandated act. If they do harm in the name of Islam, then other Muslims are required to take the religious justification of violence seriously, and contest their discursive use of Islam.

The truth is that our only understanding of Islam is what Muslims know it is. Even if one accepts the Kantian notion of the thing in and of itself, the artifact is known to us only through the knowledge we have of it as human beings. Thus, whatever Islam is in its ideal formation, the version we know of it is only the imperfect and flawed one we have as imperfect beings. The heavenly attempt to make sure we get the closest version to perfection of Islam was undertaken via prophecy. From then onwards, we require neither a divine incarnation to make sure we remain perfect nor an infallible authority to tie our feet to the chains of authority.

Often authoritarian interpretations of Islam argue that entrenched practices and beliefs are not mere constructions, but that they are indeed practices that have consistently been replicated in Muslim societies over centuries. If one makes a claim that Muslims have prayed five times a day, paid their taxes according to a set formula designed by the first believers, outlawed certain trade practices, and followed an ethics of war according to uniform and non-negotiable norms, then the burden is to prove the validity of such claims.

In order to find such proof, one is at the mercy of history and its contingencies and perils. Surely it will not be difficult to prove that Muslims believed in the obligation of five daily prayers. But it will be inordinately difficult to prove that they prayed in an identical manner. For among different Muslim schools of law and doctors of interpretation there are major differences in the practice of rituals themselves. If for the Shafiʿi school reciting the chapter called the "Opening" is an obligation in every ritual prayer including congregational prayers, then in the Hanafi law school for a follower to recite any liturgical passage in a congregational prayer comes close to invalidating his or her prayers. While all schools of law acknowledge five daily prayers, the Sunni schools insist that each prayer must be performed in its appointed time slot. The Shiʿi law schools permit the noon prayer to be joined with the afternoon prayer and for the evening prayer to be joined with the night prayers in two time slots on a regular basis. Some Sunni law schools offer such concessions only when a person is traveling. Certain trade practices may be perfectly legitimate in the eyes of one law school, while in the view of another they may be totally invalid or forbidden.

So any claim that an unbroken chain of practice serves as the incontrovertible evidence for an authentic and unchangeable tradition, as some Muslims do claim, can only be a figment of the imagination. For any such assertion can rest only on ideological fictions or specious generalizations, not on the grounds of history or even idealism, for that matter. It is only when one begins to compare practices of Muslims over time, and then dares to confront the details of such practices, that one encounters the complexity of traditions. Once one becomes aware of the historical processes by which human communities take shape, then the emphasis on the authority of a text or the authority of some infallible person or coercive capacity of consensus evaporates like mist in the rays of the sun.

Surely, what threatens the inscrutable authority of authoritarians is history. Any serious and close study of the Muslim tradition will unmistakably vaporize claims of uniformity and absolute obedience to authorities. To their utter disbelief, protagonists of authoritarianism will discover that Muslim societies in the past, as in the present, have always been diverse, differentiated, dynamic, but also in a state of contestation as all organic human social formations naturally are. The false utopias of ideal and perfect Muslim societies in the past, widely touted by ideologues of authoritarianism, will not survive the scrutiny of history.

DEBT TO MUSLIM MODERNISTS

Contemporary Muslim thought is profoundly indebted to the labors of Muslim modernist thinkers of the nineteenth and twentieth centuries. Given that modernity, according to the German philosopher Jürgen Habermas, is itself a work in progress, it is not surprising that we have come to recognize many of the errors of Enlightenment thinking and modernity as legions of scholars engaged in post-modernism have pointed out.[8] In some ways, post-modernism can be seen as a corrective as well as a continuation of modernity. In the light of what we have learnt about the pitfalls of modernism, we are compelled to ask whether the tradition of scholarship known as modernism is Islam's redeemer, nemesis, or perhaps a bit of both?

For what we do know is that some of the key figures of Muslim modernism, like Sir Sayyid Ahmad Khan, Shibli Nu'mani, and Muhammad Iqbal all from India, Muhammad Abduh, Rashid Rida, 'Ali 'Abd al-Raziq in Egypt, as well as important figures in Turkey, Iran and elsewhere in the Muslim world, were tremendously impressed by both the ideals and realities of modernity. They truly believed that Muslim thought as they imagined it from its medieval incarnation had an almost natural tryst with modernity. Modernity and "Islam" were not mortal enemies, but rather, as many of them suggested, Islam itself anticipated modernity.

In their definition, modernity was synonymous with innovation and openness to new knowledge. Thus to be modern, they argued, was historically an integral process of Muslim thinking. They pointed out that Muslim thought was sufficiently flexible to foster innovation and adapt to change commensurate with time and place. This was both a legitimate and natural process whereby the Muslim tradition could survive the rigors of time. Innovative thinking *(ijtihad)* and renewal *(tajdid)*, they argued, was emblematic of Muslim discourse. Critical to this understanding was also the place of reason and rationality as a way of objectively ascertaining the truth.

THE BURDEN OF MODERNITY

The way Muslim modernists understood modernity presents a very different picture from the way we perceive it today. Some of the ways in which we perceive reason, self, and truth might be very different from how early modernists of all stripes construed these very concepts. Reason in the past was seen as universal, held by all to articulate a set of rational true beliefs, to distinguish reason from tradition and emotion. Now we have to admit that reason is not a self-evident faculty but a socially constructed one. It exists within practices and discourses; reason is embodied. The idea of the self was once understood to be exclusively unique and transcendent. This is no longer the case. Now we acknowledge that the self is a product of language and discourses. The correspondence between language and reality exerted a strong influence in the modern period and this contributed to our understanding of truth. Today, we have a healthy skepticism about what passes for the truth. Truth is the result of agreement. We do not say there is no truth, or that the truth is arbitrary. What we do say is that the truth is not static, an end-state at which we arrive at once and for all.

What Muslim modernists most profited from in their encounter with modernity was the idea of rationality. Armed with rationality they felt that they could effectively achieve several things. Firstly, it served as a defensive weapon in apologetics. In competition with the West, Muslim modernists could argue that the best ideal in the West, namely reason and rationality, was already an artifact of Muslim civilization. Most modernists viewed the Mu'tazila school and other thinkers such as Ibn Rushd and Mulla Sadra as epitomizing the rationalist tradition. Secondly, rationality was employed to combat superstition as part of the onslaught against popular religious practices. The desired goal was to transform Muslims into autonomous rational agents. Thirdly, modernists believed it was highly desirable for such rational individuals to lessen their dependence on authority, be it the charismatic authority of the Sufi mystics and saints or the religious authority of the scholars of religion ('ulama). Muslim modernists effectively despaired of rehabilitating both groups. Fourthly, educated Muslims with a rational bent, they believed, could derive their inspiration and guidance directly from the Qur'an. Furthermore, they held that with the rise of print and the circulation of knowledge, lay people could educate themselves in matters of religion without any retrogressive mediating authority.

Nineteenth- and early twentieth-century modernist Muslim reformists viewed modernity as an ally. Twenty-first-century critical Muslim scholars are much more apprehensive of its allure and offer a critique of modernity. Of course it is partly unfair to level critique at early Muslim modernists in their assessment of modernity, since our critical appreciation of modernity has the hindsight of at least a century of critical reflection. This should moderate our criticism of this group of courageous thinkers of the nineteenth century; our criticism should be more a reflection of the different kinds of modernity that each generation of Muslim scholars has inherited.

Nevertheless, it is also true that nineteenth- and early twentieth-century Muslim modernists utilized the discourse of modernity differently. *Vis-à-vis* those outside the Muslim community, they used the modern discourse to demonstrate that Islam was very much in tune with progress and social evolution. A few of them, for instance, justified women's rights and justified the study of science and technology on modern grounds when traditionalists resisted these ideas. However, when it came to applying the intellectual harvest of modernity, namely the phenomenal developments in knowledge, to the study of religion itself, this elicited a different response. At that point modern knowledge was viewed with skepticism accompanied by a fear that it would undermine the canonical knowledge of Islam.

With some exceptions, the critical light of modern knowledge developed in the humanities did not illuminate the Muslim modernists' theories, as applied to the interpretation of scriptures, history and society, the understanding of law, and theology. What they did not undertake or in some instances refused to undertake was to subject the entire corpus of historical Islamic learning to the critical gaze of the knowledge-making process (episteme) of modernity. They of course correctly suspected that a complete embrace of modernity as a philosophical tradition would result in an Islam that they would not be able to recognize. They still felt that the pre-modern Muslim epistemology as rooted in dialectical theology (*'ilm al-kalam*) and legal theory (*usul al-fiqh*) was sufficiently tenacious, if not compatible with the best in modern epistemology. With a few exceptions, this expedient attitude towards modernity is an indication of both the good faith as well as the naiveté of some of the modernist Muslim reformers.

Some Muslim reformers did adopt new ways of writing history in order to "appreciate the teachings of Islam in the light of that knowledge," as Iqbal proposed. This becomes evident in the work of Sir Sayyid Ahmad Khan, Iqbal, Shibli Nu'mani, and others. However, it was not a thorough-going approach. Iqbal's caveat of an "independent attitude" for some signaled a caution and resistance to the allure of modern knowledge, a sentiment that was widely shared by most other reformers. How Iqbal expected far-reaching and different understandings of early Islamic teachings to take place without taking the risk of embracing the modern episteme, he never elaborated. In fact, most reformers viewed modernity and its philosophical legacy as an instrument; as an aid to advance and explain the pre-modern tradition and knowledge of religion, but never to internalize modernity entirely.

In fact, at the slightest hint of the application of modern knowledge to the traditional Islamic sciences, traditional *'ulama* called for the excommunication of the above-mentioned Muslim modernists. The result was a discursive battlefield filled with corpses of those charged with heresy. Notable among those who partially adopted a modern approach in the investigation of knowledge about religion were modernists such as Ahmad Muhammad Khalafallah, 'Ali 'Abd al-Raziq, and Nasser Hamid Abu Zayd in the Arab world, and Sir Sayyid Ahmad Khan, Muhammad Iqbal, and later Fazlur Rahman in the Indian Subcontinent. All were effectively harassed, their lives turned into a misery, ultimately resulting in their marginalization or exile.

Iqbal, it seems, understood the magnitude of a serious reform project and was understandably intimidated by its weight as well as its far-reaching consequences. Given his insight, it is not surprising that he vacillates when it comes to the application of his modernist vision. The twentieth-century Indian thinker Asaf Fyzee was perhaps among the few courageous voices to advocate far-fetching reforms practically. He spoke movingly and passionately. "After serving the cause of humanity for some seven centuries," observed Fyzee, "Islam came under a shadow. Its spirit was throttled by fanaticism, its theology gagged by bigotry, its vitality was sapped by totalitarianism."[9] He was among a very few to advocate that a modern approach to Islam requires a separation between religion (belief) and law.[10] He clearly understood the dilemma of *Shari'ah*. It is a composite concept that involves both religion and law. For this reason Fyzee argued that in every age the Qur'an has to be "interpreted afresh and understood anew."[11] Fyzee endorses a post-Enlightenment notion of religion in which belief is a matter of individual conscience and law is a public matter that is enforced by the state. He of course did not provide any detailed argument as to how one justifies such a separation, even though the idea makes eminent sense.

More convincing was the Egyptian thinker 'Ali 'Abd al-Raziq, who at the beginning of the twentieth century advocated the separation of religion and politics. Through painstaking intellectual work, he argued that there is no obligation on Muslims to follow a specific historical model of statecraft that resembles the first community at Medina. With this he opened a door for experimenting with democracy and government that was accountable, all systems that were lacking in Muslim societies. Unfortunately, the ideas of Iqbal, Fyzee, and 'Abd al-Raziq did not get a favorable hearing from the religious scholars. I think these ideas and visions need to be re-visited and require critical re-engagement by critical Muslim scholars today.

CRITICAL ISLAM: BEYOND APOLOGIA

Of all the intellectual issues facing Muslim communities, the one area that is most troubling is the area of Islamic law *(Shari'ah)*. This is especially problematic when the Qur'an endorses elements of the law. In a tradition where the revelation is viewed as the eternal word of God, the law framed in such terms does present a conundrum. The verses dealing with the law do not exceed six hundred (out of over six thousand verses in the whole of the Qur'an) yet somehow receive disproportionate scholarly attention. The bulk of the verses that more importantly address the aesthetics of the Muslim imagination get neglected. Ordinary Muslims of course feel obligated to act upon the mandate of these legal verses. However, untrained in the various exegetical and interpretive traditions, lay people are not aware that a complex methodology is applicable to materials dealing with law, even if these are stated in the revelation.

One of the features of the dominant Muslim discourse in almost all its variants, including modernist discourse, is reification. This is where Muslim traditions, by which I mean living subjective experiences and practices, are reduced and transformed into various concepts, ideas, and things. Thus the way the Qur'an offers women a share in inheritance or assuages their position in seventh-century Arabia is reduced to meaning that the Qur'an advocates justice as personified in that historical model. Flowing from that is an inference that the form of justice as embodied in the Qur'anic statement is applicable to all times and places. For instance, the limited measures introduced to manumit slaves as penances for certain moral violations as stated in the Qur'an, or the measures adopted by the Caliph 'Umar to prohibit the sale of slave women who have children by their masters are all held up as instances that are indicative of notions of freedom.

These can be deemed as essentialist categories, reducing complex problems and practices to their bare essentials in order to score an ideological point. Terms such as the "spirit" of Islam are employed in order to argue that the spirit of Islam is justice, egalitarianism, equality, or humanism – either as single signifiers or combinations of these qualities. These qualities are held metonymically to represent the entirety of Islam. Often history is invoked to argue that these ideals were evident at the very inception of Islam as a tradition in the seventh century. This is of course done at the expense of exploring exactly *how* these ideas became manifest in the practices and behavior of early Muslims.

It is not very clear whether 'Umar was actuated by concerns of freedom in limiting the sale of female slaves who had offspring or whether he wanted to prevent the proliferation of incest. For there were real concerns that a young female slave separated from her offspring when sold off could years later unknowingly be sold as a concubine to her wealthy offspring. It is also uncertain whether the inheritance system intended to further justice. However, there are clear indications that the new system of intergenerational succession attempted to further a specific form and system of kinship based on patriarchy.[12]

Nowadays, not only Muslim modernists make these arguments, but even orthodox traditionalists and revivalist groups are becoming expert in such apologetics. The real problem with these kinds of arguments is a more acute one. For one thing, they are apologetic and try to justify the past by today's standards. In the process, they inevitably distort history. Since modern Muslim sensibilities are offended by the rules regulating women, such as corporal punishment or the minimum marriageable age for women in Muslim antiquity, they try either to wish them away or to argue them away. There is of course the misplaced belief that the past is embarrassing. For, surely, closer scrutiny shows that in all patriarchal cultures – Christian, Jewish, and Hindu – during antiquity, women were married off at a very early age, in some cases even before they showed their first signs of menstruation.

If we have changed these practices in our world, then we have done so for our own reasons: our sense of justice, equality, and reasons consistent with our political-economy. For a whole set of reasons, we no longer consider marriage to what our modern culture deems minors, corporal punishment, and the death penalty to be acceptable practices. But surely in changing our practices we are not condemning millions of people before us and judging them as reprobate for being different from us? So why should we debate the past as if it is the present? The predisposition among many Muslim apologists is not to understand history, but rather to try to fix or correct it, with the enormous condescension of posterity.

But this desire to find justification in the past, in a text or the practice of a founder, suggests that Muslims can act confidently in the present only if the matter in question was already prefigured in the past. Such a perpetually retrospective approach to religious understanding is the sign of a profound lack of dynamism among the contemporary adherents of the tradition. At best, this is reverse science fiction; at worst, it is a sad commentary on the state of Muslim self-confidence in the modern period. Does this mean that Muslims can engage in discourses of justice, egalitarianism, freedom, and equality only if there is some semblance that the scripture or the Prophet or some of the learned savants (imams) of the past endorsed, hinted, or fantasized about the possibility of such discourses?

What this mentality suggests is that Muslims discredit the legitimacy of their experience in the present and refuse to allow this experience to be the grounds for innovation, change, and adaptation. In order to persuade people in public discourse today, the most effective psychological trick to play on unsuspecting Muslim audiences is to say that some past authority – Tabari, Abu Hanifa, or al-Shafi'i – held such an enlightening position on matter X, so why do you lesser mortals not adopt it? The greater the vintage of the authority, the more persuasive the argument will sound to folks, even if the rationale of the argument and its substance make no sense at all. These may sound like anecdotal stereotypes, but this happens repeatedly in Muslim communities, even among secularly educated lay Muslims. Now what happens if we are faced with problems and issues that al-Shafi'i et al. never even dreamt of, let alone confronted in their lives? Are we going to fictionalize and fabricate statements and attribute these to them in good faith? This is exactly how a great deal of prophetic reports *(ahadith,* sing. *hadith)* were invented and attributed to the

Prophet and the early authorities of Islam in order to give new ideas and changing practices some credibility, legitimacy, and authority.

If this kind of mentality has a longer history, then it certainly has reached pathological proportions among modern Muslims. Among the many reasons for this is the outlook that only the past was good in Muslim history; indeed it was perfect, if not a utopia. This suggests that Muslims lack confidence in their abilities and is symptomatic of their despair. It implies that the present is always despised and viewed as fallen. Ironically, despite the amazing and brilliant success Muslims had in history, for many modern Muslims the present, their time and opportunity in history, is viewed to be as dreadful as the original sin. Perhaps the words of Charles Baudelaire, who said that "you have no right to despise the present," have more relevance than ever before.

Some contemporary readings of the Qur'an are predisposed to text fundamentalism, a feature evident among modernists, fundamentalists, and neo-traditionalists. There are several problems attached to text fundamentalism. Sure, some of these interpretations do provide rhetorical allegiance to history by arguing that the verses of the Qur'an are accompanied by historical contextualization that locates the revelation within a material context, called "occasions of revelation" *(asbab al-nuzul)*. The doctrine of textual abrogation *(naskh)* is also employed to show that a very rudimentary form of historiography is at work in the commentary tradition of the Qur'an. While this does provide some help, it still falls far short of making the complexity of the text understandable and intelligible to modern audiences, especially if the past is presented in apologetic and defensive terms. Such an approach prevents an honest, critical, and open understanding of how the revelation functioned in societies radically different than ours.

On other occasions there has been a predilection to provide a purposive interpretation of the text. This follows the method developed in jurisprudence called the purposive approach *(maqasid)* to legal passages in the Qur'an. Each legal verse or cluster of verses, scholars argue, attempts to fulfill a larger social, ethical, or religious function that is the real intention of the verse. It is these intentions that one must take seriously and not the literal intent of the verse. While this approach has no doubt brought some relief to really knotty problems, it remains inadequate. For without adequate historical support this approach can lead to the bowdlerization of the text. For then it means the more equipped the interpreter, the more effectively he or she could read meanings and intentions *into* the text or read meanings *off* the text as derivations from the text. In this case, the text remains sovereign, ignoring the reader or marginalizing the "community of the text" and their experiences as credible participants in the textual process. After all, what is a sacred scripture worth if it does not have a community of participants, listeners, and readers? All the sacred scriptures already exist in the mythical Preserved Tablet *(al-lawh al-mahfuz)* anyway, so why send it to humans when the angels already adore it more perfectly than us humans? From the misplaced pre-occupation with the sovereignty of the text *sans* community of the text, it is but a small step to the deification of the text that unfortunately already occurs. What many Muslims fail to discern is that the Qur'an is not God; the word of God can never be God, and to imagine it as such certainly raises very serious problems of a theological nature.

On further reflection, it will become apparent that the Qur'an itself prefigures a community of listeners and participants: without this audience it ceases to be the Qur'an. Let me explain. Literally the word *qur'an* means a "recitation." As a revelation it is recited by the human voice and heard by the human ear. In the final instance the message must both be heard and understood by the "heart," as the Qur'an literally puts it. In all this a fundamental presumption persists: the Qur'an as revelation requires an audience of listeners and speakers. In other words, a community is integral to it being a revelation. If one does not take that audience and community seriously, implicitly one has not taken revelation seriously. This audience is not a passive audience, but an interactive audience that engages with a performative revelation.

Something has happened in the reading of the Qur'an in modern Islam that goes in the opposite direction. Many Muslim audiences have little sensibility for the complex ways a revealed and performance text like the Qur'an is interpreted. The fact is that how the interpretation of the Qur'an is to be approached is not as easily available as free copies of the holy book. Instead many people read it like one reads a medical textbook or an engineering manual. So the Qur'an has been turned into a sovereign, passive, non-interactive text. In other words, it ceases to be a revelation that melts the heart of the reciter and/or listener. It no longer makes reverent readers' skin shiver in awe of the Divine. Instead of having readers being in awe of God, fierce warrior-readers of the Qur'an these days scare the wits out of believers and non-believers alike. Gone is how the Qur'an itself describes its effect on listeners and reciters. "God bestows from on high, the best of all teachings in the shape of a divine writ, fully consistent with itself, repeating each statement in manifold forms – [a Divine writ] that makes the flesh [literally, skin] of all those who stand in awe of their Sustainer shiver; but in the end their flesh and their hearts soften at the remembrance of the grace of God" (Q. 39:23).

Several attempts to introduce an element of complexity in the understanding of the Qur'an are beginning to lift our veil of ignorance. The work of Mohammed Arkoun, Nasr Hamid Abu Zayd, Khaled Abou El Fadl, Farid Esack, and Abdulkader Tayob among others is doing just that. A commonsensical reading of this complex text would be far too inadequate. The Qur'an as a text is alive within contemporary Muslim communities and is subject to multiple uses. In the past too it had contexts where it negotiated multiple agendas of the society in which it was first revealed; in short it has a political history. By "political history," I mean it also occurs against the backdrop of power and history. In its multiple iterations, the Qur'an continues to develop new and multiple histories as it is embodied in communities. In other words, we need to know not only the detailed social contexts in which God's revelation is played out in history but also how it plays out in history. For this reason it is so crucial to study the different communities of the Qur'an. Without that voice of the communities engaged with their scripture, we can hardly make sense of revelation and the various communities of revelation.

There has been a pattern in contemporary Muslim scholarship to let the sovereign voice of the Qur'an speak without the community of the Qur'an speaking and interacting with the Qur'an in deep and life-transforming conversations. For instance, modern Muslim interpreters, especially Muslim feminists, make too much of a few verses of the Qur'an that suggest reciprocal rights and duties between unequal spouses and then hasten to suggest that the Qur'an advocates egalitarianism as norm. In order to accept this one must pretend to be blind to the welter of evidence that suggests an outright patriarchy as the "textual" norm. Generations of Muslim scholars have correctly stated that the Qur'an advocates patriarchal norms, since that was the historical condition in which the Qur'an was revealed. By privileging a few verses and then suggesting that these isolated and singular verses should control the meaning and interpretation of numerous other verses, using the adage that "part of the Qur'an explains other parts" (*al-qur'an yufassiru ba'duhu ba'dan*) is nothing short of hermeneutical acrobatics or a hermeneutics of wishful thinking. It may be preferable to hear the Qur'an in its patriarchal voice but to understand it with the sensibility of an actor/reader/listener/reciter immersed in the process of revelation. It is that listener/reciter who discovers through her or his history, experience, and transformed inner sensibility that gender justice, equality, and fairness is a norm for our time, and not patriarchy.

Having once done the former kind of interpretation myself, I increasingly find it unfulfilling and unsatisfactory. I am more inclined to give history and the performative role of the revelation a greater place in an interpretive schema. A closer look at text fundamentalism suggests that it sustains several fictions.

Such interpretations attempt to exclusively seek authority in some founding text. However, in doing so they fail to engage the revelatory text in an interactive manner. It is precisely such interactivity that transforms the human being who is ultimately the subject of revelation, and who has to embody the qualities that combat patriarchy and endorse justice and equality. Glossing the text with anti-patriarchal virtues is not the warrant of liberation or egalitarianism. Text fundamentalism in part perpetuates the fiction that the text actually provides the norms, and we merely "discover" the norms. The truth is that we "make" the norms in conversation with the revelatory text. If one reads medieval Muslim legal texts, one will note how the discursive formation orchestrated by the jurists constructs the norms. For this reason, many people are surprised how early Muslim jurists could give verdicts seemingly contrary to the explicit sense of the revealed text.

The answer is both simple and revealing: the earlier scholars gave greater credence to their specific social context and often gave the context decisive authority in the interpretation of the text by employing a very sophisticated hermeneutic. Thus, we find that some classical jurists argue that causing injury to the wife by means of beating is a ground for divorce, despite the Qur'an saying that a disobedient spouse can be chastized. Abu Hanifa has no objections to non-Muslims entering the holy city of Mecca, despite an explicit text of the Qur'an that deems the polytheists to be unclean and prevents them from entering the sacred mosque. For him the Qur'anic passage had a once-only application at the inception of Islam, when the holy sanctuary had to be dedicated to the faith of Islam, and has no subsequent mandate.

What is required is to explore the multiple interpretive methods that were employed by scholars in the past to discover the creativity they invested. In addition, we need to explore and develop new ways of interpretation of especially the revealed text in order to allow its full breadth and vision to speak to us in a transformative way.

CONCLUSION

This moment in history, more than any other, places an extraordinary burden on Muslim intellectuals. In short, there is an almost impossible expectation on us to provide solutions in places where none appears on the horizon, offer hope in times of utter despair, and address issues that are overwhelming in their magnitude and proportions. And yet, we dare not retreat. If anything we need to offer hope. Hope, as the novelist Anne Lamott says, is a revolutionary patience. The painstaking and soul-searching intellectual quest must be embraced boldly, creatively, and patiently. The uncomfortable questions have to be asked. If we do not, then the responsibility of learning and faith has gone unanswered.

ENDNOTES

1. Orhan Pamuk, *My Name Is Red* (New York: Alfred A. Knopf, 2001), 161.
2. My use of the term "Orthodoxy" must be distinguished from other uses of this term. I use it the way Talal Asad employs it, in which orthodoxy is not merely a set of opinions but a relationship of power, where this power is used to exclude, correct, and undermine. In short, orthodoxy is a discursive practice. See Talal Asad, "The Idea of an Anthropology of Islam," (Washington: Center for Contemporary Arab Studies, Georgetown University Occasional Papers Series, 1986), pp. 15–16.
3. Muhammad Iqbal, *The Reconstruction of Religious Thought in Islam* (London: Oxford University Press, 1934; reprinted, Lahore: Shaikh Muhammad Ashraf, 1960), 97.
4. Orhan Pamuk, *My Name Is Red*, 168.
5. Sumit Sarkar, "The Relevance of E.P. Thompson," in *Writing Social History* (Delhi: Oxford University Press, 1998), 53.
6. E.P. Thompson, *The Making of the English Working Class* (New York: Pantheon, 1963), 12.
7. Abu 'Uthman 'Amr b. Bahr b. Mahbub al-Basri, "Kitab al-Futya," *in Rasa'il al-Jahiz*, ed. Muhammad Basil 'Uyun al-Sud, 2 vols (Beirut: Dar al-Kutub al-'Ilmiyya, 2000), 1:223.

8. Maurizio Passerin d'Entrèves and Seyla Benhabib (eds), *Habermas and the Unfinished Project of Modernity: Critical Essays on the Philosophical Discourse of Modernity* (Cambridge, MA: MIT Press, 1997).

9. Asaf A.A. Fyzee, *A Modern Approach to Islam* (Bombay: Oxford University Press, 1981), 112.

10. Ibid., 84–113.

11. Ibid., 110.

12. Martha Mundi, "The Family, Inheritance, and Islam: A Re-examination of the Sociology of Fara'id Law," in *Islamic Law: Social and Historical Contexts*, ed. Aziz al-Azmeh (New York: Routledge, 1988), 1–123.

5

ON BEING A SCHOLAR OF ISLAM: RISKS AND RESPONSIBILITIES

Tazim R. Kassam

This essay reflects on the conditions and contexts in which scholars of Islamic studies have found themselves, especially in the wake of the tragedy enacted in New York, Washington, and Pennsylvania on September 11, 2001. It raises the question of what it means to be a specialist in Islamic Studies teaching in the United States at the turn of the twenty-first century.[1] These reflections emerge primarily out of experiences informally shared by scholars through email exchanges, personal conversations, list-serves and websites.[2] Scholars of Islam currently face a reality consisting of both opportunities and risks. Working and living in the United States has many benefits, including the freedom to think, to speak, and to investigate; an environment of civil discourse that encourages the peaceful co-existence of a plurality of beliefs, ethnic backgrounds, and lifestyles; opportunities for self-expression, creativity, and industry in all walks of life; and the orderly exchange of material, cultural, and intellectual goods. Consisting of a multiracial, multicultural society, ideally speaking, it is a place that offers citizens and immigrants a space of freedom within which to identify and to address common needs and concerns and to help build civil society through civic engagements with other communities, neighbors, and co-workers while also preserving and enriching one's own heritage. For the younger generation, it offers a place of hope to start afresh and put to rest older divisions and hatreds of their ancestral homes.

Notwithstanding these opportunities, being a Muslim in the Western world and, particularly in the United States, is cause for increasing concern following the fateful events of September 11, 2001. One wonders whether teachers and scholars of Islamic studies, Muslim and non-Muslim, are fighting a losing battle in their effort to make Muslim societies, their aspirations, cultural richness, intellectual traditions, and modern challenges intelligible to a wider audience. The many challenges scholars face include: the widespread demonization of "Islam"; the tense atmosphere of public opinion; the increasing levels of state surveillance; the tacit restrictions on airing dissenting opinions; and the battle over who speaks for Islam among Muslim groups and Islamic specialists. Muslim scholars of Islam, who themselves come from highly varied ethnic, geographical, linguistic, and intellectual backgrounds, additionally face considerable challenges in the three settings of academe, Muslim communities, and Western society at large, settings in which their Muslim identities are either called into question as biased or upheld as voices of legitimacy and authenticity. This essay will discuss some of these challenges and consider the various roles played by scholars of Islam, including Muslim scholars, today.

The genesis of this *Progressive Muslims* volume took place in the aftermath of the September 11 attacks on the World Trade Center and Pentagon. Individually and as a group, scholars of Islam,[3] who represent a diversity of specializations, were as horrified and stunned by the attacks and the wanton destruction and loss of life as the public. Muslim academics in particular were distraught at the damage these attacks had done to the reputation of peaceful and law abiding Muslims everywhere. They worried that the event would be misused to give confirmation to harmful theories that set up "Islam" as the post-Cold-War-enemy of "the West." In the following pages, I will briefly explore the implications and fallout of September 11 to which scholars of Islam have had to respond. This includes the ongoing necessity of putting into historical and socio-political context the events of September 11 as well as other conflicts in the Middle East within an already inhospitable atmosphere in which all things Muslim and Islamic are demonized. Unfortunately, the attacks of September 11 and the American global "war on terrorism" has given a new lease of life to stereotypes and suspicions about the "other" in the so-called Western and Islamic world, and has dealt a blow to the efforts of teachers, scholars, and activists who work hard to reduce this unhealthy and dangerous state of mutual incomprehension. The chapter will consider the deleterious cost of ignorance and of the perpetuation of discourses of hatred which foil hopes of achieving lasting peace, security, and justice for Muslims and non-Muslims alike in an irreversibly interdependent global village. It will also raise issues pertinent to the roles of scholars of Islam in the Western world with particular emphasis on their responsibilities for "speaking truth to power," to borrow Edward Said's phrase, and to highlight the intimidating and silencing accusations of disloyalty and treachery which are received by those who dare to speak up.

The September 11 crisis brought into sharper focus a number of challenges and risks already faced by experts in Islamic and Middle Eastern studies prior to the tragedy. Most scholars of Islam and the Middle East were called upon to juggle divergent roles and to play a balancing act that was simultaneously sympathetic, dispassionate, and critical. Scholars were pressed into service in a variety of contexts. Muslim student associations and Islamic centers expressed fears of reprisal and anti-Islamic, anti-Arab sentiment and they wanted and expected scholars of Islam, especially Muslim scholars, to defend their religion and culture. Americans, young and old, were angry, confused, and worried about further terrorist attacks, the implications of declaring a state of war, and the potential loss of life and civil liberties in the U.S.A. which heightened security measures would entail. Together with newspapers, TV stations, radio talk hosts, civic associations, and church organizations, citizens wanted information, explanations, rationalizations, debates, and discussions on Islam, the Taliban, Osama bin Laden, Wahhabism, jihad, *fatwas*, and so on. Specialists with knowledge of Arabic, Afghanistan, and radical Islamist movements were called upon to assist the Federal Bureau of Investigation and the State Department in their criminal investigations. Some experts were engaged in providing scholarly rationalizations for going into war in Afghanistan and, more vaguely, against terrorism while others argued that a unilateral show of American military force in countries speculated to harbor terrorists and lying in the dubious "axis of evil" would only serve to fuel the very social, economic, and political conditions that are hotbeds for terrorist organizations. Scholars of Islam were in demand in women studies programs, the media, and at other venues to discuss the plight of women in Afghanistan and the place of women in Muslim culture generally. In sum, highly complex issues had to be discussed in contexts that pushed for simplification, taking sides, and drawing conclusions.

Tragically, the September 11, 2001 attack on the World Trade Center and Pentagon revived centuries-old prejudices of "Islam" as a force to be feared and of Muslims as an inherently violent and irrational people, prejudices that have antecedents reaching back to the Christian Crusades. This event has made the already difficult task faced by scholars and teachers, enlightened journalists, and Muslims themselves of dispelling the negative stereotypes that abound of "Islam" virtually impossible. Among the many questions people asked in the wake of the horror and destruction of that day were: Why do *they* hate us? Why do Muslims oppose modernity and the West? How do Muslims relate to Christians and Jews? Why are Muslim women oppressed? Not just Americans, but people around the world (including Muslims) were shocked and traumatized by the event. Not surprisingly, as the identities of the terrorists came to be known, greater hostility and anger were expressed towards Muslims, and especially Arab Muslims. The event played into the cynical predictions of commentators such as Bernard Lewis, Samuel Huntington, and Martin Kramer whose sensationalist, polarizing, and contemptuous views of Muslims and Islamic cultures have been fed to an unsuspecting and misinformed public.[4] In this respect, the actions of the suicide bombers have damaged the reputation and, practically speaking, the future of Muslims worldwide who must live with the slur, albeit unfair, that has been cast upon them. The judgment of guilt by association, while unfair, will inevitably be invoked by some to justify their oppression.[5]

It cannot be denied that there are groups among Muslims who, although representing a minority, have given credibility to negative stereotypes of "Islam" for generating their own vituperative black and white rhetoric against "the West." Whereas scholars of Islam can and do make a contribution to rectifying stereotypes of the Islamic worlds, the events of September 11 have awakened many Muslims to their own obligation of restoring the image of their faith and traditions by manifesting attitudes and behaviors that are humane, just, and generous and by assertively speaking out against and eschewing all forms of terrorism, violence, and hatred in their midst. For many reasons, most especially feelings of being under siege, the voices of moderate Muslims who recoil from aggression are infrequently heard in the public domain. Now more than ever, however, following the Islamic precept to "command good and forbid evil," Muslims increasingly recognize that their silence is tantamount to acquiescence and tacit approval of such immoral and futile acts. If, indeed, the purpose of the suicide bombings and terrorist acts was to aid Muslim causes, it is necessary to ask whose lives in the Islamic world were actually improved by the senseless destruction of September 11. Ironically, the tragedy offers a call to the so-called invisible majority of peaceful Muslims to stand up and show itself through deeds reflecting an active social and ethical conscience. Failing to repudiate strident voices of extremism in their midst will simply give credence to the views proliferated by writers such as Samuel Huntington, Bernard Lewis, and Dinesh D'Souza – namely, that to be Muslim means to be wilfully destructive, oppressive, and regressive.[6] September 11 has shown that if Muslims do not make serious and concerted efforts to reject hateful speech and violence justified in the name of "Islam," and if they do not address the concrete social, economic, and political causes at the root of such profound wrongdoing, they risk hurting their own faith and heritage.

Many scholars have documented the fact that suspicion and fear of Muslims and Islam as a monotheistic faith is deeply rooted in the Euro-American imagination about the "other." This prejudice began long before Muslims appeared on the world stage as conquerors, and culminated with the horrors of the Crusades, which were further perpetuated by waves of European colonization and occupation of Islamic lands.[7] Scholars have observed that Christian Europe developed a rhetoric against Islam in order to define itself by demonizing the powerful and illustrious "other" that it was not. Europeans projected their own anxieties on Islam by calling it an inherently violent religion.[8] While Europe was being divided by warring feudal lords in the early Middle Ages, Arabs and Persians were immersed in recovering the intellectual heritage of Plato and Aristotle in the libraries of Alexandria, Baghdad, and Asia Minor. They translated this learning and wisdom from Greek and Syriac into Arabic, adding to it with their commentaries. Muslim commentary and expansion of the Greek heritage was eventually shared back with the European world. Thus, at one time Islamic civilization was the yardstick by which Europe measured itself and, indeed, the European Renaissance owes a great but frequently unacknowledged debt to the Islamic world. Karen Armstrong, among others, speculates that Islamic civilization in the Middle Ages was everything that Christian Europe aspired to be but was not: "Islam was the quintessential foreigner, and people resented Islam in Europe much as people in the Third World resent the U.S. today. One could say that Islam then was the greatest world power, and it remained so up until the early years of the Ottoman empire. Muslims were everywhere in the Middle East, Turkey, Iran, South East Asia, China. Wherever people went, there was Islam, and it was powerful, and people felt it as a threat."[9] It is more likely that European resentment turned Islam into "the quintessential foreigner," exaggerating the differences between Christians and Muslims, since, in actual fact, the monotheistic and prophetic faith of Islam was part of the Abrahamic traditions. Both for religious/polemical and expansionist/political reasons, Christian Europe experienced Muslims and their empire as a threat. This helps put into context its impetus to deal with Islam as an entity or totality that had to be discredited outright as barbaric and false.

Added on to this long and complicated history of hostility, caricature, and power struggles which were strengthened by religious dogmatism and imperialism, in more recent times public and media attention in the West has focused on the Islamic world primarily in times of strife and conflict: the Algerian War; the Iranian Revolution; the American hostage crisis; the Iran–Iraq War; the contest over Kashmir; the Gulf War; the Palestinian–Israeli conflict, and so on.[10] When the framework of inquiry into another culture or faith is locked into questions of violent conflict, national defense and security, access to oil reserves, geopolitical and economic interests, human rights abuses, and so on, even genuine efforts to understand the worlds of Muslims are doomed to failure. Moreover, the capacity to sift what is accurate from what is distorted in different sources is hampered by the lack of rudimentary knowledge of the Islamic world in the American public education system. While this is slowly changing, primary and secondary education in the United States has failed to provide adequate historical knowledge not only of Islamic but of African, Asian, Native American, and other indigenous histories and cultural traditions. Well-researched and informative materials on Muslim cultures and societies in the primary and secondary school curriculum have been virtually non-existent until very recently.[11] The few textbooks that do exist are marred by inaccuracies and biases.[12] When general knowledge of Islamic histories and cultures is so low, it is possible for instant experts and opinion makers to trade on the public's ignorance. In addition, it has taken disasters such as the Iran hostage crisis, the Gulf War, and now the September 11 tragedy for departments in the humanities and social sciences to argue for new positions in Islamic studies as an urgent and compelling priority given local and international events, and to galvanize college and university administrations into raising funding to support curricular enhancements for the study of Muslim histories, cultures, literatures, and institutions so that citizens develop the abilities necessary for a sensitive and informed engagement with Muslims and the Islamic world.

Thus, given this profound level of ignorance about the second largest and fastest-growing religion in the world, the almost total dependency of ordinary American citizens on the press, TV experts, talk shows, conservative Christian groups, and right-wing organizations for "information" on the Islamic world can only be described as flawed at best and dangerous at worst. Add to this the cacophony of voices, the captivating lyrics of songwriters who have expressed a variety of sentiments about September 11 through the powerful medium of popular music.[13] It is thus clear that in crisis situations such as September 11, the only times when interest in Islam is kindled, even serious attempts to communicate intelligently are bound to have limited impact. The public's desire for simple answers "in a nutshell" and the educational necessity for complex analysis "rich in detail" come to loggerheads. In a democracy that depends on the capacity and intelligence of well-informed citizens to vote with their conscience, this issue of the formation of opinion based solely on a diet of news and popular media is relevant not only to the handling of the subject of Islam but also to many other sensitive political, social, economic, and ethical issues that require in-depth information and analysis before judgment is made. It should be noted that the public in this context includes Muslims, who add to the problem of oversimplification when they present "Islam" in a totalizing, homogeneous, ahistorical, and decontextualized manner.[14] As educators, scholars of Islam are engaged in the task of helping students develop their intellectual gifts, analytical skills, and knowledge base with the hope that when they assume their roles as citizens and future leaders of society, they will sensitively assume their civic duty of creating a more just and humane society. The events of September 11 have shown that the educational role of scholars of Islam has had to be extended beyond the classroom into public venues to benefit a wider public that for the various reasons already outlined has been deprived of basic factual knowledge about the faith, interpretations, and histories of Muslim societies.

In the aftermath of September 11, scholars of Islam, who are often the sole experts on the religion, culture, and history of Muslims in their respective university campuses, received a deluge of requests for interviews and radio and TV appearances. Many found the experience of communicating about complex issues within the limiting constraints and agendas of the programs taxing and frustrating. Few scholars have the commanding presence, dexterity, and eloquence of an Edward Said or a Hanaan Ashrawi to convey information and critique in the flash of an interview and still make a lasting impression. It takes considerable skill to deal successfully with the media and yet to preserve the integrity of one's message. Apart from learning how to convey ideas in sound bites, scholars have to contend with the fact that they never know in what context a sentence will be quoted and what spin will be put on it. In addition, taking on such a public role comes at a huge cost of the scholar's time and privacy. As Rashid Khalidi points out with reference to Edward Said, "engaging the media is often a most uncongenial task, and always a tiring one, for those who have to do it regularly and who care about the topics they are asked to comment on."[15] Public appearances might also entail provisions for personal security when the views that are being expressed are unpopular, provocative, and perceived as politically incorrect. It is inevitable in such contentious circumstances that some members of the audience will take offense and object to this or that statement depending on their own positions and interpretations. Thus, scholars pressed into service during the September 11 crisis struggled with whether or not they ought to assume such a public role given the costs in energy, time, security, and peace of mind. At the same time, they also had to weigh the fact that not doing so would leave an uninformed but genuinely interested populace open to more distortions, propaganda, and confusion.

Given deeply entrenched prejudices and the various interests that maintain them politically through the media, think-tanks, hate groups, and the publishing industry, it seems unlikely that the negative perceptions and attitudes are going to change in the near future. The veritable growth industry of publications which has sprung up in the last few decades bearing eye-catching and alarming titles on Islamic jihad, fundamentalism, extremism, terrorism, and so on demonstrates that negative and ideologically motivated views about the Islamic world sell.[16] The insulting depictions of Muhammad and distortions of Muslim beliefs articulated by a prominent pastor at a major Southern Baptist Convention in St Louis and echoed in other evangelical contexts may be discounted in polite conversations, but they may well express largely unarticulated sentiments of many people on the street.[17] At the very least, the reach of such voices may continue to influence public opinion and maintain stereotypes. Sales of the Qur'an and books on Islam boomed after September 11. This does not mean, however, that readers were necessarily enlightened given the variety of opportunistic and often misleading books that were made available. Many readers simply found in them a confirmation of their pre-existing misconceptions. In a town meeting after September 11 at which the Qur'anic injunction against suicide and arbitrary killing was quoted, a person in the audience proclaimed he had read the Qur'an from cover to cover and found many justifications for engaging in jihad or holy war. Justifications for violence against enemies can be found in virtually any scripture. Unfortunately, Muslims and non-Muslims alike read the Qur'an without any sense of historical perspective, or knowledge of the religious, sociological, and political background of seventh-century Arabia. It is essential to call into question the use of scriptures as self-evident artifacts which stand independent of time and context, and whose meanings can be deduced quite apart from the historical evolution of language and rhetoric, formations of communities of interpretation, and social and political mechanisms for controlling divergent readings.[18]

In the college classroom, despite encouraging and genuine attempts by students at understanding the complexities underlying the events of September 11, displacing the vivid images of destruction and hate with a more balanced view of the diversity and range of Islamic histories, literatures, and cultures was an almost impossible task. Enrollments in various courses on Islam increased markedly after September 11, but, as with the public, students too had to struggle hard to come to terms with their understandable identification with those who were lost in the attacks and the feelings evoked by watching repeatedly televised images of the destruction of the Twin Towers, pictures of the suicide bombers, and video clips of Osama bin Laden taunting the West. Even after working through and analyzing primary sources on Islam, the history and the diversity of interpretations of concepts such as jihad, and the socio-economic and political dimensions of post-colonial Islamist movements, some students could not see Islam as anything but a monolithic faith permitting and promoting violence. This ambivalence was matched by reactions of Muslim students in the classroom who were justifiably angry and hurt, firstly because they felt an unfair judgment of guilt by association had been passed on all Muslims, and secondly because of the double standard regarding the value of life which they detected in media reports and reactions of American politicians. A Muslim student described his resentment at "being identified as one of *them* who is being examined under a microscope like a specimen." Another argued that while outrage was expressed at the loss of American or Israeli lives, few seemed to care about the loss of lives of innocent civilians in the war in Afghanistan[19] or the cumulative loss of Palestinian lives as a result of the Israeli occupation[20] or the rape and massacre of Bosnian Muslims when they were supposedly in a safe zone under U.N. protection in 1995. The material and psychological causes for the festering resentment and anger in parts of the Muslim world against America involve specific U.S. capitalist and military interventions which often do not demonstrate a consistent ethical framework. Many of these policies have helped advance the wealth and power of the ruling class to the detriment of the working classes in Muslim countries.

Adversarial modes of engagement with the Islamic world obscure the profound and mutually enhancing interactions between the cultures and peoples on every side of the divides generated by those who objectify the "other," whether the other is Muslim or not. There has been no more critical time than the present to bring these interactions into view. Attempting to understand – not necessarily condone – the varieties of Muslim revolutionary activities in each of their discrete contexts bears the double burden first, of trying to unravel the complexities attached to particular economic and political struggles for power, and second of trying to generate discussion, critical analysis, and debate in a context in which such rational inquiry is increasingly perceived as anti-American and unpatriotic because the complexities attached to the former have a direct bearing on the latter. For instance, an assessment of the role of colonialism, the

Cold War, and American foreign policy in the destabilization of a given region's political economy necessarily requires students and citizens to engage in an unsettling self-examination and scrutiny of the U.S.A.'s and Europe's role in supporting oppressive regimes and underwriting the strife, restrictions, and terror that these regimes have imposed on their own citizens. The list is endless: the Shah of Iran before the Iranian Revolution; Saddam Hussein before the Gulf War; Osama bin Laden before Soviets pulled out of Afghanistan; and so on.

The global demonization of Islam and Muslims is further facilitated by linking the "war on terrorism" with the rhetoric of evil which places entire (and almost entirely Muslim) countries on the "axis of evil." This linkage gives *carte blanche* to governments outside the U.S.A., but who count on U.S. support, to oppress and repudiate their own Muslim minorities, who are criminalized when they show forms of resistance even when they are non-violent. Whether in Chechnya, Kashmir, or Israel and the Occupied Territories, the use of terrorism including suicide bombings as a counter-hegemonic strategy invoked by Muslims (and non-Muslims) has provided the opportunity for governments to exercise force regardless of the legitimate concerns of the populations, and to further reinforce the view that Muslims behave irrationally and violently even in self-defense. If only irrational people were willing to die for a cause, no nation would have police forces, armies, or firefighters. What is defined as terrorism and war in one context is described as revolution and the fight for freedom and independence in another. One needs to look at each specific situation to assess this question carefully. Furthermore, while terrorism and Islam have been made synonymous in the popular imagination because of sustained media and press coverage, terrorism is not unique to individuals who profess Islam. People in all parts of the world, Muslims and non-Muslims, misguidedly use terror tactics to achieve their ends and are motivated by a variety of causes including ideology, economic disparities, class conflict, poverty, injustice, oppression, and religious zeal. Terrorists can be found among the Irish Republican Army, Tamil Liberation Tigers, Sikh Khalsa, Algerian freedom fighters, Japanese Aum Shinrikyo, and others. Americans too have their home-grown terrorists in Timothy McVeigh and the Unibomber. However, while the contextual and historical factors of non-Muslim forms of revolution and terrorism have been explored by the academy, the media, and groups who have a stake in the matter, in the case of terrorists who are Muslims religion is immediately and in a facile manner made responsible for this tool of the weak on the one hand and of the tyrannical on the other.

But for scholars of Islam, at a time when civil liberties are in danger of being withdrawn to fight an all encompassing "war against terror," the risk involved in contributing to the knowledge, analysis, and discussion of the many complexities attached to the study of Islam and those parts of the globe where political tensions are exceedingly high is immense. There is no question that terrorism as such, whether motivated for a just or an unjust cause, is unacceptable because of the irreparable harm it does to all involved. Nor is there any question that those who commit such crimes against humanity must be brought to justice. The problem arises when the term "terrorism" is blithely used to cover all forms of revolution and resistance and when it is deliberately misused to repress legitimate voices of protest and dissent. Hence, such an open-ended war threatens to reduce access to candid investigative studies and intellectual analysis by scholars and reporters who thereby risk facing unfounded accusations of supporting terrorism on the one hand and lacking patriotism and concern for American (and global) security on the other. In the heat of conflict, it is often overlooked that the capacity for dispassionate critical self-examination is the basis of renewal and progress at both the individual and collective level. The curtailment in the U.S.A. of civil liberties such as freedom of inquiry and the expression of dissenting opinions constitutes one of the most troubling repercussions of September 11. Scholars and intellectuals have discovered that even judicious attempts to explain why there is such strong anti-American sentiment not just in parts of the Muslim world but around the globe generally are dismissed, denounced, and silenced as unpatriotic and apologetic.

For example, a report issued two months after the September 11 attack by the American Council of Trustees and Alumni, a conservative academic group founded by Lynne Cheney, former President of the National Endowment of the Humanities and wife of the U.S. Vice-President Dick Cheney, chided forty college professors including the President of Wesleyan University for not showing enough patriotism in the aftermath of September 11 and accused college and university faculty as being "the weak link in America's response to the attack."[21] This censorship of diverse and dissenting views is problematic at any time, but especially so after September 11 when Americans are coming more fully to grips with their superpower status and the responsibilities that come with such power, wealth, and privilege. As Americans recognize that they can no longer live as if in a self-contained, impregnable fortress, many feel a genuine desire to comprehend the reasons for the hostility felt towards them, and the complexity of problems abroad and how these conflicts relate to American involvements in the regions in question. Hence, instead of admonishing scholars for their contributions to informed and thoughtful analysis, and for advancing sensitive and situated knowledge of other cultures, it is necessary to appreciate the urgency and importance of educating the American public – including Muslims – about the complexities involved. The fundamental question that thus looms ahead before scholars of Islam is what roles they can play to address this vital need to understand truthfully, compassionately, and critically the relationships between events and conditions in the Islamic and the Western world without fear of reprisal from all sides.

What is the cost of continued ignorance and mutually reinforcing stereotypes? What are the consequences of concealing or distorting facts, remaining silent when conditions are inhumane, when people suffer degradation and despair as a consequence of economic sanctions and foreign policies, and when preachers and politicians mislead and incite their congregations and constituencies? Islamophobia on the one hand and hatred of the West on the other hand are two sides of the same coin. As Armando Salvatore argues, the antagonisms are perpetuated by a growth industry of publications, audio-visual materials, internet sites, and pop cultures on both sides that frame the Other as irrational and fanatical or imperialist and exploitative, respectively.[22] The more that Euro-American discourses and policies attack and distort Islam and Muslims, the more fuel this provides to Islamic extremists to generate their own anti-Western rhetoric and provocations. So much so that it is perhaps true to say that these constructions mutually create and sustain each other. The Algerian Muslim philosopher and critic Mohammed Arkoun argues that we need both to criticize and to expose the mythologization and ideologization of Islam by militants, state-sponsored 'ulama, and Muslim apologists; and at the same time, to criticize the static and fragmented portrait of Islam given by many Western scholars and Orientalists "under the pretext that they are only faithfully transcribing the discourse, both ancient and contemporary, that Muslims have generated about their own religion."[23]

Orientalist conceptions of Islamic radicalism have at their heart a picture of "an Islam in movement, where the movement is prompted by basically irrational impulses to turn 'religion' into 'politics.'"[24] The views of Orientalists are mirrored and matched by equivalent revolutionary self-images within Islamist movements which insist upon the conflation of faith and politics under the guise of an Islamic awakening. What is synopsized as "Islam" by Orientalists and Islamists (both totalizing terms in need of further qualifications) alike is thus a fringe, revisionist, ideological, post-colonial phenomenon ironically supported by the interests of an "oiligarchy."[25] These contemporary "imaginaries" of Islam totally obscure the rich and diverse history of Islamic cultures and civilization. According to Arkoun, "the 'imaginary' of an individual, a social group, or a nation is the collection of images carried by that culture about itself or another culture – once the product of epics, poetry, and religious discourse, today a product primarily of the media and secondarily of the schools."[26] Both Islamist and Orientalist imaginaries are premised upon the necessary conflation of faith and politics in Islam and any attempt to undo this identification is met with enormous resistance on both sides. To the detriment of all, hate and contempt sell. They also create conditions ripe for human rights abuses, international injustice, and global insecurity. The enormous resources expended on all sides to prop up false perceptions of the other could be put to much better use solving real problems of humanity such as hunger, disease, poverty, child abuse, women's oppression, illiteracy, and crime.

In 1941, President Roosevelt proclaimed that four freedoms were essential for democracy (and, one might add, the global village) to flourish: (a) freedom of speech and expression; (b) freedom of worship; (c) freedom from want; and

(d) freedom from fear. It is now evident that the pursuit of these freedoms in the U.S.A. is intimately tied to its willingness – since it has the capacity – to facilitate these same liberties in other parts of the globe. But analysis of a number of U.S. foreign policies since the foundation of this great republic indicates otherwise. Often governed by economic and geopolitical interests of the day and subject to the vagaries of internal politics, U.S. foreign policy has exhibited double standards in dealing with different nations. For example, during the Cold War, the U.S.A. encouraged and financially supported Islamist groups, but once the communist threat ceased to exist, Islamists themselves became the target. Similarly, at one time it served U.S. geopolitical interests to promote Saddam Hussein – until he posed a threat to American access to Kuwaiti oil reserves and the stability of the Middle East. U.S. foreign policy also supported autocrats like the Shah of Iran and Gamal Nasser of Egypt despite the atrocities they committed against their own peoples.

Thus, for observers abroad, the standards and moral criteria exercised in U.S. dealings with other nations, if there are any, appear to be opportunistic and, since the end of the Cold War, ever more autocratic. National interests are used to justify many measures that may be at odds with humanitarian interests and international justice. For instance, a confusing signal is sent when the United States asserts that its soldiers cannot be arraigned under international law but feels no compunction in detaining in custody without due process any individual held under suspicions of terrorism.[27] It suggests that an American's life is more valuable than the lives of Africans (as demonstrated in the treatment of those hurt in the bombings at the U.S. Embassy in Kenya), ordinary Iraqis (whose children suffer the consequence of U.S.-enforced sanctions), and Afghanis who first served as U.S. foot soldiers in the war against the Soviets only to be abandoned when they were no longer needed, thereby creating a vacuum and an opportunity for the Taliban and Osama bin Laden. A critical examination of many U.S. foreign policies reveals a double standard that all human beings are not, in fact, conceived of as equal in respect to the individual's right to life, liberty, justice, and happiness. The freedoms and protections spoken of by Roosevelt are all too often the privilege of but a few. Simply in terms of changing demographics, sustaining these stark disparities in basic quality of life factors between the rich and powerful and the poor and weak is growing untenable in this global village.[28] Although Americans have diverse views on these policies and there is vigorous debate and disagreement as well as criticism of them, it is not difficult to see why observers of U.S. foreign policy, especially those adversely affected by it, develop feelings of hostility, mistrust, and anger towards the U.S.A. The fact that the U.S.A. is the sole superpower also leads to the opinion that its unilateral policies and conduct are an abuse of its superpower status.

Already, the consequences for Americans who rightly pride themselves for their hard-won rights and freedoms have been adverse. Many Americans keenly feel this conflict between safeguarding national security interests and civil liberties. It must not be forgotten that before September 11, the worst act of terrorism committed on U.S. soil was by an American citizen, Timothy McVeigh, a Christian and a decorated soldier in the U.S. Army who served in the Gulf War. Whereas the bombing of the Federal Building in Oklahoma did not leave a scar on Christianity and condemn all Americans as violent, September 11 has unfairly been allowed to demonize Muslims, revile the Islamic faith, and castigate the Arab world. To protect its national and security interests, the U.S.A. also needs to pay attention to the concerns of its own dispossessed and dejected citizens who struggle against a system that benefits some sectors of society and marginalizes others. The status of the United States as the world's only superpower is less than two decades old, and the nation's extraordinary success is premised on the cherished principles of liberty, fairness, democracy, meritocracy, justice, freedom of inquiry, and protection of civil rights. However, in an increasingly interdependent globe, can the U.S.A. sustain an imperialistic outlook without sacrificing some of these very principles? If the dialogue of the deaf between the West and the rest continues, it is likely to lead to a decrease of civil liberties as Americans are expected to give them up, albeit begrudgingly, to protect their security interests. The massive surveillance apparatus being implemented under the newly established office of Homeland Security shows that September 11 has effected a siege mentality in the U.S. Republican government. Clearly, other constructive alternatives are necessary, such as a concerted focus on economic aid and development strategies that place common human interests at the forefront and offer all societies hope and confidence in the future.

In conclusion, the multiple roles of teacher, scholar, critic, advocate, public intellectual, media expert, policy advisor, human rights activist, and so on bring into focus the enormous responsibilities that were suddenly and unwittingly assumed by many scholars of Islam after September 11. In addition to teaching and doing research, scholars of Islam tried to make substantive contributions to the public's understanding of the rich history, diversity, and complexity of the Islamic world, which are intimately intertwined with those of European and Asian civilizations. They shouldered the obligations of public intellectuals to explain highly complex matters such as the genesis of conflicts within the Muslim world, to examine the multiple interactions between former colonial and neo-colonial powers and their subjects, and to link larger issues of civil society, international justice, and political economies to U.S. foreign policy, aid, and investments in other parts of the globe. To promote intellectual exchanges within spaces of tolerance and civility, they have had to bring into conversation the obstructive perceptual frameworks generated by Muslims and non-Muslims. In speaking truth to power, they have had to be able to question, analyze, and critique adversarial discourses and activities of both the Euro-American and the Muslim worlds.

Clearly, there are severe risks and consequences involved for academics, intellectuals, and critical and dissenting voices who speak up in countries whose state apparatus underwrites education, research, and the media. Muslim intellectuals in other parts of the world who have not towed the party line have been persecuted or incarcerated or have paid with their lives.[29] Salman Rushdie's definition of freedom of expression would be unthinkable in those contexts and yet it remains vital in order to sustain a participatory democracy: "What is freedom of expression? Without the freedom to offend, it ceases to exist. Without freedom to challenge, even satirize all orthodoxies, including religious orthodoxies, it ceases to exist."[30] It can only be hoped that the conditions for free and open inquiry will remain robust in the U.S.A. for scholars and academics to work their balancing act between the equally oppressive forces of Islamic obscurantism and Western demonization. In the embattled atmosphere of current events where emotions run high, there is an urgent need to find ways to communicate sensitively about very contentious matters without inflaming the situation further but at the same time without remaining silent about (and complicit in) the multiplicity of factors that contribute to it. To create discourses of the middle way, scholars of Islam must keep working at two major problems that seem insurmountable at times, namely, resisting the polarizing and generalizing language used for discussing contentious issues and continually addressing the lack of specific historical and cultural knowledge in the Western world about Islamic civilization and in the Islamic world about Western civilization.

ENDNOTES

1. I have deliberately avoided the use of the term "Islamicist" since it has taken on meanings which obfuscate its usual reference to an "Islamic (special)ist." For instance, even the usually reliable and astute Ahmed Rashid incorrectly uses the term "Islamicist" instead of "Islamist" when he writes, "The Islamicists denigrated tribal structure in pursuit of radical political ideology in order to bring about an Islamic revolution in Afghanistan." *Taliban: Militant Islam, Oil and Fundamentalism in Central Asia* (New Haven: Yale University Press, 2001), 19. Another instance of this confusion was Jerry Falwell's reference to a respected scholar of Islamic studies, Michael Sells, as an "Islamist" instead of "Islamicist." Falwell objected to assigning Sells's book *Approaching the Qur'an: The Early Revelations* as required reading for all incoming freshmen at the University of North Carolina (UNC), Chapel Hill. See "Hypocrisy in Education," July 31, 2002, *BP News* (www.BPNews.net). In the court documents submitted by the group suing UNC for this requirement, "Islamicist" has been defined as "someone who is sympathetic to or subscribes to Islam." This further muddles the meaning of this term, ascribing to it the connotation of religious affiliation rather than academic qualification. In academic usage, "Islamicist" usually refers to an academic who specializes in Islamic studies, whereas "Islamist" usually refers to those who use Islam as an ideology for engaging in revolutionary and/or extremist activities. "Muslim" simply refers to one who professes Islam as a personal faith. The *Oxford English Dictionary* states that "Islamist" can refer to an "orthodox Muslim" or to "an expert on Islam." Given these confusions, it may be necessary to develop another academic designation such as "Islamologist" to replace "Islamicist."

2. In particular, the list-serve of members of the Study of Islam section of the American Academy of Religion (islamaar@bard.edu) exchanged information and resources and discussed many issues subsequent to the event. Also see the website created by Omid Safi at http://groups.colgate.edu/aarislam/response.htm. The site includes a statement by the members of the Study of Islam section, documents the reactions of Muslims and non-Muslims around the globe, and provides links to useful resources about September 11.

3. At the outset, it is important to problematize the notion of Islam as a singular, undifferentiated phenomenon. Properly speaking, scholars have expertise in a few of the multiple forms and expressions of Muslim communities that have existed within specific historical and geographical contexts. In this article, while the word "Islam" is used, properly speaking, it may be more accurate and appropriate to use "islams" to resist the totalizing connotation of Islam as a homogeneous entity.

4. Bernard Lewis gave currency to phrases such as "Muslim rage" and "the clash of civilizations" which have been picked up by journalists and policy analysts such as Samuel Huntington. See Bernard Lewis, "The Roots of Muslim Rage," *Atlantic Monthly,* September 1990, 52–60; Samuel Huntington, *The Clash of Civilizations: Remaking of the World Order* (New York: Simon & Schuster, 1996); and Martin Kramer, *Ivory Towers on Sand: The Failure of Middle Eastern Studies in America* (Washington: Washington Institute for Near Eastern Policy, 2001).

5. An interesting study would be to look at how Muslims and other minorities who resist their own governments in countries around the world have become the target of state oppression on the basis of their alleged terrorist activities (which might involve unarmed resistance or civil disobedience). Soon after the U.S.A. declared its "war on terrorism," the Bush administration released a list of terrorist organizations and put on notice any country that harbored such groups. Undoubtedly, this move, which was primarily intended to demolish the al-Qaeda and similar networks, was a critical step in securing a safer world. However, the Bush administration's list of terrorist groups has given governments cause to pursue their own interests against sections of the population who oppose them for a variety of reasons. For example, one of the groups on the terrorist list is the Lord's Resistance Army, a quasi-religious movement that mixes Christianity with African spiritualism located in the remote bushland of Uganda. The conflict between government forces and rebels had cooled down, but after the list was released the Ugandan government announced Operation Iron Fist, its version of the American war in Afghanistan, to root out the rebels. Since the fighting resumed between the rebels and government forces, half a million people have been displaced and tens of thousands have been killed. A Roman Catholic Archbishop who is trying to bring about a peaceful settlement aptly said, "When two elephants battle, the grass is what suffers." Marc Lacey, "Uganda's Terror Crackdown Multiplies Suffering," *New York Times,* August 4, 2002.

6. In his book *What's so Great about America* (Washington: Regnery, 2002), D'Souza argues that George Bush's and Tony Blair's attempts to resist the identification of Islam and terrorism is misguided because Islam, that is, the faith itself, is a threat to America, for it provides the rationalization and rewards for terrorists to engage in their attacks.

7. For discussions of European views of the Muslim worlds, see: Edward Said, *Orientalism* (New York: Vintage, 1979); Maxime Rodinson, *Europe and the Mystique of Islam,* trans. by Roger Veinus (Seattle: University of Washington Press, 1987); Norman Daniel, *Islam and the West: The Making of an Image* (Edinburgh: Edinburgh University Press, 1960); and Benjamin Kedar, *Crusade and Mission: European Approaches to the Muslims* (Princeton: Princeton University Press, 1984).

8. "Some details of this fantasy reflect Christian anxieties about their own emergent identity. Islam was stigmatized as the 'religion of the sword' during the Crusades, a period when Christians themselves must have had a buried worry about this aggressive form of their faith which bore no relation to the pacifist message of Jesus." Karen Armstrong, *Muhammad: A Biography of the Prophet* (New York: HarperCollins, 1992), 27.

9. Interview with Karen Armstrong, "The Feel of Religion," by Omayma Abdel-Latef, *al-Ahram Weekly Online*, 593, 2002, www.ahram.org.eg/weekly/2002/593/intrvw.htm

10. Edward Said, "Impossible Histories: Why the Many Islams Cannot Be Simplified," *Harper's Magazine*, July 2002, 70.

11. The Council for Islamic Education (www.cie.org) was founded by Shabbir Mansuri to address the lack of reliable information on Islamic cultures in primary and secondary education. The Council has worked closely with publishers on addressing the quality of materials on Islamic civilization found in primary and secondary school textbooks. In a video on *Islam in America* produced by the *Christian Science Monitor*, Mansuri relates that he decided to found this organization when he saw his daughter's eighth-grade social sciences textbook. The chapter on Islam was introduced with a picture of a camel whereas chapters on other cultures began with a picture of a key historical figure.

12. Grassroots Muslim organizations such as the Council on American–Islamic Relations have made an effort to address this problem by giving seminars to teachers, administrators, and curriculum writers. For further information, visit its website at http://www.cair-net.org.

13. Songwriter and country singer Steve Earle has released a song titled "John Walker's Blues" which tries to figure out why John Walker Lindh decided to fight alongside the Taliban. The song begins, "I'm just an American boy raised on MTV/ and I've seen all those kids in the soda pop ads/ but none of 'em looked like me," and concludes, "Now they're dragging me back/ with my head in a sack/ to the land of infidel." For more songs touching on September 11, see Kris Axtman, "Patriotism vs. Protest," *Christian Science Monitor*, July 31, 2002, www.csmonitor.com/2002/0731/p03s01-ussc.html

14. This is particularly evident in the pamphlets produced and circulated by Islamic groups in the West for proselytizing (*da'wa* and *tabligh*) activities. The materials normalize, ritualize, and standardize this diverse faith into a uniform mold through a process that might be called the "five-pillarization" of Islam.

15. Rashid I. Khalidi, "Edward Said and the American Public Sphere: Speaking Truth to Power," in *Edward Said and the Work of the Critic: Speaking Truth to Power*, ed. Paul A. Bove (Durham, NC Duke University Press, 2000), 154.

16. A search of titles on amazon.com with words including "Islamic threat," "terror," "jihad," "fundamentalism," "politics," etc. gives a sobering idea of the extent of publications available in this genre.

17. Rev. Jerry Vines, pastor of the First Baptist Church in Jacksonville, Florida, "called Muhammad a 'demon-possessed pedophile,' asserting that his 12th and final wife was a 9-year-old girl, and declared that Muslims worshiped a different God than Christians." See Susan Sachs, "Baptist Pastor Attacks Islam, Inciting Cries of Intolerance," *New York Times*, June 15, 2002.

18. The Algerian philosopher Mohammed Arkoun argues that among the many unthinkables in traditionalist and conservative Islamist discourses is to analytically reflect upon the nature of the Qur'an before it became a fixed corpus. Even to raise questions regarding the historical formation of a closed corpus is blasphemous, for it would signify a time in Islamic history when the "timeless" Qur'an was not as it is known and handled by Muslims (and non-Muslims) today, namely, a total, fixed, divinely sealed text. For further discussion, see Mohammed Arkoun, *The Unthought in Contemporary Islamic Thought* (London: Saqi, 2002), especially chapter 1, "A Critical Introduction to Qur'anic Studies," 37–65.

19. Numbers are hard to nail down, but reportedly some three thousand Afghans lost their lives as a result of "collateral damage," thousands were maimed in the war and countless others displaced by it. Afghans continue to suffer as the U.S. military forces "accidentally" strike targets suspected of harboring al-Qaeda forces. For instance, an American plane bombarded a village in southern Afghanistan on July 1, 2002 and killed forty-eight people, mostly women and children, and injured 117 people who had gathered for a wedding party. For the full report see Carlotta Gall, "Expecting Taliban, but Finding only Horror," *New York Times*, July 8, 2002.

20. For instance, President Bush was "furious" and "outraged" by the Palestinian bomb that killed seven students, including Americans, at Hebrew University in Jerusalem, but merely chided Israel for its "heavy-handedness" when Israeli forces killed eleven Palestinians including seven children while targeting Sheikh Salah Shehadeh, a Hamas leader in Gaza. For the report, see Suzanne Goldenberg, "12 Dead in Attack on Hamas: Seven Children Killed as Israelis Assassinate Military Chief," the *Guardian*, July 23, 2002.

21. Patrick Healy, "Conservatives Denounce Dissent," *Boston Globe*, November 13, 2002. The full report can be found online at http://www.goacta.org. In astonishing remarks made on multiculturalism on October 5, 2001, Lynne Cheney actually criticized the call for greater understanding of Islam.

22. Armando Salvatore, *Islam and the Political Discourse of Modernity* (Reading, NY: Ithaca Press, 1997), xvii.

23. Mohammed Arkoun, *Rethinking Islam: Common Questions, Uncommon Answers*, trans. Robert D. Lee (Boulder: Westview Press: 1994), 2.

24. Salvatore, op. cit., xvi.

25. This term was used by Woody Harrelson (who played Woody Boyd in the TV show *Cheers*), in an interview with Tim Cooper. Harrelson was describing his views on the U.S. handling of September 11 and said, "Blaming things on Bush is like blaming the hood ornament on a car on the accident [*sic*]. It's his whole 'oiligarchy' – that's what I like to call it. They have a certain agenda. It's all about oil, it's all about money. And the voice of dissent? It's a frightening time in America." *Hot Tickets Magazine*, July 19–25, 2002.

26. See Arkoun's discussion of the Western "imaginary" of Islam in *Rethinking Islam*, 6–13.

27. Attorney General John Ashcroft "vowed to use the full might of the federal government" and "every available statute" to hunt down and punish "the terrorists among us." This resulted in the detention of twelve hundred people suspected of violating immigration laws and having some connection to the terrorists. Not surprisingly, "the government's effort has produced few if any law enforcement coups. Most of the detainees have since been released or deported, with fewer than 200 still being held." Adam Liptak, Neil A. Lewis and Benjamin Weise, "After September 11, a Legal Battle over the Limits of Civil Liberty," by *New York Times*, August 4, 2002.

28. It is a sobering fact that the average woman in Yemen can be expected to have seven children in her lifetime. If birthrates remain the same for three generations, she will have forty-nine grandchildren, 343 great-grandchildren, and 2500 great-great-grandchildren. In comparison, the average family in many parts of Europe and the U.S.A. is barely more than one child. An American mother will have one grandchild, one to two great grandchildren, and two to three great-great-grandchildren. Source: *Religious Consultation Report*, 5(2), 2, www.religiousconsultation.org/

29. To give but one example: in July 2002, Mr Sa'ad Eddin Ibrahim, who holds a U.S. passport, was sentenced to seven years' hard labor by a court in Egypt for promoting democracy. This ill sixty-three-year-old man's crime was that his Institute at the American University in Cairo was helping Egyptians learn how to register to vote, fill out a ballot, and monitor an election. The State Department said it was "deeply disappointed" by Mr Ibrahim's conviction. Reporting on this, Thomas Friedman says, "Disappointed? I'm disappointed when the Baltimore Orioles lose. When an Egyptian president we give $2 billion a year to jails a pro-American democracy advocate, I'm 'outraged' and expect America to do something about it." Thomas Friedman, "Bush's Shame," *New York Times*, August 4, 2002.

30. Salman Rushdie, *Imaginary Homelands: Essays and Criticism 1981–1991* (New York: Granta, 1992), 396.

part II

PROGRESSIVE MUSLIMS AND GENDER JUSTICE

6

TRANSFORMING FEMINISMS:
ISLAM, WOMEN, AND GENDER JUSTICE

Sa'diyya Shaikh

INTRODUCTION, POSITIONING AND CONTEXT

I will begin by making my positioning explicit. My name is Sa'diyya Shaikh, an Arabic name. I am South African, born and raised solely on the continent of Africa, and my ancestry is Indian. I have, to date, never visited India although the first language I learned to speak was an Indian language called Gujarati and the staple diet of my family is still curry. I am most fluent and comfortable speaking the English language. I am a Muslim woman, whose existential, spiritual, and ethical universe is based on an Islamic worldview, a religion whose roots are to be found in seventh-century Arabia. The first time I ever visited the Middle East was on pilgrimage at the age of nineteen.

My coming of age was formulated within the socio-political context of apartheid South Africa. The aspect of my religious tradition that resonated most strongly in confronting this reality was the fact that Islam spoke to a humanity that transcended boundaries of race and that demanded human agency in the quest for social justice. In my confrontation with patriarchy in my social and cultural milieu, sometimes paraded under the guise of religion and tradition, it was this same social justice imperative that urged me to struggle with what exactly constituted Islam and the Islamic legacy – and what it means to be a gendered human being as well as a believer. My academic pursuit of Islamic studies is premised on a view of the integrity of the relationship between intellectual pursuits, social responsibility, and spiritual commitments.

By this extended introduction I am not only intending to situate my own ideological and personal positioning but also to make salient the notion of plurality and diversity encapsulated within the world of Islam, which encompasses realities of people from varying socio-cultural and political realities. Therefore, my positioning is also an explicit rejection of those intellectual, political, and popular idioms that argue for a homogeneous religious civilization, a reductionist assumption that is most pervasively prevalent in depictions of Islam.

Within the diverse worlds of Islam gender issues have been indigenously engaged with, argued about, harmonized, problematized, synthesized, negotiated, and re-negotiated in varying ways throughout history. In this era there are Muslim women and men who find Islam to be a source of human well-being and profound social egalitarianism. There are also, however, Muslim women in many parts of the world who experience oppression and marginalization that is justified in the name of Islam. Currently, one can find Muslim leaders who hold forth endlessly about the fact that Islam accords women high status and liberation while simultaneously promoting hierarchical and discriminatory power relationships between men and women. There are, however, also Muslim leaders who contest sexism and resist the masculinist bias of inherited traditions, many of whom relentlessly strive on the path of gender justice in Islam.[1]

There are also some Muslim women who have internalized the patriarchal dimension of their heritage and become its proponents, while, at the other end of the continuum, there are those who have exited the religious tradition as a response to experiences of patriarchal realities. Moreover, different groups of Muslim women come from varying cultural and geographical backgrounds, so that Jordanian Muslim women are often grappling with very different realities from Indonesian or Senegalese Muslim women.[2] The realities of gender dynamics in Islam are as complex and polymorphous as the realities of women in other religious, social, and political contexts.

Among those unwilling to compromise on the Islamic imperative to gender justice, there are some who define themselves as feminists, while there are others who do not sit comfortably with such an identification. Let me define at the outset what I understand by the term "feminism." It includes a critical awareness of the structural marginalization of women in society and engaging in activities directed at transforming gender power relations in order to strive for a society that facilitates human wholeness for all based on principles of gender justice, human equality, and freedom from structures of oppression.[3]

However, the current debates on feminism, gender, and women's rights in Islam are ideologically charged, since they are embedded in a history of larger civilizational polemics between the Islamic world and the West.[4] Gender discourses in contemporary Islam are prefigured by the history of a political conflict between Islam and Christianity, the European colonial encounters in different parts of the Muslim world, and the nationalist responses by colonized peoples. The processes of globalization, in tandem with neo-colonial configurations of power, currently pervade not only the concrete economic and socio-political spheres of most parts of the world but also the areas of knowledge production.[5]

From the perspective of many Muslims, Euro-American cultural hegemony remains coupled with a xenophobia directed at Islam and Muslims. This is reflected in the enduring legacy of problematic types of orientalist scholarship on Islam and, on the popular level, the continuing stereotyping of Islam as a violent, medieval, and, especially, misogynist religion. In many Muslim societies, gender issues have acquired a symbolic field that extends beyond simply redressing prevailing injustices, to the politics of cultural loyalty.[6]

American scholar Gisela Webb points out that one of the unfortunate consequences of misrepresentations of Muslims in the West is the creation of a siege mentality among many Muslims.[7] This mindset reinforces a reactive and defensive posturing towards the West. Alternatively, in some parts of the Muslim world the overall ascendancy of Euro-American powers in an increasingly shrinking globe, together with a sense of economic and political frustration with local despotic governments that are sometimes financed by Western powers, also contributes to strongly anti-Western sentiment.

Akbar Ahmed suggests that Muslim religious leaders who adopt a blanket opposition to the West are "in danger of rejecting the essential features of Islam such as love of knowledge, egalitarianism and tolerance because these are visibly associated with the West."[8] Moreover, part of this siege mentality ironically contributes to an occidentalist view that perpetuates similar "othering" constructs relating to Western immorality, greed, and brute force. This type of dichotomous categorization of "Islam versus the West" *à la* Samuel Huntington results in monolithic constructions that efface the complex nature of realities and multiple ethical discourses prevalent in both Muslim and Western societies.[9] It also eclipses the reality that there are growing communities of Muslims in the West, many of whom are culturally Western as well as religiously Muslim. These contemporary socio-political dynamics have especially strong ramifications for discourses of gender and feminism in Islam.

LEGACIES OF IMPERIAL FEMINISM

Many Muslims view contemporary Euro-American feminist approaches that reinforce reductionist views of Islam as a peculiarly sexist religion as part of the broader Western enterprise to discredit and misrepresent Islam. Ironically, many of these same Muslims also misrepresent feminism by stereotyping it with all that is considered negative and problematic in Western culture. Azza Karam, a contemporary Muslim scholar, summarizes these tensions in describing some of the difficulties in using feminist discourse in the Muslim world:

> The term "feminism"... in post-colonial Arab Muslim societies is tainted, impure and heavily impregnated with stereotypes. Some of these stereotypes are that feminism basically stands for the enmity between men and women, as well as a call for immorality in the form of sexual

promiscuity for women ... some religious personalities ... have associated feminism with colonialist strategies to undermine the indigenous social and religious culture.[10]

Some Muslim scholars have reacted with blind defensiveness to this perceived Western feminist attack on Islam. In legitimately attempting to repudiate the unpalatable and inaccurate stereotypes of certain orientalist discourses, these Muslim scholars have unwittingly become equally reductionist by romanticizing the Muslim legacy as one that has unequivocally empowered Muslim women.[11] This stance makes it increasingly difficult to approach the questions of gender relation in an honest manner, seeking to identify and redress realities of injustice.

Moreover, those Muslims who have invested in the maintenance of a patriarchy use the civilizational polemic with which Western feminism has been associated in order to discredit and malign Muslim women who are involved in feminist activity as agents of Western colonialism.[12] These accusations are particular charged due to the legacy of imperial feminism, missionaries and other emissaries of the empires having justified their political attacks on Islam and Muslim cultures by suggesting that their colonial "civilizing mission" was also intended to free the poor oppressed women in Islam. The ideological hypocrisy of this colonial narrative is exemplified by the case of the British Consul General in Egypt, Lord Cromer, who in the late nineteenth century was the champion of Egyptian women's unveiling while in his homeland, England, he was the President of the men's league for opposing women's suffrage.[13] While this reflects some European men's manipulation of Western feminist discourse in furthering the project of imperialism, many Western feminist women were also enmeshed in the colonial mindset as reflected in their interactions with women from colonized nations.

A particularly illustrative case is the nature of relationships between the Euro-American and Arab feminists in the International Alliance of Women (IAW), an international feminist organization.[14] This group began as a Western suffragist alliance; in 1923 it expanded its focus to broader questions of women's empowerment and invited "Eastern" feminists to participate. The ideological tensions between Eastern and Western feminists came to a head in 1939 when Western members of the organization registered protests and appeals for the release of a Czech Jewish member incarcerated by the Nazis, but refused to do so when a Palestinian member was imprisoned by the British.[15] Arab women saw this as symptomatic of the double standards and ideological biases of Western feminists. For Arab women the limits of international feminism became apparent due to the "failure of western feminists to confront imperialism and its negative implications for democracy and feminist ideals."[16]

Dominant strands of Western feminism were subject to extensive and continuing critique into the latter part of the twentieth century, not only by

Arab women but also from a spectrum of other women outside of the centers of white, Euro-American privilege.[17] This body of criticism by various women, including African-American and Chicana women as well as women from the many parts of the Third World, sparked extensive debates that articulated some of the central problems with second-wave feminism well into the 1980s.[18]

THIRD WORLD FEMINIST CRITIQUE AND ISLAM[19]

Many Third World women have argued that while the genesis and historical development of Western feminism primarily reflected Eurocentric realities, Euro-American feminists regularly assumed that they could speak for the experiences of all women.[20] Feminists from the Third World and African-American womanists argued that this presumption of a universal womanhood represented only the realities of a particular group of women, namely, First World, white, middle class women.[21] Such discourses marginalized and eclipsed the realities of women with different experiences and who came from diverse contexts. Subsequently, many Western feminists, particularly from the 1980s onwards, have acknowledged their own positioning and have significantly responded to issues of pluralism, representation, and hegemony.[22] However, I would argue that when it comes to issues of Islam and Muslim women, feminists more easily discard judicious analysis and reiterate negative stereotypes. Thus some Western feminists, who would otherwise be sensitized to questions of diversity, persist in making sweeping claims about Muslim women or Islam without engaging the necessary levels of complexity and specificity. Moreover, as I will illustrate, such Western discourses on Muslim women are predicated on unquestioned cultural and social assumptions that do not allow for the engagement of specific Muslim societies in their own terms. Thus I believe that some of the key critiques offered by feminists from the Third World continue to reflect the conceptual difficulties and ideological biases experienced by many groups of Muslims with regard to certain developments in Western feminism. I will explore two specific dimensions of a Third World feminist critique that apply to certain Western feminist discussions on Muslim women, particularly relating to questions of cultural hierarchy and representation.[23]

CULTURAL HIERARCHY AND REPRESENTATION:
THE EXAMPLE OF VEILING

Firstly, within many Western feminist discourses about Third World women, the standards of First World women have often been used as the superior norms against which Third World and non-Western women are measured. Often, Western cultural ideals are imposed on women coming from very different religious and cultural traditions.

Secondly, the homogenization of women within dominant Western feminist paradigms relates to the construction of women as *a priori* victims and as "powerless."[24] This approach does not examine particular material conditions and ideological frameworks that generate a certain context of disempowerment for a specific group of women. Instead, various examples of disempowered women are used to prove the general thesis that women as a group are "powerless."[25] Women become identified as an oppressed group prior to the process of analysis. The crucial fact that groups of women are constituted through the processes and structures of social relations is obscured.

In exemplifying the way in which these two critiques of Western feminist analyses apply to discourses on Muslim women, I will examine some of the popular Western understandings of Muslim women's veiling, head covering, or *hijab*. While the term *hijab* literally means "barrier" or "curtain," in this context it has come to signify the notion of concealing garments that women wear outside their homes in keeping with an Islamic ethic of modesty.[26] Conceptually it encompasses a range of different forms of covering that Muslim women adopt which are contingent on socio-historical factors and range from a headscarf to loose clothing to a veil.

It is certainly true that some discourses of the *hijab* are based on the coercion, the "othering," and the subjugation of women. This is most apparent in cases where women are forced to veil and are punished if they resist, as in the case, for example, of Afghani women under Taliban rule. However, this type of coercive discourse is by no means universal. Those Western feminist discourses that represent the *hijab* as simply symbolic of Muslim women's subjugation miss both the particularity of such a phenomenon as well as the multiple levels of meanings that it may have for different Muslim women.

For example, during the British colonial occupation of Egypt many Muslim women adopted the *hijab* as a symbol of their resistance to colonial definitions.[27] During the 1979 Iranian Revolution many middle class Iranian women donned the *hijab* as a symbol of their resistance to the Shah and Western cultural encroachment. The latter represents a very different meaning of the *hijab* from the post-revolutionary Iranian enforcement of *hijab* on women. In a contemporary study of Islamist movements, anthropologist Fadwa el Guindi found that educated and professional Islamist women have deliberately donned the veil as an assertion of their identity which reflects a syntheses of modernity and tradition.[28]

Hijab within Muslim societies does not constitute a singular symbolic field. It has come to represent varying meanings within multivalent realities. On the one hand there are large numbers of women who believe it is a religious requirement exemplifying the Islamic requirement of modesty and they choose to wear it because they seek to be obedient to God. Other women have stated explicitly feminist and anti-capitalist motivations for their veiling. They argue that the veiling detracts from patriarchal prioritization of women's physical and sexual attractiveness. Moreover it provides resistance to a perceived Western consumerism in which money and energy are constantly spent in keeping up with changing fashions that in reality keep women hostage to their appearance and to the market.[29] Finally, it is necessary to remember that norms for dress are socially and culturally specific and there is no reason that Muslim women's clothing needs to be measured against specific Western norms of dress.

Moreover, numerous sociological and anthropological studies have illustrated the ways in which veiling has increased female mobility in different parts of the Muslim world. In Iran and Egypt, for example, as in other parts of the Muslim world, the wearing of the *hijab* has neutralized public space for many traditional families, thus making it more acceptable for women to occupy such space.[30] This has led to a greater female presence in various aspects of public life, including the crucial areas of education and skills training, and has for the most part facilitated increasing participation of women in the public sphere.

It is worth considering the position that veiling reinforces the patriarchal assumption that public space is a sexualized, male space and thus women who enter it need to erase the femaleness of their bodies in order to be legitimately present. However, it should also be noted that the reality of a sexualized male public space is not unique to the Muslim world: in many parts of the Western world, one's visual space is constantly assaulted by pictures of scantily clad women advertising commercial products.

Ultimately in any study of dress and *hijab* among Muslim women, it is necessary to look at the complexity of the varying narratives and to treat Muslim women as subjects instead of objects of research. Such an approach will prioritize Muslim women's self-understandings, it will look at the varying ways in which veiling operates in relation to women's agency, it will recognize sites of resistance as well as contradictions and ambivalence within the discourses, instead of treating veiling as evidence of the monolithic victimization of women.

Furthermore, to the extent that Muslim women engage in this debate, there is much diversity in the ways in which we discourse upon the question, meaning and necessity of the particular forms of religiously appropriate dress, a diversity that has often remained unrepresented in many Western feminist discussions of veiling. One-dimensional Western feminist depictions of Muslim women as always oppressed by the phenomenon of veiling are thus both misrepresentative and reductionist. An example of contemporary feminist scholarship on Islam that most aptly encapsulates both misrepresentation as well as victim constructions of Muslim women is the 1997 edition of a sociology textbook by feminist sociologist Linda Lindsey called *Gender Roles: A Sociological Approach.*[31] Whereas the titles for the sections on Judaism, Christianity, and Hinduism merely give the name of the respective traditions without any adjectives, the section examining Islam is titled "Islam and Purdah: Sexual Apartheid." This immediately reduces all the complexity of Muslim gendered practice to the issue of the veil, a misrepresentative caricature of the complexity of Muslim societies and Islam. Moreover, it forecloses any serious engagement with aspects of this religious tradition that are potentially or actually liberating for Muslim women. These types of homogenization, generalization, and objectification of Muslim women result in the perpetuation of dominant patriarchal and colonial discourses that freeze women and the colonized into rigid categories. Such approaches suppress the ways in which particular groups of women challenge, subvert, and resist patriarchy at various points. They thereby undermine a politics of resistance and the construction of women as subjects capable of agency and transformation.

ALTERNATIVE PARADIGMS

In reviewing some of the alternative conceptualizations of women, Third World feminism offers a broader paradigm through which some of the concerns of Muslim women may be articulated. Indian feminist Chandra Mohanty asserts that there are no monolithic "Third World women," or "Third World situations" for that matter. Rather the term "third world" is utilized as "an analytical and political category" that makes connections in terms of the struggles of women in the Third World against racism, sexism, colonialism, and neo-colonialism in the context of particular balances of power in the world.[32] This definition thus refers to "a common context of struggle" which facilitates the formation of politically oppositional alliances and coalitions in the face of specific exploitative structures.[33] The alternatives posed by many Third World feminists are premised on the understanding that the gendered social subject has a number of simultaneous social identities that overlap, interlink, and position particular women at the nexus of different social hierarchies.[34] The recognition and representation of such heterogeneity is an initial and fundamental premise from which any study of Third World women may proceed.

Similarly, feminists working in the area of post-modern and post-structuralist theory have also contributed to the debunking of essentialist notions of "women" and "feminism." The post-modern approach undercuts singular feminist narratives through embracing cultural diversity, recognizing multiple feminist epistemologies, and focusing on the specificities and particularities of the women's different contexts.[35]

Post-modernism, Third World feminism, and critiques from other women on the margins have resulted in the development of varying understandings and different articulations of feminism over the last two decades. Thus there is a reconfiguring of the contours of feminism, one that is more attuned to specificities of different groups of women and acknowledges the varying forms of feminist praxis. Within this type of fluid and dynamic understanding of feminisms, it is possible to detect a range of Muslim women's gender activism or Islamic feminisms.

ISLAMIC FEMINISMS

While some Muslims eschew the term "feminist," increasing numbers have begun to utilize the term to describe themselves. The value of retaining the term "feminism" is that it enables Muslim women to situate their praxis in a global political landscape. This in turn creates greater possibilities for alliances, exchanges, and mutually enriching interaction among different groups of women. These connections enable varying groups of women to share and learn from each other's experiences, whether this is an exchange of feminist tools of analysis, or of varying ways of implementing activist initiatives, or simply an exposure to other forms of justice-oriented gender praxis. Furthermore the use of feminist language is helpful in that it creates a finely tuned vocabulary for a constellation of ideas that are linked to a critical consciousness surrounding gender politics. To accept feminism as a Western concept is in the last analysis to concede the most visible discourses around women's rights and gender justice as the property of the West and to marginalize the indigenous histories of protest and resistance to patriarchy by non-Western women. Therefore I use the term "feminist" as a description of Muslim women's activities that are aimed at transforming masculinist social structures.[36]

Muslim women and men with feminist commitments need to navigate the terrain between being critical of sexist interpretations of Islam and patriarchy in their religious communities while simultaneously criticizing neo-colonial feminist discourses on Islam. The fact that Muslim women resist both narratives while sometimes moving between their critiques is a consequence of the way in which they are situated within this larger minefield. miriam cooke describes this adoption of different speaking positions as a "multiple critique."[37] I find her notion of multiple critique compelling in that it allows one to conceptualize the notion of dynamic and multi-layered subjectivities of Muslim women in varying contexts as well as the reality that one's speaking position is influenced by one's audience. However, cooke's position and theorization of this concept reflect some fundamental problems as well. She suggests that the "term Islamic feminism invites us to consider what it means to have a difficult double commitment, on the one hand to a faith position, and on the other hand to women's rights both inside the home and outside."[38] I would contend that implicit in this statement of a "difficult double commitment" is an acceptance of the assumption that Islam and women's rights belong to essentially different domains and that Muslim women bring them together strategically as "an act of radical subversion" as part of the "postcolonial women's jockeying for space and power" (as cooke puts it). I would argue that this account runs contrary to the self-definitions of many Muslim feminists who see their feminism as emerging organically out of their faith commitment and whose contestation of gender injustice is more than simply the result of a post-colonial power struggle.

Nonetheless the notion of multiple critique is useful in capturing the complexity of Muslim women's positioning. Most Muslim women reject those feminist discourses that have been implicated and continue to be implicated in attacking Islam and Muslim culture. However, in relationship to our own faith communities, we are positioned simultaneously as critics of the assumptions of male normativity, and as female believers who present an alternative way of understanding and approaching gender relations in Islam.

Among the most revolutionary elements in the works of Islamic feminism is the view that feminist commitment is integral to Islam and responsive to the core Qur'anic call to justice. The primary incentives for some feminist Muslim scholarship is the reality that there is dissonance between the ideals of Islam which are premised on an ontology of radical human equality and the fact that in varying social contexts Muslim women experience injustice in the name of religion.[39] Some look at the way in which Islamic teachings are subject to social contexts and argue that patriarchal interpretations are the result of the exclusively male constitution of much of institutional Islam.[40] Others acknowledge the tension between patriarchy and egalitarianism in the Islamic legacy but argue for the primacy of egalitarianism as representative of the spiritual and ethical ideals of Islam, ideals that need to be constantly worked towards.[41]

There is a significant group of Muslim scholars whose feminist work appears to be permeated with strong spiritual and religious bases. American feminist scholar Elizabeth Fernea also demonstrates this point on the basis of interviewing Muslim women in various parts of the world:

> Islamic belief is also the stated basis of most behavior I felt to be feminist ... In Egypt, Kuwait, Turkey and the U.S., Islamic women begin with the assumption that the possibility for equality already exists in the Qur'an itself. The problem as they see it is malpractice, or misunderstanding of the sacred text. For these Muslim women, the first goal of a feminist movement is to re-understand and evaluate the sacred text and for women to be involved in the process, which historically has been reserved for men.[42]

Some Muslim women scholars have argued that while women indeed have multiple identities which are contingent on specific contextual realities, among many Muslim women there is an overarching sense that a belief in Islam provides a core existential ground for one's way of understanding the world, one's self, and the ultimate purpose of human life.[43] This then suggests that for some Muslim feminists Islam is not one among many equally weighted identities but rather a primary source of understanding one's very being in the world. This does not, however, imply that all Muslim women's understandings of Islam are the same or that there is a monolithic Islamic identity that stands unaffected by other social, political, and cultural factors. Indeed the manner in which Islam is understood and experienced in diverse contexts is mediated by numerous factors, including national, ethnic, economic, and cultural forces. However, the essential components of belief and one's existential relationship to God and the world, the five pillars of Islam, are significantly shared dimensions of how Muslims experience their existence, cosmology, and eschatology.

Islamic scholar Maysam Faruqi points out that while many other dimensions of identity like race or gender are not necessarily subject to one's own choice, being Muslim in the world is a choice that implies a particular constellations of theological, spiritual, and religious beliefs.[44] In analyzing this paradigmatic assertion one may argue that this Muslim woman sees her religious identity as a primary identity which is then mediated by a number of secondary identities, including gender, nationality, ethnicity, and class.

Whether Muslim women see their religious identities as core to their self-definition or not, I believe that it is accurate to suggest that Muslim feminists are committed to

> questioning Islamic epistemology as an expansion of their faith position and not a rejection of it ... and offer[ing] a critique of some aspect of Islamic history or hermeneutics, and [that] they do so with and or on behalf of all Muslim women and their right to enjoy with men full participation in a just community.[45]

SCHOLARSHIP AND ACTIVISM

There is currently a vibrant presence of Muslim women scholars and activists in various Muslim communities around the world. In reviewing varying types of Muslim women's gender activism in different parts of the world, feminist scholar Margot Badran has identified different modes of feminist expression among Muslim women. These are, firstly, various types of *feminist writing* from scholarship to fiction; secondly, *everyday activism*, including initiatives in social services, education, and professions; and thirdly, organized *movement activism*, including political and even confrontational movements for women's emancipation.[46]

Particularly within the last few decades, Muslim women are engaging some of the primary sources of the religious legacy, namely the Qur'an and *Sunnah*, not only individually but also as a political initiative. Many of these scholars are deeply committed to their faith and religion and are invested in redressing the male bias of the inherited legacy. Here one finds radical and illuminating understandings of Qur'an, Islamic law, theology, and mysticism from the perspective of women. For example, in contemporary Iran, there is a plethora of emerging women's discourse on Islamic law and Qur'anic exegesis which contests women's marginalization in society. This has occurred most explicitly in the popular women's journal *Zanaan*, where feminist scholars have explicitly contested and decentered the male clerics from the domain of interpretation and have advocated the reading of the Qur'an as a woman.[47]

Similarly, African-American scholar Amina Wadud has authored a book that has gained international popularity: *Qur'an and Women: Rereading the Sacred Text from a Woman's Perspective.*[48] This was published first in Malaysia and has since been translated into Indonesian, Turkish, and Arabic and used as a formative text in approaching gender justice in Islam. Fatima Mernissi, a Morrocan sociologist, has provided a feminist detective work on retrieving the history of powerful women in Islamic history in her *The Forgotten Queens of Islam.*[49] In another work, *The Veil and the Male Elite*, Mernissi has re-visited authoritative *hadith* regarding the Prophet and the early Companions.[50] Using traditional Islamic *hadith* methodology she illustrates that some of the misogynist traditions are inauthentic and have been fabricated to serve the interests of a particular narrator and respond to historical exigencies. In the book *Women and Gender in Islam*, Egyptian historian Leila Ahmed focuses on the ways in which gender discourses evolved historically within the formative Muslim communities and examines how both patriarchal and egalitarian gender discourses have since developed within some Muslim societies.

On the ground, organizations like *Sisters in Islam*, based in Malaysia, have provided a critique of wife battery from an Islamic perspective and have lobbied for stronger penalties for male offenders. They have also been actively involved in educational and consciousness-raising activities among Malaysian women. In South Africa, the *Muslim Youth Movement* and the *Call of Islam* have promoted women's leadership, including *inter alia* questions of sermon giving, mosque attendance campaigns, and gender egalitarian reformulation of Muslim personal law. In the United States, *Karamah* (Muslim Women Lawyers for Human Rights), whose members have varying levels of expertise in both Islamic and American law, has worked to protect Muslim women from sexist applications of Islamic law while simultaneously working to protect the civil rights of Muslim Americans.[51] These are but a few examples of the gender activism and feminist work of different groups of Muslim women.

I maintain that activities emerging from a commitment to the imperative of gender justice in Islam are crucial to the articulation of genuinely engaged and transformative Islamic feminisms. Rejecting colonial feminist representations of Muslim women as the "victimized" and voiceless "other," Muslim women are contributing to the re-definition of feminist discourse that includes the authentic self-representations of heterogeneous groups of women. This approach is one that embraces the particularity of context and the multiple identities of women. By definition it makes salient the question of religious identity in the experience of Muslim women. It allows for the collusion of feminist discourse with Muslim women's articulation of their engagement with gender issues. It also creates the space for meaningful dialogue and "horizontal comradeship" between groups of Muslim women and women from other religio-cultural contexts. Islamic feminism and the broader gender activism of Muslim women are flowering in many parts of the Muslim world. In the last analysis, Islamic feminism is, in my view, one of the most engaged contemporary responses to the core Qur'anic injunction for social justice of our time.

ENDNOTES

*An earlier version of this essay appeared as "Islam, Feminisms and the Politics of Representation," in *The End of Liberation? Liberation in the End! Feminist Theory, Feminist Theology and Their Political Implications*, ed. Charlotte Methuen and Angela Berlis (Leuven: Peeters, 2002).

1. In South Africa, the resistance of Muslim activists to patriarchy and sexism in their religious communities has been embraced as the "gender jihad."
2. For a discussion on the varying realities of Muslim women from different parts of the world see Azizah Al-Hibri, "Islamic Law," in *A Companion to Feminist Philosophy*, ed. Alison M. Jaggar and Iris M. Young (Cambridge, MA and Oxford: Blackwell, 1998), 541–9.
3. Qur'anic scholar Amina Wadud describes feminism as the "radical notion that women are human beings." See the preface to the second edition of *Qur'an and Women: Rereading the Sacred Text from a Woman's Perspective* (New York and Oxford: Oxford University Press, 1999).
4. Clearly neither "the Muslim world" nor "the West" exists as homogeneous or discrete entities. I am simply using them as descriptive categories to the extent that they reflect perceptions of shared identity among respective communities.
5. For an incisive analysis of Islam and post-colonial relations of power see Majid Anouar, *Unveiling Tradition, Postcolonial Islam in a Polycentric World* (Durham, NC: Duke University Press, 2000).
6. For a discussion of the politics of gender and identity see Lila Abu-Lughod (ed.), *Remaking Women: Feminism and Modernity in the Middle East* (Princeton: Princeton University Press, 1998).
7. Gisela Webb, "Teaching Islam as a World Religion to Undergraduates: Challenges and Opportunities in the Age of Globalization and Multiculturalism," *Religion and Education*, 25:(1–2), 1998, 31.
8. Akbar S. Ahmed, *Postmodernism and Islam: Predicament and Promise* (London: Routledge, 1992).
9. Huntington's argument regarding the inherently conflicting relations between Islamic and Western civilizations was first articulated in his article "The Clash of Civilizations," *Foreign Affairs*, Summer 1993, 22–49. Huntington's thesis – while no doubt influential – has been severely criticized by a host of anthropologists, political scientists, historians, and others. For one insightful example, see Roy Mottahedeh, "Clash of Civilizations: An Islamicist's Critique," *Harvard Middle Eastern and Islamic Review*, 2(2), 1996, 1–26.
10. Azza M. Karam, *Women, Islamisms and the State* (New York: St Martin's Press; Basingstoke: MacMillan, 1998), 5–6.
11. For a discussion of this type of apologia see Barbara Stowasser's examination of Shaykh Sha'rawi's work in Barbara Stowasser, *The Islamic Impulse* (London: Croom Helm, 1987).
12. Margot Badran, *Feminists, Islam and the Nation* (Princeton: Princeton University Press, 1995), 24.
13. Leila Ahmed, *Women and Gender in Islam: Historical Roots of a Modern Debate* (New Haven: Yale University Press, 1992), 153.
14. A detailed account and rich analysis of the relationship between the IAW and Arab feminists is offered by Margot Badran, *Feminists, Islam and the Nation* (Princeton: Princeton University Press, 1995).

15. Ibid., 33.
16. Ibid., 246.
17. For such critiques see the following collections: Cherríe Moraga and Gloria Anzaldúa (eds), *This Bridge Called My Back: Writings by Radical Women of Color* (Watertown, MA: Persephone Press, 1981); Chandra Mohanty (ed.), *Third World Women and the Politics of Feminism* (Bloomington: Indiana University Press 1991).
18. Second-wave Western feminism began in the 1960s and was characterized by the formation of active networks of women's groups in the U.S.A. and parts of Europe. Its inception is often dated from the publication of Betty Friedan's *The Feminine Mystique* (New York: Norton, 1963) in America. While there was a diversity of perspectives within second-wave feminism, including liberal, radical, and socialist/Marxist approaches, much of this work presumed a universal womanhood without attending to differences of race, culture, First World / Third World locations, etc. See Rosemarie Tong, *Feminist Thought: A More Comprehensive Introduction* (Boulder: Westview Press, 1998) for greater details on the different strands of second-wave feminism.
19. There is clearly no singular Third World woman or Third World situation. The terms are used to describe the relationships of structural domination between First and Third World peoples while fully recognizing the diversity of experiences and realities among different groups of Third World people. "Third World women" has also been used interchangeably with the description "women of color." For a more extensive discussion of defining "Third World feminism," see Chandra Mohanty, "Cartographies of Struggle: Third World Women and the Politics of Feminism," in *Third World Women*, 1–47.
20. See Valerie Amos and Pratibha Parmar, "Challenging Imperial Feminism," *Feminist Review*, 17, 1984, 3–19; Chandra Mohanty, "Under Western Eyes: Feminist Scholarship and Colonial Discourse," in *Third World Women*, 51–80.
21. A classic example of this approach in second-wave feminism is reflected in Betty Friedan's *The Feminine Mystique*, in which the plight of women is described as the boredom and unfulfillment of being mere housewives who were put on a false pedestal and not integrated into the public sphere of work. In *Feminist theory: From Margin to Center* (Boston: South End Press, 1984), 2, African-American scholar bell hooks points out that the "generic" woman described by Friedan does not remotely represent women of color or poor and working class women, who often had to work "as maids, as babysitters, as factory workers, as clerks, or as prostitutes and did not belong to the leisure class of housewife." Similarly, black South African women were often political activists, breadwinners, and heads of households in black townships where men were absent because of the politico-economic apartheid structures of the migrant labor system in South Africa, which caused many black men to leave their household in the search for employment. The effects of migrant labor included disintegrated black families, urban prostitution, and a gender imbalance between rural and urban areas. Black women often became the heads of single-parent families and were left alone to face the rigors of earning an income, raising children, and maintaining a home, often under economically and socially debilitating circumstances.
22. Much of the critical and vigilant work among Western feminists addressing issues of representation, difference, and authority emerged in the latter part of the 1980s and 1990s. This includes works such as Elizabeth Spelman, *Inessential Women, Problems of Exclusion in Feminist Thought* (London: Women's Press, 1990); Nancie Caraway, *Segregated Sisterhood* (Knoxville: University of Tennessee Press, 1991); and Anne Russo, "We Cannot Live without Our Lives: White Women, Antiracism and Feminism," in *Third World Women*, ed. Mohanty, 297–313. This type of non-hierarchical scholarship was limited and marginal during the formative period of second-wave Western feminism.
23. For a broader discussion of such critiques in relation to other Third World women see Mohanty, "Under Western Eyes," 51–69.
24. Ibid., 56.
25. Ibid., 57

26. See Barbara Stowasser's comprehensive discussion on the term and concept of *hijab* in her article "The *Hijab*: How a Curtain Became an Institution and a Cultural Symbol," in *Humanism, Culture and Language In the Near East: Studies in honor of Georg Krotkoff*, ed. Asma Afsaruddin (Winona Lake, IN: Eisenbrauns, 1997), 87–104.
27. Leila Ahmed, *Women and Gender in Islam*, 164.
28. Fadwa El Guindi, "Veiling Intifah with Muslim Ethic," *Social Problems*, 28, 1981, 465.
29. Even this is not universal, since there is evidence that the Egyptian fashion industry has responded to women who are interested in a more fashion conscious mode of *hijab*. Accordingly, the industry has marketed all kinds of head coverings, which include berets and pillbox hats to be worn over the scarf. See Stowasser, "The *Hijab*," 87–104.
30. See Ziba Mir-Hosseini, *Islam and Gender: The Religious Debate in Contemporary Iran* (Princeton: Princeton University Press, 1999), 7.
31. Linda L. Lindsey, *Gender Roles: A Sociological Approach* (Upper Saddle River, NJ: Prentice Hall, 1997).
32. Chandra Mohanty, "Cartographies of Struggle: Third World Women and the Politics of Feminism," in *Third World Women*, 4
33. Ibid., 7.
34. See Desirée Lewis, "Feminisms in South Africa," *Women's Studies International Forum*, 16, 1993, 538.
35. Azza Karam, "Feminisms and Islamisms in Egypt: Between Globalization and Postmodernism," in *Gender and Global Restructuring*, ed. Marianne March and Anne S. Runyan (London: Routledge, 2000), 207, warns, however, that even within this approach there are researchers who duplicate the older ideological biases of focusing on investigating the specificities of Muslim women's oppression rather than looking at newer ways to study the specificities of women's empowerment strategies.
36. For a discussion on different types of feminisms among Muslim women see Azza Karam, *Women, Islamism, and the State* (New York: St Martins Press, 1998).
37. miriam cooke, *Women Claim Islam* (New York: Routledge, 2000).
38. Ibid., 59.
39. See the collection edited by Azizah Al-Hibri: "Women in Islam," *Women's Studies International Forum*, 5(2), 1982.
40. See, for instance, Riffat Hassan, "Equal before Allah? Woman–Man Equality in the Islamic Tradition," *Harvard Divinity Bulletin*, 17(2), 1987, 2–14, and Amina Wadud, *Qur'an and Women: Rereading the Sacred Text from a Woman's Perspective* (New York: Oxford University Press, 1999).
41. See, for instance, Leila Ahmed, *Women and Gender in Islam*, and Fatima Mernissi, *The Veil and the Male Elite* (New York: Addison Wesley, 1991).
42. Elizabeth Fernea, *In Search of Islamic Feminism: One Woman's Global Journey* (New York: Doubleday, 1998), 416.
43. For discussions by Muslim women scholars on the centrality of Islam in their advocacy of gender justice and the rejection of secularist biases in some contemporary forms of feminism, see interviews with Azizah Al-Hibri, Amina Wadud, and Heba Rauf Ezzat in Fernea, *In Search of Islamic Feminism*, and Maysum Faruqi, "Women's Self-Identity in the Qur'an and Islamic Law," in *Windows of Faith: Muslim Women Scholar-Activists in North America*, ed. Gisela Webb (Syracuse, NY: Syracuse University Press, 2000), 72–101. Webb's volume is one of the best contemporary collections of essays by Muslim women scholars.
44. Maysam Faruqi, "Women's Self-Identity in the Qur'an and Islamic Law," *Windows of Faith*, ed. Webb, 74.
45. miriam cooke, *Women Claim Islam*, 61.
46. Margot Badran, "Feminism," in The *Oxford Encyclopedia of the Modern Islamic World*, ed. John Esposito (New York: Oxford University Press, 1995).
47. For a detailed discussion of the politics surrounding the feminist exegesis that takes place in *Zanaan* see Ziba Mir-Hosseini, *Islam and Gender: The Religious Debate in Contemporary Iran* (Princeton: Princeton University Press, 1999).

48. Amina Wadud has contributed another of the essays to this volume, titled "American Muslim Identity: Race and Ethnicity in Progressive Islam."

49. Fatima Mernissi, *The Forgotten Queens of Islam,* trans. Mary Jo Lakeland (Minneapolis: University of Minnesota Press, 1993).

50. Fatima Mernissi, *The Veil and the Male Elite* (Bloomington: Indiana University Press, 1987).

51. *Karamah* has a useful web site, which serves as a resource for many Muslim women in North America: http://www.karamah.org.

7

PROGRESSIVE MUSLIMS AND ISLAMIC JURISPRUDENCE: THE NECESSITY FOR CRITICAL ENGAGEMENT WITH MARRIAGE AND DIVORCE LAW[1]

Kecia Ali

Progressive Muslims have a difficult relationship with Islamic law. Many progressive Muslims have undertaken alternative close readings of the Qur'an, or have delved deeply into ethical and mystical aspects of Islam to find teachings that can be used as a cornerstone of a progressive Islamic interpretation. But we have been reluctant to enter into serious conversations about Islamic law, which is generally seen as the realm of more conservative scholars. Partially as a result of this hesitancy, discussions of Islamic law today tend to reflect only different degrees of conservatism and fundamentalism. Debates over implementing *Shari'ah* revolve around issues like the stoning of adulterers or amputating the hands of thieves. For those living in the Muslim world, negotiations with Islamic law as it is enforced through personal status codes are a practical necessity. Muslims who live in the West, however, encounter Islamic law only to the extent that we choose to apply it in our personal dealings. For many, that means most especially in matters of family. Paradoxically for progressive Muslims, this is the arena where traditional Islamic law is thought to be most conservative.

Despite the fact that Muslim marriage is not generally thought of as a progressive institution, even progressive Muslims generally want to get married. We do not want our relationships to be bound, however, by the strictly hierarchical rules that we assume to be enshrined in Islamic law. A few Muslims in the West simply leave aside Islamic law in personal matters, choosing to abide exclusively by secular laws, which tend to be more egalitarian. These couples work to keep the spirit of Qur'anic proclamations on the nature of marriage alive in their relationships, but do not consider its legal pronouncements literally applicable. Other progressive Muslims, perhaps most, follow the key elements of classical marriage in the wedding, but may reduce the dower to a symbolic amount due to discomfort with its "commercial" connotations. There is an implicit understanding, in these unions, that traditional legal rules – such as those allowing the husband to take additional wives or to forbid his wife from leaving the marital home without permission – will not govern the spouses. Both of these approaches are based on an understanding of Islamic marriage law as inherently biased against women; therefore, it is avoided or observed primarily in the breach. Islamic law, in this view, does not accurately embody the ideals of Islam regarding relations between spouses, which are mutuality, respect, and kindness. A third stance, however, calls for selective appropriation of provisions of classical law, allowing for the spouses to customize their marriage contract through the inclusion of numerous conditions, generally favoring the wife, that modify traditionally accepted rules for spouses' marital rights.

Proponents of this approach argue that, in fact, women are guaranteed numerous marital rights by Islamic law, some of which surpass rights granted by secular Western laws; women simply need to learn how to protect themselves by invoking them. The lawyer Azizah al-Hibri is the most prominent, though by no means the only, advocate for this view, which has gained widespread attention in recent years and has been adopted by many Muslim women's organizations. It is also quickly becoming conventional wisdom among some non-Muslim feminists concerned about avoiding orientalist stereotypes surrounding "women's status" in Islam.[2]

Al-Hibri was recently featured in "Talk of the Town" in *The New Yorker*. There she explained that women have rights in Islamic law that are often unknown and unutilized, with the right to make stipulations in marriage contracts primary among them. According to the article,

> A woman can secure her right to work outside the home at any job she likes; she can reassert her right to have her husband support her financially, even if she has a job or is independently wealthy; she can keep her finances separate from his and invest them wherever she wishes; she can specify the sum of money she expects to receive should the marriage end in divorce or should she be widowed; she can negotiate the right to divorce her husband at will, should he, for example, take another wife; [and] she can reserve the right not to cook, to clean, or to nurse her own children.[3]

This picture does not resemble at all the laws governing most Muslim women's marriages today. If implemented, however, such rights would seem to guarantee women a life of ease and comfort. Further, to the extent that these rights can be supported by opinions from texts of classical jurisprudence, they are more likely to achieve acceptance than attempts to rework marriage law entirely, since they can claim an "authentic" Islamic pedigree.

In this essay, I will argue that this approach misses the forest for the trees. While its adherents may or may not be right about any particular contractual stipulation[4] (and often they significantly overstate the extent to which specific conditions are enforceable), they fail to address the basic parameters of the marriage contract itself and the assumptions it is based on. By focusing on isolated rights without paying attention to how they are embedded in a system of interdependent spousal obligations, al-Hibri and other advocates for women's legal rights implicitly accept the basic structure of the marriage contract as understood by Muslim jurists to be the divinely sanctioned norm for Islamic marriage. However, this framework is not God-given but rather was developed by men working at a particular time and place, governed by certain assumptions. Before we simply accept the traditional legal understanding of marriage and move to modify its practice with conditions attached to marriage contracts, its basic premises must be subjected to sustained analysis and careful critique.

One purpose of this essay is to present such an analysis of the traditional jurisprudential understanding of marriage. I will demonstrate, through an exposition of the views of early Sunni jurists, that the overall framework of the marriage contract is predicated on a type of ownership (*milk*) granted to the husband over the wife in exchange for dower payment, which makes sexual intercourse between them lawful. Further, the major spousal right established by the contract is the wife's sexual availability in exchange for which she is supported by her husband. This basic claim, which would have been accepted without controversy as an accurate portrayal of the legal dimensions of marriage by virtually any pre-modern Muslim jurist, is unthinkable today for the majority of Muslims, including those who write about Islamic law. This portrait of how traditional jurists conceived of marriage is a necessary precursor to the evaluation of contemporary discourses on marriage in Islamic law that I undertake in the second half of this essay.

I will address two types of modern discourses on Islamic law: neo-conservative and feminist-apologist. Both attempt to appropriate the authority of traditional Islamic law through various means, in each case upholding some of its substantive doctrines while setting others aside. Neo-conservative authors suggest that the rationale for men's and women's differing marital rights and duties is the natural difference between husbands and wives that results from a divinely ordained "complementarity" of males and females. Though presenting their views as simply restatements of traditional law, these authorities allow some rights previously granted to women to lapse, since they do not make sense as part of the new framework.

Feminist and reformist approaches that take women's rights and needs as their main concern make different interpretive moves from those of the neo-conservatives. In some cases, they reject juristic interpretations and turn instead to the Qur'an and, to a lesser extent, the *hadith* collections as source of legal guidance. In this essay, though, I am concerned with the way these discourses focus on particular substantive rules of jurisprudence. Claiming back rights that have recently gone unnoticed or even been denied outright, those working from this perspective attempt to promote and defend wives' rights by appeal to traditional legal authority. In doing so, however, they provide new justifications and interpretations for these rights that do not accurately reflect their original place in a system of spousal rights and obligations.

In my view, neither contemporary approach profiled here accurately or thoroughly engages with traditional jurisprudence. To do so would be to acknowledge that traditional Islamic legal understandings of marriage and divorce are unacceptable from a modern perspective. A serious analysis of traditional jurisprudential logic leads me to the conclusion that a new jurisprudence is required. It cannot be achieved piecemeal, or through strategies of patching together acceptable rules from different schools. Nor can it be sidestepped by an exclusive focus on scripture. There is no getting around law; we must understand it, then work to replace it. This essay is a preliminary step in the direction of comprehension.

A significant amount has been written in the last decades on Muslim men's and women's marital rights and duties, from a variety of perspectives. Despite the diversity of views, there is a trait common to most of this literature: little attempt is made to distinguish between types of norms and sources of authority. When authors make claims about what rights "Islamic law" (or sometimes simply "Islam") grants to spouses, they might mean Qur'an, or prophetic tradition, or the classical jurisprudence of one or more legal schools, or even the modern, codified laws of a particular Muslim country.[5] If it is traditional jurisprudence that is meant, seldom is it specified whether the text is from the fourth/tenth century or from the fourteenth/twentieth century, or whether the view presented is the majority view or a minority one, perhaps held by only few jurists. Claims that "some jurists" or "many jurists" held a particular view are especially difficult to investigate. This collapsing of different discourses into the category "Islamic law" allows one to claim a broad authority for one's own view without needing to specify the source for that authority. By remaining so vague, it also prevents others from critiquing the claims and being able to weigh independently how authoritative they wish to consider a particular doctrine to be. And shifting from one set of sources to another – taking a majority view from classical Sunni jurisprudence when it suits, turning to the Qur'an when it doesn't, and drawing from modern statutory reforms when necessary – leaves one open to charges of inconsistency.

This essay will use Sunni[6] legal texts from the third century *hijri* / ninth century CE to illuminate how marriage was understood contractually in traditional Islamic jurisprudence.[7] My choice of this period requires a note of explanation. While the following centuries produced important texts – the classical works from the fourth/tenth to the sixth/twelfth century are particularly significant[8] – the literature from the formative period of the third/ninth century is a manageable body of work, making it possible to adequately survey the primary texts themselves. Given the importance of the issues under consideration, I think it is important to have a solid, thorough comparative approach, rather than using selected passages from a variety of texts from different centuries and different schools, or relying on modern summaries of earlier doctrine which may misrepresent crucial positions. That said, I think my general characterization of the marriage contract and its associated rights and duties applies to later Sunni texts as well, though in a few minor respects later classical doctrines may differ in their particulars from those described here.

I want to be absolutely clear to avoid any misunderstandings: I am not making any argument as to what Islamic marriage ideally should be or what the Qur'an or *Sunnah* says about spouses' rights. Nor should my portrait of legal doctrine be taken as a description of Muslim women's lives, either historical or contemporary.[9] When I state that Islamic jurisprudence grants husbands a type of ownership over their wives, I do not mean that 'Islam' sanctions this, that God intends it, that the Qur'an requires it, or that the Prophet approved it. Rather, I intend to characterize the system of gendered rights and obligations developed by the jurists whose works I am discussing.

One basic fact is very important to keep in mind throughout: there is not now, nor has there ever been, a single, unitary Islamic law. Though Muslims agree that the *Shari'ah* – God's law for humanity – is complete, infallible, and universal, it cannot be known directly but only through the work of human interpreters. Historically, these interpreters have been the jurists. Their attempts to understand, develop, and implement *Shari'ah* are human, imperfect, and shaped by the constraints of their specific historical contexts. This boundary between revealed law (*Shari'ah*) and jurisprudence (called *fiqh* in Arabic, which means "understanding" or "comprehension") has been obscured in the modern period as nations have adopted the term *Shari'ah* to describe their legal codes. Even before the modern period, the human element in the creation of legal rules was often overlooked, particularly by non-specialists. Even among the jurists, conformity with school doctrine (*taqlid*) became important, and the particular rules themselves took on an air of inevitability. However, jurists themselves always recognized that it was their efforts that were central; the term *ijtihad*, used to refer to independent legal reasoning, refers to *striving* for results not the attainment of correct answers. The jurists knew of significant differences between the schools; there is a vital literature of dispute and polemic. While one finds, at times, disparaging remarks about legal doctrines held by other groups of jurists, one also frequently finds a disclaimer, most often after the expression of a ruling on which there is significant disagreement. The jurists state simply, "And God knows best." There can be no clearer recognition of the inability of human reason to fully comprehend and implement God's revealed law.[10]

FORMATION OF ISLAMIC LAW: SOURCES, METHODS, AND JURISTIC DISAGREEMENT

The Qur'an was revealed beginning in the year 610 CE; its revelation continued until Muhammad's death in 632. In addition to general pronouncements on the nature of the relationship that should exist between spouses – love and tranquillity, good conduct – the Qur'an addressed a number of specific issues relating to marriage and divorce. These included dower, a payment from the husband to the wife at the time of marriage; polygamy; the waiting period to be observed following the end of a marriage to determine if the wife was pregnant; and various types of divorce including unilateral repudiation and divorce for compensation. Muhammad also adjudicated in numerous disputes himself, establishing precedents separate from, and sometimes in tension with, the words of the Qur'an.[11] In the decades following his death, the Prophet's Companions gave *ad hoc* decisions in cases brought to their attention. Some cases were decided in accordance with what a Companion recalled to have been Muhammad's practice in similar situations; others were based on what they expected he would have done in such a circumstance; others simply on a sense of community norms. Sometimes, Companions drew on the Qur'an as support for their decisions, though they differed on the proper understanding of numerous passages.

In later generations, into the eighth century, a process of recording these decisions and various other types of historical accounts from and about Muhammad and his Companions was underway. It eventually resulted in the compilation of books of traditions (*athar, ahadith*), the most famous of which was the *Sahih Bukhari*, completed in the ninth century. At the same time these traditions were being collected, a more systematic effort to explore legal issues was undertaken by jurists. Schools of law (*madhahib*, sing. *madhhab*) formed, with a base of shared doctrine and methodology, though jurists within each school sometimes diverged from the majority opinion on a given topic.[12] Today, these schools survive as four Sunni schools (the Maliki, Hanafi, Shafi'i, and Hanbali) as well as one primary and several smaller Shi'i schools.

The legal schools of the formative period differed substantially on a number of issues related to marriage and divorce: how far a father's right to marry off his virgin daughter without her consent extended; whether an adult woman had the right to contract her own marriage; whether three repudiations pronounced at once took effect together or only counted as one divorce; whether a minimum dower should be set; whether a woman had the right to contractually stipulate monogamy or that her husband could not take her away from her hometown; and whether a woman could stipulate the right to divorce her husband under certain circumstances. One should not assume that some schools held a "liberal" position and others a more "restrictive" one with regard to women's rights. The Hanafi school, which held that adult women were free to contract their own marriages without needing a male representative (*wali*) to act on their behalf, also held that a woman could not obtain a divorce from an unwilling husband on any grounds except total impotence or possibly leprosy, and even then only so long as the marriage had not been consummated.[13] The Maliki school provided the most extensive grounds for a woman to seek divorce, including failure to support and the broad category of "harm" (*darar*, also "cruelty").

Nonetheless, its jurists permitted a father to marry off his never-married daughter against her wishes even if she were forty and independently wealthy. Only the Hanbalis held that there were consequences if a husband violated his contractual stipulation not to move his wife from her hometown or to take another wife; other schools considered these conditions meaningless and unenforceable.

Thus, it is clear that there were significant – and for actual women, quite real – implications to being under the jurisdiction of one legal school or another; the differences between the schools were not, as some have asserted, merely in matters of detail.[14] Nonetheless, there was indeed a shared understanding of the contractual relationship of marriage that prevailed at that time. This common view was based, in large part, on cultural assumptions shared by the jurists as a result of their social location in a particular and, according to Leila Ahmed, particularly patriarchal environment. She has shown that the 'formation of the core discourses of Islam' including jurisprudence took place in an era of hierarchy, social stratification, and the widespread practice of slavery. One characteristic of this environment was the "easy access" of elite men to slave women. She argues that "for elite men in particular, the distinction between concubine, woman for sexual use, and object must inevitably have blurred."[15]

Indeed, the jurists were influenced in their elaboration of a system of marital rights and obligations by the norms governing slavery. Slavery and particularly slave-concubinage were normal and accepted facets of social life, and it was assumed by jurists of the ninth century that one could usefully draw analogies between marriage and slavery, husbands and masters, wives and slaves. At its most basic, the jurists shared a view of marriage that considered it to transfer to the husband, in exchange for the payment of dower, a type of ownership (*milk*) over his wife, and more particularly over her sexual organ (*farj, bud*'). As evidence presented below will show, it was this ownership, while distinct from the outright ownership of another's physical body in slavery, that legitimized sexual intercourse between husband and wife. It also gave the husband the unilateral right to terminate the marital relationship at any time, by repudiating his wife for any, or no, reason. As the jurists frequently noted, this was analogous to the master's freedom to manumit a slave at any time.

Although marriage contained an element of ownership, this ownership was established by a contract that also gave rise to other rights and obligations between the spouses. These rights were interdependent – a wife's rights were obligations upon her husband and vice versa – and strictly differentiated by gender. A wife's most important marital duty was sexual availability, in exchange for which she was to be supported by her husband.[16] The primacy of, and linkage between, these particular rights is clearly illustrated in a passage from the *Umm*, the main Shafi'i work of the period: "Al-Shafi'i said: It is among her rights due from him that he support her, and among his rights to derive pleasure from her [*istimta'a minha*]."[17]

The wife's obligation to be available to her husband was set apart from other types of domestic duties. Maliki, Hanafi, and Shafi'i jurists emphatically denied any wifely duty to perform housework. (Ibn Hanbal's responsa do not discuss this topic.) She need not even cook for herself, let alone her husband. The words of the third-century Hanafi jurist Ahmad b. 'Umar al-Khassaf demonstrate this. He was asked, "What if she doesn't have a servant and her husband supports her, must she bake bread and labor to prepare [food] for herself?" He replied, "If she says, I won't do it, she is not compelled to. Rather, his claim on her is her making herself available for her husband [*tamkin al-nafs min al-zawj*], not for these tasks."[18] Al-Khassaf goes on to contrast the wife's situation to that of a servant, who, if she refuses to perform these services, is not due support and may be turned out of the house. Al-Khassaf was not alone in this view; rather, he was representative. Service is excluded from a wife's duties in the *Mudawwana* in an unequivocal way: "I said: Must a woman serve herself or perform household service or not according to Malik? He said: She need not serve herself or perform any household service."[19] Al-Shafi'i suggested that whether or not a husband had to support a servant for his wife depended on whether or not "someone like her" was accustomed to serving herself; however, he was also adamant that even a woman who did not have a personal servant should be provided with prepared food and someone to bring her water so that she need not go out to collect it.[20] In all of these cases, the wife's performance of household duties is not expected, and is certainly not a condition of her support. Her maintenance is due, instead, as a result of her availability to her husband for sexual enjoyment.

The husband's right to derive pleasure from his wife, in exchange for his support of her, led the jurists to grant him total control over her mobility. A man could restrict his wife's movements in order to keep her available to himself, including forbidding her to go to the mosque or to visit her parents. The *Mukhtasar* of Shafi'i jurist al-Muzani notes that a woman's husband even had the legal right to forbid her to attend the funerals of her parents or her children, though the jurist preferred that he not do so; jurists from other schools held similar views.[21] A woman who left the house without permission would be guilty of *nushuz*[22] – a term variously translated as "recalcitrance," "disobedience," or "rebellion." The Hanafis and Shafi'is agreed that she would lose her right to support so long as she remained unavailable to her husband, while the Malikis and Hanbalis do not directly discuss the suspension of a wife's maintenance for *nushuz*.[23]

For the Shafi'is, a wife's sexual refusal while remaining at home also constituted *nushuz* and was grounds for suspension of maintenance. For the Hanafis, a wife's sexual refusal was not grounds for loss of maintenance. However, this was because she was still considered "available" to her husband; he was entitled to force her to have intercourse.

> If she is in his house but she withholds herself from him is maintenance
> due to her from him? It is due ... Is it lawful for the husband to have sex

with her against her will …? It is lawful, because she is a wrongdoer [*zalima*].[24]

These passages, in addition to illustrating the link between maintenance and a wife's sexual duties to her husband, make clear the extent of a man's sexual rights over his wife according to the early jurists.

Though the wife had a duty of sexual availability, she did not have a right to sex. Though today it is almost a cliché that Islam recognizes women's sexuality,[25] the legal reality in the early texts is that women's rights to sex in marriage were virtually nonexistent. In all four Sunni schools, a woman could have her marriage dissolved for impotence if the husband proved unable to consummate the marriage; she had to complain to a judge then wait for a year. In one other case, if the husband took a vow to abstain completely from sex with her for a period of more than four months (*ila'*), she could seek to have the marriage judicially dissolved on that basis if her husband continued to abstain after four months had passed according to jurists from the Maliki, Shafi'i, and Hanbali schools. (The Hanafis considered a vow of forswearing to result in automatic divorce if not broken or expiated during the four months.)

However, after consummation, simple abstinence without a vow was not grounds for divorce in any of the four schools. Ibn Hanbal, when asked about a man who had intercourse with his wife one time, declared, "He is not impotent, and the couple are not separated. I hold this opinion even if he does not have intercourse with her again, and she has no right to request him to."[26] The Maliki texts record the same position, as in this passage from the *Muwatta'*:

> Yahya related to me from Malik from Ibn Shihab from Sa'id ibn al-Musayyab that he used to say, "Whoever marries a woman and is not able to touch (i.e., have intercourse with) her, a deadline of one year is set for him. If he touches her, [fine], and if not, they are separated."… Malik said, "However, someone who has touched his wife then avoids her (*i'tarada 'anha*) I have not heard that there is a deadline set for him or that they are separated."[27]

In the *Mudawwana*, Ibn Shihab states simply that "I have not heard [that] anyone [would] separate a man and his wife after he touched her, and that is practice among us."[28] The Maliki jurists do make one exception: if the husband's total abstinence constitutes deliberate or negligent harming of the wife (*darar*) it may be grounds for judicial divorce. (However, if the husband becomes impotent or suffers an injury that renders him incapable of intercourse, the wife has no such right.) This position reflects juristic ambivalence about a wife's right to sex. On the one hand, it is acknowledged that depriving a wife of sex can be harmful to her; on the other hand, while "harm" is grounds for divorce (for the Malikis), lack of sex *per se* is not. This unwillingness to grant wives regular rights to sex is part and parcel of the strict separation between male and female rights that early jurists maintained.

The jurists did, however, grant the wife a right to a portion of her husband's time, subject to certain limitations. A man's duty to divide his time among his wives did not prevent him from traveling or spending a portion of his time with his concubines instead of his wives. A woman had no absolute claim on his time, but rather only claim to equal treatment with her co-wives. A man with more than one wife had a duty to allot his nights between them equally, and very strict rules governed how he was to make up missed turns.[29] Some jurists recommended that he have sex with them all regularly, but despite this, there was no penalty for a husband who did not. Al-Shafi'i voiced the consensus view when he stated that the husband's "division (of time) is based on staying, not having sex." He added – apparently unaware of the irony – that "intercourse is a matter of pleasure, and no one is compelled to it." Of course, he meant that no man is compelled to it; women's continual sexual availability was a condition of their support, and "refusal," again in al-Shafi'i's words, was *nushuz*.[30]

I have shown that if the wife failed in her duty to be sexually available, the jurists agreed that she would lose her right to support. However, in the case where the failure to perform an obligation was the husband's – if he could not support her – the jurists were divided on the consequences. If she could borrow in his name, or liquidate his assets to provide herself with support, she was permitted to do so.[31] However, even if he were unable to support her and had no property upon which she could draw, Hanafi jurists refused to grant her dissolution no matter how long the non-support persisted.[32] In sharp contrast, Shafi'i jurists allowed a wife to seek judicial divorce after as little as three days of non-support.[33] Furthermore, during the three days he was not supporting her, she was allowed to leave the house without her husband's permission in order to obtain what she needed through work. This vast difference in these two schools' treatment of the non-supporting husband (the other Sunni schools fall in the middle of the spectrum between these opposites[34]) illustrates clearly that early Islamic jurisprudence was not monolithic. On topics such as this, some positions were quite favorable to women, and others were anything but. Nonetheless, these specific rules were all embedded within a system of rights and obligations based on the premise of male support for female sexual availability.

CONTEMPORARY DISCOURSES: NEO-CONSERVATIVES

The neo-conservatives are the most prominent faction in debates over the proper legal and social rights of Muslim women today.[35] Their views are represented in publications subsidized by the Saudi government and organizations like the Jamaat-i Islami, and distributed as pamphlets and booklets in mosques and conferences of Muslims everywhere; they are likely to be the most influential group in mosques in the West. Though they often support adherence to Islamic law, they do not have the political zeal of the fundamentalists, nor are they seeking a return to a pristine, original law. Rather, they support the continued enforcement of law as developed by jurists through the classical period and, in its transformed form, by legislatures in Muslim nations. I have lumped together in this group both those with traditional religious education (the *'ulama*) and those non-specialists – far more numerous – whose support for Islamic law is a matter of principle, but whose understanding of the law is derived from contemporary notions. Even though there are some differences between these groups that might warrant separate consideration, I treat them together in part because in both cases the discourses with which Islamic law is explained and justified take on a decidedly non-traditional tone. Neo-conservative authors may believe in adherence to classical legal doctrines (though, as will be seen below, this is not always the case), but they justify them with language that is, more than anything else, Victorian.

This phenomenon can be seen clearly in a treatise on *nushuz* by Saalih ibn Ghanim al-Sadlaan, a professor from the College of Shari'ah at Muhammad ibn Saud Islamic University in Riyadh. While the author is clearly trained in the doctrines and methods of jurisprudence, and his study draws on these sources, he adopts a tone of biological determinism that is alien to classical *fiqh* discourses:

> The woman is naturally conditioned and created by Allah to perform the functions of pregnancy, giving birth, and taking care of the internal affairs of the house. Man, on the other hand has been endowed with more physical strength and clearer thought and he is, therefore, more befitting to be the leader of the household and the one responsible for providing the means of livelihood, protecting the family and bringing about security and continuance in the family.[36]

While the notions of male superiority and headship of the family, and even of men's greater intellectual and physical capacities, are consonant with earlier jurisprudential treatments of spousal rights, the link the author draws between women's capacity for childbearing and their duty to "tak[e] care of the internal affairs of the house" is not merely a restatement of traditional jurisprudential views. Rather, this formulation assimilates early *fiqh* rules about male support to a male breadwinner / female housewife model that is more in keeping with ideas about 1950s America. As the previous section has shown, this model is inaccurate to describe the early jurists' rationale for male support of their wives. In the case of this particular work, despite the adoption of non-traditional rhetoric, the legal doctrines presented regarding its main topic, *nushuz*, are generally in keeping with the provisions of traditional jurisprudence. However, with regard to a woman's responsibility for "taking care of the internal affairs of the house," Al-Sadlaan departs from the established views of early jurists. His brief mention of this point illustrates a much larger phenomenon: in many cases, what is advocated by the neo-conservatives as the "traditional" Islamic view is not in fact historically the position adopted by the early and classical jurists.

The neo-conservative treatment of housework as well as women's work outside the home illustrates clearly the differences between early *fiqh* doctrines and contemporary apologia for them. Two examples suffice as evidence. The first is from *Marriage in Islam: A Manual* by Muhammad Abdul-Rauf.[37] First published thirty years ago, and now in its seventh printing, its chapter "A Happy Conjugal Household" gives listings of husbands' and wives' duties, which include the following:

> A husband is responsible for the protection, happiness and maintenance of his wife. He is responsible for the cost of her food, clothes and accommodation. Although she may have to cook, he has to buy her the raw materials and cooking and kitchen facilities, as may be required and applicable.[38]
>
> The management of the household is the wife's primary responsibility. She has to take care of meal preparation, house-cleaning and laundry. Whether she undertakes these tasks herself or has them done under her careful supervision, it is her task to manage them in the best interests of the family. She may expect some cooperation from her husband, but this should depend on what he can afford to do. What is important is the mutual goodwill and love which will no doubt stimulate each party to alleviate the burden of the other as much as possible.[39]

Not only do these passages assign to women the task – meal preparation – that earlier jurists most emphatically exempted her from performing, it sets up an explicit relationship between the husband's support of his wife and her responsibility to do cooking and other household chores. However, the author hesitates a bit: he must pay for food; she *may* have to cook it. Rather than declaring outright that the wife has to perform the listed services (a term he studiously avoids), Abdul-Rauf states that she must "take care" of these "responsibilit[ies]" and "manage" these "tasks."[40]

My second example is drawn from the much-read *Woman in Shari'ah* by 'Abdul Rahman Doi, a text frequently used by English-speaking Muslims as an authoritative resource on Islamic law.[41] Doi, making extensive use of biological and "natural" arguments for women's place in the home and society, avoids any hedging around women's domestic duties. He states, "When a wife is not employed the household becomes her first occupation. By household is meant the rearing of children and all domestic services required for maintaining a clean and comfortable habitation." Doi goes further, however, touching on the subject of women's work. He reserves for the husband the right to prevent his wife from working – acknowledging, though not explicitly, the authority legally granted to the husband to prevent his wife from leaving the marital home for any reason. Yet he departs from traditional jurisprudence when he states that if a man allows his wife to work, "Any gain from work realized by the wife belongs to the family and cannot be considered as her personal property."[42] In traditional doctrine, there is no marital property regime; the jurists never countenance a married woman's obligation to support herself, let alone her husband or children.

These few examples demonstrate that neo-conservative interpretations diverge from the traditional model in several ways, generally to women's detriment. The majority of North American Muslims rely on pamphlets and quasi-scholarly books such as these, which claim to present authoritative and authentic information, for their knowledge of Islamic law.[43] It is against this backdrop of pseudo-traditional doctrine that the feminist and reformist discourses to which I now turn must be understood.

CONTEMPORARY DISCOURSES: FEMINIST APOLOGETICS

A number of authors concerned with promoting Muslim women's rights in matters of marriage and divorce have discussed women's legal rights "in Islam." These authors oscillate between, on the one hand, upholding specific rules as an example of how Islamic law protects women and, on the other hand, critiquing traditional jurisprudence when patriarchal assumptions lead the jurists to unreasonable decisions.[44] In the latter case, these reformers turn to the Qur'an to challenge, often quite persuasively, juristic interpretations. However, I am concerned here with their attempts to defend the basic precepts of traditional jurisprudence on marriage.

In seeking to counter both stereotyped portrayals of women's legal rights and the negative consequences of neo-conservative interpretations, these authors point to provisions of classical law that guarantee women certain protections. These doctrines serve as evidence that Islamic law is not unremittingly patriarchal. They also provide practical guidelines for Muslim women seeking to ensure more egalitarian marriages for themselves. Both goals are laudable, and the strategy of promoting detailed marriage contracts is, in the short term, potentially quite effective at securing for women rights that are ignored today. However, there are two serious flaws in this approach. First, the strategy of including contractual stipulations is not, jurisprudentially, nearly as straightforward as it is often made out to be. Second, and far more importantly, adding conditions onto a contract does not change its basic essence. I will address the validity of stipulations first.

Among the clauses al-Hibri suggests women can include in their marriage contracts are some rights that accrue to women anyway according to traditional jurisprudence (such as to be supported by her husband or to not have to cook or clean) and some that are only hers if agreed upon in the contract (such as to work outside the home).[45] In this latter category are the oft-mentioned stipulations that a husband will not take any other wives or will not relocate his wife from her hometown. Al-Hibri writes that

In fostering change, the Qur'an resorts to what has been known as recently in the West as affirmative action. In a patriarchal society, even a general declaration of equal rights is not sufficient to protect women. Consequently, divine wisdom gave women further protections. Paramount among these protections is the ability of the Muslim woman to negotiate her marriage contract and place in it any conditions that do not contradict its purpose. For example, she could place in her marriage contract a condition forbidding her husband from moving her away from her own city or town.[46]

The Qur'an, it should be pointed out, does not refer to stipulations in the marriage contract. So Al-Hibri is using the phrase "divine wisdom" to describe the jurisprudential doctrine of stipulations. However, according to Maliki, Hanafi, and Shafi'i jurists of the formative period, the stipulation that the husband will not move his wife from her hometown is completely void; the Hanbali jurists alone allow it.[47] Even in the Hanbali case, the wife is given a choice as to whether or not to divorce her husband in this circumstance; she is not allowed to bind him to remain with her in her town. My discussion here will focus on the related issue of stipulations against polygamy, illustrating that the current discourses about these stipulations misrepresent the provisions of traditional jurisprudence on the subject. I will further argue that even if this provision can be satisfactorily formulated so as to be legally binding, it still fails to address the underlying inequities in spousal rights.

When a contemporary author mentions putting a condition in the contract that the husband will not take another wife, or that she has a choice to divorce him if he does so, she or he is lumping together two entirely different mechanisms for ensuring the wife's "right." The first is a simple contractual stipulation; the second is conditional delegated divorce. According to Maliki, Hanafi, and Shafi'i texts from the formative period, contractual stipulations that a husband will not take additional wives (or any concubines) are meaningless.[48] For the Hanbalis, if the husband breaks the condition by taking an additional wife, the first wife has the option to divorce him.[49] However, in none of these cases is the validity of the second marriage affected.

The second mechanism is more potent. In this type of stipulation, the husband delegates his power of repudiation to the wife if he performs a certain action. Thus, a husband can state in the contract that "If such-and-such occurs, your affair is in your hands." If the wife learns that the condition has come to pass, she has the option to divorce him.[50] There is difference of opinion on whether such a choice is only good during the particular encounter where she learns of it or whether she retains the right even after that meeting so long as she has not had intercourse with her husband. For the Hanbalis, however, a woman can lose her right to divorce by having intercourse with her husband *even if she did not know that the event giving her the right to divorce had taken place*: "If her husband has intercourse with her, the wife in question no longer has the option of separating from him, regardless of whether she was aware of her option before the act of intercourse."[51] In this case, under Hanbali law, a woman who had not put a stipulation in her marriage contract that her husband would not take an additional wife, but rather relied on delegated divorce at a later date, would lose her freedom of choice if her husband simply concealed the second marriage long enough to have intercourse with the first wife. (Remember that she is legally obligated to have intercourse with him whenever he desires.)

There is one additional way that a wife can attempt to regulate her husband's taking of another wife: through having him pronounce a suspended repudiation. For all of the schools, if the husband makes an oath of repudiation conditional on his taking a second wife ("If I marry again, you are repudiated") the repudiation is effective. As a practical matter, when a woman has no other option for assuring her right to be separated from a polygamous husband, this conditional repudiation can be a useful strategy. But what makes the strategy possible is the unfettered nature of a man's right to repudiation. His repudiation automatically takes effect when he marries again simply because of his absolute right to repudiate his wife. The same would be true if he said, "If you ever speak to so-and-so, you are repudiated" (or "If I ever speak to so-and-so ...") or even "If it rains on Tuesday, you are repudiated." To hold up a woman's right to divorce on her husband's taking another wife as an example of how Islamic law protects women's rights ignores the specific legal rationale for validating such a divorce. It occurs in a context in which the woman has no way to protect herself from an unwanted repudiation, which is valid without her consent, participation, or even knowledge.

I have demonstrated that insuring against polygamy through a condition in the marriage contract is not the simple affair it is made out to be by contemporary authors. Yet even if one could find a way to construct stipulations against polygamy in a binding manner, it would not address this basic imbalance in men's and women's marital rights, or the definition of the marriage contract as being unilaterally in the husband's domain (*fi yadihi*). There is no condition that can restrict the husband's right to repudiate his wife at any time, for any reason or no reason at all. Raga' El Nimr acknowledges this, in an apologetic piece that differs only subtly from the views put forth by Abdul-Rauf, but does not explore its implications.[52] For El Nimr and others who stress women's protections in Islamic law, however, the dower serves that function by acting as practical deterrent or an economic safety net. I now turn to a consideration of how dower (*mahr* or *sadaq*) is understood in these discourses. Some stress its economic importance, while others suggest that a large deferred dower provides a disincentive to capricious repudiations, since the balance will become due at divorce. El Nimr considers that dower is intended "to safeguard the economic position of women after marriage." Drawing from Qur'anic verses on dower, El Nimr argues that dower is a critical means through which women can secure their well-being. She writes that "The object is to strengthen the financial position of the wife, so that she is not prevented, for lack of money, from defending her rights."[53]

Al-Hibri likewise stresses the dower's importance for women, providing a slightly different description of its purpose:

> Mahr, therefore, is not a "bride price" as some have erroneously described it. It is not the money the woman pays to obtain a husband nor money that the husband pays to obtain a wife. It is part of a civil contract that specifies the conditions under which a woman is willing to abandon her status as a single woman and its related opportunities in order to marry a prospective husband and start a family.[54]

In comparison, the Maliki jurists of the formative period express a quite different role for the dower, stating that a free woman "is due her dower, and her vulva [*bud'uha*] is not made lawful by anything else."[55] Nor do the jurists shy away from considering the dower a price. Indeed, Al-Shafi'i explicitly uses the term "price" (*thaman*) on numerous occasions for the dower, stating that "dower is a price among prices."[56] Various discussions in the *Umm* illustrate that dower is "a price for the vulva" (*thaman al-bud'*),[57] and that "a woman's fair dower is the fair value of her vulva" (*qima mithl al-bud'a mahr mithlaha*).[58] The commercial aspects of the marriage contract are unremarkable for the jurists. For example, in discussing a situation where a slave was specified as the wife's dower, Al-Shafi'i states that "she sold him her vulva for the slave" (*ba'athu bud'aha bi 'abd*).[59]

I do not give these examples to prove that marriage was a sale, for the jurists also made analogies that differentiated marriage from sales in particular respects. I simply want to demonstrate that jurists of the formative period did not have any hesitation whatsoever in using the terminology of sales and purchases to discuss marriage. The discomfort with these comparisons is our own, and was not shared by the pre-modern jurists. The explanations of dower given by Al-Hibri and El Nimr gloss over the logic and language of traditional jurisprudence, accepting its substantive rules but providing them with more palatable interpretations.

As with dower, Al-Hibri and El Nimr champion women's exemption from domestic duties in traditional jurisprudence, but provide a new rationale for it. In these discourses, a woman's lack of duty to cook or clean is an example of her marital rights. El Nimr writes that

> With regard to domestic duties, Islam has relieved women of all manual drudgery. According to strict Islamic injunctions, it is not obligatory for a woman to cook the food for her husband or children, or to wash their clothes or even to suckle the infants. A woman can refuse to do any of these things without this being made a ground of legal complaint against her. If she undertakes these duties, it is an act of sheer grace.[60]

While with regard to dower, El Nimr turns to the Qur'an for her explanation, here she refers only to "strict Islamic injunctions" – meaning, undoubtedly, jurisprudence. Though she makes the point forcefully that women do not have household or childcare duties, she does not offer any explanation of what responsibilities they do have as wives or why it is that they are exempt from the obligation to perform these services.

Al-Hibri's treatment of the same subject offers a glimpse into her interpretive strategy:

> Islam also views marriage as an institution in which human beings find tranquillity and affection with each other. It is for this reason that some prominent traditional Muslim scholars have argued that a woman is not required to serve her husband, prepare his food, or clean his house. In fact, the husband is obligated to bring his wife prepared food, for example. This assertion is based on the recognition that the Muslim wife is a companion to her husband and not a maid. Many jurists also defined the purpose of the marriage institution in terms of sexual enjoyment (as distinguished from reproduction). They clearly stated that a Muslim woman has a right to sexual enjoyment within the marriage.[61]

Al-Hibri, like El Nimr, is correct in her characterization of the traditional jurisprudential position that a wife has no obligation to do household chores (though she perhaps underestimates how prevalent this position was, attributing it only to "some prominent traditional Muslim scholars"). Seizing on the view that women are not required to do housework, Al-Hibri argues that this indicates that Muslim women were recognized to be "companions" to their husbands rather than maids. However, for the early jurists, as discussed above, wives were bound to provide service, but sexual rather than domestic.

The wife's sexual responsibilities are entirely sanitized by Al-Hibri's next statement that "Many jurists also defined the purpose of the marriage institution in terms of sexual enjoyment." This phrasing obscures the reality that sex in marriage was almost exclusively a female duty and a male right. While it was recommended that a husband satisfy his wife sexually, women had no enforceable rights to sex. Indeed, Al-Hibri's assertion here about women's right to sexual enjoyment is undercut by her later statement that "some traditional jurists gave women the right to seek judicial divorce if they had no conjugal relations with their husbands for more than four months."[62] Apparently, of the "[m]any jurists" who "clearly stated that a Muslim woman has a right to sexual enjoyment within the marriage" only "some" considered that a husband's abstention for more than four months constituted grounds for separation. Indeed, even this overstates the case; four months, as my discussion of the formative period jurists indicated, is only the relevant period of sexual abstention where a husband has completely forsworn his wife; it does not apply to cases of abstention without a vow.

CRITIQUE AND ANALYSIS

The early and classical Muslim jurists had a clear logical system underpinning their conception of marriage and the interdependent rights of spouses within it. The basic purpose of marriage was legitimizing sexual intercourse: the jurists formulated an interdependent system of spousal rights that put the wife's support and the husband's right to sex at its center. This system was predicated, at a very basic logical level, on an analogy to slavery and other types of ownership. Furthermore, its specific rules were based on the widespread availability of slave-servants. Thus, the jurists' debate was not over whether women were required to maintain their husbands' homes, cook, and clean, but rather whether the husband had to support only one of his wife's servants or more than that. Admittedly, this likely bore little resemblance to reality for the majority of Muslim women. But it served as a basis for the elaboration of many different rules that are unintelligible if removed from this framework and held up independently as an example of what "Islam" guarantees women.

Neo-conservative authors, even as they press for the observance of certain substantive rules that are the product of early *fiqh*, balk at using the commercial terminology and analogies to slavery that were part of the jurists' accepted language. While often upholding the spousal rights that were agreed upon in that model, they provide new rationales for them, as can be seen in their discussions of a husband's duty to maintain his family. For the early jurists, "a husband must maintain his wife, whether she is rich or poor, for restricting her for himself so that he may derive pleasure from her [*bi habsiha 'ala nafsihi li'l-istimta'a biha*]."[63] The jurisprudential rationale for a husband's support of his wife is entirely separate from the rationale for any person's support of other relatives, including minor children or parents. For the neo-conservatives, however, a man's duty to support his family is part and parcel of his male nature that makes him fit for earning a living and supporting his "dependents." No distinction is made between wives and children. The wife's role is conceived of in a complementary fashion: her nature makes her suited for caring for the home and children. In the process, certain traditional female rights (such as a wife's exemption from housework) tend to fall by the wayside, as they are incompatible with the new understanding of male and female roles in marriage. When women's advocates seek to resurrect these rights, they do so by appeal to the authority of traditional jurisprudence. Like their neo-conservative antagonists, however, they frame these rights in a different conceptual vocabulary than that originally used by the jurists.

Feminist discourses that seek to promote more egalitarian Islamic laws are, undoubtedly, strategically useful. In particular, highlighting women's legal exemption from housework or childcare is a useful corrective to neo-conservative discourses that presume wives have an obligation to perform these services because of a natural aptitude for them. Likewise, the attempt to promote the inclusion of conditions in marriage contracts governing the husband's taking of additional wives or the wife's right to work and keep her earnings can be an important means of setting forth the spouse's expectations for the marriage. This appeal to traditional legal views, however, is not without its perils. Though potentially quite effective in securing for women rights that are not respected today, it runs the risk of further cementing the authority of the traditional opinions. With regard to women's work outside the home, while traditional jurisprudence rejects a man's right to take any of his wife's earnings, it upholds, as I have noted, his right to prevent her from working entirely – indeed, to forbid her from leaving the home at all. Some would suggest that a condition in the marriage contract would resolve that; it is an iffy proposition with regard to traditional law.[64] Even where conditions can be made enforceable, and where rights can be upheld, the feminist rhetoric of women's marital rights in Islamic law distorts traditional legal rationales – if not its substantive doctrines – at least as seriously as does the neo-conservative discourse.

Al-Hibri, El Nimr, and others fail to grapple with the way that the specific rights they point to as evidence of women's legal protections are part of a larger logical understanding of what is being contracted for in marriage. If women reserve the right not to do any household service or childcare, *and* to be entirely supported by their husbands, while at the same time being free to pursue whatever work they choose, *and* maintaining sole control over their earnings from that work, what rights does the husband have? What responsibilities does the woman have in this situation? What is the basic aim of marriage, in either case? If the husband no longer supports his wife and no longer controls her mobility, then what is the point, legally speaking? Such a marriage no longer serves the purpose for which it was regulated according to traditional jurisprudence: ensuring a woman's sexual availability in exchange for male support. If it is a different type of marriage, then it needs a different type of law. Half-measures to make the best of an existing situation are insufficient. It is necessary to question the traditional model that obliges a husband to support his wife and grants him the right to control her movements in return and expect sex at his whim. This will require a radical rethinking of Islamic marriage, beginning with a fresh approach to the Qur'an, above all.

A number of scholars, including Al-Hibri, have undertaken this effort to flesh out a new exegesis of sacred texts as a means of arriving at an alternative view of relations between the sexes in society, including in marriage. Their work is important, and challenges the androcentric nature of traditional interpretations. Al-Hibri turns to the Qur'an in those cases where traditional law does not offer a resolution to the problems she sees. Others such as Riffat Hassan, Amina Wadud, and Asma Barlas have focused on the Qur'an to the exclusion of jurisprudence. Their ground-breaking studies have inspired a willingness on the part of other progressive Muslims to address legal issues through new approaches to the Qur'an.[65] In and of itself, there is nothing wrong with such an approach; indeed, the Qur'an must be at the center of Muslim piety and thought. However, in focusing so single-mindedly on the interpretation of the Qur'an, discarding centuries of jurisprudential texts as irredeemable, progressive Muslims run the risk of leaving the field of jurisprudence entirely to those trained in its methods and committed to its traditional assumptions. Scriptural exegesis, no matter how sophisticated, is not a legal methodology; the Qur'an is not a law book. Though the Qur'an does contain specific commands and prohibitions as well as moral and ethical guidance, it does not provide explicit regulations covering all possible circumstances. Some means of applying its provisions to the nearly infinite cases that arise among Muslims will always be necessary. The battle for egalitarian Muslim marriages will be fought on numerous fronts, and jurisprudence will undoubtedly be one of them.

Progressive Muslims cannot afford to ignore jurisprudence. There is a need for a thorough appraisal and analysis of the rules and methods of traditional jurisprudence. Such analysis will demonstrate, as I have done in part in this essay, that its doctrines are entirely inadequate to serve as the basis for laws governing Muslim families, communities, and societies today. However, it should also illustrate the phenomenal intellectual effort that went into creating the logical systems that produced law to govern millions of Muslim lives through the centuries. I would even venture to say that the legal method used by the jurists is basically sound, including the use of analogy. The issue is the assumptions from which they began, including the notion that marriage can be usefully compared to slavery or to commercial transactions. This does not mean, however, that doctrines should be simply modified, piecemeal, until we come up with something we can live with. Rather, whatever elements of traditional jurisprudential method are used, the process of regulating marriage and divorce will have to begin anew. Qualified Muslims must begin working to shape new laws, beginning from new assumptions – including those that feminist and progressive Qur'anic scholars have brought to the fore. The most critical of these insights is that men and women are ontologically equal, and that ultimately our equality as human beings in the sight of God matters more than any distinctions based on social hierarchy.

CONCLUSION

Azizah al-Hibri posits that the Islamic marriage contract "is a vehicle for ensuring the continued well-being of women entering matrimonial life in a world of patriarchal justice and inequality."[66] I agree that it can be; a large deferred dower is often successfully used as a disincentive to hasty repudiation, for example.[67] Certain other stipulations may secure rights that would otherwise be unenforceable. However, this formulation fails to address the complicity of jurisprudential institutions and doctrines in, at the very least, perpetuating the patriarchy and inequality that make such measures vital. The husband's unrestricted right to unilateral repudiation, for example, is not a *necessary* interpretation of scripture and prophetic tradition, yet traditional jurisprudence has affirmed his right to exercise it while denying women any parallel privilege. Since men have this unilateral power, contractual stipulations and practical strategies such as deferred dowers become crucial for women, a means of negotiating a patriarchal terrain. But given that jurisprudence itself is largely to blame for the state of affairs that requires women to implement these "affirmative action"[68] strategies, praise for the protections it extends to those women knowledgeable and powerful enough to invoke them seems misplaced.

Acknowledging the deeply patriarchal and discriminatory elements in Islamic jurisprudence is not cause for despair. It does not mean accepting that God intends Muslim women and men to live in hierarchical, authoritarian marital relationships. On the contrary, as I have illustrated, a thorough exploration and analysis of traditional jurisprudence will reveal the extent to which its rules are seriously flawed; they cannot be Divine. The role of human agency in the creation of these laws is evidenced by the diversity of legal views as well as the creation of a system of male marital privilege and sharply differentiated spousal rights that does not simply emerge wholly formed from the Qur'an. This system is the result of an interpretation, indeed of numerous acts of interpretation, by particular men living and thinking at a specific time. Their jurisprudence is shaped not by any malicious misogyny, or so I choose to believe, but rather by the assumptions and constraints of the time in which it was formulated. Our contemporary recognition that the traditional scheme of marriage law is compromised beyond repair liberates us to pursue a new jurisprudence, one based on assumptions that do not liken women to slaves or marriage to purchase. A marriage law that foregrounds the mutual protectorship of men and women (Q. 9:71) rather than male providership (Q. 4:34), or that focuses on the cooperation and harmony of spouses inherent in the Qur'anic declaration that spouses are garments for one another (Q. 2:187), can represent a starting point for a new jurisprudence of marriage. The result will be a closer – but still only human, and therefore fallible – approximation of divinely revealed *Shari'ah* than what currently exists. And God knows best.

ENDNOTES

1. An early version of this essay was delivered as a lecture at the University of Missouri – Columbia in March 2002 as "Marriage and Divorce in Islamic Law: Contemporary Debates in Historical Perspective." I would like to thank the Women's History Month Committee for that invitation and the lively exchange that ensued. I would also like to thank Kate Albright, Ellen Dunning, Ann Kim, Khaleel Muhammad, Harvey Stark, and especially Omid Safi for their comments and suggestions. Of course, I am responsible for any errors of fact or interpretation that remain.
2. For a scathing critique of this type of discourse, see Haideh Moghissi, *Feminism and Islamic Fundamentalism: The Limits of Postmodern Analysis* (London and New York: Zed, 1999).

3. This is the reporter's summary, not al-Hibri's. Rebecca Mead, "Comment: A Woman's Prerogative," *New Yorker*, December 2001. It accurately conveys Al-Hibri's views as presented in that piece and several other published articles. For this essay, I draw from two articles by Al-Hibri: "An Introduction to Muslim Women's Rights," in *Windows of Faith: Muslim Women Scholar-Activists in North America*, ed. Gisela Webb (Syracuse, NY: Syracuse University Press, 2000), 51–71 (hereafter, "An Introduction"), and "Islam, Law, and Custom: Redefining Muslim Women's Rights," *American University Journal of International Law and Policy*, 12(1), 1997, 1–44 (hereafter, "Islam, Law, and Custom").

4. *Shart*, pl. *shurut*.

5. For example, in an article discussing honor killings, Lama Abu Odeh uses the heading "The classical jurisprudential treatment of crimes of honour" for a section dealing exclusively with contemporary Arab criminal codes. "Crimes of Honour and the Construction of Gender in Arab Societies," in *Feminism and Islam: Legal and Literary Perspectives*, ed. Mai Yamani (New York: New York University Press, 1996), 146. No mention is made of *fiqh* doctrines. I point this out not to disparage the article or its conclusions, but to emphasize that the terminology used to discuss Islamic law in its varied manifestations is seldom applied in a precise fashion.

6. I do not discuss the Shi'i legal schools here, in part because the role of *mut'a* ("temporary") marriage in Shi'i law makes comparison difficult. However, in its broad outlines the Shi'i view of marriage (*nikah*) is similar to Sunni law. See Shahla Haeri, *Law of Desire: Temporary Marriage in Shi'i Iran* (Syracuse, NY: Syracuse University Press, 1989), especially chapter 2, "Permanent Marriage: *Nikah*."

7. This is the body of literature that I survey in my doctoral dissertation, "Money, Sex, and Power: The Contractual Nature of Marriage in Islamic Jurisprudence of the Formative Period" (Duke University, 2002). However, the dissertation does not discuss Hanbali jurisprudence, which I include here. This essay draws on the following texts: for the Maliki school, the *Muwatta'* of Malik ibn Anas (d. 179/795) and *Al-Mudawwana al-Kubra* (hereafter, *Mudawwana*) of Sahnun al-Tanukhi (d. 240/854); for the Hanafi school, *Kitab al-Hujjah 'ala Ahl al-Madina* (*Kitab al-Hujjah*) attributed to Muhammad al-Shaybani (d. 189/805), and two other works attributed to him: a recension of Malik's *Muwatta'* (*Muwatta' al-Shaybani*) and *Al-Jami' al-Saghir*; as well as the *Kitab al-Nafaqat* of Ahmad ibn 'Umar al-Khassaf (d. 261/874); for the Shafi'i school, *Al-Umm*, attributed to Muhammad b. Idris al-Shafi'i (d. 204/820) and the *Mukhtasar al-Muzani 'ala 'l-Umm* of Isma'il b. Yahya al-Muzani (d. 264/878); for the Hanbali school, a compilation of Ahmad b. Hanbal's (d. 241/855) legal responsa (*masa'il*) edited from manuscript sources and translated by Susan Spectorsky as *Chapters on Marriage and Divorce: Responses of Ibn Hanbal and Ibn Rahwayh* (*Chapters*). My citations of the Arabic volumes include the titles of the chapter and subsection to which I am referring, to make it easier for those using different editions of the texts to locate the relevant passages. Unless otherwise noted, all translations from the Arabic are mine.

8. Baber Johansen has addressed some of these issues for the classical period using Transoxanian Hanafi texts. See "The Valorization of the Human Body in Muslim Sunni Law," in Devin J. Stewart, Baber Johansen, and Amy Singer, *Law and Society in Islam* (Princeton: Markus Wiener, 1996), 71–112.

9. Numerous scholars have investigated these subjects and found compelling evidence of female agency and juristic effort to protect women's interests. Despite women's clear disadvantages in legal doctrine across the schools, in practice women were able to exercise many rights, especially to property. Further, they often gained advantages that, in strict doctrinal terms, they should not have had. Scholars working with court records and collections of *fatawa* (juristic opinions, sing. *fatwa*) have demonstrated that judges were often, in their application of the law, amenable to women's claims and flexible in their judgments. This was often done by sidestepping, rather than directly challenging, problematic doctrines. To take only one example, in Hanafi communities, a woman's inability to obtain divorce from an unwilling, non-supporting husband was dealt with not

by changing the school's position, but by appointing a deputy judge from another legal school to pronounce the divorce. For an online bibliography of works on women, gender, and Islamic law, see www.brandeis.edu/departments/nejs/fse

10. Khaled Abou El Fadl has made this point eloquently in *Speaking in God's Name: Islamic Law, Authority, and Women* (Oxford: Oneworld, 2001), 32.

11. One well-known subject on which prophetic precedent is generally agreed to differ from Qur'anic revelation is that of punishment for a married person (*muhsan/muhsana*) guilty of illicit intercourse (*zina*). While the Qur'an prescribes flogging as a punishment for *zina*, some *hadith* record the Prophet as setting stoning as the penalty for adulterers, reserving flogging for fornication.

12. Several recent scholarly works have explored the early development of the Sunni legal schools and their methodologies. Two particularly useful studies are Wael B. Hallaq, *A History of Islamic Legal Theories: An Introduction to Sunni Usul al-Fiqh* (Cambridge: Cambridge University Press, 1997) and Christopher Melchert, *The Formation of the Sunni Schools of Law, 9th–10th Centuries C.E.* (Leiden: Brill, 1997).

13. Occasionally, one or two other equally serious diseases were included by analogy to leprosy.

14. Farida Shaheed, writing about feminist criticism of Muslim laws, states in a footnote, "On the question of women's rights, status, and role, the four [Sunni] schools agree in principle. The differences between them relate to details of legal procedure." See "Controlled or Autonomous: Identity and the Experience of the Network, Women Living under Muslim Laws," *Signs: Journal of Women in Culture and Society*, 19(4), 1994, 1004, n. 7. In *Women in Islam: From Medieval to Modern Times*, rev. edn (Princeton: Markus Wiener, 1993), 50, Wiebke Walther writes of the four Sunni schools of law, "They are to be found in various regions of the Islamic world, but they do not vary very much in their dogmas."

15. Leila Ahmed, *Women and Gender in Islam: Historical Roots of a Modern Debate* (New Haven: Yale University Press, 1992), 85. See also p. 67 and chapter 5, "Elaboration of the Founding Discourses."

16. Two aspects are important in the consideration of sexual availability: "deriving pleasure" (*istimta'a*) and "exercising restraint" (*habs*, later *ihtibas*). For purposes of this article, the two are combined in the notion of sexual availability, though there were some important distinctions between the two.

17. Muhammad b. Idris al-Shafi'i, *Al-Umm* (Beirut: Dar al-Kutub al-'Ilmiyya, 1993), K. al-Nafaqat, "Bab al-rajul la yajidu ma yunfiqu 'ala imra'atihi," 5:132.

18. Ahmad b. 'Umar al-Khassaf, *Kitab al-Nafaqat* (Beirut: Dar al-Kitab al-'Arabi, 1984), K. al-Nafaqat "Bab nafaqat al-mar'a 'ala al-zawj wa ma yajibu laha min dhalika," 33.

19. Sahnun b. Sa'id al-Tanukhi (Malik b. Anas), *Al-Mudawwana al-Kubra* (Beirut: Dar Sader, n.d.), K. al-Nikah IV, 'Fi ikhtilaf al-zawjayn fi mata'at al-bayt,' 2:268.

20. "And if someone like her does not serve herself, maintenance of a servant for her is obligatory for him." *Al-Umm*, K. al-Nafaqat, "Al-nafaqa 'ala 'l-nisa,'" 5:153; see also "Wujub nafaqat al-mar'a," 5:127.

21. Isma'il b. Yahya al-Muzani, *Mukhtasar al-Muzani*, published as vol. 9 of Al-Shafi'i, *Al-Umm* (Beirut: Dar al-Kutub al-'Ilmiyya, 1993), K. al-Nikah, "Mukhtasar al-qasm wa nushuz al-rajul 'ala 'l-mar'a ...," 9:199.

22. See Vardit Rispler-Chaim, "*Nusuz* between Medieval and Contemporary Islamic Law: The Human Rights Aspect," *Arabica*, 39, 1992, pp. 315–27; Kecia Ali, "Women, Gender, Ta'a (Obedience) and *Nuṣuz* (Disobedience) in Islamic Discourses," in *Encyclopedia of Women and Islamic Cultures*, ed. Suad Joseph (Leiden: Brill, forthcoming); and Sa'diyya Shaikh, "Exegetical Violence: Nushuz in Qur'anic Gender Ideology," *Journal for Islamic Studies*, 17, 1997, 49–73.

23. One fifth/eleventh-century Maliki text suggests that Ibn al-Qasim (d. 191/806–7), the main authority for Malik's views in the *Mudawwana*, considered the maintenance of a *nashiz* wife to be obligatory. See Ibn 'Abd al-Barr (d. 463/1071), *Al-Kafi fi Fiqh Ahl al-Madina al-Maliki* (Beirut, Dar al-Kutub al-'Ilmiyya, 1987), K. al-Nikah, "Bab fi 'l-nafaqat 'ala

'l-zawjat wa hukm al-a'sar bi 'l-mahr wa 'l-nafaqat," 254. However, I found no evidence of this in the *Mudawwana*. Perhaps further study of Maliki manuscript sources for the formative period will turn up additional information that can substantiate this claim and provide a rationale for it.

24. Al-Khassaf, *Kitab al-Nafaqat*, "Bab nafaqat al-mar'a 'ala 'l-zawj wa ma yajibu laha min dhalika," 35–6.

25. A representative statement is that of Asifa Quraishi: "In Islam, sexual autonomy and pleasure is a fundamental right for both women and men." See Asifa Quraishi, "Critique of the Rape Laws of Pakistan from a Woman-Sensitive Perspective," in *Windows of Faith*, ed. Webb, 131. Quraishi's comments in the note to this passage reference sources dealing with women's right to sexual pleasure. Though jurists may seek to protect women's right to sexual pleasure in any given act of intercourse, they do not require the husband to have intercourse with his wife in the first place. This is because of the strict separation of male and female rights in marriage that I am arguing for in this paper.

26. Susan Spectorsky (trans.), *Chapters on Marriage and Divorce: Responses of Ibn Hanbal and Ibn Rahwayh* (Austin: University of Texas Press, 1993), 113. See also p. 234: "[W]hen a man has had intercourse with his wife once, he is not impotent."

27. *Muwatta*, K. al-Talaq, "Bab ajal alladhi la yamassu imra'atahu," 375; see also *Mudawwana*, K. Nikah IV, "Ma ja'a 'l-'innin," 2:265.

28. Ibn al-Qasim reiterates this view: "I [Sahnun] said: If he has sex with her one time then keeps away from her, is he set a year's deadline in Malik's opinion? He [Ibn al-Qasim] said: No deadline is set for him if he has intercourse with her according to Malik then he avoids her." *Mudawwana*, K. Nikah IV, "Ma ja'a fi 'l-'innin," 2:265. The same view is expressed in Hanafi and Shafi'i texts. See Muhammad al-Shaybani, *Al-Jami' al-Saghir*, (Beirut: 'Alam al-Kutub, n.d.), K. al-Zihar, "Masa'il min Kitab al-Talaq lam tadkhul fi 'l-abwab," 241–2; *Mukhtasar al-Muzani*, K. al-Nikah, "Ajal al-'innin wa 'l-khasi ghayri majbub wa 'l-khuntha," 9:191; *al-Umm*, K. al-Nikah, "Nikah al-'innin wa 'l-khasi wa 'l-majbub," 5:65.

29. Equally between free wives, that is; Hanafis, Hanbalis, Shafi'is, and at least one prominent authority cited by the Malikis (Sa'id b. al-Musayyab) argued for two nights for a free wife to each night for a slave wife. Malik, on the other hand, defended an equal division between free and slave wives. See *Mudawwana*, K. al-Nikah IV, "Al-qasm bayna al-zawjat," 2:271; K. al-Nikah II, "Fi nikah al-ama 'ala 'l-hurra wa 'l-hurra 'ala 'l-ama," 2:204–6. It should be emphasized that a slave wife belonged, of necessity, to another master. Though a man could take his own female slaves as concubines, he could not marry them without first manumitting them or selling them to another owner, who then needed to give permission for the marriage. A slave concubine was not entitled to a share of her owner's time.

30. *Al-Umm*, K. al-Nafaqat, "Nushuz al-mar'a 'ala 'l-rajul," 5:285.

31. For a strong statement of this view by Ibn Hanbal, see Spectorsky, *Chapters*, 230.

32. Muhammad al-Shaybani, *Kitab al-Hujjah* (Hyderabad: Lajnat Ihya' al-Ma'arif al-Nu'maniyah, 1965), K. al-Nikah, "Bab al-rajul yatazawwaju al-mar'a wa la yajidu ma yunfiqu 'ala imra'atihi," 3:451–69.

33. "He said: If he finds his wife's maintenance day by day, they are not separated, and if he does not find it, he is not granted a delay of more than three [days], and he does not prevent his wife during the three [days] from going out to work or ask (i.e., ask for food). If he does not find her maintenance, she chooses [whether or not to divorce him] ... And if they are separated then his situation improves it (i.e., the separation) is not rescinded. He does not possess the right to return to her during the waiting period, unless she wishes with a new marriage." *Al-Umm*, K. al-Nafaqat, "Bab al-rajul la yajidu ma yunfiqu 'ala imra'atihi," 5:132.

34. For the Maliki position, see *Mudawwana*, K. al-Nikah IV, "Fi farad al-sultan al-nafaqa li 'l-mara'a 'ala zawjiha," 2:258–63. For the Hanbali position, see Spectorsky, *Chapters*, 80, 190.

35. One could argue for other terms to describe this group, including traditionalist or neo-traditionalist. I do not attach any importance to the term "neo-conservative" beyond its simple descriptive nature.

36. Saalih ibn Ghaanim al-Sadlaan, *Marital Discord (al-Nushooz): Its Definition, Cases, Causes, Means of Protection from It, and Its Remedy from the Qur'an and Sunnah*, trans. Jamaal al-Din M. Zarabozo (Boulder: Al-Basheer, 1996), 13. Though published by an obscure press in the U.S.A., by the time of its translation the book was already in its third Arabic edition.
37. Muhammad Abdul-Rauf, *Marriage in Islam: A Manual* (Alexandria, VA: Al-Saadawi, 2000; reprint of 1972 edition). Many sections of this work are accessible online, giving some indication of its wide acceptance. See, for example, www.jannah.org/sisters/relations.html
38. Abdul-Rauf, *Marriage*, 47.
39. Abdul-Rauf, *Marriage*, 55.
40. See also a modified version of this sentiment, which reflects the special attention devoted to food preparation among a woman's duties: "If the wife is sick and cannot perform her household duties or she belongs to a rich family and refuses to do her domestic work with her own hands or she regards it to be below her dignity, then she may be provided with cooked food. But it is better to do her domestic work with her own hands and as a housewife it is her responsibility. The duty of a husband is to provide means and a wife should manage and run the house." Muhammad Iqbal Siddiqui, *Family Laws of Islam* (Delhi: International Islamic Publishers, 1988), 108–9. This formulation preserves the traditional rule that a wife is not required to perform this work, but emphasizes her domestic duties nonetheless.
41. 'Abdul Rahman I. Doi, *Woman in Shari'ah (Islamic Law)* (London: Ta-Ha, 1994). This work is one of the sources used by Raga' El Nimr in her article, discussed in the following section. Despite its generally accurate portrayal of various legal doctrines across the Sunni schools, the book has a few significant errors and numerous minor ones. Mistakes include: failing to acknowledge traditional rules allowing for the forced marriage of minors (35); stating that Malikis consider a marriage guardian's power of compulsion (*ijbar*) to apply to widows and divorcees (36); failing to note juristic disagreement on when and how apostasy causes a marriage to be dissolved (43) and how return (*raj'a*) is effected during a woman's waiting period (86–7); failing to differentiate between irrevocable and absolute repudiation (86–7); claiming that there is no possibility of divorce oaths before marriage (89); misidentifying a woman in a *hadith* (93); affirming that compensation in *khul'* divorce is limited to the dower amount (96); mis-stating the time that must elapse before Maliki and Shafi'i jurists will grant judicial divorce for non-support (107); and asserting vehemently that a marriage contracted for an unlawful dower "is null and void. All the jurists of the 4 schools agree upon this point" (160–1). In fact, *none* of the Sunni schools holds that view. While the specified dower would be invalid, the marriage is *at most* (e.g. for the Malikis) subject to dissolution (*faskh*), and even then only if not consummated; this is quite different from being void (*batil*), which implies having no legal effects whatsoever. Such errors in a work of this type are particularly unfortunate, because those knowledgeable enough to spot the mistakes will not be relying on this work for their understanding of Islamic law, and those who rely on it, unknowingly, will be misled.
42. Ibid., 107. However, he later states that if she runs a lawful business, she may "keep the whole income to herself. Islamic law does not put any responsibility for domestic expenses on her." (154). Doi does not note any contradiction or attempt to reconcile these positions.
43. In a more recent phenomenon, the predominance of this type of information on the web parallels its presence in Muslim communities. Khaled Abou El Fadl's *Speaking in God's Name* illustrates, through its analysis of Saudi *fatawa*, that this type of thinking is not present only in the United States.
44. Al-Hibri refers to this type of arrogant and "self-serving worldview" as "Satanic logic." "An Introduction," 51; see also p. 57, n. 19.
45. The specific issue of working outside the home at a salaried job is anachronistic, though of course women did earn money through commercial activities in the first Muslim centuries. The closest proxy by which to examine this right is the wife's stipulation that she may come and go as she pleases. Alternatively, one could look at the husband's right to determine the

marital domicile unilaterally, since the wife's right to maintain stable employment is obviously compromised if the husband may relocate her at his whim. In both cases, wherever these stipulations are discussed in Maliki, Hanafi, and Shafi'i texts they are simply deemed void. Hanbali jurisprudence, in contrast, allows these types of stipulations. See Spectorsky, *Chapters*, 183–4, 232.

46. Al-Hibri, "An Introduction," 58.
47. It should be pointed out that this stipulation, along with a prohibition against taking additional wives, has been used by numerous Muslim women through history, with a greater or lesser degree of success in judicial enforcement. On the distinction between judicial decisions (*qada'*), which are binding on litigants but do not set precedent, and juristic opinions (*ifta'*), which are precedent-setting but not binding on anyone, including those who have requested the *fatwa* (opinion), see Muhammad Khalid Masud, Brinkley Messick, and David S. Powers, "Muftis, Fatwas, and Islamic Legal Interpretation," in *Islamic Legal Interpretation: Muftis and Their Fatwas*, ed. M.K. Masud, B. Messick, and D.S. Powers (Cambridge and London: Harvard University Press, 1996), 3–32.
48. Maliki views: Malik ibn Anas, *Al-Muwatta* (Beirut: Dar al-Fikr, 1989), K. al-Nikah, "Bab ma la yajuzu min al-shurut fi 'l-nikah," 335, *Mudawwana*, K. al-Nikah II, "Fi shurut al-nikah," 2:197–200; Hanafi views: *Kitab al-Hujjah*, K. al-Nikah, "Al-rajul yatazawwaju 'ala shay' ba'duhu naqd wa ba'duhu ila ajal," 3:210–2; Shafi'i views: *al-Umm*, K. al-Sadaq, "Al-shart fi 'l-nikah," 5:107–9, *Mukhtasar al-Muzani*, "Al-shart fi 'l-mahr . . .," 9:195–196.
49. Spectorsky, *Chapters*, 183–4.
50. These texts do not specifically address this type of delegation occurring at a second marriage, but the principle is the same as in those events they do discuss. See Spectorsky, *Chapters*, 206–7, 219–20.
51. Spectorsky, *Chapters*, 206. Ibn Hanbal makes this statement when questioned about another jurist's opinion "that if a husband has intercourse with his wife without her knowing that she has the option of choosing to be separated from him, she is asked to swear that she did not know of the option during intercourse. If she swears that she did not, then she is given the option of separating from him. If she did know of her option, she has lost it by the act of intercourse." The option does not concern the husband breaking a stipulation against taking an additional wife, but the same logic applies.
52. "The wife may not legally object to the husband's right of divorce. The marital contract establishes her implicit consent to these rights. However, if she wishes to restrict his freedom in this regard or to have similar rights, she is legally allowed to do so. She may stipulate in the marital agreement that she, too, will have the right to divorce or keep the marriage bond only so long as she remains the sole wife." El Nimr does not explain how it is that "if she wishes to restrict his freedom in this regard ... she is legally allowed to do so" if, as she affirms, a "wife may not legally object to the husband's right to divorce." El Nimr, "Women in Islamic Law," in *Feminism and Islam*, ed. Mai Yamani (Ithaca Press: Reading, 1996), 96.
53. El-Nimr, "Women in Islamic Law," 97.
54. Al-Hibri, "An Introduction," 60.
55. *Mudawwana*, K. al-Nikah V, "Fi ihlal," 2:292.
56. For example, disagreeing with the Maliki (and Hanafi) position that a minimum dower is necessary, Al-Shafi'i states, "The dower is a price [*thaman*] among prices, so whatever they consent to as a dower that has a value [*qima*] is permitted, just as whatever two people engaged in a sale of anything that has a value [consent to] is permitted." See *Al-Umm*, Kitab Ikhtilaf Malik wa'l-Shafi'i, 7:376.
57. *Al-Umm*, K. al-Sadaq, "Fi 'l sadaq bi aynihi yatlafu qabla dafa'ahu," 5:92.
58. *Al-Umm*, K. al-Nafaqat, "Ikhtilaf al-rajul wa 'l-mar'a fi 'l-khul'," 5:300.
59. *Al-Umm*, K. al-Sadaq, "Sadaq al-shay' bi aynihi fa yujadu mu'ayban," 5:111. See also *Mukhtasar al-Muzani*, K. al-Nikah, "Sadaq ma yazidu bi budnihi wa yanqasu," 9:194, and *al-Umm*, K. al-Sadaq, "Fi 'l-sadaq bi aynihi yatlafu qabla dafa'ahu," 5:92.
60. "Women in Islamic Law," 97.

61. Al-Hibri, "An Introduction," 57–8. On housework, see also her "Islam, Law, and Custom," 22.
62. Al-Hibri, "An Introduction," 70.
63. *Al-Umm*, K. al-Nafaqat, "Wujub nafaqat al-mar'a," 5:128.
64. Furthermore, this does not necessarily affect the social recognition of these rights. At an Islamic Society of North America session I attended in Chicago in 1994 or 1995, a woman raised a related issue before a panel of male "experts." She had stipulated in her marriage contract that she was to attend medical school. Her husband, however, was objecting now that she sought to do so. The panelist who responded to her acknowledged the validity of the condition, but counseled her to drop her plans for medical school in order to preserve family harmony! What type of harmony can exist when it is predicated on the negation of women's legitimate aspirations?
65. I do not mean in any way to suggest that these scholars have erred by not addressing jurisprudence; to the contrary, progressive Muslims must be grateful for the work they have done and the conceptual frameworks they have introduced. Nor do I intend to imply that exegesis is only a precursor to work on law. Rather, I mean that *some* progressive Muslims must devote attention to jurisprudence; it is a *fard kifaya*, a collective obligation the performance of which by a portion of the community exempts others from the duty to undertake it.
66. Al-Hibri, "An Introduction," 60.
67. See, for example, Lisa Wynn, "Marriage Contracts and Women's Rights in Saudi Arabia," in *Women Living under Muslim Laws. Special Dossier 1: Shifting Boundaries in Marriage and Divorce in Muslim Communities*, ed. Homa Hoodfar (Montpelier, France: WLUML, 1996), 106–20. This topic has been discussed in numerous sociological studies. Today, the use of deferred dower is widely accepted in many parts of the world, and has been for centuries, as studies based on Ottoman court registers attest. Indeed, dividing a dower into prompt and deferred portions is common in North American Muslim communities. Yet while a fixed term for deferring payment of some portion of the dower was acceptable for jurists of the formative period (e.g. one or two years), the idea of deferring part of the dower's payment until death or divorce was controversial and, at the very least, disapproved of. See, for example, *Mudawwana*, K. al-Nikah II, "Fi shurut al-nikah," 2:197; *Kitab al-Hujjah*, K. al-Nikah, "Al-rajul yatazawwaju 'ala shay' ba'duhu naqd wa ba'duhu ila ajal," 3:211–2.; *al-Umm*, K. al-Sadaq, "Al-shart fi 'l-nikah," 5:107–9; and *Mukhtasar al-Muzani*, "Al-shart fi 'l-mahr …" 9:195–6.
68. Al-Hibri uses this term; see "Talk of the Town," and "An Introduction," 51 and *passim*.

8

SEXUALITY, DIVERSITY, AND ETHICS IN THE AGENDA OF PROGRESSIVE MUSLIMS

Scott Siraj al-Haqq Kugle[1]

This study is dedicated to Hamid Nastoh, for bravery despite despair.[2]

> In the name of God, the Merciful and Compassionate. Praise be to God, the marvels of whose creation are not subject to the arrows of accident. Minds do not reflect on the beginning of such wonders except in awe and bewilderment. Praise be to God, the favor of whose graces continue to be bestowed upon all creatures. These graces come in succession upon the created beings whether or not they wish to receive them. One of God's marvelous favors is creating human beings out of water, causing them to be related by procreation and marriage, and subjecting creatures to desire through which God impelled them toward sexual intercourse and thereby preserved their descendants.[3]

With this majestic praise of sexual intercourse, Imam al-Ghazali begins his book that deals with sex, procreation, marriage, and romantic relations. Imam al-Ghazali is very forthright in talking about sex. In this respect, he represents the whole tradition of Islamic scholars, who never shied away from a frank (and often delightfully raunchy) discussion of sex with all its dangers and delights, following in this way the footsteps of the Prophet Muhammad. If we can judge by the traditions passed down from him, it appears that Muhammad challenged his society not only in the realms of faith and ritual, but also in the realm of sexual pleasure and the complex relationships it creates.

In comparison with many other religious traditions, it has often been noted that Islam is a religion that has evaluated sexual life positively. Articulating the integral relationship between spirituality and sexuality is one way that the Prophet Muhammad challenged his society. It remains for us, today, to continually struggle with that challenge. The system of norms, rules, and laws created by Muslims in the past (a collective body we call *Shari'ah*) does not absolve us of this challenge. It may, in fact, create complexities that drive us to reinvestigate the topic while presenting obstacles to a just resolution of those complexities. Scholars in the contemporary period have not lived up to the standards and frankness of pre-modern Islamic scholars, and much work has yet to be done on the question of sexuality in Islamic scripture, law, and society. Many scholars and Islamic leaders in the present shy away from honest discussions of sex and sexuality, with all its promise and problems. Muslims in pre-modern times certainly were not shy about discussing matters of sex, so why should we be prudish? The most basic goal of this essay is to return to us contemporary Muslims the "awe and bewilderment" that al-Ghazali felt when considering sexual pleasure.

Sexuality is connected not just to spirituality, but to politics as well. What is required of us in political situations is an acute sense of justice, but we often ignore or obscure justice when it comes to matters of sex and sexuality. We need to think more clearly about "intimate citizenship," how the personal, emotional, and sexual dimensions of our lives (which are often locked away as "private") actually have very public and often political consequences.[4] Questions of sex and sexuality become incendiary when members of a religious community feel threatened by or in conflict with external "enemies." Under such conditions, religious communities maintain restrictions and develop ideologies governing sexuality and gender. In our contemporary age, this is a serious problem, in both Muslim-majority societies in Africa, Asia, the Middle East, and also among Muslim minorities in the West. We see fundamentalist groups securing political power through the persecution of women, sexual minorities, and gender minorities. Even in North America, where many in the Muslim community feel threatened, the discourse around sexuality and especially homosexuality can become quite ideological and even violent. The Qur'an demands an acute sense of justice from all Muslims. Justice does not allow us to displace political tensions and economic inequalities onto sexual and intimate relationships. Conversely, open discussion of human sexuality helps us perceive more clearly ethical issues in the more public social fields of politics, economics, and criminal law.

What do we mean by sexuality? We certainly mean more than lust. The concept of sexuality identifies an integral dimension of each individual's personality: "an indicator of our core being, a sexuality which interweaves thoughts, desires, motivations, acts and psychological and mental well-being within its meaning."[5] The critical re-evaluation of sex and sexuality grows out of the feminist re-evaluation of gender and the constraints that gender imposed on women. As feminist scholars critique the assumed superiority of patriarchal masculinities, space is opened for a deeper introspection about sex – not in the light of gender alone but also in the light of sexuality. The success of any project to free sexual practices from the constraints of patriarchy depends ultimately on the success of freeing women (and eventually men too) from the same dominance of patriarchal structures of power.

SEXUALITY AND EROTIC LIFE AMONG MUSLIMS

The mass media in the West assert that Islam is a "repressive" religion. However, comparison with other religious traditions reveals that Islam is a sex-positive world religion. In Muhammad's teachings (as in the Qur'an), sexuality is not an obstacle to spirituality in general. Rather sexuality is a field where spirituality plays out, as it does in economic life, ritual practice or political struggle. Even conservative religious scholars saw sexuality in a positive light.[6] The Qur'an does not blame sex or sexual desire for the "fall" of Adam and his mate from Eden, nor do Muslims in general see sex as part of fleshly corruption in the life of this world. Rather, sexual desire is part of creation and expresses Allah's wisdom. It brings divided people together, forces them to confront spiritual and ethical truths, and allows for continuity between generations.

This characteristic distinguishes Islam from its Abrahamic cousins. Authorities in the Judaic tradition often see sex as positive only in procreative results, and Christianity (like many interpretations of Buddhism) harbors deeply negative assessments of sexual activity. Early Christian leaders struggled with the question of whether the faithful should have sex at all, and speculated with horror whether the resurrection would be "bodily" with sexual organs and sexual desires. In contrast, the Qur'an depicts a heaven that is not just bodily, but sensually delightful and even sexually blissful.

> In posing the radical legitimacy of the practice of sexuality, Islam helped in the formation of a specific form of culture. The continuous outpouring of oneirism [cultivation of dream visions], combined with the most delicate and most elaborate eroticism, gave birth to a particularly original and attractive mode of life ... To be attentive to one's own body, to assume it in its totality, to take one's own fantasies seriously, to make the quest for orgasm an essential aim of earthly life and even of the life to come, are some of the aims of Islam.[7]

With these words, the Tunisian sociologist Abdelwahab Bouhdiba tries to preserve the Islamic challenge of connecting eroticism with spirituality.

The Prophet Muhammad is remembered as saying, "Three things were made beloved to me in this world of yours: women, perfume and prayer."[8] This saying has given generations of Muslims pause to consider the intimate connection between beauty, sexual desire, and worship of the One God. The general picture that emerges from the traditions preserved about the Prophet's teachings is that sexual activity is an important form of worshipful pleasure. It embraces sexual play (the giving and receiving of erotic pleasure) in many forms as a good in and of itself, without being restricted to procreative acts. One *hadith* scholar, 'Ali Muttaqi (who died in 1567 CE) relates these prophetic traditions about the benefits of sexual play with one's partner:

> A man's sexual play with his partner, when accompanied by sincere intent, causes him to be rewarded by Allah. As the Prophet is reported to have said, "Allah is pleased with a man's playing with his wife, and records a reward for him and makes a worthy provision in the world for him because of it." There is another hadith that says "When a man gazes at his wife and she gazes at him, God looks at them both with a gaze that is compassion and mercy."[9]

This openness to sexual play is within established relationships, in which partners acknowledge their relationship through some kind of contract. Such relationships were not historically limited to formally matrimonial relationships (*nikah*), but included sexual relations through informal contract (*mut'a*), ownership in slavery, and other less formally legalized relationships.[10] Contemporary Islamic communities, especially in the West, tend to demand exclusively matrimonial relationships. However, this was never the exclusive norm in pre-modern Islamic societies, where other kinds of sexual relationships were legal and socially sanctioned.

Islamic society's acceptance of sexual pleasure as a good in itself explains its openness to the use of contraception.[11] Beyond its procreative function, sexual play was valued for establishing effective and emotional bonds of caring between partners. The Qur'an addresses the question of non-procreative sexual acts directly and affirms them (in Surat al-Baqara 2:223, though interpretation of this verse was always the subject of contest and debate).[12]

In summary, the Islamic tradition has valued the pursuit of sexual pleasure positively. Sexual play was not limited to marital relations, but was permissible in other kinds of contractual relationships. Sexual pleasure was not restricted to procreation, but was seen as spiritually and socially beneficial in itself, such that some kinds of contraception were encouraged. This positive assessment of sexual pleasure was traditionally limited to sex between a male and a female. A "heterosexist" assumption underlies all these positive assessments. Accordingly, Muslim jurists saw their primary duty to regulate sexual activity that might lead to the birth of illegitimate children or situations of unclear parentage.

However, is it honest to assume that all Muslims are heterosexual in their sexual orientation and practices? Is it factual to assert that genders are clearly divided by physical nature rather than by socialization? Is it realistic to pretend that sexual desire is always only between a man and a woman? The ambiguities that arise from exceptions to the heterosexist assumption are always a challenge to any human community, and Muslims are no exception. Muslim scholars and jurists of the past certainly confronted these issues and offered certain answers to the questions they raise.

In the light of new biological knowledge about genetics and sociological knowledge about personality development, the traditional answers may no longer be convincing. This is especially true now that several generations of Muslim feminist scholars have questioned the patriarchal assumptions behind so many practices that Muslims popularly consider integral to their religious tradition. Inspired by feminist critiques, some Muslims who are attuned to sexuality are taking the contemporary situation as an opportunity to return to the sources of Islamic religious beliefs in order to reassess questions of sexuality and its diversity. An honest and subtle examination of these sources (the Qur'an, the prophetic traditions, and the decisions of Islamic jurists) reveals more ambiguities than the defenders of "orthodoxy" care to admit. This study will illuminate these ambiguities to show how they are productive ambiguities. These ambiguities should urge those Muslims with a keen sense of justice and a firm hold on reason to entertain the possibility of reassessing the Islamic tradition's stand regarding homosexuality as part of rethinking its stand on sexuality in general.

This study begins with what might seem like a radical notion, that Islam does not address homosexuality. It might be conceivable that particular Muslims in particular situations addressed issues related to something we currently call "homosexuality."[13] We must be instantly suspicious of statements like "Islam says ..." or "The Shari'ah says ..." as if these abstractions actually speak. Things do not speak. Only people speak. Although all Muslims revere the Qur'an and respect the Prophet Muhammad, statements about these sources of divine guidance are interpretations of them. Such interpretations are always expressed and advocated by people. And people, even Islamic leaders, are never infallible. There must be room for an educated and sensitive dialogue about even these most intimate (and sometimes scandalous) topics.

DIVERSITY AND SEXUALITY IN THE QUR'AN

Before turning to the topic of homosexuality in all its controversy, let us return to the more general category of sexuality. We should approach homosexuality from the wider perspective of diverse sexualities. We should begin by asking whether the Qur'an positively assesses diversity in creation and among human beings. We should observe the Qur'an's positive assessment of diversity in gender, race and ethnicity, color, language, and culture, and then turn to ask whether this positive assessment might include diversity in sexuality as one more dimension of the creation of humanity.

Such a basic question might seem absurd to Muslims who identify as gay or lesbian. Like many Christians and Jews, Muslims tend to put religion behind them when they begin to identify as gay or lesbian, in reaction to the rejection they experience from their families and religious communities. They tend to leave behind the active participation in religion (as ritual or community) even if they feel nostalgia for the sense of belonging that religion promises or retain a sense of distinctive identity in coming from a Muslim background. Many gay and lesbian Muslims feel that Islam is antiquated, oppressive, or hopelessly corrupted by a patriarchal elite. In avoiding the Islamic community, many embrace gay and lesbian communities, hoping to feel comfort and belonging under the rubric of "homosexuality" that they were denied under the rubric of "Islam."

For gay and lesbian Muslims, the term "homosexuality" represents the acknowledgement that there is a natural diversity in sexuality in human societies. For them, it may be disquieting to examine the origins of that term "homosexuality." When it was invented and interpreted in Europe and America in the late nineteenth century, "homosexuality" did not represent an acceptance of diversity in sexuality. The term was popularized in medical clinics to identify a "deviant" sexuality in order to classify people, control their behavior, and "cure" them or confine them. Western societies are still deeply divided over whether there is and should be a natural diversity in the sexuality of its members, though more and more thoughtful people are accepting that homosexuality is not a sickness, weakness, or sin, but rather is a natural variation in human character.[14] This should give gay and lesbian Muslims reason to be courageous and optimistic, for terms mean what they mean as a result of discussion, debate, and struggle. Like the term "homosexuality," the term "Islam" can (and inevitably does) mean different things to different generations and communities. It may not be inevitable that "Islam" stands in opposition to "homosexual" in a relation of contradiction.

A basic strategy for questioning dominant Muslim interpretations of Islam is not to reject Islam as an entire tradition. Rather we should return to Islam's most basic principles, knowing that the details of dominant interpretations may not be in accord with the basic principles.

At its most basic level, Islam is a religion that positively assesses natural diversity in creation and in human societies. Despite the chauvinism of many Muslims, the Qur'an announces the radical idea of diversity in religion. Allah has sent many Prophets, speaking in different languages, bringing ethical teachings and exhortations to different nations, giving rise to a confusing array of ritual practices and legal norms. Islam has a unique history of being a confessional, universal, and missionary religion that nonetheless accepts and protects other religious communities, guaranteeing the security of their members. As a corollary, the Qur'an accepts diversity in tribal, ethnic, and national groupings. The Qur'an's vision stands in stark contrast to the Biblical portrayal of the Tower of Babel (in which God scatters humanity into different groups with mutually incomprehensible languages as a punishment for their competition with God). The Qur'an addresses humanity, saying, "We created you different tribes and nations so that you may come to know one another and acknowledge that the most honorable among you are those that stay the most conscious of Allah" (Surat al-Hujurat 49:13).[15]

The Qur'an respects diversity in physical appearance, constitution, stature, and color of human beings as a natural consequence of Divine wisdom in creation. Muslim feminists have shown that the Qur'an celebrates the creation of women as equal to men, asserting that the differences between them are complementary and are an ethical challenge. The Qur'an does not portray Eve as having been created from Adam's rib, as if she were derivative or inferior.[16] Islamic scholars have traditionally acknowledged that Allah created two genders and also created people who cannot be categorized through a binary construction of gender. One Islamic scholar, 'Ali Muttaqi, displays this acknowledgement clearly in the introduction to his book on marriage and sexual play.

> In the name of God, the Merciful, the Compassionate. Praise be to God who created male and female as partners, then mixed the two in a display of Divine power by creating hermaphrodites as well. Praise be to the One who favored humanity over all the rest of creation and made the continuation of the world to rest upon the conjugal union of the male with the female.[17]

Beyond the fundamental category of gender, the Qur'an asserts that human beings are created in variety and assesses this variation positively. "From among Allah's signs is the creation of the heavens and the earth and the difference of your tongues and the variation of your colors [alwan]" (Surat al-Rum 30:22).[18] Alwan is the plural of the word lawn, which literally means "color" but figuratively stands for shade or type, and can describe variation of texture, flavor, and kind (as in dishes of food).[19] Alwan therefore implies the existence of variations among people, not in outward appearance only but also in inward disposition. Another verse declares "that everyone acts according to his or her own disposition [shakila]" (Surat al-Isra' 17:84). This suggests that human nature that has been created diverse, not just in language, ethnicity, and appearance, but also in inward disposition and personality.

It is not a long step from these profound examples to ask whether the Qur'an accepts diversity in sexual disposition and orientation. The Qur'an never states this clearly, since there is no term in the Qur'an for "sexuality" in its abstract meaning (just as there is no term in the Qur'an for "gender").[20] The above examples show that the Qur'an asserts that creation is diverse on so many levels and that this variation is not random or mistaken and is never to be assessed negatively. With the Qur'an's vivid portrayal of diversity at so many levels of the natural and human world, it would be logical to assume that this diversity of creation plays out on the level of sexuality as well. It is also plausible to assert that, if some Muslims find it necessary to deny that sexual diversity is part of the natural created world, then the burden of proof rests on their shoulders to illustrate their denial from the Qur'anic discourse itself. The Qur'an certainly implies that some people are different in their sexual desires than others when it mentions "men who are not in need of women" (Surat al-Nur 24: 30).[21] The Qur'an includes such men in a list of people whose presence does not require of women social modesty or seclusion (along with male relatives and children who have not attained sexual maturity). It is not clear what inner disposition caused such men to not be attracted to women. Perhaps they simply have no sexual desire (due to age, illness or self-control that involves an inner disposition that could be characterized as "asexual") or perhaps they experience sexual desire that is not attuned to women (which suggests an inner disposition that involves sexual orientation that could be conceived as "homosexual"). In either case, the Qur'an offers an example without negative judgment about men who do not conform to patriarchal assumptions that men are always, inevitably, and uncontrollably attracted sexually to women.[22]

This example from the Qur'an is suggestive, but not indicative. It is clarified by the fact that the Prophet Muhammad knew of men in his era who belonged to this category of "men who are not attracted to women." In Arab society at the time of the Prophet, there were men who lived outside the patriarchal hetero-normal sexual economy (*mukhanath*), as described in the detailed study of Everett Rowson.[23] The evidence presented by Rowson from early Islamic literature shows that the Prophet accepted these men-who-acted-like-women as citizens in Medina, as long as they did not transgress certain ethical rules. They attracted the criticism of the Prophet only when they helped arrange clandestine affairs between men and women (since they were in the unique position of having access to both women's secluded spaces and the more public space of men).

It is therefore reasonable to conclude that the Qur'an accepts the existence of diversity in sexuality and sexual orientation. This is the basic fact that must be acknowledged before moving on to address any particular legal regulation of sexual acts or sexual relationships. In other words, Islamic discourse based on the Qur'an did not use a discourse of "natural" or "unnatural" to describe sexualities. European Christians introduced this concept of "natural" versus "unnatural" to describe variation in sexuality and sexual actions. It has remained the keystone of denunciations of homosexuality long after Christianity ceased to function as the moral touchstone for Western societies. Contemporary Muslims who explicitly denounce homosexuality as "un-Islamic" adopt this dichotomy of natural and unnatural, and apply it as if it were indigenous to the Islamic tradition and to the Qur'an.[24] This is a sign of bad faith, and a signal that contemporary Muslim moralists are not insulated from modernity, even as they depict gay and lesbian Muslims as corrupted by modernity. Gay and lesbian Muslims are certainly not required to accept the posturing of self-righteous defenders of a "tradition" that they anachronistically defend with conceptual tools from Christian thought and modern Euro-American culture. These same moralists and fundamentalists blithely assert that there are no homosexual people in Islamic communities (or if they are they should be killed). On the contrary, when one looks through the historical and literary records of Islamic civilization, one finds a rich archive of same-sex sexual desires and expressions, written by or reported about respected members of society: literati, educated elites, and religious scholars.[25] This is so much the case that one might consider Islamic societies (like classical Greece) to provide a vivid illustration of a "homosexual-friendly" environment in world history. In fact, medieval and early modern Christian Europeans have often engaged in polemics against Muslims by accusing them of being "sodomitical" and of engaging openly in same-sex practices; this rhetoric was an integral part of the Christian campaigns to re-conquer Spain.[26]

How ironic, then, that modern Western scholars have averred to Muslim jurists' views of sexual morality, those jurists who were always a minority voice and often had no social power to enforce their views. It is surprising that most modern Western scholars consistently ignore the observations of medieval European scholars as well as the rich literary and historical examples of same-sex relationships among pre-modern Muslims. The situation among Western scholars has not changed since the time of John Addington Symmonds (who first used the word "homosexual" in English prose in 1883), who remarked that homosexuals are a topic that scholars "touch with reluctance and dispatch with impatience."[27]

If medieval Westerners condemned Muslims for being completely permissive, modern Westerners have recognized only the most repressive elements among Muslims as spokespersons for their religious beliefs and practices. In this, modern Western scholars are certainly acting out their own indigenous forms of homophobia in the mis-recognition or erasure of gay and lesbian Muslims, who might protest, along with the poet Ghalib, that they were not created by mistake no matter who may seek to erase their presence.

> Oh Lord, why does time move to obliterate my every trace?
> I'm no misspelling chalked on the tablet of the universe
> In punishment, go ahead, torment me any way you see fit
> I'm no infidel in the end, but just a simple sinner[28]

It is as if Ghalib were echoing (with a note of sarcasm) the benediction of Imam al-Ghazali: "praise be to God, the marvels of whose creation are not subject to the arrows of accident." If sexuality is inherent in a person's personality, then sexual diversity is a part of creation, which is never accidental but is always marvelous.

Here we have to pause, and scrutinize this evident clash of pre-modern and modern terms of understanding sexuality. Under the conditions of modernity, as it developed in Europe and America, the terms for the debate over sexual diversity are "homosexuality" with its derivative terms "heterosexuality" and "bisexuality." As mentioned above, these conceptual terms are unique to modern societies. While we cannot avoid the terms, we admit that they are contested and debated. It is also crucial for the Muslim community to understand the subtlety of these terms before refuting or denouncing them. Many contemporary analysts are uncomfortable with the term "homosexuality," since it is clinically prescriptive and was invented at the end of the nineteenth century. The term presumes a binary and irreducible opposition between two sexual orientations: "heterosexuality," which is normative, and "homosexuality" which is derivative (and therefore judged to be perverted, inverted, sick, criminal, or somehow unnatural or undesirable). Some historians of sexuality posit that "homosexuals" did not exist before the creation of the term "homosexuality"; they claim that homosexual people, like the term "homosexual" itself, are products of the peculiar conditions of modernity. This argument is the cornerstone of a political position that religious traditions have nothing to say about homosexuality or modern homosexuals, since their ancient scriptures have no term to describe them. Other historians of sexuality take a less nominalist position and argue that "homosexuality" is a particularly modern lens through which to see types of people, behaviors, and dispositions that exist in a more universal way in all societies.[29] They argue that an apple is an apple whether one calls it *Apfel, tufah,* or *sib,* even if the word/concept in English, German, Arabic, or Persian might have different metaphoric associations and cultural connotations. The argument between "essentialists" and "constructionists" over the usefulness of the term "homosexuality" has been a very productive argument with no easy resolution.

Many historians of sexuality have reacted against the binary opposition asserted by the language of "homosexuality" and "heterosexuality." Many now prefer to use a more open-ended term, "queer," to describe all sexual orientations and practices that fall outside the narrow constraints of patriarchal procreative sexuality (called "hetero-normativity"). "Queer" would include same-sex eroticism between men and men or between women and women. It would also include variations of bisexual eroticism in which men might engage in sexual attraction or practices with both men and women (either in series or simultaneously) and women might engage in the same with both women and men. At its conceptual frontier, "queer" would also include celibacy as a sexual practice that falls outside hetero-normative sexuality. More complex would be sexual practices that include gender-crossing identification, as with men who take on social roles described as "female" (through dress, language, or behavior), or women who take on roles described as "male."

The term "queer" allows for a more descriptive and complex analysis of a variety of sexual orientations and practices that are very distinct, but united in their common difference from hetero-normative sexuality. "Queer" is also a literal translation of the Arabic term *shudhudh* which is currently applied to the phenomena of homosexuality in humanistic studies and journalism. *Shudhudh* literally means "odd" in the sense of numerically unusual or rare. "Queer" also has a further merit, in that even heterosexual and normative sexual practices of the past may seem "queer" to heterosexuals in the present. For instance, the notion that Islamic law and prophetic example permitted sexual relationships with slaves who were "owned" rather than "married" appears to many contemporary Muslims very strange and even shameful (since most Islamic communities today do not habitually own slaves any more, with some exceptions). Investigating queer people of the past makes us realize the general "queerness of the past."

HOMOSEXUALITY THAT IS NOT IN THE QUR'AN

With this background of basic Qur'anic principles about diversity and modern concepts of sexuality, what can we say about homosexuality? We can make some statements that may seem radical, but actually come from an insistence on respecting the literal specificity of the Qur'an as revelation. The Qur'an contains no word that means "homosexuality" (as an abstract idea denoting a sexuality of men who desire pleasure with other men or a sexuality of women who desire pleasure with other women). The Qur'an contains no word that means "homosexual" as a man or woman who is characterized by this type of sexuality as forming a core part of his or her identity. The terms that became popular in Arabic in later times (*Liwat* for acts associated with same-sex relations, and *Luti* for persons associated with these acts) are not found in the Qur'an at all. The Qur'an does not explicitly specify any punishment for sexual acts between two men or two women. Most modern commentators and demagogues insist that the Qur'an does do all these things, but their insistence is not rooted in a close reading of the Qur'anic verses with attention to specific terms and their narrative context.

Let us address each of the above points one at a time, since they may strike many Muslim readers as not just controversial but beyond serious consideration. The Qur'an contains no word that means "homosexuality." Nor does it contain a word that means "heterosexuality." The very concept of "sexuality" as an abstract idea is a characteristic of modern societies. This is why sociologists who write in Arabic have had to invent new words to describe homosexuality in the later part of the twentieth century, and have come up with *al-shudhudh al-jinsi* (which means literally "sexually rare or unusual"). Had there been a Qur'anic term for this idea, it would have entered the Arabic language through common usage and modern scholars would not have had to invent a new one. The Qur'an does contain terms that describe desire (*raghba*) and lustful appetite (*shahwa*) which are certainly components of sexuality in the abstract. But without the idea of sexuality, the Qur'an does not have specific terms for either homosexuals or heterosexuals.

That said, it is admitted that the Qur'an assumes a heterosexual norm among its listeners. This does not automatically mean that the Qur'an forbids homosexuality or condemns homosexuals – it means only that the Qur'an assumes that sexual desire between men and women is the norm and that addressing and regulating this desire is the basis for establishing a moral society.

Heterosexuality is certainly a numerical norm. In any society, homosexuals are a numerical minority and are discursively located at the margins of ethical regulations: whether they are condemned or admired, they are always unusual. This is exactly what the modern Arabic term *al-shudhudh al-jinsi* means: a sexuality that is uncommon, outside the general norm, and rare. However, despite being a numerical minority, homosexual women and men are also present in society and numerically persistent. In every historically documented society there is evidence of homosexual desire and activity and there are persons characterized by such desire and activities.

The closest the Qur'an comes to directly addressing homosexual people is the phrase "men who are not in need of women (or have no sexual guile before women)." The Qur'an presents this phrase descriptively in neutral tone, not linked to denunciation or legal proscription. To such people, the Qur'an does not explicitly address its discourse. Commentators and jurists have drawn analogies and presented arguments to conclude that the Qur'an does address such sexually unusual people, despite the Qur'an's lack of a term for them or the actions that characterize them. Those are, however, arguments of jurists and commentators; they are not the words of the Qur'an itself.

The Qur'an does not contain abstract analytical terms like homosexuality or homosexual, yet it does have words for certain acts. Its verses contain terms that designate actions that transgress ethical norms, like *fahisha*: some acts deemed *fahisha* could be sexual in nature. The most explicit term for sexual transgression is adultery, *zina*, but that is clearly applied to sexual penetration between a woman and man outside the bounds of a contractual relationship. As we will see later, many jurists sought to draw equivalence between "adultery" (*zina*) between a man and woman and other sexual acts between two men or between two women. However, this equivalence is based on analogy (*qiyas*) utilizing a legal fiction and is not based on the explicit wording of the Qur'an. Such analogies were the subject of intense debate and little agreement in classical Islamic law.

The Qur'an does specify an abstraction for the underlying moral attitude that gives rise to behaviors and actions that are deemed *fahisha* or transgression; it calls this attitude *fisq* or *fusuq*, which is usually translated as "corruption." As an action, *fusuq* means to break out of the bounds of moral restraint. As an attitude or spiritual condition that causes such action, *fusuq* means not being bound by obedience to the ethical demands of God and is synonymous with the worship of idols. Often in sermons or moral advice, well-meaning preachers will use the word *fusuq* to denounce sexual acts or sexual minorities, in utter disregard of the Qur'anic use of the term. In the Qur'an, the term is both general and deep, specifying a person's or community's inward spiritual state that either accepts God's presence through the Prophets' teachings or conversely rejects them. *Fusuq* is deeply linked to *kufr*, or denying that God is One who sends Prophets who are many. In the view of this writer, those who claim that *fusuq* is a term referring mainly to sex, specific sexual acts, or types of sexuality grossly disregard the ethical and spiritual specificity of the Qur'anic message.

Since the Qur'an does not provide explicit terms for homosexuality or homosexuals, why have Muslims traditionally felt so confident in declaring that the Qur'an forbids homosexuality and condemns homosexuals? This is a very complicated subject, demanding that we assess the ways in which Muslims have read the Qur'an in the past. Nobody simply "reads" a text, especially when it is a scripture or sacred text. We have "ways" of reading. These "ways" refer to practices through which we come to the text, engage the text, and apply the text to people, situations, and events that are not the text. We do not come to the text naïvely. We come as human beings with our pre-conceptions, prejudices, experiences, and "pre-understandings." Our minds and hearts are already full of concepts and ideas (hard-wired, we could say in this computerized age) that we bring to the text before we ever open its pages and pronounce its words.

> Every interpreter enters the process of interpretation with some pre-understanding of the questions addressed by the text – even of its silences – and brings with him or her certain conceptions as presuppositions of his or her exegesis ... One can proceed to examine and discuss the legitimacy, usefulness and justice of particular pre-understandings in contrast to others. Pre-understanding is a condition of living in history ... the ethics or absence of them, are located in an acknowledgement or denial of its [pre-understanding's] presence.[30]

These pre-conceptions both enable us to read and also limit our reading. It is unethical to ignore their presence even in the most respected of classical interpreters. Feminist scholars have shown how traditional readings of the Qur'an have been "male" readings of the Qur'an, entirely shaped by assumptions of masculine prerogative, privilege, and patriarchal power. Feminists have accused male readers of distorting the sacred text by importing into it patriarchal assumptions that may not be present in the Qur'an itself. Contemporary scholars attentive to injustices against gay and lesbian Muslims approach the question with the same moral agenda as feminist scholars. They use the same critical techniques of rereading the scriptural texts through new lenses in order to free the text from its former patriarchal confinement.

This is a very weighty undertaking. It is a project in process. This study can only sketch the preliminary scope and method for such a project. Let it be admitted at the outset that gay and lesbian Muslims are not certain what will be found after a thoroughly critical reassessment of scriptural and juridical texts of their religious tradition. They are only certain that no reassessment has yet been made that takes into account differences in sexuality as well as gender. This article hopes to contribute, in a small way, to this project. It cannot address all the details, but it can highlight the crucial importance of this project and some of the preliminary insights that might be gained from it. It asserts that there is reason to doubt the reasoning behind the traditional condemnation of homosexuality. More urgently, there is reason to doubt the justification of capital punishment for homosexual acts. This article will address texts and traditions in their order of importance to Islamic jurisprudence: the Qur'an, the *hadith* reports attributed to the Prophet Muhammad (*Sunnah*), legal reasoning by analogy (*qiyas*), and the consensus of jurists (*ijma'*).[31]

INTERPRETING THE QUR'AN DEPENDS ON THE EXPERIENCE OF THE INTERPRETER

There is, at present, no complete interpretation of the Qur'an from a non-patriarchal perspective. Islamic feminists have boldly begun this project, but it is hardly complete. Scholars like Amina Wadud, Riffat Hassan, and Fatima Mernissi have asserted that the Qur'an does not picture women as devoid of reason, biologically inferior, or inherently subject to men's control, despite the interpretations given to the Qur'an by traditionalists, jurists, and commentators. Gay and lesbian readers of the Qur'an have much to contribute to a non-patriarchal reading of the sacred text, but have only recently become empowered to join this project in the footsteps of their feminist heroines. As they do, they will use the same interpretive tools that feminists have developed (and these are the same tools that modernist, even politically radical, interpreters have used for liberationist purposes). Let us call this kind of interpretation "sexuality-sensitive" interpretation, as short-hand to compare its results to feminist interpretation and liberationist interpretation.

Sexuality-sensitive interpretation is attentive to the fact that sexualities are always multiple in society. It is attentive to the fact that variation is always arranged in hierarchical orders of power, leading to marginalization and disempowerment of the non-normative groups, such as gays, lesbians, or those whose gender is not easy to categorize as male or female. An elite is always empowered by silencing and oppressing the marginal few; the elite claims to speak for the norms of society, while subtly or explicitly supporting the oppression of other groups, like women or political dissidents. "Sexuality-sensitive" as a descriptive term for this kind of interpretation is a direct translation of the Arabic term *hassas*, meaning literally "a sensitive person" but used colloquially to denote "a homosexual person."[32]

Two basic interpretive strategies are important for sexuality-sensitive readings of the Qur'an: semantic analysis and thematic analysis of the Qur'an. These strategies are designed to move beyond "traditional" Qur'anic interpretation with its verse-by-verse analysis that decontextualizes moments of revelation, freezes their meaning, and specifies their interpretation according to a word-for-word replacement. It will become clear that word-for-word replacement, as practiced by classical Qur'anic commentators, has led to very narrow interpretations of the Lut story in the Qur'an. The Lut story in the

Qur'an is the same as the Lot story in the Bible, yet it is told in a very different way, with contrasting emphases and contradictory details. The stories are comparable but not collapsible. This study insists on naming the Prophet Lut (with Arabic spelling) in order to draw this distinction from the story of Lot, which may be more familiar to many readers. The Lut story is the constant reference for Muslims' understanding of same-sex relationships. Word-for-word replacement in classical commentaries has given rise to the dubious equation of the Divine punishment of Lut's people with a condemnation of homosexuality and juridically enforceable punishment for same-sex acts. This is a conclusion that looks less inevitable (and less intelligible) when we pursue different techniques of interpretation, like semantic or thematic interpretation.

First, let us review how classical commentators have interpreted the Qur'an. I do not say "traditional" commentators, for in their time they were pioneers not traditionalists. Only in retrospect have their works come to represent immutable tradition, as later readers of the Qur'an were too modest or were disempowered from giving alternative readings. Let's look at the example of al-Tabari, whose commentary on the Qur'an is accepted as one of the foundational texts of this genre. In his commentary on the verse in which Lut admonishes his people for "approaching the transgression" (Surat al-A'raf 7:80–81), al-Tabari writes,

> The transgression [*fahisha*] that they approach, for which they were punished by Allah, is "penetrating males sexually" [*ityan dhukur*]. The meaning is this: it is as if Lut were saying "You are, all of you, you nation of people, coming to men in their rears, out of lust, rather than coming to those that Allah has approved for you and made permissible to you from the women. You are a people that approach what Allah has prohibited for you. Therefore you rebel against Allah by that act." That is what the Qur'an means by going beyond the bounds [*israf*] when Lut said, *You are a people who go beyond all bounds.*[33]

It is clear from this passage that al-Tabari's basic strategy is definition and substitution. He takes a term that is pivotal to the verse and defines it: "transgression" equals anal sex between men. Al-Tabari supplements definition with substitution. He substitutes his own words for the words of the Qur'an in order to add weight and validity to his interpretation: "It is as if Lut were saying" this and that. This strategy allows al-Tabari to make a speculative assertion as if it were a foregone conclusion: "This reproach [declaring anal sex between men hateful] was the content of Lut's prophetic message [*risala*]; his purpose was to make this act forbidden."[34] This speculative assertion is not certain from the Qur'an itself. It is not clear that Lut was sent as a Prophet solely (or even primarily) to declare anal sex between men to be forbidden. It is not clear from the Qur'anic text that Lut's entire prophetic message revolves around sex acts. Rather, this is the conclusion that al-Tabari engineers through his strategy of definition and substitution.

Al-Tabari's techniques of commentary are very limited and give a very limited interpretation. However, it is the dominant mode of commentary in the classical period, and al-Tabari's interpretation is echoed in almost all later commentators. Once they were enshrined in classical commentaries, such conclusions were repeated in most commentaries through the present day, especially in commentaries that pretend to be simple "translations." If we take Abdullah Yusuf Ali's popular English "translation" of the Qur'an as an example, we find him engaging in very irresponsible translation that promotes a dangerously reductionist way of thinking. In his translation of Surat al-'Ankabut 29:28–35, where the Qur'an talks about "the lewdness that not has come to before in the wide worlds," Yusuf Ali describes this "lewdness" as homosexuality which is a "crime against the laws of nature."[35]

Al-Tabari's commentary conflates sexual acts of a specific nature with sexual desire of a particular orientation. He does not distinguish between sexual acts, sexual desire, or sexuality. These terms must be carefully dis-aggregated, according to sociological facts about the human personality and sexual diversity. Does the Qur'an talk about a sexual identity characterized by erotic orientation? Does it address a coupling between two people characterized by this identity? Or does it refer to specific sexual acts? These are specific questions that al-Tabari does not ask or answer.

In fact, his interpretive strategy pointedly precludes the possibility of asking these questions of the Qur'an. Sexuality-sensitive interpretation of the Qur'an needs to ask these questions. When we use methods of analysis and interpretation that are more complex and ethically alert, it becomes clear that the story of Lut is not about homosexuality or homosexuals in any general sense. Let's turn to two methods of interpretation that can give us new insights into the Qur'an. They can give us insights precluded by the simple denunciation of homosexuality which is content to take a few words or phrases out of context in order to interpret the verses by definition and substitution.

Semantic analysis of the Qur'an is a technique of reading that does not trust simple translation. The Islamic scholars have long been skeptical of the ability of translation to capture the meaning of the Qur'an in another language. Semantic analysis takes this skepticism further and makes an analytic technique out of refusal to trust a word-for-word translation of Qur'anic terms. The Japanese scholar of Islam Toshihiko Izutsu provided the most sophisticated explanation of this technique and demonstrated what it can contribute to Qur'anic interpretation.[36] He explained that words have meaning only by being enmeshed in a web of relationships to other words. This is especially true in regard to the Qur'an, which was revealed as scripture and represents the "Speech of Allah" that belongs to its own realm of discourse. The ethical imperatives of the Qur'an can be understood by looking at how its words relate to each other; in effect, its words "define themselves" by grouping into clusters of relationships in "semantic fields."

One scholar has applied this technique to the sexuality-sensitive interpreta-tion of the Qur'an, in the first serious critical attempt to reassess the Qur'an's view of same-sex relationships.[37] Amreen Jamel analyzed the passages from fourteen surahs of the Qur'an that mention Lut and his relationship to the community of people to whom he was sent as a Prophet.[38] While it is clear that Lut's people were wicked and were destroyed by Divine punishment for their wickedness, it is not clear at all whether the Qur'anic terms that describe their wickedness and destruction are terms that specify same-sex relationships. Jamel's goal is

> to discover the nature of the moral judgements within the Qur'an by raising questions about the Qur'an's perception of sin. The question that needs investigation is whether the specific moral terminology used within the Lut saga as well as in the rest of the Qur'an provides a direct link to attitudes toward same-sex sexuality.[39]

To do this, Jamel's article highlighted the seventeen Arabic root-words that appear in the story of Lut (which carry the weight of ethical condemnation of Lut's people). The article then analyzed their range of meanings both in the Lut story and throughout the Qur'an where they appear without any relationship to Lut's people. Jamel charted whether these terms specified sensual or sexual acts or attitudes and whether they were clearly positive or negative in their moral weight. Semantic analysis was used to discover how the Qur'an gave these terms a range of meanings, dependent on how the terms were related to each other and how they were repeated in different contexts.

This method gives a very "literal" reading of the text. It respects the words of the Qur'an not as defined not by human authorities who assign them meanings by definition and substitution, but rather as defined by their placement in relations to other words in the Qur'an itself. The results of Jamel's systematic and comprehensive study confirm that there is great ambiguity in the Qur'anic retelling of the story of Lut.

> While there are no terms in the Qur'an that are uniquely attached to same-sex sexuality, certain terms (e.g. from the roots sh-h-y [as in shahwa] and f-h-sh [as in fahisha]) are frequently associated with same-sex sexual practices ... However, these terms are used to qualify morally opposite-sex and non-sexual activities as well. Same-sex indiscretions are, in fact, put on the same ethical plane as all sorts of inappropriate opposite-sex and non-sexual activities. In that form, same-sex sexual abominations [sic] are just another form of alienation from God, no different than anything else ... It is possible to suggest that Lut's people (specifically the men) were indeed destroyed right after they threatened to assault Lut's male guests sexually; however, there are others, like Lut's wife, who are destroyed for non-sexual indiscretions. This example alone

confirms the premise that same-sex sexuality is not the ultimate abomination that causes people to be alienated from God.[40]

Jamel's analysis is the first step in a serious analysis of the Qur'an from a sexuality-sensitive perspective. Yet the conclusions are very moderate in comparison with the data the study raises.[41] Jamel notes that the terms that the Qur'an uses to denounce Lut's people are not unique to Lut's people; some imply sexual activity but are not limited to sexual activity. Jamel's conclusions could go one step further, to question whether the overall condemnation of Lut's people was either about their sex practices in general or about the sexuality of specific persons in the community. It is certainly hard to imagine a just God, whose most basic message through the Prophets is that "whoever does an atom's weight of good will see the results and whoever does an atom's weight of evil will see the results" (Surat al-Zalzala 99:7), would destroy women and children because of acts of anal intercourse that could occur only between men. From this vantage point, it would seem that it was not sexual behavior or sexuality for which they were all punished, but rather something far more basic.

It is crucial to pursue this point in Qur'anic analysis beyond the initial study by Amreen Jamel. That study notes how Lut's people were destroyed after some of their men "threatened to assault Lut's male guests sexually." Why did these men threaten to assault them? What was the social, political, and moral context of this assault? Should readers of the Qur'an understand this "sexual assault" as an expression of sexuality (let alone homosexuality) or rather as an exercise of coercive power through rape? These are questions that cannot be answered through the technique of semantic analysis alone. We have to turn to a second technique, to "thematic analysis," to supplement Jamel's study and take its analysis to a deeper level of critical re-evaluation of tradition.

Thematic analysis of the Qur'an is based on the insight that the Qur'an is a unique scripture in its form and texture. Unlike the Hebrew Torah, the Qur'an is not a chronological account of a distinct people or tribe; unlike the Christian Gospels, it is not a biographical account of a founding religious figure. The Qur'an's verses are organized into chapters whose structure is more like a kaleidoscope than a chain. Its central themes radiate out in patterns from a central point (where Divine will impacts human language in the consciousness of the Prophet). These patterns are not subordinated to a chronologically organized story. In the Qur'an, narratives comes as reminders. They are told in short sequences, interspersed with parables, directives, or ethical exhortations, only to be repeated or continued in a different place. This contributes to the Qur'an's unique power to communicate and move its audience. But this also creates a daunting challenge for those who seek to interpret "what the Qur'an says" about a particular topic. An interpreter cannot just pick one verse and use it as a proof-text to make an authoritative statement, for the same theme could come up, in different contexts with different shades of meaning, in other places in the Qur'an.

Thematic analysis of the Qur'an embraces this structural characteristic of the Qur'an, while classical commentaries ignore it. A thematic analysis identifies a single theme (be it a concept, an image, or a character) and traces its multiple appearance throughout the Qur'an. It tries to provide a composite picture of the theme, based on its multiple and varied single instances, without privileging one verse over another and trusting that the Qur'an provides a thematic unity underneath all these instances. This type of analysis is basic to all reformist interpretation that searches for an inner unity of the Qur'an beyond the juridical rulings enshrined in the *Shari'ah*.

> Reformist scholars all agree that the task of interpretation today must consider the time, location and an understanding of how tenets and directives respond to the contemporary context. They also share a commitment to the inner unity of the Qur'an and a rejection of random and selective citation.[42]

To see how this works, let's take a simple example. When one reads a Qur'anic passage about "water" one should not interpret it solely based on the lexical meaning of "water" as "liquid H_2O" or on the grammatical placement of the word "water" in a sentence. One should not stop at "water" as a particular subject related to the verse before it or the verse after it. Rather, thematic analysis urges us to interpret "water" in relationship to all other instances in which the Qur'an mentions "water." This gives us a more holistic basis for interpretation, in which any mention of "water" is not isolated but has a greater meaning created by the varied repetitions of water imagery: as rainfall, as seas, or as a means of ritual purification. The meaning of "water" is more fully and more deeply understood if we take account of the multiple and varied contexts in which it is embedded, rather than ignoring these contexts in order to interpret a single verse. The Qur'an's repeated and varied references to water is a key to our thinking about *rizq* or how Allah distributes provision to all creatures, forcing us to consider the economics of distributive justice in our societies. Through thematic analysis, "water" forces us to examine the way our economies destroy the environmental interconnectedness that is the apparent conduit for Allah's continuous creation and provision. In addition, water is linked to sexuality through procreation, for (as al-Ghazali asserted in the quotation that heads this study) "Allah created all things from water," and al-Ghazali interprets "water" to mean the meeting of male and female sexual fluids with their procreative potential.

This method of analysis is especially useful, even indispensable, when we come to the Qur'an's more narrative passages. These are frequently about the Prophets who came before Muhammad, including the Prophet Lut. This study will focus here on the narrative of Lut's struggles as a Prophet, since it is from verses in this narrative that commentators and jurists have made assertions about homosexuality. The Qur'an does not present this narrative completely in one place. Rather, various parts of Lut's story are mentioned in different places as reminders. Thematic analysis has trained us to be wary of interpreting one part of this story separate from the composite whole that is created by the repeated and varied presentation of parts of the story in scripture. The deeper meaning of Lut's struggles will be lost to us if we do not try to construct these textual incidents into a cohesive narrative while simultaneously being attentive to the context of their incidence.

Since the classical period, Muslim scholars have been engaging in thematic analysis of the Qur'an (without announcing the fact) by telling stories of the Prophets. They developed these "narrative re-constructions" into a new genre, called "Stories of the Prophets" (*Qisas al-Anbiya'*). Though this genre was distinct from classical commentaries (*tafsir*), the Stories of the Prophets were in reality a kind of commentary on the Qur'anic verses that mention the various Prophets. Tradition presents the practices of telling these stories as just as old and just as authentic as making explicit commentaries on the Qur'an.[43] We have no books that date from this early period. For this study, we will focus on the Stories of the Prophets written by al-Kisa'i.[44] Although he wrote in the twelfth century CE, al-Kisa'i quotes from earlier books that no longer exist.[45] Al-Kisa'i is one of the earliest texts that we have in this genre in Arabic, along with other similar books in Persian, to which this study later refers.[46]

Al-Kisa'i interprets the Qur'anic verses about Lut by telling Lut's story. He arranges all the verses about Lut in a narrative sequence, buttressed by what the Islamic tradition had preserved of historical and sociological knowledge about "the Cities of the Plain" and the society that thrived there. Let's listen to his interpretation as an example of a thematic analysis of the Qur'an.

There were five cities known as the "Cities of the Plain" and the chief among them was named Sodom. The cities were each surrounded by high walls of iron and lead. In each lived thousands of inhabitants. The king of the realm was called "Sodom son of Khariq" and was from the family of Nimrod. The people of this realm were more skilled than any in the whole world in cheating in accounts and shooting at thrown clay targets. They were well-known for sins like clapping their hands, playing sports with pigeons, lining up fighting birds, playing with tooth-picks, chewing gum, setting up dog-fights and cock-fights and worshiping graven idols. Their king established special temples for the idols which were intricately sculpted and set up. Special seats for the idols were bedecked and decorated.

The people of these cities took to building gardens within the walls of their houses to avoid the public. In this privacy, they would retire to partake of beautiful and pleasant pass-times. Then a famine came and they fell into poverty. Iblis the accursed took this opportunity to come to them, saying, "This famine has befallen you all because you prevented other people from entering your homes but did not prevent them from entering your orchards which are outside your homes!" They had gardens inside their homes that were hidden from the public, and gardens and orchards outside their homes which they left open for the rest of the people who might be travelling through and need to stop at night to take rest and provision.

So the people asked the Tempter [Iblis], "How can we guard against strangers and travelers entering these public orchards?" Iblis replied, "Make it your custom that if any strangers come and enter the orchards of your land you will fuck them from behind and steal all their belongings! If you do that, nobody will dare stop there in their travels to spend the night!"

On hearing this, the people went outside the city walls, searching for people whom they could debauch [yafjuruna bihi]. Iblis then appeared to them in a different form: the form of a young man, handsome and richly-dressed. The people overtook him, stole all his belongings, and fucked him. The people all decided this was a good thing. It became a habitual custom for them with any stranger who wandered onto their lands. Corruption spread among them.

Then Allah revealed to Ibrahim that his cousin, named Lut, has been chosen as a warner and a messenger to those corrupt and degenerate people.[47]

At this point, the apostlehood of Lut begins in earnest. Into this narrative reconstruction, al-Kisa'i embeds the verses from the Qur'an that mention Lut. The Qur'anic words are rendered here in italics, to make clear how he quotes scripture interspersed with commentary.

So Lut set off and traveled until he came to the cities [of the plain]. He stopped just outside the area, not knowing in which city he should begin. Then he entered the city of Sodom since it was the largest city and the residence of the king.

When he reached the market place, he raised his voice and announced, "Oh people, stay conscious of Allah and obey! Restrain yourself from these transgressions [fawahish, in the plural] that no other people has practiced like this before you! And quit worshipping idols! For indeed, I am the messenger of Allah sent to you!" It is as Allah said in the Qur'an, And [remind them of] Lut, when he said to his people: Do you come to the transgression that nobody in the universe has before you? And Allah also said, Do you come to the men in your lust disregarding the women? Indeed you are a heedless and headstrong people! (Al-A'raf 80–1 and al-Naml 27:55).

His people simply answered him by retorting, *Let us expel Lut and his family from this city of ours, for they are people who pretend to be purer!* (Al-Naml 27:56). They meant purer than them by abstaining from these transgressions [*fawahish*]. These are the things Allah indicated in the verse: *Indeed you come upon men and rob wayfarers and practice reprehensible things in your gatherings* (Surat Al-'Ankabut 29:29) meaning short-changing and cheating people, clapping their hands [*tasfiq*], playing sports with pigeons, wearing clothes dyed scarlet [luxurious clothes]. *Then the people answered Lut immediately, saying* "Bring on the punishment from Allah if you are a sincere speaker of truth!" (Surat Al-'Ankabut 29:29).

News of this confrontation reached their king, who demanded that Lut be brought before him. Lut came into his presence and the king asked, "Who are you? Who sent you here? And why?" Lut answered "Surely it is Allah the Exalted who sent me to you as a messenger that you might put an end to these transgressions [*fawahish*] and return to obedience to Allah."

Hearing this, the King's heart was struck with fear. He said to Lut, "I am one with my people – as they answer you so I answer you." So Lut left the king and went out to the people. He beseeched them to return to obedience to Allah and forbade them from continuing their rebellious ways, warning them about the punishment of Allah and preaching to them about the destruction of former nations who were oppressive.[48] The people rushed upon him from every side, *shouting If you don't desist, Lut, you will surely be driven out!* (Surat al-Shu'ara 26:167) meaning driven out of their land. So Lut rebuffed them, *saying I am surely of those who stands above what you practice!* (Surat al-Shu'ara 26:168) meaning that he was one of those who find what they do reprehensible. [Lut prayed] *My Lord, save me and my family from what they are doing.* (Surat al-Shu'ara 26:169).

In al-Kisa'i's interpretation of the story, Lut is helpless. He lives among the people of the cities for twenty years, during which time his first wife dies (who had come with him from outside). He marries a new wife from among the people of Sodom. Now partly integrated into their society,

He persisted in preaching to them, but they heaped insults on him and beat him while continuing their ugly behavior. This continued until he had lived among them forty years. They continued to ignore him and refused to follow him and never desisted from their custom. This continued until the earth beneath them rose in tumult because of their awful deeds. So Allah revealed these words to the earth: "I am most restrained and patient and I never rush against those who rebel against me, until their appointed time comes about" (echoing the phrasing of Surat al-Dhariyat 51:30). Yet still the people persisted in deeming this messenger of Allah as trivial and not heeding his call to return to obedience to Allah.[49]

The solution to this troublesome situation comes from outside the Cities of the Plain. Lut had an integral connection to the Prophet Ibrahim (Abraham). Lut was related by family ties to Ibrahim, and their prophetic missions were similar in opposing idol worship and espousing an ethic of care for vulnerable, weak, and marginalized people of their societies. As if to assert this integral connection between the two Prophets, the four angels who are sent to destroy the Cities of the Plain first stop at the camp of Ibrahim, in the form of human beings. Ibrahim welcomes them as his guests, "For it was his custom not to eat except with guests with whom to share his food, and he had not had any guests for three days in a row."[50] He greets them by saying, "Peace be upon you, strangers from an unknown people" (Surat al-Dhariyat 51:24). He invites them to stay with him and eat of his food. He grows suspicious and frightened when the guests do not eat, fearing that the risk he took to help them would be repaid by their intending harm against him (Surat Hud 11:69–70).

This sets up a narrative tension that explains the story in more depth. The hospitality, generosity, and care for the poor, strangers, and travelers that was exhibited by Ibrahim and Lut contrasts vividly with the "practices of the people of Lut" in the Cities of the Plain. They do not host strangers; they chase them away. They do not feed travelers; they rob them. They do not take care of guests and the needy; they rape them sexually by force as an operation of power over them.

Thematic analysis of the Qur'an has the goal of finding the deep structural motifs of the Qur'an and relating individual images or verses to these deeper motifs. In this way, thematic analysis of the Qur'an tries to make clear the most basic and profound ethical principles expounded in the Qur'an. At its deepest and most meaningful level, the Qur'an argues that humane values come from belief in one God while inhumane values come from idolatry. Belief in one God is the basis for generosity, hospitality, and an ethic of care for the needs of others. On the contrary, belief in idols is the basis for pride, hoarding wealth, denying the rights of others and exploiting their weakness in every way possible (through wealth, property, coercion, objectifying others, and using them). Sexual relations are not exempt from this ethical dynamic. They can express care for others or abuse of others, depending on the ethical situation, the moral intention and the social context in which they are practiced. Clearly the sexual acts of the people of Sodom are only one expression of their overall ethical corruption. Their acts are not important as sexual acts (as expressions of sexuality) but rather as expressions of their disregard for the ethical care of others and most specifically their rejection of the prophethood of Lut.

This is the repeated message of the Qur'an, which becomes clearer as al-Kisa'i re-constructs a narrative context for the story. It is the message that comes across clearly even as the angels enter the cities and Lut tries to take responsibility for hosting and protecting them as strangers and wayfarers.

> Then the angels left Ibrahim and traveled to the cities where Lut lived. They arrived just before evening. The eldest daughter of Lut, named Rabab, spotted them approaching as she was irrigating the fields. When she saw how beautiful and attractive they were, she approached them and said, "What are you doing coming to these corrupt people? Especially when there is nobody to give you hospitality and protection except that old man over there. He is their Prophet, against whom they are remorselessly cruel in their opposition."[51]

This narrative commentary does not interpret the verses against their literal meaning; it places them in a social and historical context in which their literal pronouncements make sense. This context focuses not on sex acts as expressions of sexuality that might be called "homosexuality" or could be judged as "unnatural." Rather the context of the narrative focuses on acts of greed, selfishness, and inhospitality, which are taken to the extreme of violence against strangers. The sexual acts of the narrative are acts of violence more than acts of sexual pleasure; they are contiguous with acts of coercion and robbery. Worse, all these incidents of violent inhospitality are concentrated in rejecting the prophethood of Lut and disbelieving in the God whom Lut claims to represent. The narrative is clearly about infidelity through inhospitality and greed, rather than about sex acts in general or sexuality of any variation in particular.

One possible critique of this narrative style of commentary on the Qur'an is that it frames the Qur'anic verses in a "fictional" story. Critics might rush to point out that al-Kisa'i does not cite any reports from the Prophet or the early Companions to authenticate the elements of this story. However, other scholars who wrote narratives of the Prophet Lut in Stories of the Prophets have presented similar narratives in the form of reports from the Prophet and early Companions with an authenticating record of transmission (*isnad*). One example is the book by al-Rawandi, written in the late twelfth century CE.[52] He quotes a series of *hadith* attributed to the Prophet Muhammad, with full *isnad*, which support elements of the narrative framework presented by al-Kisa'i. For instance, one *hadith* presents Muhammad asking Jibra'il why and how the people of Lut were destroyed. Jibra'il answers,

> The people of Lut were a people who did not clean themselves after excreting, and did not wash after sexual ejaculation. They were stingy and covetous in refusing to share food generously with others. Lut stayed among them for thirty years, living amid them without ever becoming like them, entering into intimate terms with them or establishing a family

among them. Lut called them to follow Allah's command but they never heeded his call or obeyed him as their Prophet.[53]

This *hadith* stresses that the sinful nature of the people of Lut was greed, avarice, covetousness, and a cruel lack of generosity. It supports the basic framework of al-Kisa'i's narrative interpretation of the Qur'an.

This is even more explicit in another *hadith* quoted by al-Rawandi. The report has Abu Ja'far asking the Prophet Muhammad to describe the consequences of stinginess in refusing to share with others (*bukhl*). The Prophet is reported as reciting the Qur'an – "And those who protect their souls from stinginess, they are the spiritually successful" (Surat al-Hashr 59:9) – and then he answers,

> I will tell you about the consequences of miserliness. The people of Lut were inhabitants of a city that refused to share its food with others. This miserliness consequently became a disease that had no cure that infected their sexual organs [*furuj*] ... Their city was on the main highway between Syria and Egypt, so caravans and travelers used to halt there and stay as their guests. This situation increased until their means were stretched to the limits and they grew dissatisfied. Greed and miserliness bid them follow its call, to the extent that if any strangers stopped to ask for their hospitality, they would rape them [*fadahahu*] without sexual need, in order to dishonor them. They persisted in this behavior until they began to search out men and force themselves on them.[54]

Again, al-Rawandi asserts that the "sexual acts" of the people of Lut were acts of violence to drive away strangers, travelers, and those in need. They were not sexual acts expressing a distinct sexuality or even fulfilling the desire for sexual pleasure. They were acts of coercion expressing their miserliness, greed, and rejection of the ethic of care that was the hallmark of the Prophets. Rape is not primarily about sexual acts, pleasures, or relations. It is primarily about power and authority (as recent evidence from the war in Bosnia, involving the rape of women or police brutality cases involving anal rape of men, demonstrates).

This argument can be extended to explain why Lut offered his daughters to the crowd that rushed to his home intending to violate Lut's guests. Many interpreters have stressed the gender difference between the daughters who were female and the guest-angels who were male, explaining this episode as confirmation that females are the appropriate sex-objects of males to the exclusion of other males. However, this episode can be explained in a different way that highlights the ethics of hospitality rather than the hetero-normative conflation of gender difference with sexual desire.

As the head of a household, Lut had the duty to protect two kinds of people: his kin and his guests to whom he had offered food and shelter. Offers of hospitality were not just a matter of sharing a meal, but also cemented a social bond including the duty to protect guests from threats in the surrounding community. The people of Lut rejected his prophethood by violating his right to offer hospitality and protection to strangers and visitors. Their attempt to abduct his guests and rape them most graphically demonstrates this rejection. When Lut offers up his family members (who happen to be female daughters) in exchange for his guests (who happen to be male visitors), he displays in most extreme terms the sacredness of protecting guests who are elevated even above the status of offspring. The difference in gender between the female characters in the narrative and the male characters obscures the more important underlying message, that caring for those in need is a sacred duty that overrides the duty to protect one's own family. How many of us, homosexual or heterosexual, can claim to live up to that ethical principle?

In this way, the genre of Stories of the Prophets acts as a commentary on the Qur'an, beyond the technical limitations of the *tafsir* genre. One could argue that authors of Stories of the Prophets are actually articulating the fundamental ethical principles of the Qur'an better than do the authors of *tafsir*, since they are not confined to grammatical and lexical commentary on each verse. They are freer to compare verses to come up with an intelligible narrative that does not contradict the explicit word of the Qur'anic verses that inform it. Their goal is to present each Prophet as a character who upholds ethical values in the face of rejection and opposition by their community, ethical values that can and should inform the Muslim community that strives to follow the whole line of Prophets.

JURISTS, SEXUAL ACTS, AND LUT'S PEOPLE

There is an instructive contradiction here. In populist religious discourse (*muwa'iza*), sexual acts between men are always condemned in reference to the people of Lut. However, in juridical discourse, there is nothing in the Qur'anic verses about Lut on which to base legal rulings. Jurists refer to Lut's people only rhetorically, not juridically. As short-hand, they call the act of penetration of a penis in another's anus "the act of the people of Lut." To construct legal rulings about this act, jurists rely on either *hadith* or, more often, reports of the decisions of the early followers of the Prophet. It is to this body of textual sources for the law they we must now turn.

Let's look closely at commentaries on the Qur'an that were written by jurists. Their concern was not to give a semantic or thematic analysis of the Qur'anic discourse, but rather to give legal rulings for the ordering of society. Their commentaries were meant to highlight those Qur'anic verses from which legal rulings could be deduced. Jurists were concerned with acts rather than intentions, and they focused rather obsessively on the act of anal intercourse between men. While gay men can rightly protest that anal sex is not the definitive feature that characterizes them, and many gay men do not practice anal penetrative sex at all, it is the case that this is how the Islamic juridical tradition pictured all same-sex desire.[55] It will become clear that jurists in the classical period did not reach a consensus about the legal status of anal sex between men. It will become even clearer that they did not even address something called "homosexuality" in the abstract. The jurists argued over how to understand the term *fahisha* in the Lut story, and whether it was, in legal terms, equivalent to *zina* or sexual intercourse between a man and a woman who are not related by marriage, contract, or ownership.

Let's begin with al-Qurtubi, a Maliki jurist who died in 1273 CE. He wrote a detailed commentary on the Qur'an, and tried to argue that anal sex between men was a *hadd* crime requiring capital punishment. A *hadd* crime (pl. *hudud*) is a crime that is explicitly defined in the Qur'an and for which specific punishment is demanded in the Qur'an. There are five crimes with *hadd* punishments that are explicitly mentioned in the Qur'an: murder, highway robbery, theft, adultery between a man and a woman, and false accusation of adultery. Al-Qurtubi argues that anal sex between two men is also a *hadd* crime, even if this is not explicitly stated in the Qur'an, since this sexual act is the legal equivalent of *zina*. *Zina* is an act of sexual penetration between a man and a woman who are not joined by a contractual relationship or marriage, and the punishment for *zina*, under certain legal conditions, is death by stoning. To make this argument, al-Qurtubi lines up a series of assertions, all of which are open to question and critique.

In the Qur'an, Lut says to his community, "Do you approach the transgression [*a ta'tuna al-fahishata*]?" In the commentary on this verse, al-Qurtubi gives a classic example of interpretation by substitution. He is unconcerned about the semantic range of the term *fahisha* or whether it is related to wider themes. Rather, he defines the word *fahisha* in juridical terms, by substituting it with a phrase that is explicit.

> *Do you approach the transgression* means "sexually entering males" [*idkhal al-rijal*]. Allah mentions this act with the term *the transgression* [*fahisha*] in order to make it clear that this act is adultery [*zina*]. It is just like Allah's statement in another verse, *Do not approach adultery* [*zina*] *for it is a transgression* [*fahisha*] (Surat al-A'raf 7:80–84).[56]

In classical Islamic law, the *hadd* punishment for adultery is either lashing (if the person is unmarried) or stoning to death (if the person is already married). This is the punishment that al-Qurtubi argues should apply to men who have anal sex with a man. He argues this despite the fact that the Qur'an does not specify this as a *hadd* crime and the Prophet Muhammad does not give any explicit example of having applied this punishment to the act in question. By offering a definition (substituting "entering males" for "transgression") and an analogy (sexual penetration of an unmarried man by a man is equal to sexual penetration of an unmarried woman by a man), al-Qurtubi argues that this juridical decision is in reality nothing but a simple "reading" of the Qur'an.

One could argue with al-Qurtubi that his reading of the Qur'an is not just simple, but also erroneous, limited, and misleading. His reading is not attentive to grammatical subtlety or narrative context. In the verse that communicates Lut's prohibition *al-fahisha* comes in the definite nominal form, "the transgression," whereas the verse about adultery mentions *fahisha* in the indefinite nominal form "transgression." This suggests that transgression is a general category including many different specific kinds of acts; one could speak of the particular transgression in specifying an act or one could speak of transgression in general to imply a whole range of acts that transgress the boundary of decency, righteousness, or legality. Not every term mentioned as "transgression" would be equivalent, morally or legally or punitively. In fact, the Qur'an often uses the term "transgressions" (*fawahish*) in the plural in the narrative sections about Lut and his conflict with his community. One would have to ignore grammar and narrative context to draw the one-for-one equivalence that al-Qurtubi has done.

Al-Qurtubi is quite bold about doing this, and insists that he knows Allah's intention in using particular terms. However, al-Qurtubi cannot deny that other jurists have read the same passage and come to different conclusions. He admits that "jurists have differed amongst themselves over the exact punishment for this [anal sex between men] after they have come to consensus on forbidding it."[57] The Maliki and Shafi'i jurists insist that anal sex between men is a *hadd* crime punishable by death. This contradicts the Hanafi jurists, who argue that although it is an immoral act and is forbidden, it does not qualify as a *hadd* crime. Hanafis insist that there should be no punishment of death but rather the government authorities can punish the act as they think appropriate. As a Maliki jurist, al-Qurtubi quotes Imam Malik, for whom two contradictory judgments have been recorded: one says "He should be stoned [to death] whether he is married or unmarried," while the other says, "He should be stoned if he is married and disciplined if he is unmarried." Despite the contradiction, both judgments interpret anal sex between men as a *hadd* crime, equivalent to *zina*, or adultery. Imam al-Shafi'i's judgment makes this explicit in ways that Malik leaves implicit when he is reported to have said, "He should be punished with the *hadd* penalty to adultery *by reason of juridical analogy.*"

There is a deep problem here for those who advocate capital punishment for anal sex between men. It is primarily countries that follow the Hanbali legal method (or countries ruled by fundamentalists influenced by Hanbalism) that make a state policy of executing gay men. Hanbalis are a tiny minority in the Islamic world. Only Saudi Arabia is an officially Hanbali state, though fundamentalist regimes in Sudan, Pakistan (under General Zia ul-Haqq), and Afghanistan (under the Taliban) have been overtly influenced by Hanbali dogma. Hanbalis follow Shafi'i juridical positions in regard to anal sex between men, though they degrade legal reason and analogy and advocate capital punishment as a "literal" reading of the Qur'an itself.[58] The state of Iran (since the Islamic Revolution in 1978) also has a state policy of executing gay men, which they justify through the Shi'i Ja'fari legal school. Though Shi'i Iranians are usually quick to distinguish themselves from their Sunni neighbors, in the case of execution of gay men the Iranian legal arguments parallel the Hanbali arguments. All these states argue (along the lines described by al-Qurtubi) that homosexual men are exclusively characterized by anal sex, which, they claim, is a crime with a "*hadd* penalty." It is unclear whether any of these contemporary states in practice apply the legal conditions that limit *hadd* cases, such as observation of the actual act of penetration by four adult male witnesses.

Hadd penalties are, by definition, those penalties described explicitly by the Qur'an itself. Jurists are not supposed to exercise legal reasoning and analogy in cases of *hadd* penalties. Al-Qurtubi, we noted above, had to resort to legal reasoning and analogy to argue that anal penetration between men was a *hadd* crime, since the language of the Qur'an is not explicit and exact in this case. Hanafi jurists were keenly aware of this problem, and argued that anal sex between men could not justifiably be considered a *hadd* crime.

> The punishment for adultery [*zina*] is known [from the Qur'an explicitly]. Since this act is known to be different [in nature] from adultery, it should not be treated as a hadd crime equivalent to adultery ... This act is a kind of sexual intercourse in a bodily opening that has no relation to legal marriage and does not necessitate giving a dowry or determining parentage [as adultery does]. Therefore it has no relation to the hadd punishment for adultery.[59]

The Hanafi jurists mounted a strong case against the Malikis, Shafi'is, and Hanbalis (and also, implicitly, the Shi'is), and accused them of applying a *hadd* penalty for an act that was not defined in the Qur'an as a *hadd*, thereby committing a grave injustice.

In his juridical commentary on the Qur'an, the Hanafi jurist al-Jassas (who died in the tenth century CE), addresses this issue. He argues that the Qur'an specifies a *hadd* punishment of death by stoning for adultery between a man and a woman and in this specificity the punishment applies only to adultery (not to anal sex between men or other types of sexual acts). He argues this position with two *hadith* attributed to the Prophet. "Whoever applies a *hadd* penalty to a crime that is not a *hadd* crime has committed injustice and oppression" and "The blood of a Muslim is not liable to be shed, except in these three cases: adultery after marriage, infidelity after adopting Islam, and murdering an innocent person."[60] He acknowledges that certain *hadith* were in circulation, attributed to the Prophet Muhammad, that men found "doing the act of the people of Lut" should be killed. However, he notes that these reports have weak chains of transmission containing unreliable transmitters, and therefore cannot form the basis for a juridical decision to put a Muslim to death.[61]

Clearly, there was a hot argument on this issue among classical jurists, with no actual consensus on the nature of the act, the status of punishment for it, or the relation of punishment to the words of the Qur'an. It also appears that jurists faced opposition from commentators who read the Qur'an as a narrative of ethical exhortation rather than as a legal text, as did the authors of the Stories of the Prophets. When al-Qurtubi argued that the Prophet Lut's conflict with his community was about forbidding anal sex between men and that this justified capital punishment against those men found doing this, he recognized at least two possible objections to his interpretation. Both of these objections were based on ethical readings of the same Qur'anic narrative. The first objection is that "the people of Lut were punished because of their disbelief in Allah and their calling their Prophet a liar [*kufr wa takdhib*] just like the rest of the ancient communities that were destroyed by Allah." The second objection is that "the young children and old people of Lut's community were included with the mature men in being punished, and that proves that their actions should not be considered in the realm of *hadd* crimes [were not primarily sexual intercourse]."[62] After stating these objections from anonymous critics, al-Qurtubi dismisses them. Yet the points they raise are logical and ethically important, and are based on a literal reading of the Qur'anic narratives about Lut. Al-Qurtubi's dismissal of dissenting opinions cannot be construed as indicating consensus among the jurists on the legal status of anal sex between men.

In the face of dissenting opinion, how did jurists defend the position that anal sex between men deserved capital punishment (by stoning or by other means)? To defend this decision, Imam Malik simply noted that the people of Lut were destroyed by stones as hard as baked brick (*sijjil*) that fell from heaven. This is an argument by rhetorical association, not an argument by legal reasoning. However, it is a kind of argument that would prove very effective, and seems to be based on early precedent among the Companions of the Prophet (though not on the example of the Prophet himself).

EXEMPLARY CONDUCT OF THE PROPHET MUHAMMAD

As noted above, jurists argued their cases based on the analogy that anal sex was like adultery, and that the Qur'an specified the firm and exact punishment for adultery. The earliest jurists did not make reference to specific *hadith* attributed to the Prophet Muhammad about anal sex between men. In fact, we have no evidence that the Prophet Muhammad ever punished any men for anal sex (or any women for same-sex behavior). We have no evidence that he addressed cases where people were accused of committing "the act of the people of Lut." This leads to another radical assertion of this study; the Qur'an does not address homosexuality or homosexuals explicitly *and* the Prophet Muhammad did not act to punish people as homosexuals or for acts associated with them in his lifetime.

At a certain point in history, *hadith* attributed to the Prophet Muhammad began to circulate which addressed the issue of punishing men for having anal sex. This is just one specific case of a very general problem for Muslims ever since: the existence of reports, on a whole range of subjects, that circulate in the name of the Prophet without being reliably or verifiably known to represent the Prophet's actual actions and teachings. As more and more jurists accepted Imam al-Shafi'i's argument that all legal decisions had to be based on *hadith* attributed to the Prophet, the role of these *hadith* changed radically. They had circulated informally as moral advice, but now began to harden and crystallize into formal "knowledge" about what the Prophet said and did. It is probable that such *hadith* came into being long after the Prophet had died, and were attributed to him in order to give them the force of association with the Prophet's respected and revered personality.[63]

It is very difficult to establish the authenticity of most reports that circulate in the name of the Prophet Muhammad. But clearly, many reports were projected retrospectively back upon the Prophet without being reliably attributed to him. Muslims are confronted with *hadith* in which the Prophet reportedly speaks about issues that did not exist in his lifetime: such as the Shi'i-Sunni schism, various theological "heresies," and even the systematic collection of *hadith*. Reassessment of the authenticity of *hadith* reports is the key to legal and social reform among Muslims. However, in the contemporary period, there are less and less scholars who are trained in *hadith* criticism. Wahhabi and Salafi scholars, who may have such training, have no motive to critique *hadith*, for in their zeal to escape history and return to the Prophet's own time, they reify *hadith* as unquestionable building blocks for their monolithic iconic image of the Prophet's exemplary behavior.

The *hadith* that address the issue of punishing men for having anal sex are not linked to any specific case or event in the Prophet's life. This is in marked contrast to the *hadith* that address the issue of adultery between a man and woman, which are linked to very detailed cases that preserve the names of the men and women involved during the Prophet's lifetime. A review of *hadith* from the two most reliable collections (*Sahih Muslim* and *Sahih al-Bukhari*) reveals no evidence that the Prophet asserted, in word or deed, that homosexual relations were a *hadd* crime, or were to be equated with adultery, or ever punished any actual persons for "crimes" relating to homosexuality.[64] Nor is there any *hadith* in these two most authentic collections in which the Prophet discusses Lut in relation to sexual acts or relationships.[65] This writer further suspects that the very terms *Luti* and *Liwat* are not found in authentic *hadith*, although this would take more research to substantiate.

Based on this preliminary research, we can make some general conclusions about *hadith*. Most reports in which the Prophet reportedly condemns same-sex activities have weak chains of transmission and are found in *hadith* collections that are not the most authoritative. *Hadith* scholars in the medieval period (when *hadith* criticism was still actively pursued in Muslim communities) explicitly debunked some of them for having forged chains of transmission. In the earliest period, jurists did not agree as to which *hadith* might be authentic and strong enough to form the basis of legal rulings.

It is very difficult to suppress *hadith* once they gain credibility and circulate widely. This is especially so when a report reinforces the common prejudice of patriarchal societies against same-sex relationships. Hanafi jurists earlier criticized the chain of transmission of *hadith* like "Whomever you find doing the act of the people of Lut, kill the active and the passive participant."[66] Al-Jassas rejects this *hadith*, since one of its transmitters, Amr ibn Abi Amr, is considered weak and unreliable. Similarly, he rejects the supposed *hadith* that reads "the one practicing the act of the people of Lut, stone the one on top and the one of the bottom, stone them both together," since one of its transmitters, 'Asim ibn Amr, is also considered weak and unreliable.[67] Despite these critiques, the *hadith* continue to circulate and are frequently put to rhetorical and even legal use.

There is further historical evidence to suggest that these *hadith* were fabricated long after the Prophet Muhammad had died and were retrospectively projected back onto him.[68] The earliest incident in which a man was punished for same-sex relations occurred during the rule of Abu Bakr, after the death of Muhammad. It is clear from this incident that the closest Companions of the Muhammad knew of no precedent for such punishment. The Prophet had never punished anyone for same-sex relations and had not specified a method of punishment. The Companions consulted together and decided to burn the man accused.[69]

This story is very revealing, since it shows the uncertainty of the Companions surrounding same-sex activity and confirms that the Prophet Muhammad himself had never specified it as a crime with a specific punishment. When Abu Bakr received report from a governor that he had found a whole town "doing the act of the people of Lut," he gathered the Prophet's closest Companions together to consult with them about what to do. 'Ali ibn Abi Talib reportedly said, "This is a sin that no community from the known nations has perpetrated except one single community. Allah did to them what you all know [from scripture]. My opinion is that such people should be burned in a fire." So the Companions agreed with 'Ali's idea that the punishment was burning.

This incident is certainly very disturbing. First, we don't know exactly what the governor meant by "the act of the people of Lut." If it were same-sex relations in general (or anal sex between men in particular) it is difficult to imagine a whole town being involved in a way that would be significantly different from other towns. It is highly probable that the town might have resisted the governor's authority (as this occurred during the earliest years of the Islamic conquests when their rule was new and contested) just like the people of Lut resisted Lut's assertion of authority over them. It may not have had anything specifically to do with sexual acts. If the acts were sexual in nature, how could Islamic legal procedure have been applied (with four adult male witnesses to the actual act of penetration)? It is more probable that this was a case of putting down resistance to political conquest than enforcing Islamic "family values." However, the Islamic jurists have interpreted this incident as the first case of actual punishment for same-sex activities.[70]

Even if that were the case, it shows us something more disturbing still. The earliest punishment was burning. It was based on Imam 'Ali's opinion about what to do (very roughly linked to his reading of the story of Lut from the Qur'an), but clearly not based on any precedent or oral teaching or exemplary conduct of the Prophet Muhammad. The supposed *hadith* that later circulated usually specify stoning as the punishment, not burning. This establishes that these *hadith* were later inventions, reflecting the jurists' ongoing debate about whether anal sex between men was the legal equivalent to adultery with stoning as the *hadd* punishment. The conflict between stoning or burning as the appropriate punishment signals that the Prophet had not left any specific teaching about appropriate punishment, neither in word nor in deed.

Could it be that the Prophet never addressed the issue because he did not see it as an issue of crime and punishment, but rather as one variety of indiscretion? The Prophet certainly did encounter people in his Arab society in Mecca and Medina who had uncommon sexual identities and practices that contradicted the heterosexual norm. Researchers in pre-Islamic and early Islamic Arabic literature have uncovered a wealth of examples. Salah al-Din Munajjad has documented that same-sex practices existed among both men and women in pre-Islamic Arabia (refuting ideologues who claim that these practices were unknown among Arabs until the Persians introduced them during the Abbasid revolution).[71] Everett Rowson has documented the very lively culture of "effeminate men" during the Prophet's lifetime in Medina. These men took on women's social characteristics and were especially noted as popular musicians and comedians; some of them were associated with same-sex sexual desire while others were not. These people were ambiguous in their gender and their sexuality. Yet the Prophet is not known to have censured any of them for sexual acts or sexuality in the wider sense. There is no report of the Prophet having any of them burned or stoned for sexual practices.

CLARIFYING THE QUESTION OF SEXUAL ETHICS

Jurists claimed to enforce a punishment for same-sex acts that was based solidly on a literal reading of the Qur'an and legal proscription by the Prophet Muhammad. The evidence presented above shows that their assertions are based on legal analogy, not on literal interpretation. The analogy, in addition, is quite weak and is based on sources that are of doubtful authenticity. At its most basic level, this study argues that capital punishment for anal sex between men is unjust and of questionable legal validity in Islamic law. There is not and has never been full juridical consensus that anal sex between men is a *hadd* crime (let alone less dramatic sexual acts that might be practiced in same-sex couplings).

In reading the story of Lut's struggle with his obstinate and violent community, jurists have missed the point. Why does the Qur'an tell the narratives about Lut if the story is not about forbidding homosexuality in the abstract or same-sex practices in particular? This study argues that the story is primarily ethical in intent, not juridical. The jurists' narrow focus on punishment for sexual acts obscures the deeper meaning of the story and the force with which the Qur'an tells it to an audience struggling to meet the challenges of faith and realize the fullness of the Prophets' teachings on *tawhid*. Leaving behind an obsessive attention to anal sex and stigmatizing same-sex sexuality can actually be a positive act for contemporary Muslims, one that brings new clarity to questions of sexual ethics. Addressing sexual ethics is, in the view of this author, a more faithful reaction to a close reading of the Qur'an.

To get beyond the jurists' obsessions, let's return to the project of thematic interpretation of the Qur'an as presented in the Stories of the Prophets genre. This genre highlights how the Qur'an tells the stories of Prophets with an underlying unity of intention. Their situations are different, but their ethical message is the same to each community. Through different means, each community finds ways of rejecting their Prophet, and the means are often violent. The Qur'anic discourse on Lut, therefore, mentions his unique circumstances, but always stresses his commonality with the other Prophets who preceded him and came after him, like Noah, Abraham, Salih, Hud, and others. Fragments of Lut's story are always retold in the Qur'an as part of a series about the seven exemplary punishments meted out to the communities of the past who rejected their Prophet.

To see clearly how the jurists' treatment of this story perverts its deeper message, we can compare Lut's story with that of Salih. Allah sent Salih to the people of Thamud as their Prophet. Like the people inhabiting the Cities of the Plains, the people of Thamud were wealthy, powerful, and arrogant. While the issue with Lut was giving hospitality and protection to travelers, the issue with Salih was the protection of a consecrated camel. Salih announced to his people that a certain camel was made sacred and should be allowed to wander freely, eat and drink on anyone's land, and be respected by all. The camel stood symbolically for the weak and vulnerable members of society; if the people could care for the sacred camel, they might have the spiritual insight and ethical strength to care for the needy in the midst of their society and at its margins.

Clearly, there are deep thematic parallels between the story of Lut and that of Salih. The people of Thamud rejected Salih as their Prophet and ridiculed his exhortations to live up to an ethic of care and justice. When he urged them to protect the consecrated camel, the arrogant nobles of their community hamstrung her, tied her up, and slaughtered her. As a consequence, their city with all its inhabitants was destroyed by Allah (with an earthquake and choking clouds from what appears to be a volcanic eruption). Why did they kill the camel? To repudiate their Prophet, lower his dignity in the eyes of their fellows, and reject the belief in the One God which was the foundation of his ethical message.

Nobody would take seriously a commentator who presents the people of Thamud as being obsessed by a hatred of camels or a perverted lust for camel blood that corrupted their innermost dispositions. Nobody would take seriously a jurist who argued that slaughtering another's camel is a capital crime, based on the example of the people of Thamud who were destroyed after killing a camel. Nobody would argue that anyone who slaughters an animal that does not belong to him should be punished by asphyxiation, in a rough human approximation of how Allah razed the people of Thamud by a volcanic eruption. Anyone suggesting these interpretations would be laughed out of the mosque, and would be gently reminded that he or she had missed the basic point of Salih's story.

The same is true for those who miss the point of Lut's story. The Qur'an tells these stories in a series; they are always grouped together. Further, they are told in specific contexts that encouraged Muhammad to have patience and perseverance in the face of rejection, repudiation, and oppression at the hands of the rich and powerful of the pre-Islamic Quraish nobles in Mecca.[72]

So what can the Muslim community deduce as ethical principles from the story of Lut, once the story is freed from the jurists' narrow and obsessive attention to anal sex? Lut was exemplary in revealing the challenge of hospitality, generosity, and protection of the vulnerable. He struggled with his community to get them to support the needy, the poor, and those who appeared as strangers. He challenged their arrogance, their inhuman exertion of power over vulnerable people, and their creation of a coercive system out of trade and economic relations. These are certainly challenges that Muslims face in their personal lives and collective societies. We have not lived up to Lut's basic challenge yet.

As part of this fundamental ethical challenge, it is clear that Lut also confronted his society's exploitative use of sex. He condemned its use of sexual acts as a form of coercion. This is the prohibitive side of his message. The positive side would enjoin upholding consensual agreement, reciprocity, mutuality, and care in sexual acts and relationships. For Muslims to live up to Lut's challenge would mean categorically opposing rape, whether it be men raping men or men raping women. Lut's story clearly shows that rape is only sexual on the most crass level (in that it has to do with sexual organs). It reality, rape is motivated by desire for domination, not by sexual desire or the desire for pleasure. It is a form of coercion, control, and punishment that can have no place in a society that respects the message of the Prophets.

This is important to keep in mind when we confront contemporary fundamentalist movements, like that fostered in Pakistan under General Zia ul-Haqq. The clever General declared himself ruler in a military coup and executed the democratically elected Prime Minister. To court the support of Islamist parties, like the Jama'at-i Islami, among others, General Zia ul-Haqq justified his military coup by claiming to institute *Shari'ah law* through the "Hudud Ordinances." These ordinances allowed legal prosecution and punishment for gay and lesbian consensual sex acts, while erasing any punishment for male rapes of women. In Zia ul-Haqq's Hudud Ordinances there is no term for "rape," which is simply conflated with adultery, leading to the blatantly unjust situation of a women who is raped not only finding no protection under the law but actually being prosecuted for adultery with a possible punishment of execution.[73]

Lest the reader consider such blatant hypocrisy to be concentrated in only one nation state, consider recent developments in Egypt. In 2001, police there arrested fifty-two allegedly "gay men" at a nightclub and tried them in Cairo's State Security Court, not under the national legal code but under emergency executive courts that had been set up to try "fundamentalist terrorism."[74] In order to justify trial in extra-constitutional courts (that were designed to try fundamentalists and terrorists) and to completely avoid discussing the issue of sexuality, sexual diversity, and ethics, the Egyptian government charged the men for "contempt for religion," "false interpretation of the Qur'an," and "obscene behavior." Almost half of the fifty-two men convicted were sentenced to five years of hard labor; some of those incarcerated subsequently reported having been tortured or raped. On the educational and legal levels, many Muslim communities vociferously denounce homosexuals or acts associated with them (regardless of whether these are consensual), while maintaining a silence around men who coerce others (women, men, or children) through sexual acts in homes, schools, or work places. This silence, coupled with homosexual scapegoats, actually protects men who engage in rape and sexual abuse, guarding their patriarchal privilege to use sex as a weapon to maintain their position of power over others.

What kind of society would denounce consensual sexual activity while protecting violent sexual abuse? Such a society could never be considered to uphold high ideals of justice. Will Muslims allow their societies to be counted among such as this? Will progressive Muslims allow such injustice to be legitimized through simplistic interpretation of scriptural sources? This problem highlights the interconnectedness of social ethics with sexual ethics. Muslims with a keen sense of justice should not let sexual relations be judged by the surface component of the gender of the partners, but should look rather to the content of the relationship. We judge any sexual relationship by examining its ethics and intent, in accord with the Prophet Muhammad's teaching that "Acts are according to the intentions behind them."[75]

CONCLUSION: SEXUAL ETHICS BEYOND PATRIARCHAL POWER

We must be honest in acknowledging that patriarchy existed before the Qur'anic revelation, persisted in the early Islamic community, and continued to exist centuries later during the formative period of Islamic law. The Qur'anic revelation and the Prophet Muhammad's creation of a new community seriously challenged many of the patriarchal practices that were routine in Arab societies. The young community, especially after the death of Muhammad, often did not live up to the initial challenge. It fell back on patriarchal norms in hopes of social stability and in the creation of a new Islamic elite ruling class.[76] With the advent of modernity (for all its newly introduced forms of violence and imbalance), perceptions of human nature and social organization change, and the practice of religion changes with it. This is not just a reality; it is an ethical challenge and is also potentially a blessing. Modernity gives us the chance of thinking differently and freeing ourselves from the shackles of patriarchal power.

For most of the history of Islam, Muslims assumed that the Qur'an demanded the political rule of a monarch, whether conceived as a khalifa, sultan, or king. This was true despite plenty of evidence of dissent in the earliest community, since many early followers of the Prophet rejected authoritarian rule.[77] Monarchal rule by an all-powerful male is one facet of patriarchy that is deeply woven into Islamic society and religion. This is so even though monarchy is not explicitly sanctioned by the Qur'an. In previous centuries, to be a Muslim who questioned the right of monarchs to rule was largely unthinkable. If one acted upon a critique of monarchs, one would be branded an apostate. Today, most Muslims do not live under monarchies, and most Muslims think this is a good thing. Their Islam is not less faithful because they live without monarchies; in fact it might be stronger for that reason.

For most of the history of Islam, Muslims have taken for granted that slavery was a legal and useful social institution. Islamic law adapted to the practice of owning human beings as slaves, a practice that existed before Islam and continued after Islam's advent. Rights of ownership by a wealthy male is one facet of patriarchy that is deeply woven into Islamic society and religion. This was true despite the Qur'an's clear emphasis on freeing slaves and the Prophet's example in this matter. Yet today, most Muslims do not own and sell fellow human beings. Most Muslims would consider this a good thing, and consider slavery a clear form of oppression.

For most of the history of Islam, Muslims have assumed that women were inferior to men. Some might limit this inferiority to realms of physical constitution and legal privilege, while others would extend the inferiority to piety and even rationality. The superiority of gendered males is one facet of patriarchy that is deeply woven into Islamic society and religion. This was true despite the Qur'ran's empowerment of women in many fields. Islamic law adapted to this basic assumption of patriarchy, and encoded it in all manner of legal norms and authoritative interpretations. Yet many Muslims today assert the fundamental equality of women and men in economic, social, religious, educational, and political spheres of life. Their Islam is not less faithful because they live without gender segregation and tribal honor codes; in fact their Islam might be stronger with their commitment to gender justice.

Many Muslims today cannot imagine that Islam could be a religious practice that acknowledges and respects diversity in sexuality and sexual practices. They may not even recognize the aspects of patriarchy that oppress people characterized by same-sex desire and erotic longing. This is no different from other forms of oppressive prejudice in the past that, with struggle (that is, with *jihad* and *ijtihad*), Muslims have managed to overcome with positive results for our understanding of our faith. As progressive Muslims, we have focused our sense of justice demanded by radical *tawhid* on the fields of political organization, economic ownership, or gender norms. Why stop there? Why not continue to extend this challenging focus on justice into the more intimate spaces of our sexual lives, in order to think more clearly about how our erotic lives intersect with our spiritual lives?

Many lesbian and gay Muslims who read this study will support the challenge articulated above. However, many will wonder whether any purpose is served by focusing on classical jurists and Qur'an commentators. Can there be any rapprochement with the *Shari'ah* and the authorities that support it? Or is any discussion of the *Shari'ah* a capitulation to authority that is hopelessly prejudiced against the very possibility of thinking that homosexuality is about anything beyond misplaced lust? This is a crucial question. The Islamic legal scholar Abdullahi Ahmed an-Na'im has addressed this question directly in its widest form by asking whether there is any possibility of "reforming" the *Shari'ah* in contemporary times to revive its underlying principles so that it protects civil liberties and human rights rather than suppressing them. He concludes that this is possible, but is complicated by the neo-colonial struggles of nations inhabited by Muslims for the long-deferred promises of political and cultural "self-determination."

> We have Muslim demands for self-determination by the application of Islamic law in public life. Yet such Islamic law cannot possibly be Shari'a as historically established. The only way to reconcile these competing imperatives for change in the public law of Muslim countries is to develop a version of public law which is compatible with modern standards of constitutionalism, criminal justice, international law, and human rights ... We can then proceed to resolve the conflict and tension within the framework of Islam as a whole, albeit not necessarily within the framework of the historical Shari'a.[78]

An-Na'im is arguing for the disengagement of the *Shari'ah* as historically formed from Islam as a whole. The *Shari'ah* in its historical development is not Divinely ordained: it is the creation of many generations of commentators, jurists, and *hadith* scholars who lived long after the Prophet Muhammad died and in a completely different political and cultural milieu. Radical *tawhid* demands that Muslims let nothing created by human beings stand in for Allah, the Single and the Unique.[79] From a critical point of view, it is a kind of icon worship to imagine the *Shari'ah* to be infallible, unchanging, or somehow Divine. Just as building the *Shari'ah* was a historical process, the creation of human (and fallible) minds, hands, and hearts, so the *Shari'ah* should be open to continual reform and re-creation.

A new and evolving *Shari'ah* is a politically and religiously necessary project. It would offer Muslim-majority national states in post-colonial situations a way of resolving many of the contradictions created by European colonialism's imposition of modernity through violence and domination, without having to destroy the nation state or reject some of the more valuable innovations of modernism. It would offer immigrant or indigenous Muslim communities in North America and Europe a way to reconcile their religious faith and community aspirations with the reality of living as minorities in states that enshrine secular legal traditions and cultural values. The new South Africa will be an important test case, since it has recently emerged from the apartheid regime with a politically active Muslim community. South Africa now has one of the most progressive constitutions in the world (which explicitly protects the civil liberties and human rights of women, lesbians, and gays).[80] It will be instructive to observe how Muslims there, many of whom sacrificed their lives in opposing apartheid, will come to accept and embrace the new constitution and the values it enshrines.

An-Na'im has pointed out that the central questions to be addressed in this reformation of the *Shari'ah* are those of international law, human rights, and civil liberties. Under this last rubric come concerns about women and their rights. However, as argued in this study, asserting women's rights will never be limited to the realm of women. It will necessarily change the way men behave and the way both women and men perceive sexuality. As feminism opens up sexuality as a topic for discussion, homosexuality will inevitably come up as a challenge to all Muslims with a keen sense of justice.

ENDNOTES

1. The author would like to acknowledge two friends and colleagues who helped in the revision of this text, Daayiee Abdullah and Nicholas Heer.
2. Hamid Nastoh was a fourteen-year-old in Vancouver from an Afghan family who was driven to suicide on March 11, 2000. Schoolmates persistently bullied him with accusations of being gay and he found no consolation or protection in his religious tradition as it had been presented to him. Since Hamid's death, his mother has become a local advocate for sexuality education and "gay–straight alliance clubs" in Canadian high schools.

3. Madelain Farah, *Marriage and Sexuality in Islam: A Translation of al-Ghazali's Book on the Etiquette of Marriage from The Revival of the Religious Sciences* (Salt Lake City: University of Utah Press, 1984), 45. Creation "from water" (as found in Q. 21:30) is often interpreted as sexual union and the meeting of ejaculatory fluids, while the term "sexual intercourse" is understood metaphorically from the Qur'an's use of "tillage" (*hirth*) in Qur'an 2:223.

4. Momin Rahman, *Sexuality and Democracy: Identities and Strategies in Lesbian and Gay Politics* (Edinburgh: Edinburgh University Press, 2000), 172.

5. Ibid., 21.

6. Some ascetic-minded Sufis were the exception, and saw sexual desire as a distraction from worshipful contemplation of God.

7. Abdelwahab Bouhdiba, *Sexuality in Islam* (London: Saqi, 1998), 159. This is the best study in English illustrating the continuity between Muslim sexual practices in this world and how Muslims imagine the sacred world of paradise to come. In Arabic, there are many full studies of this theme, like Ibrahim Mahmud, *Jaghrafiyat al-Muladhat: al-Jins wa'l-Janna* [*Geography of Rapture: Sex and Paradise*] (Beirut: Riyad el-Rais, 1998).

8. This frequently cited hadith is referred to by a number of authorities, such as al-Ghazali who records it in his *Ihya 'ulum al-Din* (Beirut: Dar al-Hadi, 1992), vol. 2, p. 48. See Sachiko Murata and William C. Chittick, *Vision of Islam* (St Paul: Paragon Press, 1994) 228, 350. For discussion of this *hadith*, see R.W.J. Austin (trans.), *Ibn al-Arabi: the Bezels of Wisdom*, (Mahwah, NJ: Paulist Press, 1980), 269–78, and Sachiko Murata, *The Tao of Islam: A Sourcebook on Gender Relationships in Islamic Thought* (Albany: SUNY Press, 1992), 186–7.

9. 'Ali ibn Husam al-Din al-Hindi Muttaqi, *Jarr al-Thaqil fi Suluk al-Ma'il*, [Bearing the Heavy Burden on Soul Training of Men Considering Marriage], manuscript in Lahore: Punjab University Library 4950/1937 folios 22–9, and Islamabad: Ganj Bakhsh Library (Iranian Cultural Institute) 3745.

10. Surat al-Ahzab 33:50–2 directly addresses the question of sexual relationships outside of marriage with slaves and concubines, explicitly allowing this for the Prophet (and implicitly allowing it for other believers) while contrasting such women to those formally married.

11. Basim Musallam, *Sex and Society in Islam: Birth-Control before the Nineteenth Century* (Cambridge: Cambridge University Press, 1983), supplemented by Munawar Ahmad Anees, *Islam and Biological Futures: Ethics, Gender and Technology* (London: Mansell, 1989).

12. Scholars argue whether this verse refers to anal sex between men and women, or to vaginal sex from behind, or to whether the control of timing and frequency of sexual relations should be in the hands of men or women. Fatima Mernissi, *The Veil and the Male Elite: A Feminist Interpretation of Women's Rights in Islam* (Reading, MA: Addison-Wesley, 1991) discusses the importance of this verse and its context of revelation for a feminist critique of Islamic patriarchy.

13. Athar Hussain and Mark Cousins, *Michel Foucault: Theoretical Traditions in the Social Sciences* (New York: St Martin's Press, 1984) is a good introduction to Michel Foucault, one of the most influential historians of sexuality. Foucault argued that the term "homosexuality" (as well as "sexuality") is completely modern, and cannot be justifiably applied to ideas, practices or people before European modernity and its uneven spread to the wider world. Many historians of sexuality have questioned this assertion and are suspicious of accepting Foucault's glib Eurocentric conclusions about the uniqueness of modernity.

14. John Boswell, "Concepts, Experience and Sexuality," in *Forms of Desire*, ed. E. Stein (New York: Routledge, 1992) provides an overview of the concept of sexuality, from a scholar who has wrestled, as a historian and committed Christian, with the traditional Christian denunciation of homosexuality.

15. The Qur'an is very clear here that no ethnic group is racially or cultural inferior to another, but Islamic culture has often slipped into justifying slavery in terms that approach racial chauvinism.

16. Amina Wadud, *Qur'an and Woman* (Kuala Lumpur: Penerbit Fajar Bakti, 1992; 2nd edn, Oxford: Oxford University Press, 1999).

17. 'Ali Muttaqi, *Jarr al-Thaqil*, which was a Persian commentary on al-Ghazali's book quoted at the beginning of this study.

18. In other passages the Qur'an uses *alwan* to describe different types of honey, different types of beasts, and different types of agricultural produce.

19. "Lawn," *Encyclopedia of Islam, New Edition* (Leiden: E.J. Brill, 1954–2002), vol. 5, 699.

20. The Qur'an comes closer to discussing gender than it does to discussing sexuality. The Qur'an uses the term *zawj* to mean "one of a pair of people or things." Sometimes, *zawj* is used in an abstract sense and sometimes concretely as applied to human beings or objects. At least once, the Qur'an uses the term to indicate a binary relationship of male to female: "We have made them pairs, male and female" (42:49). But the term is not used constantly in this way; at times *zawj* refers not to clearly gendered pairs, and often to non-living entities. At one point the pair is not male and female persons, but the soul and body of each person regardless of anatomical or social gender: "We made the souls joined to their pair" (Q. 81:7).

21. The phrase is *al-Tabi'in ghayr ulu al-Irbat min al-Rijal*. The phrase might also be translated as "those men among your followers who have no guile with women."

22. Muslim theologians have not yet considered the fascinating case of the Prophet *Dhu al-Qarnayn* as described in Surat al-Kahf. Qur'an commentators have traditionally identified him as the historical figure of Alexander the Great, and Yusuf Ali has recently argued very persuasively for the authenticity of this identification. Historical record clearly reveals that Alexander's major erotic attachments were to a series of men (though he did marry as his political role required). Could it be that *Dhu al-Qarnayn* as Alexander may have been a gay man who acted as a Divinely appointed Prophet? Islamic theologians have not even begun to grapple with this question.

23. Everrett Rowson, "The Effeminates of Early Medina" in *Que(e)rying Religion: a Critical Anthology*, ed. G. Comstock and Henking (New York: Continuum, 1997). Rowson has clearly shown that some of these "effeminate" men acted in ways that we would identify as "gay" but that many of them did not; what characterized them was their breaking norms of gendered behavior rather than their sexual orientation.

24. Najman Yasin, *Al-Islam wa'l-Jins fi al-Qarn al-Awwal al-Hijri* [*Islam and Sex in the First Century Hijri*] (Beirut: Dar al-Atiya li'l-Nashr, 1997), 111 uses a phrase (in Arabic) that can be translated as "unusual sexual practices that are unnatural." Islamic jurists never used "nature" to denounce same-sex sexual practices; these practices may have been forbidden, but were not "unnatural." This is a subtle but crucial distinction that reveals how much modern Muslim intellectuals (even those who write in Arabic) have been shaped by Euro-American discourses of modernity.

25. No list will be offered here, since it would be very long. Let us highlight one personality, on whom more research must be done. That is the medieval writer Ibn Dawud al-Zahiri, who was the leading jurist of the Zahiri legal school. He was also well known for having fallen into a deeply romantic love with a school friend, Ibn Jami', to whom he dedicated his book in praise of love, *Kitab al-Zahra*. Ibn Dawud al-Zahiri held that a man's love for another man is noble as long as it is "chaste" ['*udhri*] and made no effort to conceal his erotic orientation. See Massignon, *The Passion of Hallaj*, 1:80 and 338–68.

26. Norman Daniel, *Islam and the West: The Making of an Image* (Edinburgh: University Press, 1960) and Nabil Matar, *Turks, Moors and Englishmen in the Age of Discovery* (New York: Columbia University Press, 1999) document the scope and persistence of this pre-modern European condemnation of Muslims as "sodomites." Though driven by the European need to make Muslims alien, inferior, and worthy of conquest, this theme was based on a substantial contrast between medieval Christendom (which seemed obsessed with punishing "sodomites") and a medieval Islamdom (which seemed far more relaxed and accepting of same-sex eroticism, despite the jurists' condemnations depicted in this study).

27. Byrne Fone, *Homo-Phobia: A History* (New York: Metropolitan, 2000), 294. There are many examples of Western scholars who ignore or repress the presence of homoerotic

practices among Muslims in their specific subjects of study. Let one example suffice. Madelain Farah's comments in the introduction to *Marriage and Sexuality in Islam,* 37 can only be called "bad faith." She errs in stating that "The Koran addressed the subject of sodomy. It is a reference in over seventy Koranic verses." She demonstrates a lack of understanding Arabic when she writes that *liwata* in Arabic means "homosexuality" while *Lut* means sodomy (in fact *liwata* means sodomy or anal intercourse while "*Lut*" is the name of a Prophet). Farah blithely ignores the fact that Imam al-Ghazali's own brother, Shaykh Ahmad al-Ghazali, who was a respected religious scholar and Islamic leader, was well known for homoerotic sentiments in his poetry and devotional practices, like *shahid-bazi* or "gazing at beautiful men" in order to contemplate the beauty of God. Examples of Western scholars working out their own prejudices by supposedly "representing" the Islamic tradition are legion.

28. Asadullah Khan Ghalib, *Divan-i Ghalib, Urdu* (New Delhi: Ghalib Institute, 1998), 104. Translation is by the author. Ghalib repeats al-Ghazali's insight with sarcasm because Ghalib was no theologian or ascetic; rather he was a highly intellectual and aesthetically refined poet in Urdu and Persian, who is known for writing verses of love and longing for beloved men.

29. Stephen O. Murray and Will Roscoe. *Islamic Homosexualities: Culture History and Literature* (New York: New York University Press, 1997) asserts a universal gay identity that underlies any variation in history and culture. This contrasts with the careful avoidance of asserting any gay identity in Everett Rowson and J.W. Wright (eds), *Homoeroticism in Classical Arabic Literature* (New York: Columbia University Press, 1997).

30. Farid Esack, *Qur'an, Liberation and Pluralism: An Islamic Perspective of Interreligious Solidarity against Oppression* (Oxford: Oneworld, 1997), 75.

31. This study is very limited in its focus on homosexual men and anal sex. This is not ideal and will certainly not satisfy lesbian or women readers (nor should it satisfy them). However, there is a purpose to this limitation. What follows in this study is in dialogue with the Islamic legal tradition, which addresses homosexuality through condemning anal sex between men. The condemnation was the platform for a more general cultural rhetoric against homosexuality in general, including same-sex relations between women. Though anal sex (and penetrative sex in general) is not necessarily relevant to lesbian sexuality, it was the dominant theme used by jurists to condemn both men and women. Therefore, it is the starting point of this article, though future investigation of this topic should not and cannot focus solely on men. This article is also driven by a critique of capital punishment that is inflicted on homosexual men in certain countries, and this punishment seems to be directed primarily (in the knowledge of this writer, only) against men. Lesbians, by virtue of being women first, tend not to suffer publicly under these laws, though they suffer differently under other laws and under pressure to marry and procreate.

32. The term *hassas* is used this way, in a clever *double entendre*, in Morocco. Though it is a North African term for "homosexual" (which may not be used in eastern Arabic-speaking regions or in the wider Islamic world) it is conceptually understandable anywhere.

33. Al-Tabari, *Tafsir al-Tabari min Jami' al-Bayan 'an Ta'wil Ayi al-Qur'an,* ed. Bashar 'Awwad (Beirut: Mu'assasat al-Risala, 1994), 3:463.

34. Ibid., 3:464.

35. The Qur'an's Arabic makes no reference to "nature" or "laws of nature" in this passage. As noted earlier, the Qur'an has no term that can be explicitly equated with "homosexuality," and it is not clear that "lewdness" means homosexuality in particular. Yusuf Ali interprets away the reference to other crimes that are actually described in the Qur'anic narrative about Lut's community, like highway robbery and fighting in public assemblies. This last item Yusuf Ali interprets as only committing their "special horrible crime" (meaning anal sex between men) in public places. This disregards the more straightforward and literal reading of the Qur'an, and is a speculative "interpretation" rather than a linguistic "translation." Abdullah Yusuf Ali is not unusual in this regard. He is only more explicit in his footnotes than other translators who make similar reductionist moves.

36. Toshihiko Izutsu, *God and Man in the Qur'an: Semantics of the Koranic Weltanschaaung* (Tokyo: Keio Institute of Cultural and Linguistic Studies, 1964).

37. Amreen Jamel, "The Story of Lut and the Qur'an's Perception of the Morality of Same-Sex Sexuality," *Journal of Homosexuality*, 41(1), 2001, 1–88.

38. The people to whom Lut was sent are commonly associated with Sodom and its satellite cities, the Cities of the Plain. The names Sodom and Gomorrah do not occur in the Qur'an, though they do in classical commentaries. How earlier Near Eastern names, interpretations and folk-tales entered classical commentaries is a deep topic, addressed later in this study.

39. Jamel, op. cit., 5.

40. Ibid., 64. Note that the Arabic triliteral root *sh-h-y* gives rise to a host of words meaning "to lust after" or "to desire" while the root *f-h-sh* gives rise to words meaning "to transgress" or "to exceed appropriate bounds."

41. In this crucial concluding paragraph, Jamel's use of the term "abominations" to qualify the description of same-sex acts seems to slip back into the traditional rhetoric that denounces homosexuality without critical examination, despite the overall thrust of the argument.

42. Esack, op. cit., 60.

43. Hajji Khalifa, *Kashf al-Zunun* (Istanbul: Maarif matbaası, 1943) 2:1324, argues for the authentic pedigree of this genre of "telling the stories of the Prophets" as opposed to "giving the detail of the words," which is what *tafsir* literally means. Hajji Khalifa notes that the earliest traditionists and commentators, Ibn 'Abbas and Abu Hurayra, both studied with Ka'b al-Ahbar, a Yemeni Jew who joined the Muslim community and was famed for his knowledge of "sacred history" and his retelling the stories of the Prophets. Along with Ka'b al-Ahbar, Wahb ibn Munabbih was a specialist in this kind of knowledge, and was reputed to be the first to write a book in the genre. Wahb lived from 34 to 110 Hijri (654–728 CE) and was famous for his vast knowledge of religious texts and stories relating to the pre-Islamic prophets and past nations (*Isra'iliyat*). His name is attached to many reports about stories that have entered the Islamic tradition as part of sacred history.

44. 'Ali ibn Hamza al-Kisa'i, *Bad' al-Khalq wa Qisas al-Anbiya'*, ed. Al-Tahir ibn Salama (Tunis: Dar Nuqush Arabiyya, 1998).

45. Al-Kisa'i relies on the names of al-Munabbih and al-Ahbar as his sources, though it is difficult to ascertain whether he attributes reports to them in an authentic or accurate way. Al-Kisa'i claimed in the introduction to his book to have studied *hadith* criticism and mastered its complexities.

46. The two earliest Stories of the Prophets written in Persian are by Muhammad ibn Hasan Al-Dadormi or al-Dirumi (who has preserved textual remnants of an older original text by al-Tha'albi) and Ibrahim or Ishaq ibn Khalaf al-Nishapuri, whose Persian text I refer to as: al-Nishapuri, *Qisas al-Anbiya*, ed. Habib Yaghma'i (Tehran: Bngah-yi Tarjama o Nashr, 1965).

47. Al-Kisa'i, op. cit. 219–20.

48. This final phrase, "preaching to them about the destruction of former nations who were oppressive," is found in some copies of the text and omitted in others.

49. Al-Kisa'i, op. cit., 220.

50. Ibid., 221.

51. Ibid., 222.

52. Al-Rawandi, Qutb al-Din Sa'id ibn Hibbat Allah (d. 573 *hijri*), *Qisas al-Anbiya*, ed. Ghulam Riza-yi 'Irfaniyan al-Yazdi (Beirut: Mu'assasat al-Mufid, 1989), 117–25.

53. Al-Rawandi, op. cit., 117. He quotes this *hadith* on the authority of Abu Ja'far.

54. Ibid., 118.

55. The Islamic tradition is not unique in this way, but rather all patriarchal moral systems see same-sex desire as exclusively "anal."

56. Al-Qurtubi, Muhammad ibn Ahmad (d. 1273 CE), *Tafsir al-Jami' fi Ahkam al-Qur'an* (Cairo: Dar al-Qalam, 1967), 7:243.

57. Ibid., 7:248.

58. Since they reject legal reasoning and analogy, one can question whether the Hanbalis actually qualify as a "legal school" with a *bona fide* juridical method (despite the fact that they are commonly accepted as "the fourth Sunni legal school").

59. Al-Qurtubi, op. cit., 244.

60. Abu Bakr Ahmad ibn Ali al-Razi Al-Jassas (d. 981 CE), *Ahkam al-Qur'an* (Beirut: Dar al-Kitab al-'Arabi, 1978), 2:363, under the discussion of adulterers in commentary on Surat al-Nur.

61. Ibid., 2:363.

62. Al-Qurtubi, op. cit., 7:243.

63. Richard Bulliet, *Islam: A View from the Edge* (New York: Columbia University Press, 1993).

64. Salih Ahmad Al-Shami (ed.), *al-Jami' bayn al-Sahihayn* (Damascus: Dar al-Qalam, 1995), 3:505–20 is an invaluable tool for such research.

65. Al-Nuwayri, op. cit., 206 relates the text of a report in which 'Ali ibn Abi Talib reportedly used the terms *Luti* and *Mulawwat bihi* to mean "inserting partner in anal sex" and "receptive partner." These terms are not found in the majority of reports about the Prophet and the earliest Companions, and were undoubtedly projected retrospectively back into the early community from a much later date. Most *hadith* use the term "the act of the people of Lut" (*af'al qawm Lut*).

66. This *hadith* is found in the collections of Ibn Maja and Abu Dawud and, in a slightly different wording, in the collection of al-Tirmidhi.

67. Al-Jassas, op. cit., 2:363.

68. Forged *hadith* report condemning same-sex sexual relations began to circulate in earnest during the Abbasid period, when it became aristocratic and courtly fashion to own young male slaves, employ handsome wine-bearers, and flaunt same-sex romances. Many *hadiths* circulated in the name of the Prophet to address these practices, as part of the traditionalist cultural war on the cosmopolitan elite of Abbasid-era cities.

69. Al-Qurtubi also relays that men were burned to death for this act in the time of Abu Bakr and 'Umar and while Ibn al-Zubayr was ruling. Ahmad ibn Abd al-Wahab Al-Nuwayri, *Nihayat al-Arab fi Funun al-'Arab* (Cairo: Dar al-Kutub al-Misriyya, 1923), 206 preserves the text of this report. It is narrated on the authority of Muhammad ibn al-Munkadar, but without full *isnad* to verify its authenticity. The governor in question is Khalid ibn al-Walid. Some critics hold that this report is of doubtful authenticity because there is not corroborating evidence that burning was ever a criminal punishment among Muslims.

70. See al-Qurtubi, op. cit., 7:244.

71. Salah al-Din Munajjad, *Al-Hayat al-Jinsiyya 'and al-'arab min al-Jahiliyya ila Awakhir al-Qarn al-Rabi'a al-Hijri* [*Sexual Life among the Arabs from Pre-Islamic Age to the Fourth Century Hijri*] (Beirut: Dar al-Kitab al-Jadid, 1975).

72. Al-Tabari, op. cit. 3:465 makes clear in his commentary that Lut's story always comes in a series of references to other Prophets, including Salih.

73. Shahla Haeri, "Woman's Body, Nation's Honor: Rape in Pakistan," in *Hermeneutics and Honor: Negotiating Female "Public" Space in Islamic/ate Societies*, ed. Asma Afsaruddin (Cambridge, MA: Harvard University Press, 1999), 55–69.

74. Joshua Hammer, "Gay Egypt in the Dock: The Big Crackdown Might Reflect Cairo's Own Insecurities," *Newsweek International*, February 11, 2002, and Kate Garsombke, "Gay Life – and Death – in the Arab World: Persecution of Homosexuals Increases in the Middle East," *Utne Reader*, February 5, 2002.

75. Al-Bukhari hadith number 6953 and Muslim hadith number 1907. *Hadith* scholars considered this to be the key *hadith* (of all the thousands attributed to the Prophet) and it comes first in al-Bukhari's collection before thousands of other *hadith*.

76. Fatima Mernissi's research is the strongest statement of this idea from a feminist perspective, linking the emerging rule of elite men to the suppression of democratic values and women's authority in the generation after the Prophet Muhammad's death.

77. Hamid Dabashi, *Authority in Islam: From the Rise of Muhammad to the Establishment of the Umayyads* (New Brunswick, NJ: Transaction, 1989) documents varieties of resistance to Arab kingship from positions that came to be called Shi'i or Khariji.

78. Abdullahi Ahmed An-Na'im, *Toward an Islamic Reformation: Civil Liberties, Human Rights and International Law* (Syracuse, NY: Syracuse University Press, 1990), 9.

79. The central ethical and religious teaching of Islam is *tawhid*. This could be narrowly defined through theology, or more radically conceived. In talk about God, *tawhid* means radical monotheism and insisting that God is singular and unique with no partners or associates. In theology, *tawhid* means perceiving radical monotheism as the single teaching of many Prophets, not just Muhammad, and the religious communities they founded. In social life, *tawhid* means urging a plurality of people to join in a harmonious unity. In personal life, *tawhid* means struggling with alienation and fragmentation from each other person, urging them and oneself through honesty and sincerity toward a more unified whole. *Tawhid* in general means assessing honestly the alienation, violence, egotism, and hypocrisy that are the major obstacles that keep people fragmented and keep societies unjust.

80. Farid Esack, *On Being a Muslim: Finding a Religious Path in the World Today* (Oxford: Oneworld, 1999) is one of the first writings of an Islamic theologian to couple women's rights to the rights of homosexuals (both female and male) in Muslim communities. Not surprisingly Esack writes as a South African.

9

ARE WE UP TO THE CHALLENGE? THE NEED FOR A RADICAL RE-ORDERING OF THE ISLAMIC DISCOURSE ON WOMEN

Gwendolyn Zoharah Simmons

"One of the major powers of the muted is to think against the current," writes Rachel Blau DuPlessis in her book: *Writing Beyond the Ending: Narrative Strategies of Twentieth-Century Women Writers.*[1] Questioning the inherited wisdom passed down by patriarchal authorities in the Islamic tradition has been my wont just as it was forty years ago when I began to question the racist paradigms that attempted to confine me inside the narrow *Jim Crow* ghetto created by American white supremacy. There was danger then; there is danger now. In fact I find it harrowing to even think about addressing a Muslim audience of people unknown to myself on the topic of "women and human rights" in Islam or "Islam and feminism." It is a bit like what I imagine it would have felt like addressing the white community in Memphis (where I was born and raised) in the 1960s on "why white racism was wrong" or "why the Jim Crow system of apartheid in Memphis needed to be dismantled."

I must confess that any attempt to write about "women and human rights" in an Islamic context for me is extremely difficult. It is difficult because of all of my experiences with the Islamic tradition to date both in the Middle East[2] and here in the U.S.A.[3] No matter the level of rationalizations (apologetic or explanatory), what I have seen and heard regarding the status of women in Islam has been, for the most part, discriminatory to women. Frankly, I am tired of the contortions, the bending over backwards, and the justifications for the oppressive, repressive, and exclusionary treatment of women in majority Islamic societies as well as in minority Muslim communities in the U.S.A.[4] I for one cannot and do not accept the justifications or rationalizations for this current reality. To me, these practices are morally wrong. Just as slavery cannot be morally justified today, neither can the contemporary suppression of or discrimination against women be justified.

I think it is important to state up front that I came into Islam as a fully formed African-American woman who had been on the frontlines of my people's struggle against the *Jim Crow system* (racial apartheid) in the U.S. South erected by white racists a decade or so after the end of the "legal" enslavement of my African – later to become African-American-ancestors. I was a student participant-leader in the Student Non-violent Coordinating Committee (known by its acronym, SNCC). I started out as a foot soldier marching, carrying picket signs, and being arrested outside segregated restaurants, libraries, theaters, museums, and other public places that denied my access solely on the basis of the color of my skin. I was jeered, called a "nigger," a "coon," an "ape," spat upon and physically assaulted by white passers-by, hit with billy-clubs, and arrested by white policemen enforcing the "law"; a "law" that many whites believed was ordained by Divine sanctions.

Many of the white racists really believed that God had destined people of African descent, through a curse on the Biblical person Ham, to be slaves in perpetuity to all the other descendants of Noah's children. Other whites believed that they had other scriptural justifications for the enslavement and continued segregation of Africans even after "legal" slavery ended here in the United States. Some of the most ardent white racists were deeply religious people. They used Biblical passages to support their notions of white supremacy and superiority.

During the period prior to the 1960s, many black people had internalized these ideas of white supremacy and black inferiority and its religious basis. Their objective reality (of ongoing racism and oppression) plus the unrelenting reinforcement of these racist ideas via school textbooks, film, television, and public discourse caused a distortion of self-concept in many black people and they accepted the *status quo*. When other blacks (protestors like myself and others) rebelled against this dehumanization, those who had deeply internalized racism fought against those of us who sought to throw off our oppression. This is why Malcolm X's (El-Hajj Malik El-Shabazz) strident words against white supremacy and authority were so important to those of us who were fighting for our humanity and our rights. His words were a strong cup of black coffee to the sleeping, an antidote to the psychic and mental poison that was killing black people figuratively and literally.

I went on from my street protest activities to become the Project Director of the Laurel, Mississippi branch of the 1964 Freedom Summer Project.[5] It was at this time that I learned a liberating black Christian theology and about community organizing in the face of virulent and violent white racism. The black women of Laurel, and in many other towns, villages, and hamlets in the state were the backbone of the Mississippi struggle. If it had not been for them, we would never have galvanized those thousands and thousands of people who fought for the right to vote and to be active participants in the civil and political life of that state and this nation. What we did in Mississippi reverberated across the South and the entire country, gradually knocking down the barriers to black people's civic and political participation at the local, state, and national levels.

I am amazed when I reflect on the reality of what we did in Mississippi and how it has changed so much about the racial landscape in the South, particularly, and in the U.S.A. overall. In 1964, if you were black, you could be killed for attempting to register to vote in Mississippi and some other Southern states. And, of course, running for any public office as a black person was completely forbidden. Presently the U.S. Congressional delegation from the state of Mississippi has the largest number of African-Americans of any state and the Mississippi State Legislature is at least one-third African-American. This has happened in a thirty-year period. It was the Fannie Lou Hammers,[6] the Annie Devines,[7] the Victoria Grays,[8] the Eunita Blackwells,[9] the Eberta Spinks, the Carrie Claytons, the Susie Ruffins,[10] and so many other women and men, girls and boys in Mississippi who made this happen. We Mississippi female freedom fighters stood on the shoulders of Sojourner Truth, Harriet Tubman, Ida Wells Barnett, and the thousands upon thousands of African-American women known and unknown who struck their blow for freedom as they lived the destiny that was theirs. These were women of agency and power. They were strong and they did what they had to do, when they had to do it. These are my foremothers. They are my legacy; they are an important part of my heritage.

I personally became engaged in a vigorous fight for my self, for my identity as a black person who had grown up in a racist society at an early age. I was greatly aided in my struggle for self and agency by the black women in my home (my mother, my grandmother, my aunts),[11] my church (particularly the women leaders of the church), my school (wonderful women teachers who took me under their wings and nurtured my intellect and my spirit), and in my community (women community leaders who encouraged my talents and my leadership abilities). I am fortunate as an African-American woman to have been surrounded by powerful women role models who had survived incredible hardships to make a way out of no way.

I was further aided in my struggle against racial dehumanization by the African-American interpretation of Christianity, which not only imputed agency to African-Americans, male and female, but also a chosenness and a challenge to rise up from the degradation and humiliations imposed by our enemies to become a model community of faith and righteousness.[12] I was blessed to be nurtured in such a religious environment.

I came into Islam with this history, with this legacy. Therefore, it is morally, psychically, emotionally and intellectually impossible for me to accept the notion that I am a second-class human[13] because I was born in a female form. I can no more accept this idea than I could accept in the 1960s that I was a second-class citizen because I was born in a black body. My feminism has been greatly informed by my experiences gleaned in the fight for equality here in racist America.

I am further strengthened in my beliefs about the equality of women by the fact that I was graced by God to meet a Sufi mystic, Sheikh Muhammad Raheem Bawa Muhaiyaddeen,[14] who by his teachings, his example, and his very being introduced me to Islam, an Islam of justice, truth, beauty, and grace. The Islam that my Sheikh taught and exemplified is a gender, racial, and religiously egalitarian Islam. It is an Islam that teaches that all human beings are created from a divine ray of God, are all God's children and are completely equal in God's sight. It is an Islam that overtly acknowledges the feminine qualities of God, those qualities of wisdom, compassion, nurturance, and sustenance. It is an Islam that teaches that the human being has been endowed with seven levels of consciousness or wisdom through which he or she can know God personally. The way to know God personally, intimately, taught Bawa Muhaiyaddeen, is through a rigorous self-purification process whereby all ideas and feelings of separation (sexual, racial, and religious), and the ego sense are purged. To be a Muslim, taught Bawa Muhaiyaddeen, is to be in a state of purity. If one reaches this "state" of Islam, this state of purity, then one can communicate directly with God, taught Bawa. Then one is truly a *Mu'min* (a pure believer). It is then and only then that one can truly understand the Qur'an, one's duty to God and one's fellow beings, human, animal, and plant, taught Bawa. This was the Islam that captured my heart.

In my studies of Islam, I see Bawa's teachings and that of many others in the Sufi and philosophical streams in Islam as the true essence of Islam, which emerges after one strips away the cultural, racial, and ideological accretions and dross. It is then and only then, says Bawa, that the human being steps into the true radiance and beauty of God Consciousness, which recognizes no differences in the human family. In this state, all are seen as potential manifestations of God, made in the image of God, which in the physical takes two forms, male and female. It is only this physical form that has differences and these are for reproductive purposes. The soul, the *qalb* (heart), and the levels of consciousness are not differentiated according to race or gender but are potentially the same. To see differences and to make distinctions based on differences in color, class, or gender is the greatest ignorance, taught Bawa Muhaiyaddeen.

However, what I have found in Islam, as practiced, is very, very different from Bawa's teachings. Distinctions based on race, skin color, class, gender, and religion occur all the time in societies and communities that call themselves Muslim. From my Bawa Muhaiyaddeen inspired vantage, it seems that one of the primordial essences of the religion of Islam is justice.[15] The Islam that I embrace in my heart is one of peace and justice. There can be no peace where there is unrelenting injustice. The injustice to which Muslim women have been subjected cannot be said to be the will of a God of justice. When the oppression of women occurs in an Islamic society in the name of Islam, it is the result of many things, religious, cultural, and economic. Certainly one of these is men's incorrect interpretations of the Qur'an and *hadith* owing to the societal and cultural influences that shaped the early jurists' and theologians' worldview and subsequent interpretation of these texts.[16] It is not because Islam requires it any more than any of the other religions require it. These early anti-women interpretations have been compounded by later misogynist accretions to Islam's canon and the mistaken belief that what the earlier doctors of law and theology decided are immutable, unchangeable.[17] This has locked us as Muslims into a legal and theological prison that has fostered and justified violence and repression against women and religious minorities which are done in the name of God and religion.

It is true that the Qur'an and the *Sunnah* of the Prophet have provided textual sources for the development of Islamic law. However, these texts were interpreted and applied in socio-historical contexts by human beings. Using reason and influenced by diverse geographic locations and customs, early jurists developed a body of law that reflected the differences of juristic reasoning and social customs of a patriarchal society.[18] Islamic law is a human product derived from a very human process over several centuries. These laws and the process by which they were derived can and should be questioned, challenged, and changed if and when societal harm occurs because of their implementation.

The idea that changes in law are required when there is harm caused by the law is not a new idea in Islam. Najim al Din Al-Towfi (d.1316) wrote,

If a text implies any damage to the general interest [*maslaha*], it is the latter [general interest] which should prevail. – But some say that it is against the text. On the contrary, it reinforces the text, which was revealed in order to safeguard human welfare.[19]

Men defined and continue to define what is in the best interest of Muslim societies legally. Many of the male authorities did not then and do not now include the best interests of over half of their population, women and girls, in their legal formulations. Laws, for example, that continue to countenance universal and unrestricted divorce privileges for men while placing severe restrictions on women's ability to obtain a divorce; those that permit unregulated polygamy; those that place restrictions on women's rights to travel, their right to decide if they will go to school or go to work outside the home if married; and those that give reduced sentences to male relatives who commit honor killings and the like are not taking women's interest seriously and are oblivious to the harms that such restrictions can and do cause women. These laws continue to buttress and sustain male privilege, patriarchal privilege, and to enforce women's subjugation and oppression.

Islam as practiced does have a gender ideology, which is not necessarily reflective of the Qur'an, which, as both Leila Ahmed[20] and Farid Esack[21] have written, shows ambivalence about women's equality. There is, however, a significant number of verses enjoining equitable treatment for women. So much so that if the male lawmakers had been so inclined, they could have developed a gender-equitable interpretation of the Qur'an. The negative position of women in Islamic societies has been deeply affected by the writings, interpretations, and attitudes of the 'ulama of the eighth, ninth, and tenth centuries.[22] Their attitudes regarding breadwinning in the family, Islamic family law, biological differences between the sexes, differences in the socialization of the sexes, and the whole issue of men's honor being located between the thighs of a woman have been used to marginalize women in both the public and domestic spheres. Polygamy, men's easy access to divorce, and the wife's expected obedience to her husband in all matters including sexual access and when to have or not have children, have marginalized women in the private sphere. Putting men in charge of household expenditures, which is said to be the normative arrangement, is largely responsible for the socioeconomic inequality between the genders.

By and large, Muslim religious authorities and legal scholars are of the view that the man is obliged to provide food, shelter, and clothing for his wife and children. In return the woman has obligations toward her husband including obeying his sexual demands. According to male interpretations of Islam that have become the orthodox view, men because of their economic role are given the authority to manage the affairs of women and even to punish women if they do not obey.[23] It should be admitted that men's absolute control over women seriously erodes those rights given to women in Islam that Muslims are so quick to brag about – the right to own and hold property, to work outside the home and to have control over their income, etc. If a man controls your movements and demands that you stay inside the house, it is pretty difficult for you to earn an income or to manage your properties.

This whole idea that women have to be protected, looked after, and controlled must be re-examined. Also the prevalent notion that the morality of society can be upheld only through restrictions and policing of women must be challenged. Why the double standard on morality and chastity in Islamic societies and communities? The Qur'an commands chastity and sexual purity for both men and women. Certainly, we all want strong families with children who are cared for and protected by their mothers and their fathers. But if the creation and maintenance of such families become the rationale and justification for denying women human rights, then alternatives to keeping families strong and intact must be found. Resilient and together families can no longer rest on women and their behavior alone; men must assume their role as parents beyond the breadwinning function. We must challenge the idea that woman's destiny is biologically determined. The idea that women's biological differences produce an intellectual difference and an emotional difference that suits her for motherhood and homemaking exclusively must be challenged and eradicated.[24]

In 2002, I went to hear a noted African-American imam speak at a major university as a guest of a Muslim student group. I purchased three of his tapes that were being sold at that gathering. One of them was titled "The Nature of the Woman." I became very sad listening to the contents of that tape, which posits that women are created from a bent rib[25] and as such have certain negative characteristics, which are an inherent part of her nature. The upshot of his discourse was that women were created to have a highly emotional nature, since this suits them for their role as bearers and caretakers of children. Implicit in his statements was the idea that this was woman's primary role. Here is an African-American man who seemingly has forgotten his own history and the legacy of his foremothers. He has forgotten, for example, that Harriet Tubman single-handedly escaped slavery in 1849 when she was twenty-nine years old, only to return nineteen times to lead three hundred other enslaved Africans to freedom. It is said that Tubman carried a gun in her waistband and if one of her passengers became terrified on the perilous journey and wanted to turn back, Tubman would threaten to kill him or her on the spot and forced them onward, onward to freedom. Tubman had a U.S. $40,000 bounty on her head and that was a lot of money in the 1850s. Traveling by night, hiding by day, scaling the mountains, fording the rivers, threading the forests, lying concealed as the pursuers passed them, Tubman led her passengers, guided by the North Star, to freedom. To this day, none knows the paths she took. But some say it must have been God who led her and I agree. Now can you tell me that this woman was too emotional to be a leader? She was not only a leader; she was a general. Tubman was the first woman soldier in the U.S. Army. She served as a scout and a guide during the Civil War. Shamefully, Tubman was a war veteran who had to sue the U.S. government to get her pension. I am going on at some length about my foremother Tubman as an antidote to this imam's tape that says that because woman is created from a rib she is emotional, and that her nature suits her exclusively for motherhood and wifely duties. Clearly women are created to be mothers, since it is only women who can give birth to children. Unfortunately, what is a wonderful attribute given by God to women has been turned into the justification for women's suppression, repression, and oppression.

We progressive and feminist Muslims must publicly acknowledge the oppression of Muslim women and the denial of their human rights in Islamic societies.[26] And we must also acknowledge that there has been a feminist struggle against this oppression within the Middle East since the beginning of the twentieth century. It really existed before then and it can be attested to in the first written evidence of feminist thought in the poetry of Arab women published as early as 1860. The first explicit organizational identification of Muslim feminism occurred in the founding of the Egyptian Feminist Union and the public unveiling by two upper class women in Egypt in 1923.[27] This act represented a symbolic and pragmatic announcement of the rejection of a whole way of life built on hiding and silencing women. These early feminists argued that Islam guaranteed women rights that they had been deprived of because of "custom and traditions" imposed in the name of religion.

Yet feminism in Islam has been attacked as the cultural arm of imperialism or neo-imperialism out to destabilize local society and to destroy indigenous cultural identity. It has also been attacked as being anti-Islamic – undermining the religious foundation of the family and society – and for being elitist and therefore irrelevant to the majority.[28]

But the feminist movement, named and unnamed, has persevered. Contrary to the charges against it, Margot Badran in her studies of Egyptian feminism and Eliz Sanasarian in hers on Iranian feminism have found that the feminist movements in these two countries are grounded in Islam and nationalism.[29]

Badran and Miriam Cooke in their *Opening the Gates* divide feminism in the Arab world into three distinct periods:

1. There was what they call the invisible feminism period from the early 1860s to the early 1920s, which one finds evidence of in books produced by middle and upper class women.
2. The second phase they document as being from the 1920s to the end of the 1960s. This period saw the rise of women's public organized movements. Between the 1920s and the 1950s these movements existed in Egypt. In the 1930s and 1940s feminist movements were found in Lebanon, Iraq, and Syria. This same type of activity began in the Sudan in the 1950s.
3. The third phase, says Badran and Cooke, began after the 1970s and saw a resurgence of feminist expression in countries such as Egypt, Iraq, and Lebanon.

Feminist discourse among Muslim women in the Arab world has addressed universal issues including:

*   the unfettered right to education and work outside the home;
*   women's rights in marriage, divorce, and custody of children cases after divorce;
*   women's right to the vote, to stand for election, and to participate in all spheres of their society;
*   the right to travel freely and an end to gender segregation.

There is a long and wonderful history of Arab Muslim and Christian feminists as well as Muslim feminists in other parts of the Islamic world, including most notably those in Indonesia, Iran, Pakistan, and Turkey, who are striving for their full human rights. I am sure that many if not most Muslims in the world are unaware of this history.[30] It is an important part of recent Islamic history that needs to be taught to Muslims the world over. I urge all Muslim women and progressive men to teach this history of Islamic feminism to Muslims everywhere. I hope that we feminist and progressive Muslims here in America will teach this history to all the women and men converts coming into Islam as well as the immigrants (male and female) who have come to America to live. Just as African-Americans have had to wrest our true history from the lies and obfuscations of white racist American history, we feminist and progressive Muslims must learn and teach the history of Muslim women's struggle for justice against ignorance, tradition, and superstition to all Muslims, especially the young. We will face formidable opposition in our efforts. Most likely we will be driven from our mosques and community centers when we try to teach this history. We will be shunned and ostracized. But we must persevere in spite of the forces that will be arrayed against us.

This will not be a new phenomenon, for Muslim feminists have suffered all manner of abuse in their struggle to achieve women's human rights within Muslim societies. It is the same kind of suffering and abuse experienced by women worldwide as well as racial and religious minorities, slaves, peasants, and workers who have fought for their human rights.

What is so remarkable about feminist Muslim women's struggles is that their struggle has been waged in largely agrarian societies with high illiteracy rates among men and even more so among women. They are struggling in societies where the hold of religious belief is still great and where religion is an important regulator of everyday life and source of identity. This fact is critical in societies where people are taught that the oppression of women is mandated by their religion. Muslim feminists have had to contend with these deeply held misconceptions about women, which are lodged in their tradition. They have also had to contend with the legacy of the colonialism of the late nineteenth and early twentieth century as well as the American-enforced "New World Order" of today.

Just as in the past, Muslim feminists and their supporters run the risk of being discredited as anti-Islamic, anti-nationalistic, or both. They also run the risk of assassination attempts and legal efforts to charge them with apostasy or to have their marriages annulled because they are apostate. Of course this is true for progressive male reformers too. Progressive Muslim scholars such as Farid Esack and Ebrahim Moosa of South Africa have suffered immensely, including assaults on their lives, as a result of their progressive views. Even today a Muslim feminist like Nawal al-Saadawi needs bodyguards when she's at home in Egypt. When Toujan Faisal of Jordan was elected to the lower house of the Jordanian Parliament, she too had to have armed guards to protect her. She was called an apostate; Islamists attempted to have her marriage annulled on the grounds that she was an apostate. They failed in their efforts.

We Muslims, feminists, and progressives here in the U.S.A. have the opportunity to practice an Islam that is egalitarian in its precepts and its practices. We must fight to re-interpret the texts in keeping with the socio-historical context of our times. When women are going on space missions and walking on the moon, flying F-16s, performing heart transplants, and so on and so on, can we continue talking and preaching about woman being created from a rib and that this has determined that she is too emotional and mentally fragile to work outside the home or to pursue a meaningful career? The facts on the ground dispute these contentions, resolutely. We must let these myths go. We must bring the best of Islam into the twenty-first century and stop dragging those anti-woman perspectives and interpretations of medieval men into our masjids, our classrooms, our homes, and our hearts.

We have the opportunity to bring about a change. Are we up to the challenge?

ENDNOTES

1. Rachel Blau DuPlessis, *Writing Beyond the Ending: Narrative Strategies of Twentieth-Century Women Writers* (Bloomington: Indiana University Press, 1985), 26.
2. I have lived and traveled in the Middle East on four different occasions. The longest period was from June 1996 to December 1997, when I was based in Jordan on Fulbright and NMERTA Fellowships. During that time, as well as during my earlier visits in 1994, in 1995, and again in 2002, I traveled to other states in the region, including Egypt, Syria, and Saudi Arabia. Each time I met and discussed the status of women in Arab Islamic societies with men and women concerned about this issue.
3. I converted to Islam in 1972 in Philadelphia and have been actively involved in an Islamic community since that time.
4. I must point out my particular disappointment with the level of discrimination against women in many (not all) African-American Muslim communities. Given this community's long history of struggle against discrimination based on race and skin color and its generally progressive politics because of its marginalized position in society, I had certainly hoped for a more liberal gender interpretation of Islam than I have found to be the case. The lure of patriarchal domination (long denied to African-American men over "their" women as a consequence of chattel slavery, where there was only "one man," the white man who dominated black men and women equally) seems to have overridden racial solidarity concerns. Of course many African-American women scholars and cultural workers have documented black women's resistance to the sexism and misogyny practiced in black culture. On this topic, see Toni Cade Bambara (ed.), *The Black Woman* (New York: Penguin, 1970); Katie Geneva Cannon, *Katie's Canon: Womanism and the Soul of the Black Community* (New York: Continuum, 1995); Angela Y. Davis, *Women, Race & Class* (New York: Vintage, 1981); bell hooks, *Ain't I a Woman? Black Women and Feminism* (Boston: South End Press, 1981); Audre Lorde, *Sister Outsider* (Freedom, CA: The Crossing Press, 1984); Deborah Gray White, *Too Heavy a Load: Black Women in Defense of Themselves 1894–1994* (New York: W.W. Norton, 1999); Beverly Guy-Sheftall (ed.) *Words of Fire: An Anthology of African-American Feminist Thought* (New York: New Press, 1995), Gloria T. Hull, Patricia Bell Scott, and Barbara Smith, (eds), *All the Women Are White, All the Blacks Are Men, but Some of Us Are Brave* (New York: Feminist Press, 1982); Aishah Shahidah Simmons, "Creating A Sacred Space of Our Own," in *Just Sex: Students Rewrite the Rules on Sex, Violence, Activism, and Equality*, ed. Jodi Gold and Susan Villari (Lanham, MD: Rowman & Littlefield, 2000); Aishah Shahidah Simmons, *NO!*, motion picture, AfroLez Productions, forthcoming; and Kimberly Springer (ed.), *Still Lifting, Still Climbing: African-American Women's Contemporary Activism* (New York: New York University Press, 1999); among many others.
5. The 1964 Mississippi Freedom Summer Project was the brainchild of Robert "Bob" Moses and several local Mississippi activists with whom he worked in the early 1960s. The Project was sponsored by COFO (the Council of Federated Organizations), which included CORE (Congress for Racial Equality), NAACP (National Association for the Advancement of Colored People), SCLC (the Southern Christian Leadership Council), and SNCC. The Freedom Summer Project brought over one thousand, mostly white, college-age students to Mississippi to help black activists launch a massive statewide voter registration campaign, to organize the Mississippi Freedom Democratic Party (MFDP), and to generally challenge the racial apartheid system that existed in the state. For a good description of the project, see Doug McAdam, *Freedom Summer* (New York: Oxford University Press, 1988).

6. Mrs Hammer was a local leader from Ruleville, Mississippi who became nationally known as a member of the Mississippi Freedom Democratic Party when she challenged the all white Democratic "Regulars" at the 1964 Democratic Convention in Atlantic City on national television. For more information on this remarkable sharecropper turned political leader, see Kay Mills, *This Little Light of Mine – The Life of Fannie Lou Hammer* (New York: Plume, 1993).

7. Mrs Annie Devine was an outspoken leader of the Freedom Movement from Canton, Mississippi.

8. Victoria Gray was a leader of the MFDP from Hattiesburg, Mississippi.

9. Eunita Blackwell was an SNCC activist from Mayersville, Mississippi who became the first black woman mayor of her town.

10. Mrs Carrie Clayton, Mrs Susie Ruffin and Mrs Eberta Spinks were the first leaders of the Laurel, Mississippi movement. They embraced me and the other COFO volunteers when we first arrived in Laurel, taking us into their homes, providing food and shelter, placing their own lives and that of their families in jeopardy by doing so.

11. Mrs Juanita Cranford Watson, my mother; Mrs Rhoda Bell Temple Douglas, my grandmother; and Mrs Jessie Hudson and Mrs Ollie B. Temple Smith, my aunts, had a profound influence upon the development of my self-concept as a female person and as a human being.

12. For an excellent explanation of this concept of "chosenness and challenge" in African-American Christian theology, see Gayraud S. Wilmore, *Black Religion and Black Radicalism: An Interpretation of the Religious History of African-Americans*, 3rd edn (Maryknoll, NY: Orbis, 1998), especially 253–82.

13. Many Muslims who discriminate against women would argue that they do not posit that women are "second-class humans." Rather, they contend that God ordained different roles for men and women. It just so happens that these "roles" give men authority over women solely on the basis of gender. The fact remains, however, that women are placed in subordinate positions to men no matter the reason given. For a recent excellent analysis of this problem in traditional Islamic discourse see, Abdulaziz Sachedina, "Woman, Half-the-Man? The Crisis of Male Epistemology in Islamic Jurisprudence," in *Intellectual Traditions in Islam*, ed. Farhad Daftary (London: I.B. Tauris, 2000), 160–78.

14. Muhammad Raheem Bawa Muhaiyadeen came to the U.S.A. from Sri Lanka for the first time on October 11, 1971. "What we know of him prior to then we have gathered from scattered details, which begin in 1884 when he was first known in Sri Lanka. He was recognized [then] as an illuminated master while he still lived in the jungle," writes Sharon Marcus in her "Introduction" to Bawa's book *The Triple Flame: The Inner Secrets of Sufism* (Philadelphia: Fellowship Press, 2001). He was an Islamic Sufi who dedicated much of his long life to instructing people on the true meaning of Islam and the path of Sufism. Because of his saintliness, his unwavering love for all who came before him, and his depth of understanding of the Qur'an and *hadith* as well as the Hindu and Christian scriptures, he drew thousands of seekers of wisdom to his sessions over the sixteen years that he lived and taught in the United States. Information on the *Bawa Muhaiyaddeen Fellowship*, which is the repository of Bawa's teachings can be found at the Fellowship's website at www.bmf.org or by calling +1-215-879-8631 or 8604. It is located at 5820 Overbrook Avenue, Philadelphia, Pennsylvania 19131, U.S.A.

15. It is not only the Sufis who maintain that Islam's central imperative is one of justice. The eminent legal scholar Khaled Abou El Fadl, in his important work *Speaking in God's Name: Islamic Law, Authority and Women* (Oxford: Oneworld, 2001), writes "[T]he Quran often speaks of the law of God as basically constituted of the imperative of justice. Typically it states that God commands people to establish justice, or it dictates that the Prophet or Muslims implement God's law by enforcing justice" (27). Continuing, El Fadl states, "[T]he Quran dictates the imperative of justice as both an individual and collective responsibility ... [T]he obligation of justice must be discharged by the individual and by society at large" (28).

16. One of the salient points that feminist religious scholars, as well as others, have shown is the fact that all religious experience is structured by the socio-historically conditioned worldview of the believer. The noted Iranian Islamic scholar AbdolKarim Soroush speaks about the human basis of all religious knowledge also. In *Reason, Freedom and Democracy in Islam*, trans. Mahmoud and Ahmad Sadri (Oxford: Oxford University Press, 2000), Soroush states, "Religious knowledge is a variety of human knowledge subject to change, exchange, contraction and expansion. [It is] human, fallible, evolving and most importantly is constantly in the process of exchange with other forms of knowledge" (15–16).

17. As I have written prviously, "The fact that the early Muslim legal scholars, thirteen centuries ago, saw as their lawmaking task the development of a human (the only kind that they could reach as they were not prophets) understanding (*fiqh*) of God's Commands has often been lost on the faithful ... The fact that Islamic law is the culmination of hundreds of years of human intellectual activity is crucial for women and other progressive Muslims who are striving to change aspects of the law which are out of step with modernist notions of human rights and women rights." Gwendolyn Simmons, "The Islamic Law of Personal Status and Its Contemporary Impact on Women in Jordan," dissertation, Temple University, 2002, 233.

18. Joseph Schacht, in "Law and Justice", "Islamic Society and Civilization" (in P.M. Holt, Anne K.S. Lambton, and Bernard Lewis eds. *The Cambridge History of Islam*, vol. 2 (Cambridge: CUP, 1970), 539) gives numerous examples of how the early jurists subverted the egalitarian impetus in the Qur'an as it related to women and to male–female relationships (543). He also describes how the law as formulated suppressed the ethically gender neutral voice in the Qur'an and supplanted it with laws reflective of the formulators' misogynist bias (545). An example of this process, says Schacht, is the case of divorce in Islamic law. As I have written, "Divorce in Islamic law is one of the most harmful to women institutions created by the jurists. Traditionally, it has given men almost total control over the divorce process, permitting them to discard no longer wanted wives easily. Whereas women had to go through a lengthy legal process in order to free herself from an onerous marriage." Simmons, "*The Islamic Law of Personal Status and Its Contemporary Impact on Women in Jordan*," 234.

19. Muhammad Sa'id Al-Ashmawi, "Shari'a: The Codification of Islamic Law," in *Liberal Islam – A Sourcebook*, ed. Charles Kurzman (New York: Oxford University Press, 1998), 56.

20. Leila Ahmed, *Women and Gender in Islam: Historical Roots of a Modern Debate*, (New Haven: Yale University Press, 1992), 64.

21. Farid Esack, printed text of talk given at Temple University's Religion Department Conference on "What Men Owe Women," Sugar Loaf Conference Center, Philadelphia, June 1998.

22. As Sachedina in "Woman, Half-the-man?" writes, "[I]n one area the Qur'an left the status of women to become the *mawdu'* (her social substantive social context) for laws that permitted, though mitigated, an inequality of status between men and women, reducing a woman to 'half the man.' Her distinctive contribution to determining her own social context was thoroughly excluded by eliminating her as the interpreter of her own objects and situations. Patriarchal structures of Arab culture, in the form of loosely camouflaged Traditions ascribed to the Prophet, left her intellectually crippled, while the male jurists prepared text of the laws for her insidious domination by the male members of society." (169).

23. Qur'an 4:34 is the verse of the Qur'an most often quoted to justify the idea that men are in control of women and even have the right to physically chastise them if they are disobedient. Contemporary Muslim feminists have interpreted Qur'an 4:34 differently than the orthodox interpretations of the verse. See specifically, Amina Wadud's interpretation and explanation of this verse found in her ground-breaking work, *Quran and Woman: Rereading the Sacred Text from a Woman's Perspective*, 2nd edn (New York: Oxford University Press, 1999).

24. Feminist scholars across disciplines have maintained that there is a gender hierarchy in patriarchal societies that places women in subordinate positions. As Catherine McKinnon in *Feminism Unmodified* has written, "the social relations between the sexes [in patriarchal societies] is organized so that men may dominate and women must submit." *Feminism Unmodified – Discourses on Life and Law* (Cambridge, MA: Harvard University Press, 1987), 3.

25. While many Muslims believe as do their Jewish and Christian counterparts that woman was created from "Adam's rib," as described in Genesis 2:18–24, there is no Qur'anic basis for such a belief. The Islamic theologian and scholar Riffat Hassan has written exhaustively on this subject. She notes that in the thirty or so passages in the Qur'an on the creation of humanity, there is no mention of a male human being created first and a female human being created second. Rather, as she states, "An analysis of the Qur'anic descriptions of human creation shows how the Qur'an evenhandedly uses both feminine and masculine terms and imagery to describe the creation of humanity from a single source." Continuing, Hassan notes the "woman created from Adam's rib" idea comes into Islamic theology through *hadith* sources. As we find these "rib" traditions ascribed to the Prophet Muhammad in both *Sahih al-Bukhari* and *Sahih Muslim*, the two most authoritative collections of *hadith*, Muslims believe these descriptions of woman's creation to be true. See Riffat Hassan, *Women's Rights and Islam: From the I.C.P.D. to Beijing* (self-published, n.d.). These *hadith* accounts of woman's creation and the fact that they do not accord with the Qur'anic account of human creation are a problem for feminists and progressive Muslims who are working for gender egalitarian Muslim societies. Hassan and others address this problem by pointing out that these *hadith* are weak with regard to their lists of transmitters. Whenever there is a conflict between the Qur'an and *hadith* accounts on any matter, Hassan and other scholars are of the view that any *hadith* that opposes the Qur'an cannot be accepted as authentic.

26. In July 2002 the United Nations Development Program issued the *Arab Human Development Report 2002*. The report was written by a group of distinguished Arab intellectuals and scholars. The unbiased study showed that the twenty-two Arab countries have made significant strides in several areas of human development over the last three decades. Yet, the report notes that there are deeply rooted constraints within these societies that are serious obstacles to human development. These are: (1) lack of respect for human rights; (2) *lack of rights for women*; and (3) a deficit of knowledge acquisition and utilization. As a member of a political and economically marginalized group in the U.S.A., I am greatly concerned that African-American Muslims are often adopting the same characteristics that have retarded development in the Arab Islamic world, particularly repression of female leadership in Muslim communities. There is also disrespect for the views of Muslims and others who challenge orthodox Islamic views imported into the community from the Arab world. In my opinion, to shackle and muzzle half of the community's population certainly does not bode well for a community that is already politically and economically marginalized within the U.S.A.

27. Margot Badran, "Independent Women," in *Arab Women: Old Boundaries, New Frontiers*, ed. Judith E. Tucker (Bloomington: Indiana University Press, 1993), 131, 135. Additionally, there are numerous excellent works on Muslim feminism and Muslim feminist writings. Please see: Margot Badran, *Feminists, Islam, and Nation – Gender and the Making of Modern Egypt* (Princeton: Princeton University Press, 1995); Margot Badran and miriam cooke (eds), *Opening The Gates: A Century of Arab Feminist Writings* (Bloomington: Indiana University Press, 1990); Lois Beck and Nikki Keddie (eds) *Women in the Muslim World* (Cambridge, MA: Harvard University Press, 1978) to cite just a few.

28. John Esposito, "Introduction: Women in Islam and Muslim Societies" in *Islam, Gender, & Social Change*, ed. Yvonne Yazbeck Haddad and John Esposito (New York: Oxford University Press, 1998), ix–xxviii. Also see Badran, "Independent Women," 144.

29. Margot Badran, *Feminists, Islam, and Nation: Gender and the Making of Modern Egypt*; Eliz Sanasarian, *The Women's Rights Movement in Iran* (New York: Praeger, 1982).

30. Not only are many Muslims here in the U.S.A. unaware of the Islamic feminist movement, but what is even more alarming is their resistance to learning anything about it. In my "Introduction to Islam" classes, most of the Muslim students are adverse to reading books about Islamic feminists and in many cases are quite annoyed with me that I incorporate this material in the curriculum and self identify as a Muslim feminist. A number of my female colleagues who teach Islam at colleges and universities across the U.S.A. say that they get very negative reactions from their Muslim students on the inclusion of Islamic feminism in their classes on Islam. I have taught a *"Women and Islam"* class in two different semesters. There were no Muslims enrolled the first time that I taught it. Given the large number of Muslim students on my campus, I was rather surprised. The second time I offered the class there were several Muslim women enrolled, most of whom were from the Subcontinent. There was also an Arab and an African-American Muslim in this second class. The fact that they all stayed and wrote excellent research papers on feminist topics has encouraged me to keep offering this class.

part III

PROGRESSIVE MUSLIMS
AND PLURALISM

10

MUSLIMS, PLURALISM, AND
INTERFAITH DIALOGUE

Amir Hussain[1]

> Truly, there was a party of My servants who said: "Our Lord! We believe,
> therefore forgive us and have mercy on us for You are the best of all
> who show mercy."
>
> *(Qur'an 23:109)*

In this essay, I explore some of the relationships that modern North American
Muslims have had with people of various other religious traditions. As this essay
is intended for non-specialists in the study of Islam or religion, I refrain from
using jargon or situating my work in complex theoretical matrices. I will begin
with a discussion of inter-religious relationships during the lifetime of the
Prophet Muhammad, move to a broad historical survey, and then focus on
interfaith dialogue in contemporary North America. Along with other
contributors to this volume, I locate myself as someone who is both a Muslim
(from a working class background) and an academic who studies contemporary
Muslim communities. I have been involved with interfaith dialogue at local,
national, and international levels for over a dozen years.

WHAT IS PLURALISM?

It is hard to talk in public about religion these days, and that certainly goes for
pluralism. When some people hear the term "pluralism," they think of an
"anything goes" moral relativism that seeks to mix all religions into one. My
own perception of pluralism is shaped more by scholars such as Wilfred
Cantwell Smith and Diana Eck, who have championed the necessity of
thinking deeply about religious pluralism. In her book *A New Religious*

America, Diana Eck comes back to identify three important themes about pluralism:

1. Pluralism is not simply the same thing as diversity. One may have people from different religious and ethnic backgrounds present in one place, but unless they are involved in an active engagement with one another, there is no pluralism. In other words, pluralism is not and cannot be a non-participant sport.

2. The goal of pluralism is not simply "tolerance" of the other, but rather an active attempt to arrive at an understanding. The very language of tolerance in fact keeps us from the type of engagement we are speaking of here. One can tolerate a neighbor about whom one remains thoroughly ignorant. That stance, while no doubt preferable to outright conflict, is still far from genuine pluralism.

3. Pluralism is not the same thing as relativism. Far from simply ignoring the profound differences among religious traditions, a genuine pluralistic perspective would be committed to engaging the very differences that we have, to gain a deeper sense of each other's commitments.[2]

PLURALISM AND MUSLIMS: THE GENESIS OF ISLAM IN A PLURALISTIC SETTING

Issues of pluralism and interfaith dialogue are of crucial importance to Muslims, particularly to those of us who live in countries where Islam is a minority religious tradition. Islam is already (or will become very soon) the second largest religious tradition in a number of European and North American countries.[3] Muslims living in these countries have to articulate their understanding and practice of Islam in the midst of a plurality of belief systems. It is the responsibility of Muslims to help non-Muslims to understand how it is that we, as Muslims, live out our lives. Those of us who see ourselves as progressive Muslims understand that there is a need for all people to work together on our common problems. As Muslims, we can help in the construction of a world in which it is safe to be human.

Historical Islam began as a minority tradition in a non-Muslim setting. When the Prophet Muhammad received his first revelations in Mecca in 610 CE, the people around him were largely tribal and polytheistic. Even though the people of Mecca knew of Christianity, Judaism, Zoroastrianism, and other religious traditions, large concentrations of Christians or Jews were only to be found in other cities in Arabia.

As with any new religious tradition, Islam would not have developed had it not been for interfaith dialogue. After Muhammad received his revelations, he began to speak about them publicly, first to his own family and then to other people. Slowly, people began to convert from other faiths to the religion of the one true God that Muhammad was preaching. Muhammad, then, from the beginning of his first revelations to the end of his life was actively engaged in interfaith dialogue.

The Qur'an, as the revelations to Muhammad from God came to be called, assumed that the first hearers of the revelation were familiar with the stories of Judaism and Christianity. For example, a verse in the Qur'an (5:27) begins, "Recite to them in truth the story of the two sons of Adam." The implication is that the hearers are already familiar with aspects of the story, but that the Qur'an affirms and represents, and at times modifies, the previous versions of narratives. Another example is the mention of Gabriel and Michael in the context of angels and prophets (2:98). The verse does not specify that Gabriel and Michael are angels and not prophets, but assumes that the hearers are familiar with the Jewish and Christian traditions around them. A third example is found in chapter 12 of the Qur'an, entitled "Joseph." This chapter, which is referred to as "the most beautiful of stories" in verse 3 – and is the longest sustained narrative in the Qur'an – tells the story of Joseph who is sold into slavery. It does not go into details about the family background of Joseph, but does speak of Joseph and his brother being sold into slavery by their other brothers out of jealousy (12:8). Presumably, the first hearers of this revelation were familiar with the story in the book of Genesis about Joseph and Benjamin, who are sons of Jacob and his wife Rachel, while the other brothers have different mothers. A fourth example is found in a verse about Jesus (3:55): "And God said: 'O Jesus, I am gathering you and causing you to ascend unto Me and cleansing you of those who disbelieve and making those who follow you above those who disbelieve to the day of resurrection. Then to Me shall be your return, and I will decide between you concerning that in which you differed.'" Presumably, the early Muslim community who heard these verses for the first time had some idea that, besides the Qur'anic presentation of Jesus, there was a range of interpretations in previous Christian communities about the life and nature of Christ. The Qur'an was revealed in a world that knew about various other religions.

Many people are aware of the emigration of Muhammad and his earliest followers from Mecca to Medina in the year 622. However, there was an earlier emigration to Abyssinia which underscored the value of interfaith dialogue to Muhammad. The earliest biographer of Prophet Muhammad, Ibn Ishaq (d. 767), and the famed Muslim historian Tabari (d. 923) discuss this migration.[4] As people began to accept Islam they met with opposition from others in Mecca. This opposition turned to physical persecution against certain members of the early Muslim community. Muhammad gathered a group of those most vulnerable, and instructed them to go across the Red Sea to Abyssinia, a Christian country ruled by a Christian king. There, the emigrants were welcomed and accepted. Indeed, the Christian king protected the Muslims against demands of extradition by the polytheists of Mecca. The emigrants stayed in Abyssinia until they rejoined the larger Muslim community in Medina.

Muhammad's act represents the first time that Muslims, as Muslims, dealt with Christians as a community. There was no sense of enmity against the Christians of Abyssinia; instead, they were seen as a people that would protect members of the nascent Muslim community. Clearly, this is a very early example in Islam of the importance of pluralism and interfaith dialogue, and the debt that we Muslims owe to Christians.

As mentioned earlier, Islam arose in an environment where the first converts were persecuted by polytheists for their beliefs. Later, there were tensions among Muslims and Jews, as well as tensions between Muslims and Christians. Not surprisingly, there are passages in the Qur'an that say positive things about other traditions as well as passages that are critical of them. One of the challenges faced by Muslims in an honest interfaith dialogue is to come to terms with the full range of verses that address the issue of relationships between Muslim and non-Muslim communities. Given that the Qur'an was revealed over a period of twenty-three years under a number of different historical settings, it is not surprising that there are different sets of guidance given to the young Muslim community. For example, there are passages in the Qur'an, such as 5:51 or 60:1, which advise against taking "non-believers" as protectors. There is also 5:82, which reads, "You will find among the people the Jews and the Polytheists to be the strongest in enmity to the Believers." On face value, those passages seem quite different from other verses, such as the rest of the same verse 5:82, which continues, "nearest among them in love to the Believers will you find those who say 'We are Christians.'" While it is perhaps some consolation to recognize that the Qur'an never sanctions the killing of Jews and Christians, it is also important for Muslims to be aware of how the various strands in the Qur'an can be used both as a bridge-building tool and to justify mutual exclusivism. Admittedly, the situation is different for the case of polytheists, as exemplified by 9:5: "But when the forbidden months are past, then fight and slay the Polytheists wherever you find them."[5] But there are also passages that are critical of Muslims who show disregard for others. Chapter 107, "The Small Kindness," is succinct:

In the Name of God the Compassionate the Caring
Do you see him who calls the reckoning a lie?
He is the one who casts the orphan away
who fails to urge the feeding of one in need.
Cursed are those who perform the prayer
unmindful of how they pray
who make of themselves a display
but hold back the small kindness.[6]

It is crucial for contemporary Muslim and non-Muslim readers of the Qur'an to know something of the contexts of the original revelations to Muhammad.

In a remarkable passage, the Qur'an does speak about the creation of humanity, and which people are better than others: "O humanity! Truly We created you from a male and a female, and made you into nations and tribes that you might know each other. Truly the most honoured of you in the sight of God is the most God-conscious of you. Truly God is Knowing, Aware" (49:13). There are four key points in this verse. First, the passage is addressed to all of humanity, and not specifically limited to Muslims. Second, the passage mentions that the creation of humanity into distinct groupings comes from God and is a positive value. Third, it encourages people to transcend their differences and learn from each other. Finally, the passage does not say that Muslims are better than other people, but that the best people are those who are aware of God.

PLURALISM IN EARLY ISLAMIC HISTORY

Islam remained a minority tradition until two years before the death of Muhammad. From the time that Muhammad received his first revelations in 610 to the year 622, Islam was a persecuted minority religion in Mecca. In the year 622, Muhammad emigrated with his community to the city of Medina. In Medina, Islam was also a minority tradition. However, in Medina, free from the persecution of the Meccans, the Muslim community could exist openly as a community. The number of Muslims greatly increased in Medina. Through conversion, the majority of the citizens of Medina became Muslim. In 630, Muhammad was able to return to Mecca in triumph, and much of the Arabian peninsula was converted to Islam by the time of Muhammad's death in 632.

Islam is, to be sure, a missionary religion. The three largest religious traditions in the world, Christianity, Islam, and Buddhism, are all religions that encourage and engage in conversion. All three believe that there is a proper way to live in the world, and that it is incumbent upon believers to spread information about this proper way. This conviction gives rise to mutually exclusive truth claims: only Jesus's death saves us from sin; only Muhammad is the final Prophet of God; only the Buddha teaches us how we can attain enlightenment. All three of these religious traditions have, tragically, gone through phases where the "other" was converted to the truth through force and violence.

The Qur'an is clear about not forcing people to convert: "There is no compulsion in religion: the Truth stands clear from the Wrong" (2:256). When Muhammad returned to Mecca in the year 630 as the conquering ruler, he gave Muslims a clear example to follow. The psychological tensions in Muhammad's consciousness must have been extraordinary when one remembers just what was about to occur. Muhammad was born in Mecca in a branch of the noblest family in that city. He established a reputation for himself as a trustworthy and honest businessman, had a loving wife and four daughters. Then at the age of forty he began to receive revelations from God, revelations that challenged the *status quo.* Muhammad was at first tolerated for his public preaching, and then persecuted. Little more than a decade after receiving his revelations, he had to leave the city of his birth and migrate with his followers to another city. Eight years later,

Muhammad was able to return to Mecca as the conquering ruler. He literally had the power of life and death over those who years earlier had tormented and persecuted him and had killed several of his followers. By pre-Islamic Arab custom, he had the power to seek revenge, even massacre his enemies. Instead, in this most triumphant of earthly moments, Muhammad chose to display the utmost mercy, and declared total amnesty. In this extraordinary act, he came to those who had persecuted him, and recited to them the words from the Qur'an that Joseph had first spoken to his brothers when they came to him in Egypt, humbled after having sold him earlier into slavery: "This day let no reproach be upon you. May God forgive you, and God is the most merciful of those who show mercy" (12:92). There would be no forced conversion or slaughter of the Meccans.

For many converts, it is a message of justice that brings them to Islam. There is an emphasis on social justice in the Qur'an, and on siding with the poor, the orphaned, and the oppressed. The ethical monotheism of the Qur'an requires that obligations be fulfilled, whether they are due to God or to other people. For example, Farid Esack, a brilliant Muslim scholar and theologian, has written about the role of Muslims in the struggle to end apartheid in South Africa.[7] Unfortunately, there is a stereotype of Muslims forcibly converting people to Islam. Images persist of Arab warriors on horseback with the Qur'an in one hand and a sword in the other, chopping off the heads of those who refused to convert.[8] The reality is very different. For example, the first place that Islam spread to outside of Arabia was Iran. The dominant religious tradition in Iran before Islam was Zoroastrianism. It took approximately two hundred years for Iran to transform from a country where there were almost no Muslims to a country where the majority were Muslim.[9] Often, it was the Sufis, the mystics of Islam, who spread Islam by living among the people and providing them with an example of how to live their lives as Muslims. In this way, they were no different from those Christians who lived out their lives as faithful witnesses, not active instigators of the conversion process. There have, certainly, been episodes in which Muslims abused the power that they had when they were able to dictate the discourse. But the dialogues of power corrupt any noble idea, whether it be Islam, Christianity, freedom, or democracy.

I have pointed to a few incidents in the life of Muhammad because that life (Sunnah) is considered exemplary for Muslims. In Islamic history, a number of people sought to live out the model of tolerance that Muhammad lived. Another early example is that of the Caliph 'Umar, the second successor (in Arabic, the word khalifa [English: Caliph] literally means "successor") to Muhammad. 'Umar ruled the Muslim community from 634 to 644 CE. In 638 Muslims arrived at Jerusalem. Far from him being a ruthless imperial conqueror, the traditional stories tell that 'Umar walked into Jerusalem because it was his servant's turn to ride the mount that they shared. While in the city, 'Umar was given a tour of the existing religious sites by the Christian Patriarch of Jerusalem. As the time approached for prayer, 'Umar asked for a place where he might offer his prayers. Through translators, the Patriarch offered 'Umar the opportunity to pray where he stood, in the Church of the Holy Sepulchre, one of the most important of Christian sites. 'Umar refused, saying that wherever he, the first Muslim ruler in Jerusalem, was to offer his prayers, his followers would build a place of prayer (a *masjid,* or mosque). He would not let that place be inside a spot that was of crucial importance to Christians. Instead, he prayed outside of the church on what was then the porch of the martyrs. Sure enough, if one goes to the Church of the Holy Sepulchre today, across the street is the small Mosque of 'Umar, commemorating his prayers. Clearly for 'Umar, respect was due to Christians and their places of worship.

There have been times in various Muslim civilizations where there were good relations between Muslims, Christians, and Jews when Jews and Christians were the minority. One thinks for example of the city of Baghdad in the eighth and ninth centuries.[10] Baghdad was built on the banks of the Tigris River as the capital city for the Abbasid Empire (750 to 1258) by the Caliph Al-Mansur, who ruled from 754 to 775 CE. Baghdad truly was a metropolis with links to Persia, India, China, Byzantium, and the Latin West. One sees this cosmopolitan nature in the great literary classic to emerge from Baghdad, *The Thousand and One Nights,* with its mix of diverse characters and stories from various locations. Baghdad was also home to the House of Wisdom *(Bayt al-hikma),* built by the Caliph Al-Ma'mun (ruled 813–833 CE) as a center of learning and translation for scholars from around the world. A Christian, Hunayn ibn Ishaq, was appointed as the director of the translation academy. This research institute was at the center of the movement to bring the philosophical heritage of the Greeks, Persians, and Indians within the fold of the Islamic quest for wisdom.

It is important here to emphasize that Islam has long existed in Western culture, first in Europe and later in North America. The pluralism that we see in the modern Western world has ancient roots. From the eighth to the fifteenth centuries, much of Spain was Muslim, and Al-Andalus (the Arabic term for Muslim Spain, Andalucía) was a high point of Islamic civilization.[11] In the ninth and tenth centuries, Cordoba in Muslim Spain became one of the most important cities in the history of the world. Christians and Jews were involved in the Royal Court and in the intellectual life of the city. Historically, there was also an Islamic presence in Southern France, Italy, and Sicily, with Arabic being a language known to the highly educated. And of course, under Ottoman rule, there was a profound Muslim presence in Turkey, the Balkans, and Eastern Europe. The Mughal Empire was also known for its pluralism.

The Arabic language (especially via Spanish and French) has contributed to the vocabulary of English. Common English words such as "coffee," "sofa," "genie," and "alcohol," technical words such as "algebra," or "alkaline," and even archaic words such as "lute" and "alchemy" all have their roots in Arabic. Arabic words such as *hajj,* "jihad," or *hijab* have become commonplace enough as not to require translation. There is a history of Muslims, Jews, Christians, and members of other religious traditions living together in a pluralistic society. Muslims influenced and were influenced by the people with whom they lived.

The Crusades radically altered the way that Muslims, Christians, and Jews understood each other. Before the Crusades, Muslims were relatively unknown to the European public. After the Crusades, with the making of enemy images on both sides, there was a great deal of polemic in European texts about Muslims. Norman Daniel has written the classic study of this time, his magisterial *Islam and the West: The Making of an Image.*[12] The ordinary European might come into contact with Muslims as merchants, traders, seafarers, or pirates. However, the educated classes read works of Islamic philosophy, as well as classics of Greek philosophy (such as Aristotle) translated into Arabic and then into Latin. Maimonides, the great medieval Jewish philosopher, wrote *The Guide of the Perplexed* in Arabic. Muslim physicians were among the best of their day, and Muslim scientists and mathematicians (in collaboration with non-Muslims) made great advances in the sciences. Anybody familiar with Thomas Aquinas's *Summa Theologica* has felt the hovering presence of medieval Muslim scholars. This powerful presence has been beautifully represented by the great Renaissance painter, Raphael, who included Ibn Rushd (Averroes) in his painting *School of Athens.*[13]

MUSLIMS AND PLURALISM IN THE MODERN WORLD

The Qur'an set forth perennial principles of humane interfaith behaviour. For example, Qur'an 5:48 ends with the following words: "for every one of you did We appoint a law and a way, and if God had pleased God would have made you a single people, but that God might try you in what God gave you, therefore strive with one another to hasten to virtuous deeds; to God you will all return, so God will let you know that in which you differed." The Prophet Muhammad and other early leaders left Muslims with edifying examples of cooperative relations with religions other than Islam. Throughout history, Muslims have existed in dialogue with others. Whether the relationships have been productive or disastrous, Muslims have defined themselves in dialogue. They have always understood – and constructed – their "Islams" in a context of pluralism.[14] This interfaith consciousness is particularly vital in contemporary North America.

There have been modern attempts at dialogue between Christians and Muslims in Canada going back at least to the visit to Canada by Maulana Muhammad 'Abdul 'Aleem Siddiqui, also known as al-Qadiri.[15] Siddiqui was an Indian Sufi, born in 1892, who traveled extensively and made a trip to Canada in 1939.[16] On his trip to Canada, Siddiqui spoke at the al-Rashid Mosque in Edmonton, the first mosque built in Canada, which had been opened in 1938. After speaking in Edmonton, Siddiqui travelled to Toronto, where he spoke "to a largely non-Muslim gathering."[17]

Some Canadian Muslim communities were dependent on support from Christians for early meeting facilities. For example, the first public prayer service in Ottawa (1963) was held in the basement of a Christian church.[18] According to a former President of the Ottawa Muslim Association, "we have to acknowledge the help we got from Christians, especially the United Church."[19] Since 1980, the National Christian Muslim Liaison Committee has existed as an official vehicle of dialogue. Under the leadership of the largest Protestant denomination in Canada, the United Church of Canada, there have been a number of conferences and workshops on interfaith dialogue. Several useful resources have been produced as a result of these workshops.[20] This interfaith work also involves the attendance of non-Muslims at Muslim rituals and celebrations and the attendance of Muslims at non-Muslim religious ceremonies. The result is "Islams" that influence and in turn are influenced by the other traditions with which they come into contact.[21] And as members of a minority religious tradition, Muslims in North America are aware of the dominant religious tradition, Christianity. While the majority tradition has not always had to be aware of the minority traditions in its midst (even that situation no doubt is changing because of our shrinking world), the minorities must always understand the majority culture in order to survive.

Muslim leaders in North America have made a number of comparisons between their communities and the Jewish communities. They appreciate the fact that the Jewish communities in North America have been able to build not just synagogues, but educational facilities and medical centers. Many Muslims want to match the success of the Jewish communities in North America with regard to creating public institutions as well as public support for their religious tradition.

Comparisons have also been made between Muslim and Catholic communities in North America. Catholics needed to survive as a minority in Protestant North America and to create their own educational, cultural, and medical facilities. Their success is seen as another model for Muslims to follow. Catholic–Muslim dialogue has received official support since the Second Vatican Council, and Muslims and Catholics have often spoken out in solidarity with each other at conferences around the world. Currently, Georgetown University in Washington, DC, a Catholic (Jesuit) institution, supports the Center for Muslim–Christian Understanding.

Hartford Seminary in Connecticut is home to the Duncan Black Macdonald Center for Christian–Muslim Relations, and also publishes the academic journal *The Muslim World.* In June of 1990, the seminary organized an international conference entitled "Christian–Muslim Encounter: The Heritage of the Past and Present Intellectual Trends." A very useful resource volume, *Christian–Muslim Encounters,* was produced as a result of that conference.[22]

Because of the interfaith dialogue in Canadian cities such as Toronto, many non-Muslims are aware of some of the basic elements of Islam. By contrast,

American cities such as Los Angeles do not have the same level of interfaith dialogue. Having participated in interfaith dialogue in both cities, I find that in Los Angeles people ask me basic questions about Islam. By contrast, in Toronto, people have a basic knowledge and instead are interested in deeper questions.

There is also the issue of what some of the underlying assumptions of religious pluralism mean for Islamic theology in North America. Are we teaching things that are old news to our students or things that our students are not prepared to hear? As an example, when I say, "I have said Friday prayers in the Al-Aqsa Mosque and in the Dome of the Rock in Jerusalem, and I have prayed in the sweat lodge in Manitoba with my Cree elders, and I do not think that Allah distinguishes between these prayers," I get some very interesting student reactions. Some want to hear more about each of these occasions. Some are genuinely interested in connections between Islam and the religious traditions of First Nations. Others are horrified that I have prayed with non-Muslims or that I have linked the lodge with the mosque.

Unfortunately, there are Muslims in North America and around the world who have no interest in pluralism. They see Islam as the only true religion, and often see their particular way of being Muslim as the only way to be Muslim. As a teacher, I often have Muslim students who are such zealous defenders of Islam. In hearing their rhetoric of intolerance, I think back to one of my own beloved teachers, Professor Wilfred Cantwell Smith, one of the greatest North American scholars of Islam in the past century.

PLURALISM EXEMPLIFIED: THE CASE OF WILFRED CANTWELL SMITH

Professor Smith was, for many of us who study religion, the epitome of critical scholarship. From his deep knowledge, he was able to offer critique when it was needed. Of Professor Smith's scholarship, John Hick wrote, "An outstanding feature of Wilfred's work is that it is on the highest level of technical historical scholarship and yet it is at the same time driven by involvement in and concern for the worldwide human community, with a keen sense of the threatening disasters and the amazing possibilities before us. This human involvement goes back to his work in India before Partition and has continued ever since, as a constant thread running through all his writings."[23]

Professor Smith was a committed Christian, who was deeply concerned about the issues facing Muslims. He was not a Muslim. He was not an apologist for Islam. Yet his critique never did violence to what it meant for other people to be Muslim. In *Islam in Modern History* he wrote, "A true Muslim, however, is not a man who believes in Islam especially Islam in history; but one who believes in God and is committed to the revelation through His Prophet."[24] Those words were published in 1957. In his 1963 book *The Meaning and End of Religion*, he continued "the essential tragedy of the modern Islamic world is the degree to which Muslims, instead of giving their allegiance to God, have been giving it to something called Islam."[25] Those words could have been written yesterday with equal force and validity.

Professor Smith has served as a shining example of the loftiest ideals of humanity and scholarship for me and many others. Like others of his Muslim students, I often felt that he was a better *muslim* (one who submits to God) than I was, a fact that inspired me more than I can express. As alluded to earlier in the comments by John Hick, Professor Smith and his wife Muriel spent six years as missionaries in Lahore before the partition of India and the creation of Pakistan. When we first met, he commented that he had lived in Lahore, my birthplace, longer than I had lived there, six years to my four. But Professor and Mrs Smith were no ordinary missionaries. I don't know that they ever converted one person, but I am sure that they taught and influenced thousands. And they were splendid representatives of the kind of Christianity that I came to know and love in Canada. Years ago, on a television show in Canada, I had the honour of sitting on a panel with the Very Reverend Dr Bruce McLeod, a former Moderator of the United Church of Canada. Dr McLeod told me a story about Professor Smith. Someone once asked him, "Professor Smith, are you a Christian?" After his characteristic pause, Professor Smith repeated the question, "Am I a Christian?" Then he answered, "Well, maybe I was, last week, at lunch, for about an hour. But if you really want to know, ask my neighbour." For many of us who see ourselves as progressive Muslims, Professor Smith's comment captures our own various Islams. We strive to be Muslim, meaning that we live out our submission to God in a way that can be seen by those with whom we are in contact. Not that we put on a pretence for the benefit of others, but our lives are lived as an integrated whole, with no easy teasing out of our individual Islam from the poetry of our ordinary lives.

INTOLERANCE IN THE WORLD TODAY

It is not just some Muslims who are intolerant towards non-Muslims, but also non-Muslims who show callous disregard and ignorance about Islam in North America. At the beginning of the new millennium there was a rise in anti-Muslim polemic from certain Christian groups.[26] Franklin Graham, the son of evangelist Billy Graham, spoke of Islam as a "very evil and wicked religion." Jerry Vines, a former president of the Southern Baptist Convention, labelled Muhammad a "demon-obsessed pedophile" (an odd remark if one remembers that the Jesus of the Gospels was particularly concerned with casting out demons). David Benke, a minister in the Lutheran Church – Missouri Synod, was suspended for participating in an interfaith event, and was charged by his church that, "Instead of keeping God's name sacred and separate from every other name, it was made common as it was dragged to the level of Allah." Much of this rhetoric came in the aftermath of the terrorist attacks in the United States on September 11, 2001. Although every major Muslim group in North America was quick to condemn the attacks, this was not widely reported in the news media in the days after the attacks. Many individual Muslims took the initiative after the attacks to do interfaith dialogue for the first time, and speak to their friends and neighbours about Islam. Academics who study Islam were in great demand to address groups, large or small, across North America.[27]

While North Americans learned a great deal about Islam and Muslims in the months after the attacks, there were also a number of horrible sentiments that were expressed by media pundits who had overnight become "experts" on Islam and Muslim communities. One of the few groups in the United States to immediately stand in solidarity with Muslims were Japanese Americans, many of whom were Christian. Having experienced racism and discrimination during their internment in the Second World War, Japanese Americans wanted to make sure that the same fate did not befall American Muslims.

What was immensely troubling was the anti-Muslim rhetoric from a number of American Jewish leaders. Naively, I expected American Jews, with their history of having faced persecution, oppression, and discrimination, to stand with Japanese Americans alongside Muslims. Instead, some of them used the turmoil over the terrorist attacks to further their own political agendas. In October, 2001, two different Jewish groups released studies about their estimates of the American Muslim population, usually thought to be at least six million by most researchers.[28] A study conducted for the American Jewish Committee estimated a population of between 1.4 and 2.8 million. The other study by researchers at the City University of New York estimated a population of 1.1 million adults and 650,000 children. To anyone that knows anything about the Muslim population in America, these figures were absurd. A respected scholar of American Islam, Fred Denny, estimated the American Muslim population in 1994 to be around 4.5 million.[29] Yvonne Haddad and Jane I. Smith, two of the leading scholars who have studied the American Muslim population over the past twenty-five years, have put the number in the same time period at, conservatively, three to four million.[30] Every statistical study undertaken points to the drastic and ongoing rise in the number of Muslims in America, owing to continued immigration, conversion, and large family size. It is reasonable to expect that the number of Muslims in America would thus continue to grow from the mid 1990s figures reported above. Indeed, the most recent report, conducted by the Council on American–Islamic Relations, puts the total number of Muslims in America at six to seven million.[31] All of this data, conducted both by Muslim advocacy groups and independent members of the scholarly community, point to the inaccuracy of the American Jewish Committee report. This had nothing to do with objective scholarship, and everything to do with the politics of representation. That the sponsors released these studies shortly after September 11, with heightened discrimination against Muslims, was particularly problematic.

More troubling was the work of the Jewish Defence League, the Anti-Defamation League (ADL), and the Middle East Forum, which sought to slander

American Muslim leaders. At the urging of the ADL, the *Washington Post* and Fox News both reported the following words from Dr Muzammil Siddiqi, the former President of the Islamic Society of North America, a year before the attacks: "America has to learn ... Because if you remain on the side of injustice, the wrath of God will come." Even allowing for the fact that the quotation was taken out of context, I could not see why these words were regarded as problematic, since American Christian leaders often refer to God's judgment of nations and societies, including America itself. In context, the passage was even less offensive: "We want to reawaken the conscience of America. America has to learn that. Because if you remain on the side of injustice, the wrath of God will come. Please! Please all Americans, do you remember that Allah is watching everyone. If you continue doing injustice, and tolerating injustice, the wrath of God will come. But we want blessings for America. That's why we want the conscience of America to be awakened and Americans to stand on the side of justice."[32]

Even sadder, a number of academics got into the act. In an article in the *Chronicle of Higher Education* (February 8, 2002), Alan Wolfe wrote the following in a review of Diana Eck's book *A New Religious America*: "Eck occasionally lapses into cheerleading; her chapter on Muslims, in particular, stresses the degree to which they 'are increasingly engaged participants in the American pluralist experiment,' giving scant attention along the way to those adherents to Islam who continue to believe that America is the Great Satan and who, even while living here, reject this country and its values." Perhaps I am being biased here, for I consider Diana to be a colleague, and "cheerleading," although a word held in high esteem by many Americans, is not one that I would use to describe her. But it is the second part of Wolfe's sentence which is most troubling. First, I haven't seen the U.S.A. referred to by North American Muslims as the "Great Satan" in years. Second he implies that there is an equivalency here, that as many Muslims reject America as embrace it. Certainly there are Muslims – as well as those of other religious traditions – in America who don't see themselves as participants in pluralistic American society, but these represent a tiny percentage of American Muslims. Wolfe neglects to mention that a great many Muslims emigrated to America precisely because they wanted to live in a pluralistic and democratic society where they could succeed on their own merits. Abraham Verghese describes with his characteristic brilliance the situation of a young Indian intern seeking a visa to come to America. When asked by the visa officer the real reason why he wants to come to America, the intern speaks the words below, which could easily come from the mouths of countless American Muslims:

> Vadivel, who had held on to his American dream for so long that he could speak with the passion of a visionary, said, "Sir, craving your indulgence, I want to train in a decent, ten-storey hospital where the lifts

are actually working. I want to pass board-certification exams by my own merit and not through pull or bribes. I want to become a wonderful doctor, practice real medicine, pay taxes, make a good living, drive a big car on decent roads, and eventually live in the Ansel Adams section of New Mexico and never come back to this wretched town, where doctors are as numerous as fleas and practice is cutthroat, and where the air outside is not even fit to breathe." The consul gave him a visa.[33]

It is important to remember that the vast majority of Muslims in North America are immigrants or the children of immigrants. They – we – came to North America precisely because of the opportunities that were available here and not available, for whatever reason, in the country of origin.

A month after the September 11 attacks, while watching television, I came across Pat Robertson on the Christian Broadcasting Network doing a segment on Christians in Pakistan. He too spoke about Islam as a "dangerous religion," and re-visited his comments from some years earlier that there was something wrong with any American, particularly an African-American, who would convert from Christianity to Islam. He then went on to speak about the superiority of Christianity, especially with regard to what he saw as violence in Islam as contrasted with peace in Christianity.

Along with other Muslim and non-Muslim academics who teach Islam, I have received emails since September 2001 from colleagues who teach at institutions across the United States who have talked about the rise in anti-Muslim rhetoric from certain Christian groups. And I have seen glimpses of this during my talks. At one of the many churches at which I spoke, one of the audience members asked me why I thought I worshipped the same God that he worshipped. He mentioned to me that his minister had taught him that Muslims worshipped a different god than the One God worshipped by Jews and Christians. And having heard from his minister what Muslims believed, no argument from me, a believing Muslim, could persuade him otherwise.

After the attacks, there was a remarkable flow of magazine and newspaper articles, television and radio programs, websites, books, and lectures discussing Islam and Muslims. A tremendous number of opportunities were created for interfaith dialogue, particularly for those who had never participated. The question remains: what models of religious pluralism can we call upon today to guide us through these opportunities for dialogue?

THE WORLD TODAY, AND THE URGENT NEED FOR PLURALISM

In the United States and Canada, there have been tensions since 2001 between Jewish and Muslim communities, typically over Israeli–Palestinian relations. In cities such as Los Angeles, formal dialogue broke down between Muslim and Jewish groups, although individual Muslims and Jews continue to engage in dialogue. Some Jewish groups have removed themselves from Christian–Jewish dialogue when that dialogue has become critical of Israeli colonization of Palestine. For example, in April 2002 the Canadian Jewish Congress withdrew as a partner in the Canadian Christian Jewish Consultation, which is composed of representatives of Canadian churches including the Canadian Conference of Catholic Bishops, the United, Anglican, Presbyterian, and Lutheran Churches, and representatives of the Canadian Jewish Congress. With the typical concern for social justice that is a hallmark of the United Church of Canada, they wrote in response that "It is our conviction that there will be no peaceful solution that does not guarantee both peoples, Palestinians and Israelis, the right to exist in security and freedom in their own states. It is clear that no military solution can bring about peace. This means that any peaceful solution must be negotiated and built on the framework of international law. The resolution of the illegal occupation of Palestine by Israel must be addressed in any movement towards peace."[34]

In the Qur'an, Muslims are continually reminded of their relationship with the "People of the Book" *(ahl al-kitab)*. The People of the Book are those who have received an earlier revelation from God; the term is understood by most Muslims to refer to Christians, Jews, and Zoroastrians. The Qur'an allows Muslims and the People of the Book to eat together and to intermarry:

> This day the good things are allowed to you; and the food of those who have been given the Book is lawful for you and your food is lawful for them; and the chaste from among the believing women and the chaste from among those who have been given the Book before you; when you have given them their dowries, taking [them] in marriage, not fornicating nor taking them for secret concubines.

> (Qur'an 5:5)

There is an understanding in the Qur'an of a peaceful co-existence that comes from a common revelation and a common God: "And argue not with the People of the Book unless it be in [a way] that is better, except with such of them as do wrong; and say: We believe in that which has been revealed to us and revealed to you; our God and your God is One, and to God do we surrender" (29:46).

Admittedly, there is a difference in dialogue and relationships with those other than Jews and Christians. As Islam is a strictly monotheistic religion, Muslims believe that the most grievous sin is polytheism, or associating others with God. And Muslims have often had strained or hostile relationships with polytheists and atheists. However, there has also been co-existence as well. The country with the most number of Muslims is Indonesia, where the dominant religious traditions before Islam were Hinduism and Buddhism, as well as indigenous traditions and Dutch Christianity. There was no wholesale slaughter of "pagans" by the Muslims who spread Islam in Indonesia. Another country that has a large number of Muslims is India. There are political tensions both within India and between India and Pakistan. "Communalism" is the name that is given to the politics of sectarian hatred in India. However, much of the violence between Hindus, Muslims, Sikhs, and Christians in India is an example of religion being used as a powerful political symbol and force. Much like in the "troubles" in Northern Ireland, demagogues and other power-hungry political figures use religion to incite people against each other. If one looks at the cultures of North India, one finds great similarities between Hindus and Muslims in terms of dance, music, food, movies, ritual, attachment to family, worship, and notions of a just civil life.

The Qur'an repeatedly uses the word *kufr*, which is often translated as "unbelief," with *kafir* as the word for an unbeliever. While this term is often contrasted with belief in the Qur'an, it is also contrasted with the word shukr, or "thankfulness." A *kafir*, then, is not simply one who does not believe, but also one who is not thankful to God. To be sure, some Muslims have often assumed the prerogative of God and presumed who is a *kafir* and who is not. But there is nothing uniquely "Islamic" in this: Christians, for example, have killed those who were considered "heretics" or "pagans." However, the stereotype still persists of Christianity being a religion of peace and love, while Islam is seen as a religion of war and violence – as if the term "holy war" were not used by Christians for centuries.

In many ways, North American Muslims are in a position to influence what happens in the rest of the Muslim world. In countries where Muslims are in the majority, there are often restrictions and sometimes persecutions of other religious traditions. One thinks, for example, of the Baha'is in Iran or the Christians in Pakistan. It is North American Muslims who can show their co-religionists an example of the religious tolerance that occurs in North America. One can exist safely and securely as a Muslim, free to practice as a Muslim, without having to convert or torment one's non-Muslim neighbors (or, for that matter, those Muslims who aren't "Muslim enough" for the self-righteous). In order to properly do interfaith dialogue, one must have not only a deep understanding of one's own faith, but an understanding and appreciation of the faith of the dialogue partner. This can be done only in a pluralistic context, where it is possible to have a deep knowledge of more than one faith. Accepting pluralism is a sign of firm faith and confidence, not a sign of doubt. We North American Muslims need to commit ourselves to pluralism, not because we have to but because we should. It is part of the vision imparted to us by the Qur'an and the example of the Prophet.

North American Muslims can also be an example to other Muslims by taking the lead in dialogue among various Muslim groups. All too often, this is a neglected aspect of religious dialogue. In Toronto, I as a Sunni had the profound privilege of performing the Friday afternoon prayer side by side with a Shi'i colleague, the prayers being led by a Bosnian imam, in a mosque built by Albanians. In other parts of the Muslim world, for example in Pakistan, there is sometimes sectarian violence between Sunnis and Shi'is. North American Muslims can also take the lead in dialogue with Hindu or Jewish groups. In so doing, perhaps we can help toward resolving the conflicts in India and Pakistan and in Israel and Palestine.

It is important for progressive Muslims and Muslim communities in general to return to the pluralistic vision of the Qur'an, and establish cooperative relations with other religious communities, particularly at this time. There are a great many negative stereotypes about Islam and Muslims, and it is only through dialogue that these will, slowly, be dismantled. And of course dialogue is also necessary for Muslims to learn about the beliefs of those around them. It is easy to be taught to hate Christians or Jews (as for example tragically occurs in Saudi Arabia) if there are few actual Christians or Jews in one's country. In the pluralistic context of North America, it is a very different matter. The stereotypes that one may have learned, for example that Christians worship three gods and are therefore polytheistic, fall away when one is invited to a Christian worship service and realizes that it is the same One God who is being praised and worshipped.

The Qur'an is clear that God could have created people with no differences among them, but that God chose not to do so: "If your Lord had so willed it, your Lord would have made humanity one people, but they will not cease to dispute" (11:118). God speaks to us in the Qur'an about God willing our differences and our disputes. Our differences (and ensuing disputes) are not to be feared, denied, or eradicated. God teaches us through our differences. It is through dialogue that we learn about ourselves, about others, and, in so doing, perhaps also about God:

> We have made some of these messengers to excel the others; among them are they to whom God spoke, and some of them God exalted by rank. And We gave clear miracles to Jesus the son of Mary, and strengthened him with the holy spirit.
>
> If God had pleased, those after them would not have fought one with another after clear arguments had come to them, but they disagreed; so there were some of them who believed and others who denied. And if God had pleased, they would not have fought one with another, but God brings about what God intends.
>
> (Qur'an 2:253)

ENDNOTES

1. For Patrice Brodeur and Farid Esack, my brothers in submission and dialogue. And to the blessed memories of my wife, Shannon L. Hamm, and my teacher, Professor Wilfred Cantwell Smith, who introduced me to interfaith dialogue in, respectively, my personal and professional life. Thanks to Michel Desjardins and Pat Nichelson for their comments

on various drafts of this chapter, and for their continued attempts to teach me the craft of writing. My thanks also to the United Church of Canada and its members for showing me the true meaning of ecumenical: "of the inhabited earth."

2. The above is based on Diana Eck, *A New Religious America: How a Christian Country Has Now Become the World's Most Religiously Diverse Nation* (San Francisco: HarperSanFrancisco, 2001), 70–1.

3. For a recent assessment of the Muslim community in America, see Jane I. Smith, *Islam in America* (New York: Columbia University Press, 2000).

4. For a traditional Muslim understanding of this emigration, see Martin Lings, *Muhammad: His Life Based on the Earliest Sources* (Rochester, VT: Inner Traditions, 1983), 81–4. For an account of this story by a secular historian, see F.E. Peters, *Muhammad and the Origins of Islam* (Albany: SUNY Press, 1994), 173–6.

5. On this verse as it relates to the question of abrogation of verses from the Qur'an, see Jane Dammen McAuliffe, *Qur'anic Christians: An Analysis of Classical and Modern Exegesis* (New York: Cambridge University Press, 1991), 254–9.

6. Translation from Michael Sells, *Approaching the Qur'an: The Early Revelations* (Ashland, OR: White Cloud Press, 2001), 124.

7. See his *Qur'an: Liberation and Pluralism: An Islamic Perspective of Interreligious Solidarity against Oppression* (Oxford: Oneworld, 1997).

8. In a tongue-in-cheek comment, a historian friend has talked about the fallacy of this myth: owing to the Semitic notion of ritual purity, many Muslims do not hold the sacred scripture of the Qur'an with their left hand, since the left hand is reserved for cleansing oneself. If there were an army of Muslims with the Qur'an in one hand and a sword in another, they would all have had the Qur'an in the right hand and the sword in the left. No doubt the vision of an entire left-handed army is enough to give the lie to that myth. Furthermore, manuscripts of the Qur'an were far too rare (owing to the low rate of literacy) for every soldier to have had his own copy of the sacred text.

9. See Richard W. Bulliet, *Islam: The View from the Edge* (New York: Columbia University Press, 1994), 39. For a more detailed account see Richard W. Bulliet, *Conversion to Islam in the Medieval Period: An Essay in Quantitative* History (Cambridge, MA: Harvard University Press, 1979), or Michael Gervers and Ramzi Jibran Bikhazi, eds, *Conversion and Continuity: Indigenous Christian Communities in Islamic Lands, Eighth to Eighteenth Centuries* (Toronto: Pontifical Institute of Mediaeval Studies, 1990).

10. For an excellent, succinct chapter on Baghdad as well as other key cities in Muslim civilization, see Kenneth Cragg and R. Marston Speight, *The House of Islam*, 3rd edn (Belmont, CA: Wadsworth, 1988), 86–110.

11. For more on Al-Andalus, see María Rosa Menocal, *The Ornament of the World: How Muslims, Jews, and Christians Created a Culture of Tolerance in Medieval Spain* (Boston: Little, Brown, 2002).

12. Norman Daniel, *Islam and the West: The Making of an Image* (Edinburgh: Edinburgh University Press, 1960; reprint, Oxford: Oneworld, 1997).

13. For an image of this painting, and a further discussion of the link between Thomas Aquinas and Ibn Rushd, see Majid Fakhry, "Philosophy and History," in *The Genius of Arab Civilizations: Source of Renaissance*, 2nd edn (London: Eurabia, 1983), 55–76.

14. I use "Islams" in the plural rather than "Islam" in the singular as there are multiple ways of being Muslim in any given context.

15. Siddiq Osman Noormuhammad, "The Sufi Tradition in Toronto," originally published in *Message International*, 19(6), 1995. This article was expanded and updated in 1999, and is available on the web at http://muslim-canada.org/sufi/toronto.htm

16. A short biography of him exists on the web at http://members.tripod.com/~wim canada/aleem.html

17. http://muslim-canada.org/sufi/toronto.htm.

18. Zulf M. Khalfan, "Ottawa Muslims: Growing Pains," *Islamic Horizons*, 24(3) 1995, 38.

19. *Ibid.*

20. For examples, see Susan L. Scott, ed., *Stories in my Neighbour's Faith: Narratives from World Religions in Canada* (Toronto: United Church, 1999); *Faith in My Neighbour. World Religions in Canada: An Introduction* (Toronto: United Church, 1994); and *Stories of Interfaith Families: A Resource for Families and Congregations* (Toronto: United Church, 1994).
21. For an example of this, see Amir Hussain, "Shannon's Song," in *Stories in my Neighbour's Faith*, 101–6. Another example in the same collection is Zohra Husaini's "The Tragedy of Karbala," where on page 31 she connects Imam Hussain with Jesus and Karbala with Calvary.
22. Yvonne Yazbeck Haddad and Wadi Z. Haddad, eds, *Christian–Muslim Encounters* (Gainesville: University Press of Florida, 1995).
23. John Hick, "On Wilfred Cantwell Smith: His Place in the Study of Religion," in *Method and Theory in the Study of Religion*, 4 (1–2), 1992, 5.
24. Wilfred Cantwell Smith, *Islam in Modern History* (Princeton: Princeton University Press, 1957), 146.
25. Wilfred Cantwell Smith, *The Meaning and End of Religion* (New York: Macmillan, 1963; reprinted, Minneapolis: Fortress Press, 1991), 126.
26. See the commentary by Nicholas Kristof, "Bigotry in Islam – and Here," *New York Times*, July 9, 2002, http://www.nytimes.com/2002/07/09/opinion/09KRIS.html.
27. An excellent web resource was created by Omid Safi, available at http://groups.colgate.edu/aarislam/response.htm. All of us who teach Islam in North America are indebted to Omid for creating and maintaining this site.
28. For more information about these two studies and the controversy, see Teresa Watanabe, "Muslim Population Inflated, Studies Find," *Los Angeles Times*, October 25, 2001, A23.
29. Frederick Denny, *An Introduction to Islam*, 2nd edn (New York: Macmillan, 1994), 364.
30. Yvonne Haddad and Jane I. Smith, "United States of America," in *The Oxford Encyclopedia of the Modern Islamic World*, ed. John L. Esposito (New York: Oxford University Press, 1995), vol. 4, 277.
31. Council on American–Islamic Relations, "The Mosque in America," http://www.cair-net.org/mosquereport/Masjid_Study_Project_2000_Report.pdf.
32. Quotes taken from Solomon Moore, "Fiery Words, Disputed Meaning," *Los Angeles Times*, November 3, 2001, B20.
33. Abraham Verghese, "The Cowpath to America," *New Yorker*, June 23–30, 1997, 74–7.
34. From the website of the United Church of Canada, at http://www.united-church.ca/news/2002/0410.htm.

II

AMERICAN MUSLIM IDENTITY:
RACE AND ETHNICITY IN PROGRESSIVE ISLAM

Amina Wadud

> Four hundred years of black blood and sweat invested in America,
> and the white man still has the black man begging for what every
> immigrant fresh off the ship can take for granted the minute he
> walks down the gangplank.[1]

Imagine a banner draped across the port of arrival to the United States' shores: "America: love it or leave it." Then imagine these new arrivals came on slave ships from Africa.

At the heart of highly political, sensitive, racist, or even the most casual discussions about American citizenship and identity is at least some notion about "choice." Overwhelmingly, Americans are composed of immigrants who came to America's shores by choice. While identifying with their previous cultural heritages, they want something here in America. They relish the possibilities of establishing a new identity within the complexity of American pluralism. This new identity integrates the dual components of previous culture and American citizenship. While Muslim immigrants to America occasionally reference their previous cultures using the hyphenated designation, the term "Muslim-American" poses a rupture in the clarity of this identity formula. Being Muslim does not represent belonging to one monolithic culture. For example: "Egyptian-American," "African-American," "Jordanian-American" all name a cultural background plus the new American identity. The designation "Muslim-American" appears to include all Muslims despite the variety of cultural heritages among them.

In the case of American Islam, the hyphenated formula might eventually become a symbol of unity. At the present, however, it obscures profound and unreconciled differences across ethnic and racial backgrounds. It refers to an Islam that Muslims in America have in common, while simultaneously erasing latent and overt ethnic and cultural prejudices that have led to communication breakdowns and the hegemony of immigrant Muslim leadership and representation in the American Muslim context. These latent prejudices have yet to be directly addressed in community discourse, and this has resulted in further division. This essay looks at the issue of diversity in Muslim-American identities and particular concerns about the random ways that African-American Muslims are included and excluded.

I enter this discussion as an African-American Muslim woman whose experience with Islam and Muslims has not been limited to living in America. Gender, race, and class dynamics interface with matters of Islam and personal identification or empowerment in distinctive ways within each of the countries where I have resided. In the relationships between Muslims at the communal level, these dynamics create schisms incongruent with the pluralism idealized about Islam. In the larger context of progressive Islamic discourse, my concern has been focused on social justice. Some issues of social justice receive more attention than others in mainstream progressive discussions. Most often, the matter of gender hegemony is referred to, although not integrated and certainly not resolved, as part of progressive Islam. Matters of class or racial hegemony receive less direct attention. While references to Islam and culture abound, these are not focused on the relationships between the cultural identities of Muslims. Culture is one way to distinguish between essentialist articulations of Islam and its multi-variant manifestations throughout history and in various cultures.[2]

In the context of a progressive American Islamic discourse, attention to matters of race relations will not only need to address the power dynamics but also the problems of cultural assumptions and the lack of communication between immigrant and African-American Muslims. Ordinary communication problems at the level of exchanges between Muslims of different ethnicities lead to extraordinary misperceptions about the relationships between them. Misperceptions about the active roles fulfilled by various Muslims severely underestimate the real terms of Muslims' collective participation in establishing Islam in America. I have known many instances where immigrant Muslim women have handed over to their African-American sisters the organization of semi-public activities to benefit the community. While this implies some awareness of the more public role often played by African-American women, it simultaneously privileges immigrant women by shielding them from public scrutiny and censor. Furthermore, once the tasks have been initiated, African-American women are expected to hand over the fruits of their labor to male Muslims, the overwhelming majority of whom will be immigrants.

Leadership roles, authority, and public representation rest overwhelmingly upon the shoulders of male immigrants. In some instances, these roles have been won after the efforts of a wide cross-section of Muslim men and women, immigrant and African-American. However, those who participate at the grassroots level are marginalized when it comes to the establishment of authority. Immigrant Muslims privilege their own status as authorities on the basis of their centuries-long heritage of Islam. "I used to be around a lot of Eastern Muslims," says Muhammad Abdul Rahman, a member of *Masjid ush-Shura*. "They would come over here and treat us like we babes in Islam. They thought they should be our leaders just because they could speak Arabic. They would come in our *masjids* and try to be our teachers."[3] It mattered little if the Islam these people inherited was one of mere cultural transference rather than personal religious devotion and study.

Coincidently, the immigrant Muslim hegemony over leadership roles is also related to financial resources or class. Immigrant Muslims use international contacts as a source of funding to start and maintain some of their organizations or to build mosques and community centers. Undoubtedly, many immigrant Muslim communities have an overall economic advantage over the majority of the African-American communities. Indeed, many affluent African-American Muslims will gravitate toward certain affluent community centers and mosques of immigrant origin on the basis of class. While all mosques of some affluence are inclusive of members from lower income groups, affluent immigrant Muslims will not participate with the same fervor in grassroots mosques established by economically struggling African-Americans. "They come over here with their money and degrees and with an insular view of Islam," says Frederick Thaufeer al-Deen.[4] "For a people long considered second-class citizens within their own country, being treated like second-class citizens within their own religion is a sore point."[5]

Administrative styles also differ between immigrant and African-American Muslims in mosques, Islamic centers, and other community-based organizations. Most governing bodies and *ad hoc* committees retain for themselves the power of consultative counsel. In immigrant communities, the consultative bodies are fixed and formed by major financial contributors to the mosque establishment. Immigrant Muslim communities will more often exclude women except in supportive roles. Most are wives of other well-to-do men, and few will challenge the *status quo* or mainstream opinions on major issues. In African-American mosques, the imam himself is the head of the community. Should he refer to a consultative body, its membership is not fixed but organized on an ad-hoc basis relative to the issues that need to be resolved. Coincidently, African-American Muslim consultative bodies are more inclusive of women, allowing them the power to contribute, vote, and challenge major decisions concerning community activities. Indeed, African-American Muslim women are often the ones to initiate the construction of a consultative body to address specific community needs. While the imam of most African-American mosques must maintain full-time employment elsewhere, immigrant communities hire foreigners (usually) to serve exclusively as imams. The imported imam is often unfamiliar with current U.S. and local circumstances. More often than not, this also means that he is not well equipped to participate in and contribute to interfaith dialogues.[6] The imam is also not empowered to make decisions over the community, since he is an employee of those who hired him.

Between these two organizational styles, the question of representation is rarely confronted directly. I know of no Muslim community that intentionally organizes its leadership to reflect its membership with the express purpose of representing the actual demographics of the Muslim population in attendance at that mosque. The members most underrepresented at the administrative level are African-Americans. Consequently, their voice is marginalized in pluralist contexts outside of the mosques as well. Disagreements within the community may lead to the full departure of a body of African-Americans followed by the establishment of another Islamic center or mosque with very limited financial resources. Although this is a successful strategy for the proliferation of Islamic community organizations and mosques, it depletes the resources of an already less privileged body of citizens in the larger U.S. context. It also tends to produce greater fragmentation in the regional make-up of the Muslim community. This fragmentation is further represented in the degree to which regional Muslims form networks for coordinating symbolic occasions like 'Id celebration as well as for lobbying over shared political concerns in America.

Finally, these fragments result in contending claims over authority when the need arises for regional and national leadership representation. In no way are African-American Muslims represented in direct proportion to their percentage among Muslim Americans.[7] "'When folk want to know about Islam, they have always gone to the immigrant community,' gripes [Dr Aminah] McCloud. It is telling, she says, that after September 11, 'who came to the White House to represent Islam? The immigrant community. The African-American community felt very dismayed.'"[8] This was blatant after the catastrophes on September 11 and the resulting national character of Islam in America as portrayed to the general American public was overwhelmingly male and immigrant. Many African-American representatives were silenced or marginalized. In some cases, this was done specifically because they were Americans and therefore could not assist in the nagging questions about the loyalty of Muslims in America to American interests over and above foreign interests.[9]

The enmity within the Muslim communities in America over issues of race and ethnicity seems to thrive on the casual neglect of direct confrontations and critical interrogation of the root causes and multiple manifestations of these problems. Although a theoretical interrogation is insufficient to effect a full resolution of the problems, it can act as a catalyst for seeking pragmatic approaches and real strategies toward resolutions. More importantly, a resolution may result when the goal of theoretical consideration is intimately connected to the practical. After all, no Muslim voluntarily confesses to racism, classism, or ethnocentrism. All parties view these attitudes as inherent contradictions of Islam as based on its primary source, the Qur'an. Yet, Muslims in America engage in so many forms of ethnocentrism that these tendencies belittle the genuine integrity of Islam.

A TEXTUAL LOOK AT MATTERS OF RACE AND ETHNICITY IN ISLAM

The Qur'an is the major source of inspiration in the development of ideas and practices in Islam. An important two-part claim might best describe the Qur'anic precedent. The Qur'an supports and acknowledges difference between peoples but does not use those differences as a standard of judgment for human worth. Surat al-Hujurat 49:11–13 states

> Oh you who have attained to faith! No men shall deride (other men) ... and no women [shall deride other] women: it may well be that those [whom they deride] are better than themselves. Be conscious of God. Oh humankind! Behold, We have created you all from one male and one female, and have made you into nations and tribes, so that you might come to know one another. Verily the most noble of you in the sight of God is the one who is the most deeply conscious of God.[10]

In the first part of these verses, the Qur'an supports the idea of unity by exhorting the human family to respect and safeguard the dignity of one another.[11] This is followed by the second claim, to affirm distinctions between peoples using the collective terms "nations" and "tribes." It is important that the human collective is divided into categories as explicitly mentioned here. These divisions also determine certain aspects of behavior and identity. Since the Qur'an recognizes these aspects of identity, they are significant to human beings' social purpose and well-being. Human beings belong both to the larger collective and to smaller collectives. In acknowledging this, the Qur'an affirms that these are appropriate features of identity formation. More importantly, this verse uses these groups as part of the basis for an interconnection or "knowing one another." Overall, however, the Qur'an asserts a single evaluative standard: taqwa. "Verily the most noble of you in the sight of Allah is [atqa-kum] the one who is the most deeply conscious of Him." It does not support the notion that group membership is the standard of evaluation for nobility and worth.

Despite direct affirmation of distinctions between groups, the ultimate evaluative criterion for a person's worth is taqwa, moral consciousness of Allah, involving both an internal and an external component. Taqwa as defined by Fazlur Rahman is "a mental state of responsibility from which an agent's actions proceed but which recognizes that the criterion of judgment upon them lies outside."[12] In both its consciousness and action aspects, taqwa is part of responsible morality and agency within the larger framework of Islam, which neither limits nor excludes particular group membership. Hence, in the earlier part of the passage, the Qur'an specifically orders men and women not to deride each other, since "it may well be that those [whom they deride] are better than themselves." Ultimately goodness is not based on a group identification.

The Muslim-American configuration of identity claims to transcend problems of race or ethnicity, but because ethnicity is unclear, attitudes and practices of ethnocentricity are obscured and overlooked. In the politics of Muslim communities, organizations, institutions, and public representation, some parties claim more rights than others. These uneven and unreciprocal practices occur within group interactions, at the level of selective participation in community activities as well as in the selection and recognition of leaders. Meanwhile, all Muslim parties in America also claim to adhere to Western standards of universal human rights that explicitly prohibit disparity on the basis or race or ethnicity. In other words, despite the assumption of ethnic parity in the Qur'an and in the human rights standards in the U.S.A. (through which American Muslims also claim their rights), an equitable system of moral evaluation is *not* consistently operative in the North American Muslim communal context.

BRIEF HISTORY OF ISLAM IN AMERICA

The first Muslims in America were slaves taken primarily from West Africa. "For three hundred and fifty years, Muslim men, women, and children ... were sold in the New World. They were among the first Africans shipped and among the very last. When they reached the other side of the Atlantic Ocean, after a horrific journey, they introduced a second monotheistic religion ... into post-Columbian America."[13] "When the first Africans were shipped to the New World, beginning in 1501, Islam was already well established in West Africa."[14] Although Muslim slaves are an important historical reference today, Islam did not survive the American slave experience except in some customary practices whose origins in Islam would become obscured.

Later, after the end of slavery, the first collective movements towards complete human dignity for blacks in America referred to Islam as a part of a religious heritage that directly challenged post-slavery racist practices and attitudes in American policies. For some, Islam was also used to directly refute the Biblical justification for the slavery practiced in Christian America. Despite all this, slaves were only permitted to practice Christianity and this would remain the single religious choice among African-Americans for some time after the end of slavery. Historically, Islam represented the first viable and sustained religious alternative adopted by African-Americans.

The first movements among African-Americans to combat experiences of racism in America were primarily nationalist and pan-Africanist. They were quite secular in nature. Then "(i)n the first decades of the twentieth century, African-Americans began to actively form communities that defined themselves as Islamic."[15] These were alternative religious and spiritual articulations to address the problems of identity and race in America. Although these articulations would in many cases adopt symbols and history from global Islam, they would not sustain the integrity of Islamic dogma involving belief in one supreme transcendent God, Allah, and in the prophecy and living example of the Prophet Muhammad. However, these variant references to Islam eventually led to the large conversion movements among African-Americans. Studies of one development of African-American Islam trace the movement from the early configurations of the Moorish Science Temple, through the Nation of Islam, ending with the Muslim American Society under the leadership of Warith-Deen Mohammad today. Alongside this development of African-American Islam with multiple identity reformulations through the Nation of Islam, African-Americans also became Muslim through other sources of inspiration and information. One leading source of information for African-Americans was the immigrant communities. For example, in northeastern U.S. cities in the early part of the twentieth century, the Ahmadiyyah movement spearheaded a significant movement specifically addressed to African-Americans.[16] Although African-Americans did not become Ahmadis they used this introduction to Islam to study and practice orthodox *Sunni* Islam, eventually setting up their own communities between the 1950s and 1970s. In the 1970s, attempts to integrate various indigenous and immigrant Muslim communities began in earnest.

As it relates to identity, Muslim immigrants to North America have a varied history in this context. Three major phases of immigration differently affect the extent to which Islam itself played a factor in immigration to and integration into America. Like every other immigrant group to America after the African slaves, Muslims come to America seeking better opportunities. These opportunities are overwhelmingly defined in concrete terms of materialism and American civil liberties. The first groups of immigrants that concern us came from Arabic-speaking countries in the latter part of the nineteenth century and the early twentieth. Many were not Muslim but all came to America for purely secular reasons. Muslim and non-Muslim Arab immigrants linked with each other through shared cultural experiences as Arabs. Such links persist today.[17] Some efforts to maintain Islam were minimal and cultural at best. Efforts to establish Islam as a feature of an American subculture among Arabic-speaking immigrants were nonexistent. Such efforts would not take root and become widespread even among the earlier immigrants until subsequent waves of Muslim immigration.

A change in U.S. immigration laws in the 1960s opened the doors for a larger influx of Muslims who would come with greater emphasis on sustaining aspects of their cultural and ethnic identity and origins, including Islam. More Arabic-speaking immigrants followed and large numbers of South Asian immigrants began to arrive. The increase in South Asian Muslim immigrants would eventually lead to a stronger effort among immigrants to form a distinctive American Muslim identity. For one thing, the overwhelming majority of South Asian Muslims to come to North America were economically well off. They came with the expressed interest of pursuing professional development and material progress for themselves and their children. Islam was an intimate part of their cultural identity, and was also emphasized in their efforts to preserve their culture, since the faith was not in conflict with their material aspirations.

Except for the Ahmadiyyahs, banished as heretical from Pakistan in the 1960s, South Asian Muslim immigrants showed little or no interest in propagating Islam among the general American population except for some white women who either converted to Islam before or during marriage or were married despite their lack of conversion. Very few white American males would enter Islam until the development of strong Sufi movements in America in the 1970s and 1980s. Even today, Caucasian American converts are overwhelmingly female, with some estimates as high as eighty-five percent.

Islam as a feature of American communities took off in earnest during the 1970s. This public emergence was primarily local, in the form of establishing more mosques and community centers. The Muslim Student Association (MSA) started in 1963 at a number of campuses across the U.S.A. and Canada. As an umbrella organization, MSA worked with Muslim students in the universities as well as with Muslim community organizations. By the 1970s, other national immigrant and African-American institutions were organizing or re-organizing. Such movements would continue and proliferate into the 1990s.[18]

The national-level institutionalization of collectives with an explicit Islamic identity component is a key indicator of the movement among Muslims in America toward greater inclusion in American public life. As these organizations and institutions proliferate, they indicate the spread of Islam and the growth of Muslims' interest in their citizenship as Americans. They also indicate some of the schisms among Muslims. To be sure, these schisms are not merely on the basis of race and ethnicity, but also relate to perspectives on Islam and specific issues of concern to Muslim collectives. In any case, all such organizations represent a claim to autonomous identities simultaneously as Muslim and American. The need for national recognition is often indicated by the titles given to these groups and by the nature of their operations. The use of the word "American" implies at some level that they are representatives of Muslim or of Islamic interest in the American context. U.S. officials rarely inquire about their real constituency, even if noted by the organization itself. The conflict between their respective perspectives on Islam as well as the ethnic homogeneity of the participants indicate that these groups do not reflect a consensus of Muslims in the U.S.A. Yet, many of these groups continue to project themselves as representative. In a crisis like that following September 11, 2001, contention among the organizations surfaced about how accurately they represented their American Muslim constituency.

OVERCOMING OR RE-INSCRIBING ETHNOCENTRISM AND RACISM?

Before his death in 1967, Malcolm X would draw two important conclusions as a direct consequence of eighteen weeks of travel in the Middle East and Africa. First, he concluded that the problems of non-white peoples were identical against the capitalist racial hegemony of colonialism, and that all non-whites were more or less in the same circumstance *vis-à-vis* white supremacy. Secondly, Malcolm said, "America needs to understand Islam, because this is the one religion that erases from its society the race problem."[19] Malcolm believed the Muslim world and Muslim society were color-blind. "On a superficial level, it appeared that Malcolm X, like other naïve observers of Islamic countries, believed that this area of the world was free of the evils of racism. However, more substantively, we must ask ourselves how such an astute observer of human affairs could have missed the patterns of racial separatism that had such deep roots in the Islamic world."[20] How are both these perspectives simultaneously true?

Malcolm's comments reflect the duality of experience among Muslims in their own countries and those who come to America. When I have lived and traveled in the Muslim Middle East, North and South Africa, South and Southeast Asia,[21] as an African-American woman, I have felt an extreme affinity with Muslims of color. Despite this international feeling, the politics of racial and ethnic hegemony is blatant in my own home country, where I continually experienced a sense of "otherness" setting me apart from Muslim immigrants and their descendants. The contrast between these two experiences leads me to assume that there is an important factor in the American context that tends to engender this double standard. Although Muslim communities in America endeavor to hold collective and racially diverse activities, meetings, and celebrations, there are still persistent ethnic and racial sentiments that prevent us from sustaining radical pluralism in our communities.

Furthermore, these problems of race and ethnicity in American Muslim communities prevent us from achieving effective unity for overcoming larger external obstacles to our empowerment as a single religious minority in America. Indeed, it is often at the national level where the negative consequences of these yet unreconciled problems are most glaring. Various Muslim organizations continue to form on the national level. Each vies to be recognized by non-Muslim authorities and accepted by the Muslim masses as representative of Islam in America. However, racial parity in American Islam seems as illusive as gender parity globally. Often, leaders of national Muslim organizations and institutions are uninterested in gaining grassroots-level cooperation or acceptance, since they find the diversity among Muslim perspectives too tedious to overcome before they move forward with their agenda. Meanwhile, few grassroots organizations rise to achieve national recognition.[22]

Historically, many new mosques or splinter organizations and Muslim centers were formed on the basis of ethnicity; none would directly reject other Muslim ethnicities, however. According to the *Mosque Report* issued by CAIR (Council on American Islamic Relations), there is still great fluidity between cultures in the mosques and community centers across America.[23] Understandably, each collective gathers around shared symbols, past experiences, and perspectives on Islamic praxis as a basis for mutuality and understanding. But such sharing is not necessarily as Islamic as it is cultural or ethnic in origin. When others outside the dominant ethnic or racial group are present at collective gatherings, the distinctions between history, culture, and Islam often go unobserved or without comment. Sometimes what is shared are the distinctive languages or dialects, diet, or other customs.

AFRICAN-AMERICANS AND ISLAM

The overwhelming majority of African-Americans gravitating towards Islam are drawn to its humanizing articulation of social justice as well as to the divine nature of the Qur'an. As already mentioned, the extent to which actual experiences of racial justice are affirmed in the living reality of Muslim community relations is varied.

Historically, African-Americans had already experienced the abuses of power and denial of full civil liberties in the United States. Immigrant Muslim Americans have become direct victims of these abuses in a dramatic way since September 11, 2001. The African-American communities are the best place for Muslims to gain constructive insights about such U.S. abuses of power, and about strategies to combat them. Before September 11, 2001 few opportunities were offered Muslims to discuss these insights among themselves. There is need for substantive organized forums to allow meaningful dialogue along these lines and to benefit all Muslims in America. Before September 11 immigrant Muslims did not equally experience these abuses of power. Perhaps now they will see a greater imperative in addressing inter-community antagonisms and negative ethnic relations with African-American Muslims for the express purpose of addressing the larger systemic violations of civil liberties.

Each ethnic group of Muslims in America has collective experiences that act as references points and root metaphors to reinforce fundamental lessons about Islam. For African-American Muslims these references often relate to aspects of their pre-Islamic past. For example, references are made to the negative effects of drinking alcohol or to women's experiences when adopting immodest forms of dress. Overwhelmingly, the disruption of our African cultural heritage as enforced by North American slavery creates a particular identity reference. The American slave experience is the primary shared feature for all African-Americans, whether Muslim or not.

African-American Muslims are intimately linked with other Americans through the history of horrific racial slavery in the Americas and with the development pains of American pluralism in the period before the Civil War, through the civil rights movement, and even up to present. As part of their collective heritage, slavery links all African-Americans, not just African-American Muslims, in a unique way and affects our identity and relationship to America. There is never an issue for African-Americans about being "American." They never wanted to come here in the first place. Since immigrant Muslims do not share this experience, it sets them apart from the African-American experience. African-Americans read the history of Islam in America first through the slave trade: it has been estimated that as many as one-third of the slaves were from Islamic central Africa. This is part of the psychological claim to Islam among Muslim Americans of African origin. No such long running, painful, and unique "American" identity affiliation exists for immigrants, no matter how many generations they claim in America. Immigrant Muslims, who stress the origins of Islam in America with their own immigration during the nineteenth and twentieth centuries, overlook this important early feature of the American Islamic past.

In 1999, Oxford University Press published a book titled *Muslims on the Americanization Path.*[24] The very title reveals the presupposition of the volume and further accords priority to immigrant American Muslims, for whom being Muslim is presumed and Americanization must be an intentional operation. Such an articulation is impossibly prejudiced against African-American Muslim first- and second-generation converts, for whom being American is presumed and Islamization is the voluntary and intentional operation. True to the title, the contents primarily focus on immigrant Muslim concerns. One section of the book is titled "Americans towards Islamization"; all the chapters in this section focus on African-American identity. By implication, Islam is unconditionally granted to Muslim immigrants and a goal to be aspired to for Americans. Meanwhile being an American is normative for African-Americans and Islam is aspired towards. This is the crux of the contrast between African-American Muslims and immigrant American Muslims. "If African-American communities are to be included in the same text with other Muslim groups, then I believe more is needed to indicate how Black Muslims and those other groups interrelate."[25]

IMMIGRANT MUSLIMS

Though outside the immigrant Muslim community in America, I speak from within my limited experience as a Muslim American and among other Muslims worldwide. I have also entered the domestic and cultural environments of Muslims in North and South Africa, South and Southeast Asia, and the Middle East. My observations are brief, subjective, and relative to the task: national-level discourse on inter-ethnic relations. I have felt welcomed in many homes and public halls when I have visited lands with large Muslim populations who enjoy a long heritage of Islam. Attention was lavished over me as a guest in the home of extended families. I was comforted in many ways. This has led me to criticize my own African-American brothers and sisters as hosts in America. Perhaps we inherited a struggle for well-being in a culture that robbed us of our roots and heritage, leaving us displaced in this our new home. Our experiences of extended family have been ruptured since slavery. This has led us to form more diverse and complex community relations to facilitate our survival. It is not customary to put the visitor before us.

The private lives of African-American Muslims are sometimes closed to those who descend upon America, especially those who come to master a place of their own within it. Although this may seem a small matter, it bears upon our relationships with immigrants, who view America as a land of opportunity *among non-Muslim Americans*. Muslims who enter a substantial Muslim population in other countries do not expect to assume leadership or representation roles. Such deference and etiquette is neglected in the context of American Islam. It is as if Islam has no native presence, so outsiders must be its representatives at the national level. These observations have symbolic significance in the conflicts between indigenous and immigrant Muslims in America.[26]

Furthermore, many immigrant Muslims still see Islam as an ethnic identity. Collective experiences refer to or are drawn from back "home," such that a crisis in identity for the children of immigrants is viewed as a need to send the child back home. Even after a few generations have passed, the necessity to connect with the cultures of their origins marks the immigrants' foundational experience as something other than America. African-Americans look back only to past struggles in America. Immigrants have no such American identity affiliation. Thus, a kind of superficial Americanness is sometimes reflected. The claim to America is still recent and the past that calls is still other than America. They have yet to establish a lasting American legacy. For this reason, the general American population still identifies immigrant Muslims as foreigners. In the case of an international crisis, immigrant Muslims identify with foreign interests. In the case of a national crisis, they are clearly targeted for racial profiling and negative stereotyping that violate public civil liberties. This has become most blatant since the crisis of September 11, 2001.[27]

Since most Americans garner their perception of Islam only from sensational television programs and local media coverage, which continue to "other" the native cultures of Muslim origins, they view affiliation with these cultures as problematic. Indeed, many Americans view immigrant Muslims as brothers and sisters of foreign terrorists and associate them with the perpetuation of extreme forms of gender inequality and abuse. In the recent September 11 crisis, the question of loyalty to America brought all those with foreign interests and connections under wider suspicion. Many immigrant Muslim leaders and spokespersons were quick to associate themselves with mainstream America to offset this perception.[28] Others advocated the need to turn more attention toward national interest as a form of salvation. President Bush was emphatic – "You are either with us or against us" – about the war on terrorism. Muslims were appalled at the blatant acts of terrorism in the U.S.A. and elsewhere, and many immigrant Muslims were quick to express their support for American patriotism, which itself quickly got out of control.

Meanwhile, African-Americans who have been raised with a basic suspicion of white American sincerity about non-white peoples and cultures have generally tended towards a higher degree of counter-cultural confrontation. After the September 11 crisis, immigrant Muslims were given a hefty taste of this double standard and could no longer assume that the civil liberties they had come to America to experience would always be extended towards them. In this way, they came closer to understanding the experiences of African-Americans than at any other time. This led to more efforts to forge cross-organizational alliances among Muslim groups and individuals of different ethnicities. Although more efforts are needed and must continue for the sake of intra-community coalition building, it is too easy to return to old patterns of ethnic exclusivism when conflicts of interests arise or when opportunities for national-level recognition are offered.

CONCLUSION: SUGGESTIONS TOWARDS A MORE HARMONIOUS INTRA-ISLAMIC COLLECTIVITY

A concerted effort is required now to heal past hurts between Muslims in America, hurts that tap into racial, ethnic, and class divisions. We need greater levels of objective dialogue, shared experiences, and collective practices. Within the greater context of progressive Islam, this means a need for discourse about inter-ethnic relations as part of our dialogue to engage the particularities of culture and history of all our communities. Only through engaging these particularities can we hope to reach a more pluralistic understanding of Islam. In the context of Islam and America, this means stressing the plurality that is inherent in both. By "plurality," I mean acknowledging and engaging differences without an attempt to impose hegemony.

First, at a fundamental level, when Muslims in America identify themselves they should include their specific ethnic origins until such a time as the new American Muslim reality becomes racially balanced and inclusive. Just as African-American Muslims have been specified since the middle of the twentieth century, so should all other groups of Muslims clarify their ethnicity alongside their American citizenship and membership of Islam. Furthermore, the tendency thus far has been for some Muslims to identify themselves as Muslim Americans, then proceed to make statements that are specific to their own ethnic origins and exclusive particularly of African-American Muslims.

Muslims in America comprise African-American descendants of slaves, Asian Americans, Hispanic-Americans, and Euro-Americans as well as immigrants from Muslim countries in the past century from well over thirty countries. In discussion among us as well as presented to the non-Muslim public, more descriptive identification is called for under the umbrella term "American Muslim." A Pakistani American Muslim or an American Muslim of Lebanese origin should describe themselves thus. While this does not limit their desire to be identified as American, it also has the advantage of highlighting their connection to the area from which they have emigrated. Such a self-designation is also less likely to be offensive to many in America, since many erroneously presume the term "American" refers only to whites. This would especially benefit those who have submerged their ethnicity under either the title "American" or "Muslim" when representing Islam in America and would reflect the true diversity of American Islam.

Within Muslim communities, an important dimension of racial healing must result from organized forums that specifically address inter-community and inter-ethnic relations. Only since September 11 has race become directly related to intra-community Muslim dynamics among national organizations at the public level. However, these urgent public conversations about racial dynamics have not been preceded by integrated discussion about race relations, particularly discussion aimed at repairing long-standing conflicts. By planning and participating in meetings focused on conflict resolution within the context of ethnic concerns, Muslims in America may be able to face some of the double standards that have prevailed. Only then can we move forward to develop strategies for comprehensively erasing them. Race and ethnicity need to be among the topics focused upon in papers, presentations, and panels at national-level conferences and conventions. The model of directly confronting our internal racial attitudes follows the patterns practiced in America following the civil rights movement. Such a model brought effective resolution to both attitudes and practices. Racial sensitivity programs were eventually developed and utilized in businesses and other companies in order to confront dormant racist attitudes with information and public censure.

In addition to more direct racial confrontation to ferret out latent attitudes of discrimination and prejudice, the Muslim communities should establish festive occasions or community gatherings to celebrate specific cultural diversity. For example, celebrations like a Palestine week or an Indonesian potluck would help us to nurture our diverse cultural heritages in particular and as a part of Islamic and American pluralism. It is equally important to recognize the need to share the specific heritage of our plural "nations and tribes" as part of the Qur'anic mandate to establish *taqwa* as the basis of evaluation among us. Greater *taqwa* within our collective Islamic experiences should empower us to confront one of the most divisive aspects of our American Islamic experience. Once this aspect has been properly focused upon and eradicated through the moral imperative of *taqwa*, we can move towards a greater collective contribution to America, and humanity as a whole.

ENDNOTES

1. Malcolm X, quoted in *Bearing Witness: Selections from African-American Autobiography in the Twentieth Century,* ed. Louis Gates, Jr (New York: Pantheon, 1991), 144.
2. For example, Bassam Tibi, *Islam between Culture and Politics* (New York: Palgrave, 2001).
3. Quoted in Michelle Cottle, "Native Speakers – African-American Muslims, and Why Its Hard to Be Both," *New Republic,* November 19, 2001, *www.tnr.com/111901/cottle111901.html*
4. Ibid.
5. Ibid.
6. Another essay in this volume, "Muslims, Pluralism, and Interfaith Diagolue" by Amir Hussain, specifically engages the need for pluralism in the North American Muslim community.
7. African-Americans form the single largest ethnic group of Muslims in America – some forty-two percent of the total population. See Fareed Nu'man, *The Muslim Population in the United States: A Brief Statement* (Washington: American Muslim Council, 1992), 16.
8. *New Republic,* November 19, 2001.
9. One notable exception since September 11, 2001 was the public representation of Hamza Yusuf as a white American, who must have appealed to the general white non-Muslim American population by allowing them to share in his identity as neither foreign nor black.
10. Translation modified from Muhammad Asad, *The Message of the Qur'an* (Gibraltar: Dar al-Anadulus, 1980), 794.
11. Muhammad Asad includes a *hadith* from the Prophet in which he states, "Behold! God has removed from you the arrogance of pagan ignorance [*jahiliyah*] with its boast of ancestral glories. Man [*sic*] is but a God conscious believer or an unfortunate sinner. All people are children of Adam, and Adam was created out of dust."
12. Fazlur Rahman, *Islam and Modernity: Transformation of an Intellectual Tradition* (Chicago: University of Chicago Press, 1982), 155.
13. Sylviane Diouf, *Servants of Allah: African Muslims Enslaved in the Americas* (New York: New York University Press 1998), 1.
14. Ibid, 4.
15. Aminah Beverly McCloud, *African-American Islam* (New York: Routledge, 1995), 9.
16. Fareed Nu'man, *The Muslim Population in the United States,* 23.
17. The Arab Defamation League (ADL) is a national organization addressing Muslim and non-Muslim concerns in America.
18. Some examples include: Islamic Society of North America (ISNA), Islamic Medical Association (IMA), the Association of Muslim Scientists and Engineers (AMSE), the Association of Muslim Social Scientists (AMSS), American Muslim Council (AMC), American Muslim Mission, Islamic Circle of North America (ICNA), Center for American-Islamic Relations (CAIR), International Institute of Islamic Thought (IIIT).
19. Malcolm X, *The Autobiography of Malcolm X* (New York: Ballantine, 1965), 340.
20. Richard Brett Turner, *Islam in the African-American Experience* (Indianapolis: Indiana University Press, 1997), 215.
21. See my descriptions of multiculturalism in Malaysia: "An Islamic Perspective on Civil Rights Issues," in *Religion, Race, and Justice in a Changing America,* ed. Gary Orfield, (New York: Century Foundation, 1999), 159.
22. It should be noted that the most extensive grassroots organizations in Muslim communities are women's organizations primarily started and run by African-American women, even though the African-American Muslim woman is highly marginalized in the overall leadership of American Muslims.
23. http://www.cair-net.org/mosquereport/
24. Linda S. Wallbridge in her review of another volume, *Muslims in America* edited by Haddad, noted that "Islam is a religion of a diverse population in America. It is not simply

the religion of immigrants." And "[T]o have indigenous communities discussed in the same ... collection of articles with Arab and other immigrant communities can be confusing. One is not often sure whether the experiences spoken of are those of Black Muslims, Muslims in America, as a whole, or only certain groups of Muslims." *Journal of the American Oriental Society*, 112, 1992, 721.

25. Ibid.

26. The term "indigenous Muslims" is used to represent Muslim converts, even though the word "convert" is erroneously applied to their descendants; and the term "immigrant Muslims" is used to designate those Muslims who immigrated in the last century, and continues to be erroneously applied to their descendants.

27. Women in the foreign-looking traditional *hijab*, even if African-American, were lumped into this profile.

28. For just one example, see the list of quotes on the website of the U.S. State Department, which brought together many statements by Muslim voices talking about the harmony – even identity – of the American political system and Islamic ideals: http://usinfo.state.gov/products/pubs/muslimlife/speakup.htm. One quote, from Dr Muhammad Muqtedar Khan, Director of International Studies at Adrian College states, "The U.S. Constitution describes the perfect Islamic state. It protects life, liberty and property."

12

ISLAMIC DEMOCRACY AND PLURALISM

Ahmad S. Moussalli

In this article, I deal with the basic doctrines of government and politics that were developed during the history of classical and medieval Islam. I aim to elaborate and develop those basic principles that are not contradictory to, and include the seeds of, modern liberal democracy and pluralism, though the two civilizations have followed different historical paths. These principles include two sets of notions: first, political contract and consensus, and second, tolerance of differences, pluralism, and opposition.

Here I aim to both highlight, when possible, and construct, when necessary, the important ideological and religious arguments on democracy and pluralism that have been under development in modern Islamic political discourses.[1] Such arguments can be used in the progressive interpretations of Islam *vis-à-vis* reactionary and conservative interpretation. For from an historical perspective, progressive interpretations of Islam can be supported by finding the means and ways for the democratization and liberalization of Islamic thought.

The article selectively uses the historically developed religious and political formations, especially those of the period of the governments of the Prophet and the Rightly Guided Caliphate. This period is seen as formative and constitutive in the making of Islamic thought because of its distinctive religious and political impact on the minds of almost all Muslims. Most Muslim thinkers, philosophers, jurists, ideologists, and historians employ it to justify one ideology and understanding or another. Because of the importance of that period in validating any Islamic notion or system or, more importantly, in the making of a notion or system Islamic, this study also uses examples from different historical periods. Thus, these periods represent moments of historical practices and interpretations that moved closer to or away from the original ideals developed from the first model of the Prophet and the Rightly Guided Caliphate.

It is the argument of this article that the notions of democracy and pluralism are not only in harmony with Islamic thought, but that the seeds of these notions are embodied in many notions of government and politics in Islamic political and religious thought. Building upon classical and medieval thought, it shows that classical and medieval philosophy, jurisprudence, and theology are very rich with comparable notions that postulate and protect individual and communal rights, that legitimize political, social, economic, intellectual, and religious differences, and that view the people as the source of ultimate political sovereignty on earth.

By linking classical and medieval Islamic thought with current political and religious debates, this article further argues that modern Islamic thought in general, and today's moderate Islamism in particular, has absorbed and 'Islamized' the notions of democracy and pluralism.[2] At the religious and ideological level, Islamicly developed doctrines on democracy and pluralism constitute a theology of liberation and an epistemological break with the past. At the political level, they widen the individual, social, political, and philosophical space in the Arab world. At the international level, they provide the Muslim world with common ground with the West. At the cultural level, they serve as a general context and a political language of dialogue between different civilizations, religions, and political orders.

Thus, the basic argument of this article is both simple and grand. While the history of the highest Islamic political institution, the caliphate, is mostly a history of authoritarian governments, the economic, social, political, and the intellectual history of Islam abounds with liberal doctrines and institutions. In classical and medieval Islamic political thought, there are older, comparable, and much more universal doctrines of equality, freedom, and justice than those developed by traditional Islamic thought. In modern times, modernist Islamic thinkers and, now, moderate Islamist thinkers are making these doctrines comparable to modern Western notions of democracy, pluralism, and human rights. Equality (*al-musawat*), freedom (*al-hurriyya*), and justice (*al-'adl*), for example, have long been cardinal Islamic doctrines and have received throughout history different formulations and suffered various abuses. While most political studies derived from Islamic sources have focused their consideration on the rise and fall of Islamic dynasties and states and on the historical developments of "traditional" Islamic law (*Shari'ah*) in order to draw possible Islamic views on democracy, pluralism, and human rights, they miss the fact that neither the study of dynasties nor the authentication of "traditional" *Shari'ah* is more formative for Muslims than the ideological developments brought about by opposition movements or reformist attitudes. A "view from the edge,"[3] and not only from the traditional centers of power, is necessary in order to comprehend the true nature of the Islamic system of government and the doctrines of democracy, pluralism, and human rights. While Professor Bulliet argues correctly that "[t]he story of Islam has always privileged the view from the center,"[4] I show that such a view is mostly a political construct and, consequently, can be politically deconstructed. I also show that other constructs that were more liberal have been disregarded either under pressures from governments, in favor of political expediency, or in preference for the official discourses of religious and political institutions.

This is why this article attempts to make sharp distinctions between Islam as a divine belief system and the Islamic state as a humanly developed political system. The ability to make such a distinction between the human and the Divine will open unlimited possibilities of interpretation and re-interpretation as well as deconstruction and construction. As a belief system, Islam should be compared with other religions, but not with modern Western states. The rise and fall of Islamic states should be historically compared with the rise and fall of Western states. Thus, specific Islamic laws, like that of apostasy, should first be treated in the context of an Islamic state and must, then, be compared with treason in Western states. This is not to deny that many Islamic states and societies have historically misused what Muslims even consider to be Qur'anic duties – the complete individuality of women, the rights of minorities, and similar issues.

On yet another level, moderate Islamist political thought postulates pluralism and democracy as religious rights and, consequently, views their normative character as categorical. However, modern Islamic understanding of democracy and pluralism depends on the possibility of modern interpretations of the sources of religion and major extensions of the meanings of some basic doctrines. These doctrines include consultation (*shura*), consensus (*ijma'*), difference (*ikhtilaf*), minorities (*ahl al-dhimma*), enjoining the good and forbidding evil, and similar doctrines. However, one finds that some scholars and thinkers attempt to show that the historical *Shari'ah* is not capable of coping with doctrines like human rights, pluralism, and democracy.

I do not, then, aim here to provide a defense of or apologia for Islamic political thought, for I recognize the negative aspects of classical, medieval, and modern Islamic political thought. However, I attempt to show that Islamic political thought has initiated and developed throughout the ages doctrines compatible with Western doctrines of human rights, pluralism, and democracy. Their uses or abuses are not only related to intellectual and philosophical understanding but are tightly webbed into various socioeconomic and political contexts. Their proper application today requires not only their intellectual development, which is now being moved at a great speed by, especially, moderate Islamism, but, above all, liberal socioeconomic contexts that are mostly lacking in the Islamic world.

MODERN ISLAMIC THOUGHT

The later period of the nineteenth century and the first half of the twentieth century witnessed the birth of two intellectual and political responses to reform in both the Ottoman Empire and the Qajar Empire. The first response was liberal and secular and called for an epistemological and political break with the Islamic past and a rejection of all forms of Sultanic rule as well as the wholesale adoption of Westernization. Thinkers like 'Abbas Mahmud al-'Aqqad, Taha Hussein, Muhammad Husayn Haykal, Lutfi al-Zayyat, and others represented that response. Islamic modernism represented the second response that called for the absorption of Western civilization into the Islamic heritage. Some reformers like Jamal al-Din al-Afghani called for revolutions, others like Rida called for the establishment of the constitutional state, yet others like 'Abdu believed that the necessary prelude to political reform ought to be the reformation of educational systems and social institutions.[5]

World War II constituted a turning point in the history of the imperial powers that sought the domination of worldwide markets and cheap raw materials. Oppression emanating from the imperial powers led to nationalist and socialist tendencies that weakened the liberal Islamic response and strengthened the secular but authoritarian response. Egypt, which was under British mandate, might be a good example to use here because of its political and intellectual influence all over the Arab world. During that period, Egyptians were focusing on liberating their country from British colonialism, and advocated democracy, both secular and religious. However, the rise of Arab nationalism under Jamal 'Abd al-Nasir brought about secular and socialist authoritarian nationalism. The secular response was adopted but democracy was rejected.[6] And while 'Abd al-Nasir accepted Islam as one of the three circles of Egyptian foreign policy, in reality Islam did not amount to more than rhetoric. In this fashion, both the secular democratic response and the modernist Islamic response were aborted.

In recent decades, numerous movements that call for the return to the fundamentals of religion have flourished throughout the Muslim world. They have pushed for and developed a new Islamic response. Leaders of such movements believe that a modern development of Islamic spirituality, morality, and politics will definitely condemn moral corruption, glorify idealism, and lead to true representative governments. Such a development will mobilize Muslims to establish a modern Islamic civilization that re-constructs Muslim identity and consolidates Islamic power.

In modern times, the Wahhabiyya was founded by Muhammad Ibn 'Abd al-Wahhab, whose call (*da'wa*) was said to be based on the comprehensive and eternal nature of Islam.[7] The movement rhetorically called on believers to refer back to the fundamentals (*usul*): the Qur'an and the *Sunnah* of the Prophet. The Wahhabiyya has been a modern interpretation of Salafi Islam as interpreted by eminent scholars like Ibn Hanbal, Ibn Taymiyya, and Ibn Qayyim al-Jawziyya. Following the well-known medieval thinker Ibn Taymiyya, it has called for the purification of Islam by a return to the fundamentals of religion, i.e. the Qur'an and the *Sunnah*. It followed a strict line of thinking in its attempts to reconstruct society and government on the basis of divine Oneness (*tawhid*) and the doctrine of good ancestors (*al-salaf al-salih*). However, one trait shared by the Wahhabis and their intellectual ancestors is their reluctance to engage in philosophical argumentation, in literalist adherence to select texts. The Wahhabis focused more on the legal and ethical aspects of Islam, leaving political matters to politicians and traditional elites. Other important movements in modern times are al-Sanusiyya and al-Mahdiyya, which started basically as Sufi orders, but were later transformed into political movements that struggled against Western intervention in Libya and the Sudan, respectively. The two movements were puritan, aiming at the restoration of genuine Islam through political activities. Again, similar fundamentals were entertained as the road to the Islamic community's salvation.

At a higher and more substantive level, Jamal al-Din al-Afghani has had a massive intellectual and political influence in drawing the modern political agenda that is still more or less the backbone of intellectual and political reform. He was ready to think over and adopt into Islamic thought any new intellectual, political, or scientific knowledge that might trigger the progress of the Islamic nation. On the political level, he was ready to adopt those institutions and systems that could serve the Islamic world and save it from its crises. His follower and, later, colleague Muhammad 'Abdu and Rashid Rida, the inspirer of Hasan al-Banna, adopted different aspects of al-Afghani's intellectual and political thought. While 'Abdu tended more towards the modernist European aspect of al-Afghani's intellectual thought, Rida picked up the necessity of returning to the fundamentals of religion. Rida wanted to induce an intellectual revival and to develop new Islamic institutions for the establishment of an Islamic state, thus facilitating the renaissance of the *umma* and guaranteeing the ethical foundations of society.

Very much along Hasan al-Banna's line of thinking, the Egyptian Muslim Brotherhood, also greatly affected by Rida and al-Afghani, centered its thought and actions on the political aspect of Islam to promote a modern renaissance. Thus, the Muslim Brotherhood urgently advocated the importance of establishing an Islamic state as the first step for implementing the *Shari'ah*. While focusing its intellectual re-interpretation on returning to Islamic fundamentals, the Brotherhood selectively filtered into modern Islamic thought a few major Western political doctrines like constitutional rule and democracy. These doctrines are seen as necessary tools for modernizing the Islamic concept of state. Meanwhile, the Brotherhood's antagonistic dealings with the Egyptian government led some of its members to splinter under the leadership of Sayyid Qutb. Qutb continued to uphold the need for establishing an Islamic state and rejecting any dealing or intellectual openness with the West. For him, the Islamic state is not a tool but a fundamental principle of creed. It signals the community's submission to God on the basis of the *Shari'ah* and represents political and ideological obedience to God. Without such submission and obedience, any constitution is illegitimate, and the state loses any shred of legitimacy and enters into paganism, or *jahiliya*. Ayatollah Khomeini limited further the confines of a legitimate Islamic government. While the *Shari'ah* theoretically legitimizes a government, only the *vilayat-i faqih* (rule of the jurist) actualizes its legitimacy. Within the Islamic world today, the demands of the mainstream Islamist movements in Algeria, Tunisia, Jordan, and Egypt are derived from al-Banna's discourse on the Islamic state, constitutional rule, and multi-party politics; radical Sunni movements follow the discourse of Sayyid Qutb and Shi'ite political movements follow that of Khomeini.

The disintegration of the Soviet Union has hastened the focus on the political legitimacy of democracy, the social necessity of human rights, and the intellectual suitability of pluralism to both the Middle East and the Islamic world. Secular and religious thinkers alike attribute the miserable conditions of economic, social, and political life to the absence of democracy and pluralism in the Arab world. A new political process that stresses the importance of political democratization and liberalization is on the rise and is entertained within a whole range of political and social strata, including the media and academia. For instance, the widely read London-based Arabic newspaper *Al-Hayat* serialized extensively and for many days around the issues of civil society, pluralism, and democracy in Egypt and the Arab world. A few meetings, like "The Democratic Experience in the Arab World" in Morocco, "The Crisis of Democracy in the Arab World" in Cyprus, and "Political Pluralism and Democracy in the Arab World" in Amman, show clearly the emerging interest in democracy and pluralism. The Beirut Center for Studies of Arab Unity convened as well a conference in Cairo to discuss democracy in the Arab world.[8]

However, the West at large has focused on Islamic threats to Western interests and order while paying no real attention – or sympathy – to the oppression of the peoples of the Islamic world as well as the dialogues and debates that have been going on among diverse political trends over political theories and rights of people. Amazing titles in magazines and newspapers such as "One Man, One Vote, One Time," "The Challenge of Radical Islam," "Will Democracy Survive in Egypt?," "The Arab World Where Troubles for the U.S. Never End," and "The Clash of Civilizations" have further scared and pushed the West away from the Muslim world.[9] While quite a few Western academics concerned with the Middle East deal with people's real concerns, the West in general regards these concerns as negligible because their impact is localized and does not affect its interests.

Current political circumstances in the Arab world, especially in Algeria, Egypt, Lebanon, Sudan, and Tunisia, have led to ideological, political, and religious inquiries and debates on the compatibility of Islamic discourses, especially the doctrines of an Islamic state, with democracy, pluralism, and human rights as well as the West. However, a majority of Western media and scholars along with a majority of their Middle Eastern counterparts have directly viewed Islamist political thought, and indirectly Islam, as unfit for democracy because the Western sources hold Islamic movements to be exclusivist by nature and definition. There is no doubt that there are few religious groups that are truly exclusivist and believe in the necessity of radical ideological, religious, and political transformation. They believe that only through radical coups and education can they achieve any meaningful victory. However, most popular and influential Islamic political groups adhere to new interpretations of inclusion that manifest in pluralism and democracy. Ideological, religious, and political radicalism is not based on the main theological and religious Islamic doctrines and conceptions of the world, religion, knowledge, and salvation. More importantly, radicalism is a worldwide manifestation and is not restricted to a few Islamic groups.[10] Therefore, to make radicalism an essential part of Islamic doctrines or modern Islamic thought is only to miss the point.

Classical and modern Islamic thought, whether jurisprudence, theology, philosophy, or other disciplines of knowledge, contain within them roots comparable to modern day principles of democracy and pluralism. While they are not based on the law of natural rights, they are based on textual authorities derived from the Qur'an and the *Sunnah* that lend themselves to arguments favoring democratic forms of governments, pluralistic societies, and schemes of human rights. The contexts that shaped the development of Islamic thought have not been conducive to pluralistic democracy. Now, through a process of deconstruction and re-construction, modern Islamic thought has mostly adopted the principles of pluralism and democracy. For instance, the seminal consequence of prophetic arbitration on national and international levels lies in its acceptance of pluralism and diversity. However, any national and international political order that aims at ending conflicts and providing peace must acknowledge and accept substantive religious, ideological, and political differences. Thus, any political order can be legitimately set up without negating the others. That the historic Islamic political order was composed of many religious and ethnic communities opens the road to solving many long-standing modern conflicts. As opposed to those who hold the notion of a purely Islamic, or only ideological, state, an argument has been made to the effect that the fundamental law of the first Islamic state distinguished between religious authority and political authority. And although the religious authority had no choice but to call people to religion, the political authority must deal with down-to-earth social structures and human needs as well as diversified religious and ideological claims to the truth and sharp ethnic and economic struggles. Therefore, the inclusion of a political order of many religions, or a confederation of religions, as one factor, and the acceptance of the diversified social and economic structures, as another, shows the original non-dogmatic and Islamic viewpoint on political matters. This viewpoint allowed non-Muslims full partnership in the political structure, even on those sensitive issues of war and peace.

It has been made obvious that the religious and, at times, even the Divine were subject to and understood by the political; Divine arbitration became understood only through human judgment. The inability of anyone, from the majority's perspective, to claim to be God's sole representation led to the acceptance of human judgment in political matters and in religious affairs. Even in the first Islamic state – long idealized as the model community for Muslims – everyone acknowledged Muhammad's political authority, but a whole religious community, i.e. the Jews, contested his religious authority. Muhammad sometimes resolved religious disputes in his capacity as a national arbitrator, and not always as a religious authority.

It is clear from the historical events mentioned above that claiming a divine origin for a political position renders that position into an uncompromising value. However, when a religious dispute is projected as a political conflict, then there is, theoretically at least, a viability for solution. For if politics is the art of the possible, and this had allowed the inception of the first Islamic state, then the art of the impossible will most probably hinder any serious attempt to revive Islam. When Mu'awiya and 'Ali looked to their differences as political in nature, a compromise, i.e. submission to human arbitration, was possible. But when the Khawarij introduced the impossible or God's direct judgment on that matter, then the problem was reified and abstracted to an uncompromising value. For the "humanization" of the abstract conditions it to the needs and requirements of life. The history of Islam shows that any abstract and non-historical understanding turns the human into the Divine and, consequently, into an uncompromising metaphysical and meta-historical entity. However, when the Divine is theoretically channeled through a human interpretative agency and is historically subjected to human development, then it becomes in the service of humankind. Put differently, when the Divine is "humanized" it becomes a source of compromise.

The resolution of conflicts with ideologically oriented religious groups must take into account the "Divine" element of the conflict first and then deconstruct that element into its political components. Because insofar as political conflicts are rooted in Divine concepts, then a peaceful solution seems far away.

Human judgment then is the method to solve conflicts, but Divine arbitration makes that impossible, since no one can resort immediately to the Divine sources. Therefore, a theoretical return to the first Islamic state may well rekindle a new political philosophy that treats equally other states, religions, and ideologies. That the first Islamic state incorporated, for instance, non-Muslims and older structures indicates the need to adopt intellectual and political pluralistic models that incorporate freedom and fairness and shun prejudice and arbitrary judgment. Therefore, the arbitral authority of the *umma* (the community) as an expression of and interpretation of the Divine will and law should be employed today to re-organize political orders. If a political regime, from the majority's view, does not represent the Divine will, then the possibility of pluralistic understanding and tolerance is more likely. The community is then the human sovereign whose application of the Divine will is not restricted to an individual or a group. If the community is the source of all powers, no individual or a group of people, whether fundamentalist, modernist, or traditionalist, whether military or religious, can claim exclusive rights to interpretation or government. Consensus, then, whether through consultation or other means, is legitimate because the community, through its power to arbitrate, made it so.

From a majority's point of view, political rule became a religious duty because of people's agreement on the matter. Similarly, arbitration was chosen by the people to settle many of the most important and formative events in the history of Islam. Consequently, arbitration as well as government rests on the people's contractual authority to shape and reshape their life. While its multiple interpretations have, ironically, divided the community into many sects, the legitimacy of communal arbitration and judgment became almost incontestable, although later on it was historically waived in the interest of the increasing power of states. However, its legitimate employment by the majority was never questioned and might therefore be re-instituted today in order to deal with issues of political legitimacy and the exercise of political power.

Seen as the source of communal power, arbitration as a form of democratic interaction may be used to develop other principles of legitimacy and methods of action. It may be turned nowadays into a central principle of politics as well as international relations. In addition to this, its elasticity could make it as well a method for resolving the conflicts between Islamic states themselves with non-Islamic ones and with world orders. Thus an old concept, deconstructed and re-constructed in line with modern democratic connotations and reshaped by modern technology, might be postulated as a modest starting point in the authentic process of legitimate democratization in the contemporary Muslim world.

Islamic political thought that developed after the Prophet's death and during the classical and medieval history of Islam acknowledged the people's basic notions of rights. While these rights are not, could not, and do not have to be identical to modern human rights schemes in the West, they acknowledged, at least theoretically, the very basic roots of rights. In fact, these rights historically preceded modern Western schemes of rights and were responses to the needs that jurists felt were religiously required and sanctioned by the fundamental objectives of religion and the nature of social interactions.

Taking into consideration the nature of political power, numerous Muslim political thinkers and jurists tried as much as possible to make rulers good practitioners of Islamic law, in the sense of abiding by the basic notions of the *Shari'ah* that could protect individuals and societies from state tyranny. Other thinkers and jurists attempted to justify the state's oppressive nature by referring to the conditions that Muslims lived under. Nonetheless, if one examines other civilizations during that period, one may find that medieval Islamic thought was offering at that time the most advanced political discourse on human rights, political rights, and the complex duties and relationships between the rulers and the ruled. This is said not in order to exonerate the misuse of political power and the misconstruction of certain schemes of rights and duties, but rather in order to place these things within their historical contexts. For instance, when Muslims where discussing the human nature of political power and the need to reform it in accordance with *shura* (consultation) and *ijma'* (consensus), the West was still holding to the notion of the Divine nature of power. When Islamic thought acknowledged the rights of minorities as a consequence of accepting Christianity and Judaism as recognized religions, the West considered Muslims only as infidels, and Islam was not recognized or allowed to be practiced, and Muslims (and often Jews) were harassed and persecuted.

Of course, the history of Islamic governments and dynasties testifies indeed to many incidents of mistreatment, oppression, and even suppression of both Muslims and minorities. However, it also testifies to Islam's historical and theoretical tolerance, good treatment, and even mutual assistance of both Muslims and minorities. More importantly, what has been left for modern Muslims, which has not been developed into full schemes of modern human rights, is a basic scheme of human rights that must be developed in line with modernity and its concerns.

Shura and *ijma'* are two key doctrines that Muslims can use today for the religious development of democratic notions of government and politics as well as human rights. For they take away the Divine perception of political government and reduce its legitimacy to people's choice. The doctrine of *ikhtilaf* (difference) opens the door wide for the acceptance of pluralistic understanding of not only power and government but, more importantly, the multiplicity of religions and philosophies of life. Furthermore, doctrines of opposition and human or legitimate rights could be used today in accordance with modern standards of thought and living in order to make them workable, in the first place, and then to develop them further in order to change the vicissitudes of modern living and government. These doctrines could be an escape for not only minorities but also majorities from the tyranny of the modern state in the Islamic world, a way to select free governments, and a method to reduce the traditionalism of Islamic establishments.

DEMOCRACY AND PLURALISM

Democracy and pluralism, the basic ideological doctrines in the ever-increasing globalized world, are not only fundamental doctrines of modern Western political philosophy but are now emerging primary concerns of modern Islamic political thought. While the process of blending modern Islamic thought with democracy and pluralism appears to astonish many politicians, intellectuals, and ordinary people, it is currently underway and is one of the main intellectual occupations of intellectuals and political parties in the Islamic world. Furthermore, the awareness of the need for democracy goes beyond the theoretical to become a demand of Muslims themselves, especially *vis-à-vis* their governments. A majority view in Islamic intellectual circles, including even major Islamist theoreticians, with various expressions that adopt emergent Islamic doctrines on democracy, pluralism, and human rights, is now making its way in Islamic studies.[11] All justifications for tyrannical thought and authoritarian politics are collapsing, since they are now perceived to be the main historical impediments to the development and freedom of Muslim communities as well as good religious life.

The possibility of developing liberal and democratic discourses in Islam is expanding rapidly. One cannot deal with Muslims as supporters of tyranny and opponents to democracy, both in terms of philosophical and political discourses and of real politics. A new reading of Islam becomes the basic condition for starting a modern process of reformulating Islamic history and reforming Islamic civilization. However, this process in itself re-examines the tenets of political Islam and reforms the principles of political rule. The need for serious re-interpretation of Islamic literature and traditional institutions is postulated as a way for accommodating human needs with the modern conditions of living. While fundamental doctrines such as sovereignty are grounded in the Qur'anic discourse, only popular consent creates and justifies the legitimacy of discourses and institutions. If charged with the interpretation of the Divine word, then the community enjoys the only legitimate power; other powers and authorities are only derivative and subject to the approval of the community.

Again, although Divine governance is viewed as an absolute political doctrine, so is the doctrine of *shura*. In fact, the good realization of the former becomes dependent on the good exercise of the latter. Modern interpretations of *shura* normally absorb democracy within a political and religious context. Like democracy, *shura* should provide legitimate religious means for the control of government, since legitimacy is made dependent on popular approval. By denying any contradiction between democracy and constitutional rule, on the one hand, and *shura* and Divine law, on the other, modern thinkers absorb the principles of natural law in their re-interpretations of religious revelation. While the Islamists transform Islam into a system capable of absorbing modern philosophy, politics, economics, science, and history without disclaiming the validity of Islam, they also modernize interpretations of Islam and bring into it principles such as democracy and pluralism that have become essential for modern political living.

One of the basic elements in the revival of Islam is to re-examine and to demystify history and to center responsibility on human actions. The essence of development lies within human power, not within the scope of a mythical history: humans can positively effect their future. Spiritual, intellectual, political, and economic regeneration is the proper domain of humans, who are endowed by their Creator to act on God's behalf. The process of regeneration cannot freeze in history, and must be linked in practice to relative sciences and changing conditions. Linking regeneration to the relative and the changeable without neglecting the revealed leads modern Islamic thought generally to reject traditional understanding and institutions. This is why democracy is accepted and turned into a modern form of Islamic *shura*. Today, the demands for democracy and human rights are popular aspirations, and many arguments for their adoption are made in the name of Islam and are justified by the Qur'an. This is why two major practical developments are required. First, unlimited governmental powers should be limited by a process of them being filtered through popular channels and representative bodies to reflect people's needs and ambitions. Second, by this, a tolerant political context should be set up that facilitates the development of a tolerant intellectual, religious, social, and ethical context.

The arguments that make Islamic culture and Islam despotic by definition are erroneous. Classical and modern concepts and doctrines as well as institutions are the result of human manipulation, not Divine predestination. Qur'anic doctrines such as *shura* (consultation), *ijma'* (consensus), *tahkim* (arbitration), *bay'a* (oath of allegiance), *ikhtilaf* (difference), *al-hurriyya* (freedom), and *al-huquq al-shar'iyya* (legitimate rights) are religiously demanded. However, the historic and institutional practice of these doctrines has mostly shown the possibility of their manipulation by governments and their elite. Thus, for instance, *shura*, a doctrine that demands the participation of society in running the affairs of its government, became in reality a doctrine that was manipulated by political and religious elites to secure their economic, social, and political interests at the expense of other segments of society. *Bay'a*, a doctrine that should have been used to indicate people's voluntary approval of their ruler, became a formal act of forceful subjection to the ruler. Today, *shura* is not viewed merely as a religious concept but reflects initially the public will. The state institutionalization of *shura* and *ijma'* provides the state with a normative role in making basic choices in people's lives. Thus, some mechanisms and institutions should be made within the state to acquire formal legitimacy. If the *Shari'ah* is also institutionalized in the state, all attempts should be made to prevent making legitimacy an issue of formality only. More importantly, a political contract should be the legitimate means for assuming power. Because Islam is the constitutional reference for modern Islamists, these understandings of Islamic political thought should be upheld in all public choices.

In most countries of the Muslim world, today's political contexts are not much different from medieval and classical contexts, thus "democracy" is exercised as a source for acquiring formal legitimacy. While most of these countries have institutions like parliaments and parties that adhere formally to democracy, human rights, and due processes of law, none of these is really observed. In fact, these institutions are used to cover the tyrannical aspects of state manipulation. They only serve as a cover *vis-à-vis* the outside world. Such acts by Muslim regimes pushed people away from such institutions and into trying to find indigenous institutions that can be used to counterbalance the oppressive nature of Islamic regimes under the guise of important Western institutions.

This is why one should look into the modern quest for democracy and pluralism as a quest for liberation from the tyranny of regimes. It is a quest for liberation that uses religious doctrines that the state cannot challenge safely or manipulate without fear of losing legitimacy. If *shura*, for instance, is a Qur'anic doctrine, and if the state does not refer to people's choices, then the state is illegitimate. The religionization of democracy in the form of *shura* is a quest for popular empowerment *vis-à-vis* the oppressive state. This form of popular empowerment, derived from a Qur'anic doctrine, offsets the power of the state, derived from its coercive power.

This is why the modern Islamic trend that adopts democracy and pluralism does not view these issues as an exercise of academic nature. More importantly, it views them as a quest for liberation though democracy, tolerance through pluralism, and respect through human rights. They are made as solid as the Qur'anic doctrines through their association with religion, interpretation in a religious fashion, and their authentication in the Qur'an and the *Sunnah*. This is why the possibility that this trend bridges the gap between the Islamic world and the Western world is real.

What remains, however, is that the West itself should really support the quest for democracy and pluralism, instead of supporting regimes that are undemocratic, refuse any opposition or difference, and break all schemes of human rights. The West must support on the international level the process of democratization at its own expense, in the short run, in order to gain support and secure its interests, in the long run. In a globalized world, the West cannot just sit back and imagine that the Islamic world could be kept away from its borders or that its interests are kept secure by a few authoritarian regimes. The quest for democracy and pluralism is now a global quest that not only is of concern to people within specific borders but goes beyond all borders. The mixture of advanced technology, concentrated capitalism, and the quest for democracy may prove very explosive if it lacks the elements of fairness and justice, not only within countries but also among them. While these characteristics are shaping the newly globalized world, they are not to be limited to the industrial world and must surely include the Muslim world.

It has been clear throughout this discussion that Islamism, though perceived as being one exclusive phenomenon in both practice and theory, is in fact otherwise. Political movements that operate in the name of religion have now become a world phenomenon. However, it is only Islam that is identified with radical fundamentalism in an essentialist manner. As a result, traits associated with radical Islamism are transferred not only to moderate Islamism, but also to Islam itself. If an ordinary practicing or non-practicing Muslim is asked whether the Qur'an postulates God's governance in all aspects of life, the answer is "yes, of course." This belief does not, however, make that Muslim an Islamist by necessity, or, conversely, it makes almost all Muslims Islamists by definition.

The real issue and the decisive element in distinguishing a radical view from a moderate one revolves primarily around the conditions and principles of transforming a political agenda into daily life. As we have seen, Islamist movements deploy diverse methodological and practical processes to achieve their political aims. One of these is based on conceptual exclusivity and "*otherness*," whether philosophically, morally, or politically, that permit all unusual means to fulfill the real "self." Radical Islamism has perceived its own real and imagined isolation for a whole host of reasons ranging from social disunity and exploitation, and the political violence and illegitimacy of regimes, to personal impiety and corruption. As a consequence, it has reified, mostly under severe conditions of torture and mishandling, its political discourse into a purified theology of politics. Without this political contextualization, Islam cannot, from the point of view of radical Islamists, survive in the consciousness of the individual and society.

Shura is not merely a religious concept or a mechanism for elections. It reflects for the radicals the public will, a much more superior concept than individual freedom or social agreement. More importantly, it represents the Divine will, and any deviation from whatever is Divine is a religious violation. The individual cannot but submit to this will; in fact, he or she is only an appendage to it, with his or her freedom depending on it. While this will, for the Islamist radicals, may opt for a political contract with a ruler, it cannot, because of what it represents, allow pluralism and basic differences that may lead to disunity. The establishment of an Islamic state becomes for radicalism the fulfillment of this Divine will, and again, individuals and groups are consequently subordinated to the state.

Through the lenses of the *Shari'ah*, the radicals believe that the institutionalization of *shura* and *ijma'* provides the state, which expresses the general will, with a normative role in making basic choices in people's lives. The formal legitimacy that the state acquires in fact makes it unaccountable to anyone but God – or, at most through obedience to *Shari'ah*, itself institutionalized in the state. Thereafter, legitimacy becomes an internal state affair and not a social and public issue, though originally it may have been so. Therefore, insofar as the state is not going against the *Shari'ah*, no one can legitimately overthrow it, and it supervises in this context the morality of people and the application of *Shari'ah*. Thus individual religiosity is transformed by the radicals into a communal public will, itself transformed into state control, both moral and political. Parties, associations, and other civil institutions have no intrinsic validity in this hierarchy, and may only operate in a supplementary manner. Ultimately, an elaboration like this seems to demand exclusivity: it allows for no possibility of a pluralistic understanding of religion. Through the politicization of Islam as the proper Islamic interpretation, Islam itself cannot be represented except by the state. In this context, the establishment of inclusive pluralistic civil democracies and ways of life seems unworkable for theoretical and practical reasons.

However, to use the radical groups as representatives of Islamic and Arabic culture is both factually erroneous and culturally biased. Other non-Islamic religious interpretations witness very similar phenomena but are never treated in the same manner. One has to keep in mind that the employment of violence by these groups is not theoretical in origin, but is based on a theory which is historically developed. Put differently, they have not been committing violent acts because of their theories, but rather their theories justifying violence have been derived from the violence that they have been subjected to. At the very least, this is what they have perceived. In fact, practice has been reified into theory, which has now gained a life of its own. Both radical groups and most regimes are committed to recycling intellectual and practical violence and exclusivity. Violence, whether by secular or religious groups, has been exercised most of the time in reaction to the tyrannies of political regimes. 'Abud al-Zumar, serving a forty-year term in jail, attributes, incorrectly or not, the violence of the radical groups to the violence of the Egyptian regime. For him, Islamist violence is directed against those who have already liquidated Islamists.[12]

On the other hand, the absence of a pluralistic society and of democratic institutions is cited by the moderate trend as the real cause for violence. While moderate Islamists have long been excluded from political participation, they still call for their inclusion, as well as that of others, into politics and formal institutions. Their involvement in civil society, and their calls for human rights, pluralism, and democracy are still seen by many as the road to salvation for the community and individuals. Their inclusionary views do not postulate an eternal or Divine enmity between Islam's institutions and systems, and the West's institutions and systems. Properly grounded, what is Western becomes indeed Islamic. Here, I think, the moderate Islamists as well as the modernists may blend the culture of the Muslim world with that of the West, for they are providing Islamic arguments for the adoption of human rights, pluralism, and democracy, not mutual exclusivity. The conflict between the Muslim world and the West is viewed by them as being primarily either political or economic, but not religious or cultural. The two have common monotheistic grounds upon which multicultural and religious cooperation and co-existence might be built.

Moderate Islamist discourses on revivalism focus essentially on the termination of the normativeness of the past as both a history and a system. Of course, the moderate Islamists exempt the Qur'an and the *Sunnah* from such a termination, since both sources are viewed metaphysically and meta-historically as formative and constitutive fundamentals of Islam. Since the past is no longer normative, the moderate Islamists can choose to validate or negate certain aspects of past practices, such as stating that *shura* is akin to democracy, or that *shura* is not what has been practiced in the past. A necessary component of moderate Islamist thought is that, with the exception of the Prophet's society, there have not been any perfect Muslim societies, with complete collective Islamic self-awareness. This frees the moderate Islamists to push for achieving modern Islamic democratic and pluralistic societies and newly developed self-awareness and human rights. In this way, moderate Islamists are engaged in an unending process of renewal based on interpretation and re-interpretation.

Moderate Islamist quests for re-interpretation rest on developing intellectual and formative discourses that rediscover the appropriate meanings and significance of the texts within the framework of modern life. Such discourses must reformulate the religious roots or *usul al-din*. These discourses also reformulate a political theology loaded with political connotations, for it is directed not at a more substantive understanding of the Divine but at more control of the mundane, in particular the political. Questions related to Divine theology are bypassed in favor of those related to political theology; now, for moderate Islamism, the former can only be realized in terms of the latter. While obedience to God, for instance, is still an important demand for moderate Islamists, its most important manifestation is not mere individual religiosity but more essentially political doctrines such as the Islamic state, the community's choice, and individuals' rights.

Again, the most important measure of divine oneness (*tawhid*) manifests not in the individual's private conscience but in his or her commitment and actions toward the Islamization of state and society. For deep theological commitment to Islam must involve the economic, social, and political concerns of society. Practical Islamic activism signifies the deep-rootedness of belief, the moderate Islamists hold, while shallow and ceremonial non-active commitment to Islam weakens belief, if not destroys it altogether. Although Divine governance has become for moderate Islamism an absolute political doctrine, so has the doctrine of *shura*. In fact, the good realization of the former becomes dependent on the good exercise of the latter. Moderate Islamism developed *shura* to absorb democracy within Islamic political and even epistemological thought, and consequently to take the initiative from its advocates. It has also provided legitimate religious means towards the control of government, since legitimacy is linked to popular approval. By denying any contradiction between democracy and constitutional rule, on the one hand, and *shura* and Divine law on the other, moderate Islamism became capable of postulating their correspondence. All of these have become parts of the Islamists' non-historical discourses that transform Islam into a system capable of absorbing what is best in philosophy, politics, economics, science, and history without the need to disclaim the validity of Islam itself. On the contrary, this shows to the Islamists the true non-historical and metaphysical power of the Islamic revelation as an eternal message capable of meeting the needs that arise from development.

What moderate Islamism has also done is to drive a wedge in-between Muslims' understanding of history itself and Islam. For our understanding of the history of Islam is not Islam itself. This understanding is only one discourse on Islam within specific spatio-temporal conditions. Therefore, according to moderate Islamism, history and people's understanding of it, as well their understanding of Islam, have no normative status in themselves. In fact, their correctness depends on their utility to society and to Islam. However, though constitutional rule in the West and *shura* in Islamic history had quite different historical origins, moderate Islamism finds no theoretical problem in forcing their correspondence. In fact, it has no hesitation in calling for the adoption of Western models of government. An act like this is not un-Islamic, the moderate Islamists hold; rather it is Islamic, since it helps the Islamic state to run its affairs along Divine postulates. Of course, moderate Islamists reject secularism and communism, but not every Western doctrine for them is secular or communist. For moderate Islamism, Muslims can and should benefit from the other and update their thinking in order to keep pace with basic changes in the world.

What moderate Islamism has also done is to rework the meaning and formative character of history. It extracts historically loaded terms from their history in order to endue them with modern meanings. It assumes that the problems Muslims suffer from are the existence of particular doctrines that made the West victorious. While such doctrines are not necessarily wrong, more than just a transfer is needed to induce any revival. Islamic political theory and the plights and politics of Muslims up till modern times largely owe to neglecting the importance of social development and political practice in the formation of a justly constituted authority. Because a text indicates more than one meaning in moderate Islamism, it could be argued that its relative and human meaning becomes restrictive. The human interpretation of "And consult with them" (Qur'an 3:159) is binding on both the ruler and the ruled. Any deviation from such an interpretation or in its implementation becomes sufficient ground for charges of illegitimacy and active opposition to the ruler.

Shura has become for moderates and almost all of the Islamist movements the source of legitimization of any authority, while the continuation of legitimacy hinges on the application of the *Shari'ah* and people's approval. The historical experience of Muslims shows that by giving the state the power to employ and to execute *Shari'ah* in the name of the *umma,* more substantial doctrines of *Shari'ah* are overlooked in favor of a political interpretation of Islam. Thus, what is needed is to reform Islamic politics beyond just the re-interpretation of doctrines, which again might ultimately be used by some political authority.

However, one cannot but commend moderate Islamists' introduction of democracy as *shura* into the main political doctrines of contemporary Islam, at a time when one of the major practical difficulties of real politics is the authoritarian nature of politics exercised in the Muslim world. While the theoretical difficulty mentioned above is still being dealt with, the development of an Islamicly argued democracy justified by textual authorities seems better than denying altogether the important role of democracy.

Moderate Islamists' grounding of democracy in a metaphysically conceived composition reifies it into an act of worship. On the other hand, the application of *tawhid* in a democratically structured form makes it a justification for ruling. In this way, moderate Islamism transmutes the substantive *tawhid* into a form, and formalizes *shura* into a substantive principle. Therefore, the discourse is interpreted by its form. Moderate Islamism condenses thus the religious discourse into no more than a political footnote and makes creedal belief and unbelief into political belief and unbelief. Political belief depends on sound application of the *hakimiyya* (governance) of the Divinely ordained text. Political unbelief, conversely, results from depending alone on the *hakimiyya* of humankind.

In this fashion, moderate Islamism negates the usefulness of traditional jurisprudence and transforms a modern religious jurisprudence into an ideologically derived political discourse. In such an explanation of the true essence of Islam, one cannot fail to notice how politics informs all religious doctrines, even that of the metaphysical. Because no individual by themself can understand the real metaphysical meaning of a text, the only credible meaning becomes that resulting from politics, i.e. a consensual agreement, through *shura*. However, this cannot be properly conducted without the machinery of the state. For the rendering of categorical and lasting interpretation of a text requires a continuous ratifying process of all Muslim generations and the continuous existence of the Islamic state.

The disintegration of the state and of society brings back the need for another appropriate interpretive discourse. For an eternal interpretation is an interpretive impossibility, since interpretation is conditional and tentative. In their attempts to find proper channels for relative interpretations of the text, the Islamists focus their work on reviving the role of social forces. However, a Muslim society does indeed need an Islamic state that becomes the symbol of collective self-awareness and the possibility of a relatively correct textual understanding. Thus, moderate Islamism opens up, at least theoretically, a host of possible Islamic discourses that are in tune with realities but are nonetheless relative, conditional, and tentative.

As such, moderate Islamism theoretically frees Muslims from the finished products of early and medieval thinking and ways of living. It permits and in fact exhorts Muslims to modernize Islam and Islamize modernity: again, *shura* becomes democracy, and democracy *shura*. This forceful conceptual correspondence that took place through a process of historical neutralization brings closer together both modern Islamic political thought and its Western counterpart, and creates a possibility of a new political discourse and a meaningful dialogue.

A popular liberating democracy, grounded in Islamic law, is a political bridge between the Muslim world and the West. For authoritarianism and despotism are not specifically cultural or Islamic. While they have existed in both the West and the Muslim world, they are more prominent now in the Muslim world. The moderate trend adopts an Islamic interpretation of liberal democracy as opposed to the popular democracy of radical Islamism or the authoritarian nationalism of the Arab world. Thus, radical Islamism proclaims the constitutionality of Islam even in non-Islamic states and as such requires no prior popular approval and excludes the possibility of its inclusion in dialogues and cooperation whether with Arab/Muslim regimes or the West. However, moderate Islamism seems more amenable and eager to be included in dialogue and compromise, whether in party formations or the general discourses about politics, ideology, and religion within the context of a civil society.

ENDNOTES

1. For a full treatment of the topics of democracy and pluralism, See Ahmad Moussalli, *The Islamic Quest for Democracy, Pluralism, and Human Rights* (Gainesville, FL: University Press of Florida, 2001).
2. "Islamism" is another term for "Islamic fundamentalism." It is not only a set of political movements but carries also a spectrum of moderate and radical intellectual and political discourses. These discourses constitute a critique of philosophy, political ideology, and science. In a philosophical sense, though believing in the existence of objective and ultimate truth, fundamentalism claims that no individual can understand it, and thus all of our knowledge is relative. More substantially, it attempts to offer a way of life and thought based on its understanding of both God's law, *al-Shari'ah*, and the phenomenon of nature. Both constitute what religion is about. Fundamentalist political ideologies depend on adhering to divine governance (*hakimiyya*) and on refuting paganism (*jahiliya*) and the notion of people's ultimate authority and humankind natural possessiveness. Instead, it relegates that ultimate authority to God. Fundamentalist worldviews revolve around setting up virtuous, just, and equal societies that are regulated by Islam. "Islamism" or "Islamic fundamentalism" is an umbrella term for a wide range of discourses and activism which, from a high level of moderate pluralism, and thus inclusive democracy, to extreme radicalism, intolerant unitarianism, and exclusive majority rule. While some fundamentalist groups are pluralistic in terms of inter-Muslim relations and between Muslims and minorities, others are not. Again, while some fundamentalists are politically pluralistic but theologically exclusive, others are accommodating religiously, but direct their exclusivist programs to the outside – the West and imperialism. Even at the scientific level, Western science and technology are argued for by some fundamentalists as Islamicly sound, while others exclude them – because of their assumed un-Islamic nature.
3. This phrase is used by Professor Richard Bulliet as a title of one of his books, *Islam: The View from the Edge* (New York: Columbia University Press, 1994).
4. Ibid., 4.
5. Wajih Kawtharani, *Mashru' al-Nuhud al-'Arabi* (Beirut: Dar al-Tali'a, 1995), 12–18. See also Muhammad 'Abid al-Jabiri, *Al-Khitab al-'Arabi al-Mu'asir* (Beirut: Dar al-Tali'a, 1980), chapter 2.
6. Muhammad Hamadah, *Bina' al-Umma bayna al-Islam wa al-Fikr al-Mu'asir* (Casablanca: Dar al-Thaqafa, 1986), 86–134; Kawtharani, *Mashru'*, 18–24. See also Muhammad 'Amara, *Al-Din wa al-Dawla* (Cairo: Al-Hay'a al-Amma li al-Kitab, 1986), 151–72; 'Abd al-Majid al-Sharfi, "Mushkilat al-Hukm fi al-Fikr al-Islami al-Hadith," *Al-Ijtihad*, 4(14), 1992, 69–93; and Muhammad Tawfiq al-Shawi, *Fiqh al-Hukuma al-Islamiyya bayna al-Shi'a wa al-Sunna* (Ann Arbor: New Era, 1995).

7. For a further discussion and critique of the Wahhabi movement, see the article by Khaled Abou El Fadl, "The Ugly Modern and the Modern Ugly: Reclaiming the Beautiful in Islam," in this volume.

8. *Al-Hayat,* August 4, 1993, 19, 25; September 25, 1993, 14, 17. The series ran on August 2–6. See also *Qadaya al-Isbu',* September 10–17, 1993, 1–2.

9. Edward Djerejian, "One Man, One Vote, One Time," *New Perspective Quarterly,* 10(3), 1993, 49; Judith Miller, "The Challenge of Radical Islam," *Foreign Affairs,* 72(2), 1993, 54–5; "Will Democracy Survive in Egypt?," *Reader's Digest* (Canadian edn), 131(788), 1987, 149; "The Arab World Where Troubles for the U.S. Never End," *U.S. News and World Report,* February 6, 1984, 24; Samuel Huntington, "The Clash of Civilizations," *Foreign Affairs,* 72(3), 1993, 22–49.

10. For a study of violent religious movements in a comparative context that brings together Christian, Jewish, Muslim, Sikh, and Buddhist movements, see Mark Juergensmeyer's valuable book, *Terror in the Mind of God: The Global Rise of Religious Violence* (Berkeley: University of California Press, 2000).

11. See, for instance, al-Ghannushi, *Al-Hurriyyat al-'Amma fi al-Islam;* Fahmi al-Huwaidi, *Al-Islam wa al-Dimocratiyya;* and *Al-Hayat,* October 11, 1996, 21; October 12, 1996, 21.

12. *Al-Safir,* September 25, 1993, 10 and *Al-Diyar,* September 25, 1993, 14.

13

HOW TO PUT THE GENIE BACK IN THE BOTTLE? "IDENTITY" ISLAM AND MUSLIM YOUTH CULTURES IN AMERICA

Marcia Hermansen

I am an American Muslim and a Professor of Islamic Studies at a Jesuit University in Chicago. For most of my adult life I have worked with youth as a teacher and advisor. I began studying Arabic, Urdu, and Islamic studies as an undergraduate student in the 1970s. From that time until the present, I have lived for extended periods in various parts of the Muslim world including the Arab Middle East, South Asia, and Iran, often within Muslim families. In my academic research I have been concerned with both classical Islamic studies and the lived experience of Muslims, particularly in South Asia and in the West.

In terms of our volume's theme of a progressive Islam, one might expect that Muslim youth in America would be at the forefront of taking an interest in this development. However, increasingly in recent years I have seen the tide turning in the opposite direction, one in which quite a number of Muslim youth in America are becoming rigidly conservative and condemnatory of their peers (Muslim and non-Muslim), their parents, and all who are not within a narrow ideological band of what I will define as internationalist, "identity" Islam.

I would define a progressive Muslim outlook as one based on informed understanding of the tradition in its historical and multicultural context as evolving to address the needs and issues of the time in a way that is both spiritually and politically empowering. In this essay I express my observation and concern that a considerable portion of American Muslim youth seem to be moving in a direction antithetical to progressive interpretations. In fact they are moving in a direction that negates interpretation and diversity altogether, one that rejects historical development and cultural context. Furthermore, it privileges certain external markers of identity and is, in the process, anti-intellectual. I will be focusing on the youth I see most often, who are primarily raised in America and born of parents who emigrated from South Asia or the Middle East.

I observe that subsequent to the terrorist attacks of September 11, 2001, the Muslim community, like the larger American society, has become increasingly polarized along ideological lines. Many Muslims in America before September 11 had been celebrating their increasing voice and presence. This sentiment, I believe, was acceptable both to progressive liberals within the community and to those Muslims who focused on preserving and promoting more conservative and isolationist observance of religious injunctions. At the same time, observers, whether academic or in the media, of Islam in America seemed to be divided as to whether to celebrate this civic integration of Muslims or to warn of an essential element of Islamic identity that would never adapt to pluralistic and democratic institutions. The aftermath of the terrorist attacks, both immediate and continuing, has made me painfully aware, not only of my own personal struggle with conflicted identities, but also of the issues facing younger Muslims in America. I now feel alienated from the Muslim community here in ways I had not previously experienced. When I turn on my television or read the paper or emails, I often experience a similar alienation from those segments of American society which seem to feel they have a "Divine right" to ignore issues of global justice and world ecology.

I hesitate to construct this piece of writing on the basis of "problematizing" or "pathologizing" Muslim youth cultures. So often one is confronted by the concept of Muslim youth and of Muslims generally as a problem – criminalized, unable to adapt, and now as a violent threat. At the same time, even within the Muslim community, I sense a general concern over trends developing among youth. The energies of youth, like the genies in Islamic folklore, are potentially creative, powerful, and destructive simultaneously. I wish to interrogate my own imagery in the title of this piece of a genie put back in the bottle. Am I suggesting that Muslim youth should be contained and silenced? That would be far from a progressive stance. At the same time, I think there is a certain destructive, arrogant, and nasty energy that has been allowed to run unchecked and uncriticized, and has even been encouraged among youth by mainstream Muslim organizations in America. It is that energy that I would like to see named and examined more critically, and to a certain extent put into a framework of analysis, if not into an airtight bottle, so that it can be channeled in more productive directions.

I have to say that I was shocked when I encountered some Muslim students on my campus who seemed to feel vindicated by the destruction and loss of life on September 11.[1] I couldn't understand how children of Muslim immigrants, born and largely raised in the United States, could somehow twist their understanding of their own situation and history to welcome such an event as payback. In one case, I was told that the attacks were payback for the defeat of the Ottoman Empire. I could hardly fathom how such hatred and contempt for the society in which one lives could exist in those who had chosen to come here and in their children, but it led me to retrace and rethink the various trends that I had observed in Muslim American organizations and discourses, and how the young were positioning themselves with regard to their Muslim identities. Putting it bluntly, I find these tendencies troubling and therefore in this essay I want to explore them, as well as my own reactions to them.

Some Muslims may be disturbed that I would speak of these things so publicly, although I know that inside Muslim circles they are being discussed, at least by those who feel there is a problem. I, like many other Muslims in America, am tired of the attitudes that are expressed in Friday sermons and other forums of what had been, at least previously, insider Muslim discourse.

COMPONENTS OF IDENTITY

One of the main factors driving Muslim youth activities in America is the quest for identity. That this identity might be shaped (distorted) in odd ways is not surprising. The majority of immigrant American Muslims arrived only after 1980, therefore today's youth are the first cohort born in America. The struggle of a new generation for a place in the dominant society is nothing new. Muslim youth of immigrant parents are often more "different" in terms of skin color, names, and religion than the previous waves of immigrants were. The American political situation since the 1960s has, in increasing measure, constructed Islam and Muslims as the enemy or threat to the American way of life or Western civilization. At the same time, since the 1970s, a new form of internationalist Islamic ideology, combining political ambitions, anti-colonialism, and conservative religious revivalism, has often been the only oppositional voice raised against repressive regimes in the Muslim world. A litany of injustices of the West against Islam is part of Muslim collective memory and present rhetoric, and to a large extent present reality, most recent examples being the Palestinian situation, Kashmir, and the blockade on Iraq.

One can well imagine the identity dilemma of a Muslim teenager brought up largely in an American environment who has been encouraged by parents, Islamic groups, and extended family to dis-identify with American cultural and political contexts and to imagine himself or herself as being from somewhere else (Pakistan or Palestine, for example) as a critical or oppositional stance. At the same time, this young person is probably never going to make it as an authentic citizen of the imagined homeland, since he or she faces substantial inadequacies in language competency, historical knowledge, and even cultural and social assumptions about the idealized place of origin.

This simultaneous alienation both from American culture and from the culture of immigrant Muslim parents encourages the embrace of a culture-free, global Islamic militancy. Here I draw on British theorists who have understood "identity Islam" movements as yielding a positive identification in the face of

British racial rejection.[2] While the categories of race and class in America vary from those in Europe, the parallel experience of some degree of racism certainly exists.

Ironically, Muslim youth in the United States are often expected to be the "model," which is to say model minority, being streamed from childhood to enter the most lucrative and demanding fields. An alternative subculture of Muslim youth in the U.S., however, is those with gang or "gangsta" identification, linked to the most stigmatized social minorities in American culture. A polarization exists in the eyes of the community between the young person with beard or *hijab* who is a Muslim Student Association (MSA) member on the way to being an MD and the gangsta-identified youth who does poorly in school and may be suspected of drug use. Of course the great majority of American Muslim youth fall somewhere in-between; some flee from their Muslim identity, others are progressive activists, most are moderate, struggling with the anomalies of allegiance to a country that does seem to take policy decisions that are harmful to Muslims abroad and, increasingly, to the domestic population.

CULTURE AS THE PROBLEM

One of the major slogans of Muslim youth movements is the "rejection of culture." Recently I heard a young man who stated that he was "recovering" from the MSA experience saying that he had attended a play for the first time and really enjoyed it, but somehow felt guilty for associating with this "cultural" thing. I am often told that I speak too much about culture in my classes, and that we should be learning about the "true" Islam.

An ideological premise of internationalist identity Islam is that this "true" Islam is apparently floating above everything cultural. It is pristine and unassailable, politically it has established a utopian state where everyone is happy and honest, and that this state should be re-imposed on humanity today and it will make a better world. Internationalist Muslim revivalist movements such as Jama'at Islami and the Muslim Brotherhood (*Ikhwan al-Muslimin*) have encouraged this concept of a "cultureless" Islam around the world. These revivalists have been able to dominate Muslim organizations and mosques because of their commitment, pre-existing networks, external material support, and defined ideological agenda. The American immigrant Muslim community welcomed the identity element promulgated by such Muslim organizations in the 1970s and 1980s because it solved the immediate threat of assimilation into American culture, by keeping the youth "Muslim and proud of it." One can well imagine the problems of Muslim youth, often isolated by having distinctive names, physical appearance, and being associated with a stigmatized culture and religion. No wonder the concept that they were actually the superior ones, fending off the corrupt and evil society around them, rang pleasant.

An example of this is the manner in which one is constantly being warned on Muslim internet lists of the evils of Western cultural elements such as the celebration of birthdays, Halloween, and prom night – the insidious threat of paganism and worse. To be fair, a progressive critique of these practices could well be mounted on the basis of their commercial and commodified nature, their thrust toward a globalized consumerist monoculture, and so on. What I take issue with is the religious and cultural superiority that sustains what I term "identity" Islamic attitudes, the sense of Muslim cheerleading that goes on at so many organized Muslim events for youth and that seems to have been the element most strongly internalized. Identity Islam is not an intellectual critique of alternatives but rather a mindless and rigid rejection of "the Other" and the creation of a de-cultured, rule based space where one asserts Muslim "difference" based on gender segregation, romantic recreations of madrasa experiences, and the most blatantly apologetic articulations of Islam. It replaces spirituality with arrogance and a smug pride in one's superior manifestation of visible symbols of identity.

The outline of identity Islam is derived from frameworks of Salafi and Wahhabi interpretation.[3] It features a rejection of specific cultural elements that diverge from a literal understanding of Islamic norms. Thus, wearing saris or celebrating the birthday of the Prophet are seen as heretical innovations (*bid'a*). The fact is, almost anything cultural would be a *bid'a* if everything had to be done as Arabs in the Prophet's time did it. But who are these ideal Arabs? It is clear that the population in Mecca and Medina were not ideal, in fact the Prophet had constant problems with their rudeness and ignorance. It is also clear that wherever Islamic civilization took root around the world, it acculturated at the same time as it Islamicized. The idea of a "culture-free" Islam is therefore derived from modern ideologies rather than from authentic practice or historical fact.

As part of this celebration and affirmation of pure identity, any discourse purporting to be Islamic is performed and welcomed without analysis or regard for context. For example, I recall a campus MSA meeting where selections of the most naive and apologetic nature from a certain South Asian publication were read out before an audience of university students. No one commented or questioned and the few non-Muslim students in attendance were perplexed and alienated by the childish level of credulity exhibited. If any of the Muslim students had comments or criticisms to offer, they were stifled by the conformity and group-mind culture that excludes diversity and marginalizes independent thinking.

MUSLIM STUDENT ASSOCIATION SUBCULTURE

The MSA was founded in the United States by Muslim students from South Asia and the Arab world in the 1960s. The various local chapters are essentially independent, although they receive suggested directives from a central body.

Thus, it would be unfair to paint all with the same brush. Some campus chapters are exceptionally rigid and exclusionary, others are no doubt progressive. Since students matriculate and graduate, the leadership and membership are constantly changing. However, the direction I am witnessing gives me cause for concern. While in some cases Muslim students form other bodies on campuses as alternatives, MSAs tend to occupy the most accepted position as campus Muslim organizations. Garbi Schmidt, a Danish sociologist of religion, writes about the Muslim student events she attended in Chicago in the 1990s. After describing the context of MSA lectures and especially the events of the annual Islamic Awareness Week, she discussed the rhetoric of most events in terms of their dialogue with "the Other," the non-Muslim institution and its members:

> But the Other – fellow students, teachers – were more than an audience. They were a means to Islamic interpretation. Interpretations of the role of women, political issues, scientific investigations, and media presentations all pointed to an adoption of powerful topics and opinion formers within the United States. Though this at times included an "apologetic pitfall" it also included a means for collective empowerment. By attacking, formulating against, and arguing to formulate more correct views than majority authorities (scientists, politicians, journalists) Muslims appealed for social recognition. By "correcting" the errors of the Other they were convinced (and tried to convince) that although they socially were in minority, the knowledge they represented was intellectually superior.[4]

Thus, while the apologism of such events and the simplified and rigid identity Islam that they often promote may raise concerns on the part of liberal Muslims and others of the direction MSA students are taking, one can at least understand the rigid stance and triumphalism as empowering individuals feeling disempowered in other contexts.

Sympathy for the pietistic expression of identity Islam may come from the campus ministry and chaplain community who are impressed by the level of participation of Muslim students in religious observances. I note a certain nostalgic admiration of Muslim students' piety on the part of ministry workers who struggle with involving their largely secularized student populations.

Among some young Muslim ideologues, fear of being co-opted by the "Western" university system leads to a fascination with the madrasa style of learning. Online mullahs provide the most rigid and hateful *fatwas* proscribing the most picayune and oppressive regulations. Western "shaykhs" in robes and turbans purvey a new brand of authoritarian charisma.

For many children of Muslim immigrants technical fields and medicine are seen as being less corrupting than the interpretive humanities and social science subjects, and the former are sometimes justified as being of potential service "to Muslims." Furthermore, of the Muslim students who study the sciences, very few engage in fields such as the philosophy of science; most prefer to limit themselves to the applied sciences. In addition, the issues of interpretation raised by the humanities and social sciences involve the sort of nuance and multivalency that more rigid Muslim youth wish to avoid confronting in understanding Islam itself.

The lack of involvement in the humanities and social sciences by Muslim youth has been viewed by some American Muslim leaders as detrimental to the community being able to articulate its positions within mainstream society. As a result, small movements toward encouraging these other fields have been made: for example a few Muslim organizations offer scholarships to students who might pursue journalism. At the same time, certain traditionalist Muslim opinion-makers in the West encourage the avoidance of studies whose epistemological underpinnings might threaten the acceptance of a mythologized worldview.

The origin of the MSAs in the 1960s makes them contemporary to African-American Black Power movements. African-American students lobbied for black studies, and Muslim students, while not yet in a lobbying position (and they are not there yet), responded with the idea of the "Islamization of knowledge" – the call for a critique of the epistemological foundations of academic disciplines from an Islamic perspective. The Islamization of knowledge movement, while failing to dent the hegemony of Western scientific and secular paradigms to the extent of, say, feminist or even post-colonial theory, does partake to a certain extent in the destabilizing force of post-modern plural discourses.

Muslim Student Associations on university campuses may ironically fulfill the need for alternative Muslim spaces as sites of resistance to the dominant "West" and its institutions. Schmidt observes in her study of Muslim culture in Chicago that formal Islamic institutions of learning tend to accommodate to American patterns and standards because of regulations of accreditation, credentials of staff, and so on. More informal spaces such as MSA meetings and campus mosques are therefore sites in which the "imagined madrasa" can be more freely re-created and expressions of identity Islam may be articulated.[5] The extremes to which this may be taken, however, are illustrated by the case of an MSA group that would not allow their non-Muslim American professor to enter the campus mosque.

On one occasion, I heard a Friday speech in a student mosque in which the speaker said that in the traditional Islamic educational system the teachers cared for their students as kindly as if they were their own children. In contrast, he stated, modern university education in the West exploits the students so that the teachers are economically profiting from their pupils. I found this comparison especially egregious, since the problem of economic exploitation, bribery, and forcing the students to buy one's lecture notes is endemic in certain Muslim societies, where the university teachers are paid so poorly that they need to make extra money out of the situation. It may be that pre-modern madrasas cultivated long-term, family type relations among teachers and pupils, or that even today madrasas provide social welfare services such as room and board to poor students. However, to idealize the contemporary Muslim world, or even the past, in this way is a disservice to the honesty and critical assessment of fact.

GENDER: SISTERS, BROTHERS AND OTHERS

One way of asserting difference is through enforcing rigid norms of gender segregation at "Muslim" events on campus. One young woman at an MSA meeting declared that she didn't want to even know the names of any "brothers" (male Muslim students at the university), since she should have nothing to do with males at all. Ironically, she used the term "brother" in referring to the male Muslim members of the MSA. Is this what one means by "brotherhood" and "sisterhood," a level of distance that leads one to not even wish to know the other's name?[6] Muslim students who don't conform to strict dress codes, at least on campus, are ostracized and called *kafir* behind their back. *Kafir* in American Muslim youth culture has been extended to signify anyone who is different than you, rather like the semantic function of "honkey" in Black Power discourse. It migrates from the theological referent of being a denier of God to that of non-Muslim, or anyone, even another Muslim, co-opted by the majority Western system.

EXTREMISM AND FRINGE MOVEMENTS

Some extremist elements in the American Muslim community go so far as to send death threats to a host of progressive and liberal Muslims, and to exercise other forms of ostracization and intimidation. This strategy is used troublingly often among Muslims, even in America, and has to be openly condemned and exposed. In some Islamic centers if there is a contentious discussion or election to a board, one faction or the other may threaten individuals who disagree with them. One reason for the lack of public moderate and progressive voices is the explicit threat of reprisal from the community itself.

As an aid to understanding the type of extremist material circulating for the youthful Muslim audience, I offer some selections from a Hizb-e Tahrir newsletter.[7] The Hizb-e Tahrir is a radical fringe group, founded in the Middle East, which has a following among diaspora Muslim youth.[8] In a nostalgic revisioning of Muslim history, they configure the last Ottoman Sultan, Abd al-Hamid, as a religious hero and hold that restoring a universal Muslim caliphate and rejecting the West is the best political program available to Muslims today. Among their strategies are disrupting mosque meetings and lectures where moderates or non-Muslims speak.

According to a Hizb-e Tahrir publication, targeted at Muslim youth in the West,

Prior to the seventeenth century, Europe did not have an ideology; it was still caught in the feudal system. ... Whereas the Islamic state, al-Khilafah, was implementing the Islamic ideology and progressing rapidly.

How the *khilafa* (the institution of the Caliphate) becomes equated to a "state" is bewildering. The assertion that feudalism is not an ideology – while simultaneously holding that the Caliphate is – demonstrates the paucity of logic, historical understanding, and critical faculties of these groups.

A further excerpt from the same publication, which was distributed at a Hizb-e Tahrir booth operating at a major American Muslim conference, states,

The Shari'ah provides the prescriptions and prescriptions. The Shari'ah instructs the Muslim on what livelihood is permissible, when it is okay to lie, or when killing becomes a *wajib* (compulsory) act of *ibadah* (worship). While the value is the objective of the action, it is not the basis nor the goal. It is Allah who tells the Muslim on [*sic*] how to achieve the objective.

If the Muslim achieves the objective in the manner in which Allah commands s/he achieves the goal.[9]

Note the pre-occupations demonstrated by the choice of examples – killing and lying. I have heard Muslim youth in America discussing political strategies of making agreements in bad faith with the intent of violating them as an effective strategy to achieve goals. The implications of framing "killing" (uncontextualized) as an act of worship are disturbing, particularly in the aftermath of the horrific events of September 11. No wonder the articles in this magazine are unsigned – although poor grammar and logic could be a secondary reason for not admitting ownership.

The same pamphlet states, "the Islamic nation which once wielded the geo-political force of an atom bomb, no longer exists."[10] This is an odd and telling analogy – why would a pre-modern society be compared to an atom bomb? The message of lost Muslim glory, nursing grievances, and idealizing violence can thus be seen to circulate in this discourse targeted at Muslim youth. While most Muslims in America would consider this movement marginal and extreme, I hear far too few voices in the community raised against it.

PUTTING THE GENIE BACK: STRATEGIES

In the preceding remarks my intention was to raise awareness of ways in which Muslim youth identities in America are moving in increasingly rigid and troubling directions. In terms of moving forward in a constructive fashion, I propose a number of strategies and approaches.

Psychological and sociological analysis as a tool for understanding

One strategy for "putting the genie back" is information and understanding, even sympathetic understanding of the context within which these youth movements emerge. Such information assists an understanding of the phenomenon on the part of parents, advisors, and the youth themselves. The tendency to see things in binary oppositions helps neither the youth nor those trying to facilitate their development. A sense of the forces that impinge on the experiences of modern Muslim youth movements, within both internationalist Islamic movements and Western societies, helps one to put certain stances into perspective and historical context.

Scholarship focusing on Muslim youth in Canada and Britain seems to be somewhat ahead of that carried out in the United States and therefore may provide insights into emerging American Muslim youth cultures. Muslim youth in Britain have tended to be concentrated in certain cities such as London and Bradford. They also suffer greater class oppression than Muslim immigrants to America owing to the history of immigration to Britain from the ex-colonies and the different racial categories (intuitive if not official) operative in Britain.

> The emergence of the Muslim community in the dominant imagination can be seen as the latest in a series of re-creations of Asian identities in the post-war period. Starting life as colored, reinvented in the 1960s and 1970s as politically black, rediscovered as Asian in the new racist/multi-culturalist 1980s, it is the events of the late 1980s and the early 1990s that have re-imagined Asian identities along religious-cultural lines.[11]

Still, the effects of racism and the role of race and class play an important role in determining alternatives available for youth identities in the United States and this aspect needs to be further explored.[12]

In terms of understanding the dynamic underlying what I term "hyper-religiosity" among a number of American Muslim youth, the Canadian Muslim scholar of minority education Yasmin Zine observes,

> The importance of staying on the straight path becomes particularly germane to Muslims who live in non-Muslim societies. Things such as dating and premarital sex, drug, and alcohol use, which are common practices among many youth in North America, are strictly forbidden in Islam. As such, the religious values and lifestyles of Muslim can be difficult to maintain in a society based on often contradictory secular norms.[13]

Zine therefore explains the affirmation of religious identity among Muslim students not only as a way to negotiate their expressions of faith but also as a means of using these Muslim identities as a means of resistance to counteract their marginality within Eurocentric public schools.

As a future project, I recommend the undertaking of longitudinal studies that trace these youth into their thirties and forties as a means of understanding how hyper-religious zeal arises at a particular phase of personality development and gradually diffuses with the demands of career and family life. In fact many of the cliquish, aggressive, and shunning behaviors that I witness remind me of my own high school days and seem to draw on adolescent anxieties robed in Islamic identity symbols. Late adolescence is, after all, the time of the identity crisis for all, not just Muslims. In addition, many Muslim youth from immigrant backgrounds may be facing their first extended experience away from the family, and a relatively sheltered home life may result in their displaying attitudes and behaviors usually expected from a younger cohort.

I also observe that while one might expect graduates of Islamic schools to have the most problems with the shift to integration in a more diverse environment, the pressures of minority status in public schools seem to have more of a negative impact on some Muslim students. An additional factor might be that the lack of training or credentialing for mosque Sunday school teachers may make such classes arenas for the reinforcement of negative aspects of identity Islam. This also warrants further investigation.

Recognizing and fostering diversity among American Muslim youth

Just as a progressive stance recognizes and celebrates diversity in the larger society, a progressive stance toward Muslim youth subcultures needs to explore their diversities, probing the potentially empowering aspects of these differences and trying to anticipate and foster elements of chosen identities that could advance progressive attitudes. For example, South Asian youth in America differentiate themselves as to whether they are "American Born Confused Desis" (ABCDs) or "Fresh off the Boat." Interestingly, the two groups tend to avoid socializing with one another and generally find little resonance with each other's outlook. My personal impression is that those who have spent larger portions of childhood abroad find the zeal of the American-raised Muslim youths perplexing. Recently arrived Muslim youth are less likely to become hyper-religious, but may remain culturally ghettoized. Among the hyper-religious youth, distinctive strands of traditionalist versus radicalized Islamic identities may be observed, sometimes coalescing in a single individual. Various tendencies circulating in the American Muslim community inspired by Salafi, Tablighi, or Sufi movements have an impact on youthful articulations of Muslim identity. Social location of the families also impacts identity, youth who are less privileged often have wider circles of contacts across ethnic lines (i.e. Hispanic and African-American friends) because they attend public schools in the same neighborhoods.

Sponsoring Academic Presentations on Islam

A further strategy for enabling progressive attitudes rather than rigid identity is to encourage, in so far as possible, lectures on campus (or at the Islamic center) that present aspects of Islam in an intellectual, objective manner rather than pandering to identity affirmation and apologism.

For example, at a campus lecture I attended, an academic expert on the topic of women in Islam cited some of the *hadith* from the main Sunni collections, those of Muslim and Bukhari, that condemn women as being defective in intellect and religion. Some of the Muslim women students were surprised that such sentiments were recorded in the authoritative compendia of religion and therefore felt motivated to further explore historical and religious discussions of women's role in Islam. Muslim youth are often unfamiliar with the basics of their own tradition and therefore accept a sugar-coated apologism. Exposure to balanced and historical treatments by Muslim and non-Muslim scholars should be part of their educational experience. Unfortunately, Muslim youth organizations tend to maintain a very limited roster of Islamic "motivational" speakers who affirm a predictable identity and circulate the same set of apologetic platitudes.

Accountability

A recent discussion in the media of the need for more campus Muslim chaplains raised ambivalent feelings for me. Initially I was concerned that this would further entrench identity Islam among the university Muslim community. The imagined chaplain of the article was to be an ex-MSA officer who loved the experience so much that he (or she) wanted to come back to campus. I imagined not only my own marginalization by such a person but also that of liberal Muslim students who are quite comfortable interacting with American people and institutions.

After some reflection, however, I saw the positive aspects both of having adults who have at least a university education advising Muslim students and of the idea of Muslim leadership on campus having some accountability to the institution. One of the problematic issues in campus MSAs is outsider influence that tends to be ultra-conservative, ghettoized, or even radicalized. Community members, students' relatives, or students from other schools are invited to lead Friday prayers and can say whatever they want, with no accountability. At one Friday prayer, a relative of one of the Muslim students gave the sermon – it was election time – and told the students they should not vote in the elections of this "*kafir* country." At least having a chaplain who would be the person on call and who would have responsibility for campus activities might keep that aspect under control.

In this essay I have largely spoken from the perspective of my world, the university campus. At a broader level I would call for accountability on the part of Muslim organizations that have largely focused, it seems to me, on promoting identity rather than encouraging reflection and positive contributions from youth.

PROGRESSIVE RESPONSES

In the context of campus life, one finds both the greatest polarization of youth identities and the greatest potential to explore them. The National Islam

Awareness Weeks sponsored by MSAs across America are explicitly intended to expose more non-Muslims on campus to Islam. In fact, the events are often narrow and apologetic "preaching to the choir" and only the celebration of narrow identity is achieved. "Convert Testimonial" night, for example, is unlikely to be a big draw on campus (although very interesting sociologically for students of religion). At least some Muslim students realize the value of cultural elements such as food, film, or poetry in attracting others to hear about Islamic civilization and, indirectly, religion. Therefore, such events have an intrinsically progressive element and should be encouraged as a bridge among diverse Muslim and non-Muslim students. Campus events and politics also lead students to open up to alliances and the benefits of co-sponsoring with diverse groups. Therefore the more this is encouraged on campus, the more students' rigidity and isolationism can be challenged as they find common cause and interest with their peers from other backgrounds.

I conclude with the observation that we are passing through a transitional and critical period in the history of the Muslim community in the United States. The educational and social experiences of Muslim youth in the university system will play an important role in developing the orientation of this population. I feel disappointed that major Muslim organizations have consciously or unconsciously participated in reinforcing patterns of Islamic identity that will not serve youth well during their years of intellectual and social maturation. The dominant perspective and representation of Islam in America has thus far come from the perspective of immigrants. Adjustments to the American cultural context will inevitably take place as the born-in-America generation comes of age. Will these adjustments be made in the light of finding common and empowering connections between American intellectual and cultural traditions and Islamic principles, or will isolationism further fragment Muslims into assimilationists and rejectionists? Unless the genie of identity Islam is understood and channeled in more constructive directions, I fear that the energies and aspirations of Muslim youth may be spent in the pursuit and reinforcement of a brittle shell that will not withstand the test of time.

ENDNOTES

1. To be fair here, I need to point out that this is not a majority reaction but a somewhat extreme one. I have heard of other Muslim youth who were so deeply disturbed by the attacks that they questioned their own faith; others who were dismayed and immobilized; others clearly confused by the mixed reactions in the community, and frankly by the political responses from the West that continue to avoid the real injustices and disparities that exist in American foreign policy.
2. K. Gardner and A. Shakur, "I'm Bengali, I'm Asian and I'm living here: the changing identity of British Bengalis," in *Desh Pardesh*, ed. R. Ballard (London: C. Hurst, 1994), 142–64.
3. For an insightful discussion and critique of Wahhabi interpretation Islam in the contemporary Islamic world, see the essay titled "The Ugly Modern and the Modern Ugly: Reclaiming the Beautiful in Islam" by Khaled Abou El Fadl in this volume.

4. Garbi Schmidt, *American Medina: A study of the Sunni Muslim Immigrant Communities in Chicago* (Lund, Sweden: Department of History of Religions, University of Lund, 1998), 167.
5. Ibid.
6. I should point out that this opinion was not representative of most Muslim students' views on gender relations.
7. *Islamic Forum*, 1(1), 2000.
8. A historical study of the movement is Suha Taji-Farouki, *Hizb al-Tahrir and the Search for the Islamic Caliphate* (London: Grey Seal, 1996).
9. *Islamic Forum*, ibid.
10. Ibid.
11. Claire Alexander, "Re-imagining the Muslim Community," *Innovation: The European Journal of Social Sciences*, 11(4), 1998, 439.
12. One of the essays in this volume, titled "American Muslim Identity: Race and Ethnicity in Progressive Islam" by Amina Wadud, deals with issues of racial prejudice in North American Muslim societies.
13. Yasmin Zine, "Muslim Youth in Canadian Schools: Education and the Politics of Religious Identity," *Anthropology & Education Quarterly*, 32(4), 2001, 399–423.

14

WHAT IS THE VICTORY OF ISLAM? TOWARDS A DIFFERENT UNDERSTANDING OF THE *UMMAH* AND POLITICAL SUCCESS IN THE CONTEMPORARY WORLD

Farish A. Noor[1]

> We have not yet recognized the goal of Islam. We all talk about the Islamic revolution, (but) ask yourselves, what is the goal of Islam? This group, that group, "they curse one another" (*Qur'an, Surah* 29:25). This one contradicts that one, this one calls that one deviationist. But we have not yet recognized what Islam demands, what Islam is.[2]

WHAT IS THE VICTORY OF ISLAM?

Walking in the streets of London in the early 1990s, I came across a poster that bore the slogan *"The Islamic State: Coming soon to a country near you."* The poster was put up by the radical Islamist group *Hizb al-Tahrir*, which was originally formed in Palestine in the early 1950s and had spread its branches all over the world, extending as far as Western Europe. For decades groups like *al-Muhajirun* and *Hizb al-Tahrir* have been pre-occupied with the single-minded task of projecting themselves as the sole and exclusive voice of "pure Islam" in the West, confronting not only their respective Western governments but also other Islamic groups and movements that they regard as un-Islamic and "contaminated" by the evils of the Western environment.

Marginalized though they were, groups such as these were propelled to the forefront of European Muslim politics thanks to the machinations of the Western media (perpetually working on the basis of a "take me to your leader" mentality) and variable factors that were beyond the control of anyone. Events such as the *Satanic Verses* controversy, the Gulf War of 1990–1, the military coup in Algeria after the elections of 1992, and the Bosnian crisis contributed to a growing sense of insecurity and persecution among Muslims the world over. For

Muslims living in Europe, the fear of being engulfed by "the Other" and losing one's identity seemed even more acute.

In time, a host of radical Islamist groups began to appear on local university campuses in Britain and other Western countries. Many of these were made up of young, angry, and frustrated Muslim youths who were desperate for change in their own societies. Fed up with what they saw as the passivity of their elders and weakness of their community, these groups began to mobilize themselves and demand their rights on a communitarian basis. The groups themselves were a myriad assembly of different movements with radically different beliefs and orientations. While some adopted the politics of communitarianism (fighting for Muslim rights on the basis of democratic pluralism and democracy), others opted for a more radical approach by directly challenging the law of the land. Groups like *Hizb al-Tahrir* organized numerous "worldwide" rallies in cities like London which managed to attract mainly local participants and a number of foreign dissidents who graced their events. In many of their rallies and campaigns, talk was rife of the "second coming of Islam" and Islam's "final victory" over Western hegemony. Another common theme that was often brought up was the final victory over Israel and "international Jewry," calling on Muslims to unite and rise up against a common foe.

It struck me that what actually united these Muslims were the common negative tropes of the malevolent Other. On the many occasions when I attended these rallies, I was struck by the number of books and leaflets that were being distributed which spoke of the so-called "Western/Jewish/Zionist/Christian/ communist conspiracy against Islam and Muslims." There were books about how AIDS was a plot to destroy the *umma*, how population control was a Zionist/Vatican plot to stop the growth of Islam, and how young Muslims were being corrupted by the secular education they were being given in Western schools. There were also the usual sensational revelations that insults to Islam could be read in Coca Cola labels, provided one looked at them upside-down and reflected backwards in a mirror, and so on.

Here the unity of the *umma* was based on a simplistic form of dialectical opposition which invariably pitted Muslims against the non-Muslim Other. Two neat chains of equivalences were formed: Islam was equated with Muslim needs and concerns, ethics, morality, spirituality, and justice. By default, everything un-Islamic was portrayed as immoral, secular, worldly, and corrupt. A Hegelian dialectic follows suit: Islam is presented as an oppositional force that has to propel itself towards confrontation and conflict, in order to overcome obstacles placed before it before achieving its final and ultimate triumph.

Another recurrent theme that struck me was the millenarian idea of the victory of Islam over the West and the forces of *kufr* (unbelief). A harrowing image was being painted through the discourses that were circulating in these meetings. The propagandists of groups like *Hizb al-Tahrir* and *al-Muhajirun* spoke of a glorious age yet to come when Islam would reign triumphant over the

West, and the flags and banners of Islam would flutter over the gilded towers and parapets of Western capitals. The Western world, deemed corrupt and decadent to the core, would one day be brought under the heel of the Islamic Caliphate, and Islam (and Muslims) would rule the West, and by extension the world. One could only imagine the effect that such rhetoric would have on the unsuspecting populations of Western Europe (had they been invited to attend).

This state of affairs was allowed to go unchecked and to fester for years. During the 1990s the fortunes of many of these radical groups improved markedly as their leaders were quick to hog the limelight and grab the headlines with their fiery rhetoric and combustible speeches. Calls for the creation of an Islamic state in Britain, the imposition of *Hudud* law in the West, the formation of separate Islamic communes with legislatures, courts, and councils of their own – all reinforced the popular Western prejudice of Islam as a religion of exclusivism, intolerance, and dogmatism, unable to cope with the demands of the present and unwilling to live with the realities of a multicultural world.

Then came September 11, 2001, and in a flash the paranoia of the West took on a life of its own. The nightmare of a resurgent militant Islam growing in the very heart of the Western world seemed to many a reality, and there were just as many at hand to support the claim that Islam was indeed a religion of violence, conflict, and terror. Western authors like Steven Emerson were there to remind their readers that hidden Islamist "cells" had been allowed to develop all over North America and Western Europe, thanks to the liberal laws and regulations of these Western democracies.[3] Others like Rohan Gunaratna wove byzantine narratives about transnational Islamist terror networks working in basements all over the world.[4] The bottom line was simple and clear: Muslims were a hidden menace to the West; they could not be trusted; they should not have been given the same democratic rights as others (on the grounds that they were bound to abuse it); and they have a pathological hatred of the West which cannot be understood, rationalized, or engaged with.

The net result of years of radical thinking among some Islamist movements in the West and elsewhere was the reinforcement and perpetuation of the myth of Islam as a threat to the West. By living up to the stereotype of Muslims as intolerant fanatics, these radical movements had given additional support to the claim that Islam was indeed an enemy and threat to the world. A monumental own-goal had been scored by the radicals against not only themselves, but the Muslim community as a whole.

Caught as Muslims are in this mess that is partly of our own making, the question remains: how do we extricate ourselves from this impasse while maintaining our identity and right to speak about matters that are of pivotal concern for the Muslim community? How can we defend our rights, articulate our demands, communicate our anxieties, and aspire to success in a way that is inclusive and non-confrontational? In short, how do we work towards a new understanding of the *umma* (and its relationship with the Other) and political success in the contemporary world?

REJECTING THE RHETORIC OF OPPOSITIONAL DIALECTICS

One of the key features of many contemporary Islamist movements is their reliance on a form of simplistic oppositional dialectics which requires the creation of a negative Other as the constitutive alterity to the Islamist project. Such dialectical opposition rests upon a neat and clear division, usually constructed along a strictly policed boundary line that demarcates the differences between the self ("us") and the other ("them").

Such oppositional dialectics have been put to service in the quest for political success and victory by many Islamist movements. This was most clearly demonstrated in the case of the revolution in Iran, which demonstrated a conscious reliance on both traditional Islamic political notions and values, as well as the dialectical approach of Marxism. In the words of Mehdi Bazargan, one of the intellectual founders of the Iranian Revolution,

> Freedom requires ... the existence of an oppositional force, along with the power of choice on behalf of the individual or the society. Opposition promulgates movement and change, which may, in turn, lead to decline and progress, depending on the choice of the agent involved.[5]

The instrumentalization of dialectics for the sake of a political project is not new and not specific to any particular tradition. Such a dialectical approach is certainly not unique to Islamist movements. It was, after all, derived from the Western political tradition and experience of Western societies and the Islamists merely took up a strategy that had worked elsewhere. The problem with such a dialectical approach, however, is that it also introduces internal boundaries and strategies of differentiation that contribute to the bifurcation of society and the distortion of social relations. It introduces a moment of internal division and potential conflict that is necessary for the dialectic to get off the ground in the first place. Indeed, such a dialectical approach cannot possibly work without first introducing tension and division within society and, after doing so, emphasizing such divisions. Dialectics requires an enemy to be opposed. And if such an enemy cannot be found it will simply have to be invented.

Over the past few decades we have seen how such a dialectical approach has been normalized and generalized across the board among Islamist movements worldwide. In fact one of the defining features of the current Islamist resurgence worldwide is that it requires the presence of the trope of the negative Other, which manifests itself in a number of forms: secularism, the West, international Jewry/Zionism, capitalism, etc.

There are two problems that should attract our attention from the very beginning. Firstly, from a simply practical and logical point of view, the dialectical approach would be problematic for any political project aimed at diminishing the potentially conflictual side-effects of confrontational politics for the simple reason that dialectics itself rests upon conflict and opposition. While a dialectical starting point may be the norm expected of all political movements, it has to be noted that dialectics also introduced tensions and divisions that cannot simply be transcended overnight. One of the major problems faced by all movements for social change – be they pacifist or revolutionary in nature – is the difficulty that arises when the foundational revolutionary moment has passed. From then on, the revolution merely devours itself as the dialectics within it consumes more and more victims. This was the case for the French Revolution as it was for the Iranian Revolution that came nearly two centuries later.

Simply put, if a political project begins with the premise that opposition and confrontation are the engines of change, then one cannot simply discard confrontation and conflict as redundant once the initial revolutionary moment is enacted. Dialectical movements tend to be on the lookout for new enemies all the time, as an opponent is required to give the revolution its identity. This in turn means that the constitutive Other will also remain as a perpetual presence, like a ghost that does not abandon its victim. The Islamist project (like many other religious and secular dialectical projects) has been haunted by ghosts from the beginning.

The second problem relates to the relationship between ethics and politics in Islam. Islam, as we all know, places ethics at the forefront of all human relations. Even in cases of outright military conflict, ethics plays a vital role as a mediating force. Countless books have been written over the centuries to remind Muslims of their moral and ethical obligation to the enemy in times of conflict. We are told that Muslims do not have the right to torture their victims, kill their prisoners, destroy their property, do harm to civilians, and so on. What is more, so great is this moral imperative that Muslims are not even allowed to slander their opponents lest this diminishes their human identity and status as fellow creatures in the eyes of God. It is for this reason that racist caricatures and dehumanizing propaganda against the enemy are frowned upon. Muslims need to remember that even their mortal enemies are fellow human beings, the creation of the same God. This reminds us of the fundamental unity of all things, a principle emphasized time and again in the notion of *tawhid* (unity of God).

Dialectical opposition flies in the face of Islamic ethics and undermines the universal basis of Islam by creating and perpetuating not only false dichotomies but also violent hierarchies between the self and other. It dehumanizes the other, reducing the other to a subject whose human potential and status are diminished in our eyes. Islamic ethics, on the other hand, reminds us of the need to recognize the subjectivity of the other all the time. It is also there to remind us that the other can and should be seen as our friend and potential ally as soon as hostilities cease. It is often stated that Islam is a religion of peace, and this is true, but only if we realize that this peace can only be realized when Muslims acknowledge the fundamental humanity they share with others.

I would therefore argue that a dialectical understanding of the self which is based on a hierarchical division of "self" and "other" and which subjugates the other to a lower register to the self is fundamentally divisive and dangerous. Rather than bringing us any closer to the realization of the Islamic project (which is a project that seeks the full realization of our human potential and subjectivities as individuals and collectivities) it actually detracts us from it. In fact, dialectics does little service to the cause of Islam and Muslims: by perpetually framing the other as the predatory enemy, it divides rather than conquers. It introduces contingency and chaos in a world that should be redeemed and united instead. If Islam is meant to unite humanity, dialectics divides it. How, then, can dialectics serve the ends of Muslims?

It is clear that adopting a dialectical approach to the question of the other has actually marginalized and alienated us Muslims from the rest of humanity. Rather than reaching out to the world as a whole and accepting our common brotherhood and sisterhood with humanity in general, we have stuck to our own corner and engaged in a solipsistic self-referential monologue with ourselves. No amount of sincerity and conviction on our part will help us communicate the message and values of Islam to the world as long as we view the rest of the world as alien and antithetical to us. One does not "convert" an enemy by emphasizing one's radical difference and hostility to the other. What is needed here is a reconceptualization of the *umma* that gives equal recognition and respect to the other as well.

RE-VISITING THE OTHER: LIVING WITH PLURALISM
AND DIFFERENCE

Realism and flexibility are among the most important features of Islamic methodology.[6]

Looking at the state of the world as a whole in the context of the aftermath of September 11, I feel that there is a desperate need for Muslims to re-learn the norms and rules of dialogue and communication. For despite the painfully and brutally obvious suffering that has been inflicted upon us, Muslims have not been able to communicate our pain and anxieties to the outside world (which at times may even be the neighbor next door), for the simple reason that we think of them as the *outside* world. The division between inside and outside, in-group and out-group, has been so forcibly enforced by this dialectical outlook which we have foisted upon ourselves that we have effectively exiled ourselves from the rest of humanity. When the Palestinian mother cries amidst the rubble of her home, searching for the bodies of her children buried underneath, her pain is seen as somewhat "exotic" and "incomprehensible" by some. When the Bosnian son bears his heart and vows to avenge the death of his siblings who were killed by some murderous mercenaries, his cry for justice is seen instead as an irrational cry for blood. Somehow the agony of Muslims is presented as being somewhat less than human, or beyond the frontiers of intelligibility. Less than, or more than, or other than human, Muslims are often seen as being radically different. Much of this is due to our own introvertedness, born and bred in a climate of suspicion and frustration.

There is not much that we can do about the deliberate falsification and re-construction of the image of Islam and Muslims in the mainstream global media. Despite protests to the contrary, the world is still being fed a stream of instrumental fictions about Islam and Muslims that continue to frame us as being radically "Other." But we can – and I would argue, must – take the first step by abandoning such a dialectical approach ourselves in order to extricate ourselves from this hopeless impasse. The Muslim world has every right and duty to communicate its anger, pain, frustration, and fears to the rest of the world. But it must do so with intelligence, with honesty, and with compassion not just for Muslims, but for all of humanity.

The first thing that has to be attempted is a self-critique of ourselves and our own notions of identity and difference. For so long the Muslim world has been trapped in a dialectical impasse of its own making. The time has come for us to utilize the tools of contemporary social sciences and critical theory to interrogate some of the fundamental notions of identity and belonging which have shaped and colored Muslim politics for so long. The Muslim world needs to recognize, accept, and even celebrate the internal differences and plurality within itself. The myth of a homogeneous and static Muslim world, forever paralyzed in frozen time, must be exposed for what it is: a discursive strategy and little else.

In order to engage in any meaningful dialogue with the Other, the Muslim world must first begin by opening the way for dialogue within. This can only happen if we learn to accept the internal differences within our collective body, and the presence of a cacophony of voices in our midst. For centuries the heterogeneous reality of the Muslim world has been deliberately and tactically suppressed by conservatives who fear the release of a Babelian chorus of dissent and heterodoxy. There remains still today the fear of risk and contingency bordering on the pathological. Pluralism in Islam has been frowned upon, suppressed, denied, and even hounded on the grounds that it would undermine the unity of the commune itself.

But progressive Muslims would argue that pluralism is a fact of life and a feature that is found in all civilizations, cultures, and belief systems, and is certainly not unique to Islam. To contain these internal voices and energies does not erase or negate their presence: they merely mutate and disguise themselves in a multiplicity of subaltern voices, a plethora of hidden transcripts that adds to the instability of the collective itself.

If by creating the political and social conditions conducive to it we manage to open up the doors of speech, thought, and difference within the Muslim world, we will be able to look at the Muslim collective as it truly is for the first time. Rather than present to ourselves and others a static and one-sided face, we need to recognize the multiplicity of voices and faces that make up the collective Muslim portrait *in toto*. Not only would this be a richer, more colorful, and complex face, it would also be a more honest one. We need to see the true multiple faces of normative and living Islam, warts and all.

Recognizing the multiplicity within ourselves opens the way for us to recognize the multiplicity of the other as well. It would mean that we would be able to look at the West (and the rest) for what it truly is: a complex assembly of actors and agents, interests, beliefs, values, and ideas that may not be completely in harmony with each other. It may also help us realize that in the midst of that confusing and complex heterogeneity that is the other are also values, beliefs, and ideas that are common to ours. The poor in the Muslim world may come to realize that their poverty is shared by others beyond their faith community as well. Muslim women will come to realize that their lot is a common one, shared by women outside the frontier of *dar al-Islam* (Abode of Islam).

The recognition of the other as similar to the self is the first step toward building effective collaborative coalitions and alliances that may actually help us Muslims get our point of view across and to understand the point of view of the Other. Only then will the moment arrive when Muslims can work hand in hand with non-Muslims on matters that affect all of humanity as a whole, and not the *umma* exclusively.

Several examples come to mind. During the anti-apartheid struggle in South Africa and the civil rights movement in the United States, for instance, we saw how Muslim groups managed to achieve considerable political success when they realized that their lot and fate was tied to the fate of others. It was the recognition of common human concerns that allowed them to work with others, pushing for progressive change in society for the good of all. This was a non-exclusive understanding of victory and political success. It is my belief that Islam's success must be the universal success of all, and that our concerns cannot stop at the borders of the Muslim community.

ISLAM BI LA HUDUD: ISLAM WITHOUT BORDERS

My argument in this paper has been that the cause of Islam and Muslims has not been adequately served by the narrow and exclusive understanding of identity and difference on the part of some Islamist groups and movements. I have called for a different approach to the whole question of Muslim identity and its relation to the other: one that recognizes the internal differences and pluralism within the Muslim *umma* itself, one that problematizes its own identity while addressing the multiplicity and difference of the other, and one that seeks to identify the common threads that bind us to others.

Some might question or even object to such an approach on the grounds that it somehow threatens to dissolve the unity of the *umma*, or that it renders it vulnerable to critiques from outside. But this would be a groundless objection, for we have tried to problematize precisely these false dichotomies that have created the boundaries that need to be interrogated in the first place. Fear of the dissolution of the *umma* presupposes the unity and fixity of the *umma* in the first place: a discursive fiction at best that may have served politically utilitarian goals in the past but which has become a burden on the *umma* of today, living as we do in a pluralist and multicultural world. What is needed, in short, is a view of *Islam bi la hudud*, an Islam that is without borders and truly universal.

There are at least three areas where such a universal approach to Muslim concerns, extending beyond the limited confines of the *umma*, can help us all.

The question of Palestine/Israel

The enduring conflict in Palestine and the prolonged sufferings of the Palestinian people have been a major factor affecting the tone and tenor of Islamist politics worldwide. Israel's relentless onslaught on the people of Palestine and America's tacit support of its client state have helped only to complicate and worsen the situation in the Middle East. They have also contributed significantly to the radicalization of Arab resistance movements in the region, which in turn has had a knock-on effect by radicalizing Islamist movements worldwide. In fact, some might argue that the radicalization of Islamist politics the world over has been the result of the deliberate and systematic policies of persecution by the Zionist regime in Tel Aviv, and that Islamist politics worldwide has been held hostage by them.

One of the biggest problems faced by Muslim groups and movements today is to communicate the plight and suffering of Palestinians to the outside world. Despite the demonstration of sympathy and support for the Palestinian people, Palestine is still seen as a "Muslim problem" owing to the fact that it has been communicated via the medium of a religio-political discourse. But it was not always the case: the struggle of the people of Palestine began as a collective struggle fought by a pluralistic and multi-religious society. Palestinian activists have come from different religious, class, cultural, and ethnic backgrounds. The same could be said of the Moro struggle in the southern Philippines, which brought together Muslim and Christian Moros in a common struggle to resist Manila's hold on them.

These struggles, however, soon encountered serious obstacles and were dashed on the rocks of *realpolitik*. As the list of failures and compromises grew longer, morale dipped and a sense of hopelessness set in. This opened the way for radical groupings with exclusive agendas like HAMAS and the MILF (Moro Islamic Liberation Front) to appear on the scene. These groups in turn injected the struggle of the Palestinians (and Moros) with a heavy dose of religiocentric politics. The Palestine issue was transformed from a human rights issue to a religious one instead. Today there are many who think that the Palestinian struggle is fundamentally a matter of religious conflict.

For the Palestinian struggle to succeed, one of the key objectives in the short term has to be the re-universalization of the Palestinian issue itself. Rather than presenting the case of Palestine as a religious issue, we need to see it as a conflict between governments and states over territory and sovereignty.

Here is where a non-dialectical understanding of the self and other comes into play: Muslims need to realize that they share a common plight with others (and vice versa) and also to problematize their own understanding of the Other. It remains a confounding mystery why so many Islamist groups have chosen to label the Jews as the enemies of Islam and Muslims *in toto*. Doing so robs Muslims of the opportunity of forming instrumental alliances with Jews who may well be on the side of the Palestinians – and they are not few in number, by the way. Some of the strongest critics of the Zionist regime have been Jews themselves, proving the point that Jews – just like some Muslims – are far from a homogeneous community. Just like some Muslims, there are some Jews that seek to locate justice on a more global level; and just like Muslims, there are some Jews who seek an "us first, over the others" agenda. It is incumbent for us to reach out to those who put global justice before exclusivist claims. What is more, such an approach has to be based on an understanding of human rights as universal concepts that are valid, relevant, and applicable to all. To simply assume that every single Jew in the world supports the Zionist regime in Israel would be a great injustice to those who have risked their lives and careers defending the rights of Palestinians and other oppressed peoples.

The same approach should be used by Muslims when dealing with other Others as well. A cursory study of contemporary Islamist literature would show that Muslims' understanding of the West is as caricatured and stereotypical as the so-called "Western" view of Islam. Yet one cannot fight prejudice with prejudice, and racism remains obscene and evil even if it is done by Muslims. We need to remind ourselves continually of the fact that the Western world is far from uniform and that there exists a vast array of Western thinkers, leaders, activists, and citizens who care for Muslims as much as they do for their own. These are our real allies and friends, and we must never abandon or disregard them in our pursuit of justice and equity.

If we as Muslims are able to engage the world, we can help them see that the tragedies in Bosnia, in Palestine, in Gujarat, in Kashmir, and elsewhere are not just "Muslim issues," but are human catastrophes and gross violations of universal human rights. Only if we can engage the Christian and the Jew and the Hindu and the agnostic who care about the well-being of all human beings will we get them to care about the well-being of all Muslims. That will only happen if Muslims reciprocate by being as concerned about the welfare of all as about that of Muslims. And yes, that requires Muslims – including Palestinians – to care as much about loss of innocent civilian life on the Israeli side as on the Palestinian side. That means shedding a tear not only for the thousands of Palestinians who have buried their children killed by the aggressions of the Israeli military, but also for the Israeli mothers and fathers whose children have been killed by suicide bombers. The challenge is both for the world community and for Muslims: are we ready to confer full humanity to all the way we do to our own?

Gender

While talking about justice and equity, we in the Muslim world need to be honest about and cognizant of the injustice and inequalities within our midst as well. Thus far, the attempts on the part of several Muslim countries and communities to put forth a Muslim version and understanding of justice and equity have been hampered by the internal contradictions and double standards within our own community.

Recognizing the internal differences within the Muslim community means giving equal time to the subaltern voices within our midst, and granting them not only the right to speak, but also the right to profess and pronounce. This means granting the internal other within the same full subjectivity and rights that we demand for ourselves from others. Simply put, we Muslims cannot demand respect and equal treatment unless and until we show the same respect to those among us. The list of deserving recipients is a long one: workers, peasants, students, the subaltern classes, and, most obvious and evident of all, Muslim women.

Addressing the issue of gender in the Muslim world in turn opens up new avenues for political activism and action to take place.[7] By addressing gender as a serious and primary concern, we would be addressing the fundamental issues of power, inequality, and the production of such inequalities in our midst. By taking on board such concerns we pave the way for a critique of power that does not simply stop at the borders of the Muslim *umma* but which can also go beyond and thus tackle the related issue of power relations and power differentials between Muslims and non-Muslims in this lopsided and highly unjust new world order that we live in.

Gender, for me at least, has to be one of the primary starting blocks for such a critique, for the simple reason that the gender inequalities within the Muslim world remain one of the starkest indicators of the inertia and stasis that have blighted us for so long. Islam's universal message of equality and egalitarianism was delivered to us fifteen centuries ago, but countless generations of Muslim women have yet to see the final and necessary culmination of that aspect of the Islamic project.

As long as we do not address the question of gender, gender relations, and power in the Muslim world, all our protestations and appeals to universal justice will seem hollow and mere lip-service. By addressing the inequality within us, we perform the *Jihad Akbar* (greater struggle) of self-critique and self-questioning which has been at the heart of Islamic practice for so long. Only then can we commit ourselves to the other struggle to correct the wrongs of the world around us.

Globalization, the Environment, and the Future of us all

But here too, on the level of the global, we have failed dismally. Anyone who has been keeping up with the news will know that a number of truly global, transnational movements have emerged over the past few decades. The environmental movement, the pacifist movement against war and the trade of arms, the campaign for equal labor, the campaign against exploitation of children, and most recently the wave of anti-globalization have swept the world – yet the Muslim world remains largely unmoved and untouched.

At none of the major anti-globalization, anti-war, and pro-environment rallies and meetings over the past few years have we seen a significant Muslim presence. One might even come to the mistaken conclusion that Muslims do not believe that environmental concerns affect them. Lest it be forgotten, problems like the destruction of the ozone layer, the spread of AIDS, the rising cost of living, the spread of wars, and the traffic of arms affects all of us, and Muslims are certainly far from immune.

How can the Muslim world claim the right for universal recognition and a global presence if it remains isolated from the rest of the world? Surely Islam, as a religion that is universal in its scope and concerns, can and must come up with a response to these issues?

Muslims need to realize the need to address such concerns that may not be entirely religious in character yet are vitally important nonetheless. We need to demonstrate an awareness of such problems and, more importantly, to act upon them. The outlook that keeps us confined within the borders of our own faith community will, in the end, be the death of us all. The degradation of the environment, exploitation of finite resources, and destruction of local economies aggravated by the rampant march of trade liberalization and globalization processes are all problems that affect the Muslim world today. Indeed, an overview of the Muslim world at the present will present us with the unattractive but undeniable conclusion that the Muslim world is the Third World. It is high time that we step beyond the narrow communitarian concerns of our faith community and work with others to tackle these problems that affect humanity and its destiny.

What progressive Muslims are calling for here is, in a sense, an *Islam bi la Hudud* – an Islam without borders – that locates itself in the present realities of the borderless, plural, multicultural, complex, unequal, and unjust world that we live in today. We call for the rejection of the narrow and exclusive mindset and siege mentality that have robbed us of the channels of communication and cooperation that we desperately need. We call for the rejection of a dialectical approach to the Other which can only frame the other in negative terms as the enemy (or potential enemy) that has to be greeted with suspicion and fear. We also call for an introspection and self-critique that will help disabuse us of some of the myths of our own making, such as the myth of a "pure," "authentic," and "uncontaminated" *umma* that appears *ex nihilo.*

We need to forge a new chain of equivalences that equates universal concerns with Muslim concerns and universal problems with Muslim problems. The Muslim heart cannot bleed only when it sees Muslim tears. If we are not moved by the plight and suffering of others, if we cannot feel the pain and anxieties of others, if we cannot share the joy and aspirations of others, then we cannot claim the same rights and entitlements for ourselves. And we cannot claim that ours is a universal approach to Islam. The universal message of Islam cannot and will not become a reality until it is allowed to travel beyond the domain of *Dar al-Islam.* Justice does not stop at border crossings and it remains color-blind, gender-blind and blind, to the distinctions of class.

Universalism, which rests at the heart of Islam and the Islamic message, needs to be reactivated and made an article of faith among Muslims living in the world today. Our concerns for justice, equity, rights, and freedom need to be articulated in the context of a borderless world where our audience is not only ourselves but the world as a whole, both now and in the future. We need to take up, defend, and promote this form of universalism as part of our identity as Muslims. There has to come a time when being a Muslim means living not only for oneself but for a multitude of others as well. That time is now.

ENDNOTES

1. The author would like to thank Ebrahim Moosa for some of the pointers and recommendations that went into the writing of this paper.
2. Ayatollah Mahmud Taleqani's last sermon in 1979, in *Majmu'eh-e goftar-e "Pedar Taleqani"* [*Collection of Speeches of "Father Taleqani"*], (Tehran: Mujahedin-e Khalq-e Iran, 1979), 53. The translation is from *Liberal Islam: A Sourcebook,* ed. Charles Kurzman (New York: Oxford University Press, 1998), 48.
3. Steven Emerson, *Jihad in America: The Terrorists Living among Us* (New York: Free Press, 2002).
4. Rohan Gunaratna, *Inside al-Qaeda: Global Network of Terror* (New York: Columbia University Press, 2002).
5. Mehdi Bazargan, "Din va Azadi" (*Religion and Liberty*), trans. by Mahmoud Sadri, in *Bazyabi-ye Arzesh'ha* [*The Recovery of Values*], (Tehran: Nehzat-e Azadi-ye Iran, 1983), 80; English translation is from *Liberal Islam,* ed. Charles Kurzman, 81.
6. Rachid Ghannouchi, "The Participation of Islamists in Non-Islamic Government," trans. by Azzam Tamimi, in *Power-Sharing Islam,* ed. Azzam Tamimi (London: Liberty for the Muslim World, 1993), 59.
7. The essay by Sa'diyya Shaikh in this volume specifically deals with the themes of gender justice, Islamic feminism, and women's activism.

FURTHER READING

The task of identifying suitable reading materials on Islam can be a truly daunting one, especially in the aftermath of September 11, 2001: the publishing market has been flooded with sensationalist titles which approach Islam almost exclusively through a lens of violence, conflict, terrorism, fundamentalism, and jihad.

In this section, we have attempted to make some alternative suggestions for those who wish to gain a deeper, more challenging, and nuanced understanding of Islam. The titles are generally ones that can be easily obtained. The list is by no means intended to be exhaustive. It is only a convenient place to begin further explorations. In each section, the titles marked with a bullet point are the most essential ones.

FOUNDATIONAL SOURCES OF ISLAMIC THOUGHT (QUR'AN, LIFE OF PROPHET)

- *Approaching the Qur'an: the Early Revelations*, introduced and trans. by Michael Sells (Ashland, OR: White Cloud Press, 1999). Many Muslims and non-Muslims alike have stated that it can be difficult to access the oceans of meaning in the Qur'an. Michael Sells's scholarly text is a powerful and accessible way to get a sense of the sound, power, intimacy, and majesty of the Qur'an.
- Martin Lings, *Muhammad: His Life Based on the Earliest Sources* (Rochester, VT: Inner Traditions, 1983). This is the best one-volume biography of the Prophet in English. Based directly on the description of the life of the Prophet in the earliest Arabic sources, it is a wonderful way to get a sense of why Muslims have had so much love and devotion for the Prophet. It is also an imaginative

method of approaching Qur'anic verses, studying them as they were revealed in the context of episodes in the Prophet's life.

- William C. Chittick and Sachiko Murata, *The Vision of Islam* (St Paul, MN: Paragon House, 1994). This is perhaps the best one-volume introduction to the profound nature of Islamic thought and its foundation in the Qur'an and the teachings of the Prophet. Highly rooted in a mystical and philosophical understanding of Islam.
- Frederick M. Denny, *An Introduction to Islam*, 2nd edn. (New York: Macmillan, 1985). A highly scholarly study of the Islam as a historical faith, fully contextualized in the history of the Near East. Thorough, accurate, and accessible.
- The award-winning *Islamic Studies: Islam, Arabic, and Religion* website. This site, widely considered the most informative Islam website in cyberspace, is operated by Professor Alan ('Abd al-Haqq) Godlas of the University of Georgia: http://www.arches.uga.edu/~godlas/

For a complete translation of the Qur'an, one can use *The Koran Interpreted*, trans. Arthur J. Arberry (London: Allen & Unwin, 1955), which is perhaps the most poetic translation of the Qur'an in English. In spite of its Victorian language, or perhaps even because of it, the translation of the Qur'an by Abdullah Yusuf 'Ali, titled *The Meaning of the Holy Qur'an* (Brentwood, MD: Amana, 1991) is also quite popular among many Muslims.

Karen Armstrong, *Muhammad: A Biography of the Prophet* (San Francisco: HarperSanFrancisco, 1993). An easier read than Lings' work, with a helpful introductory chapter that deals with polemics against Islam and Muhammad in European literature.

Annemarie Schimmel, *And Muhammad Is His Messenger* (Chapel Hill: University of North Carolina Press, 1988).

John Renard, ed., *Windows on the House of Islam: Muslim Sources on Spirituality and Religious Life* (Berkeley: University of California Press, 1998). A useful way to document the rich historical, geographical, and cultural diversity of the Islamic heritage as preserved textually.

Toshihiko Izutsu, *God and Man in the Koran* (Tokyo: Keio Institute of Cultural and Linguistic Studies, 1964).

Karen Armstrong, *Islam* (London: Modern Library, 2000).

ISLAMIC HISTORY

- John L. Esposito, ed., *The Oxford History of Islam* (New York: Oxford University Press, 2000). A collection of essays by some of the top scholars of Islamic history.
- *Islam: Empire of Faith* (video produced by PBS). Probably the best and most historically accurate video available on the history of Islamic civilization. Exquisitely produced.

• Marshal G.S. Hodgson, *Venture of Islam: Conscience and History in a World Civilization*, 3 vols (Chicago: University of Chicago Press, 1964). This is surely a challenging read, and a long one, approaching fifteen hundred pages. It is also about forty years dated now. However, it remains the most ambitious attempt to fully situate the study of Islam and Muslims in the context of a global history.
Marshall G.S. Hodgson, *Rethinking World History: Essays on Europe, Islam, and World History*, ed. Edmund Burke III (Cambridge: Cambridge University Press, 1993).
Ann K.S. Lambton, *State and Government in Medieval Islam: An Introduction to the Study of Islamic Political Theory* (Oxford: Oxford University Press, 1981).
Norman Daniel, *Islam and the West: The Making of an Image* (Oxford: Oneworld, 1993).
The Adventures of Ibn Battuta: A Muslim Traveler of the 14th Century, trans. Ross E. Dunn (Berkeley: University of California Press, 1986).
Wilfred Madelung, *The Succession to Muhammad: A Study of the Early Caliphate* (Cambridge: Cambridge University Press, 1997).
Moojan Momen, *An Introduction to Shi'i Islam* (New Haven: Yale University Press, 1985).

ISLAM AND GENDER

• Leila Ahmed, *Women and Gender in Islam: Historical Roots of a Modern Debate* (New Haven: Yale University Press, 1992).
• Amina Wadud, *Qur'an and Woman: Rereading the Sacred Text from a Woman's Perspective*, 2nd edn (New York: Oxford University Press, 1999).
Miriam Cooke, *Women Claim Islam: Creating Islamic Feminism through Literature* (New York: Routledge, 2000).
Khaled Abou El Fadl, *Speaking in God's Name: Islamic Law, Authority and Women* (Oxford: Oneworld, 2001).
Haideh Moghissi, *Feminism and Islamic Fundamentalism: The Limits of Postmodern Analysis* (Oxford: Oxford University Press, 1999).
Lila Abu-Lughod, *Veiled Sentiments: Honor and Poetry in a Bedouin Society* (Berkeley: University of California Press, 1986).
Susan Schaefer Davis, *Patience and Power: Women's Lives in a Moroccan Village* (Cambridge, MA: Schenkman, 1983).
Muslim Women's League website: http://www.mwlusa.org/

ISLAMIC SPIRITUALITY AND SUFISM

• Carl W. Ernst, *The Shambhala Guide to Sufism* (Boston: Shambhala, 1997).
• M.R. Bawa Muhaiyaddeen, *Islam and World Peace: Explanations of a Sufi* (Philadelphia: Fellowship Press, 1987).

• Michael Sells, *Early Islamic Mysticism: Sufi, Qur'an, Mi'raj, Poetic and Theological Writings* (New York: Paulist Press, 1996).
• Sheikh Muzaffer Ozak, *Love is the Wine*, 2nd edn (New York: Philosophical Research Society, 1999).
Carl W. Ernst, *Teachings of Sufism* (Boston: Shambhala, 1999).
James Fadiman and Robert Frager, eds, *Essential Sufism* (San Francisco: HarperSanFrancisco, 1997).
Farid al-Din Attar, *Muslim Saints and Mystics: Episodes from the Tadhkirat al-Auliya'*, trans. by A.J. Arberry (London: Routledge & Kegan Paul, 1966).

ISLAMIC LITERATURE

• *The Spirit of Islam*, available through Minnesota National Public Radio at http://firstperson.org/programs/2001/10/19_spiritofislam/. This program features Omid Safi and Seemi Ghazi in a wide-ranging discussion of Islamic literature, spirituality, Qur'an recitation, and contemporary Islam.
• Farid ud-Din Attar, *The Conference of the Birds*, trans. by Afkham Darbandi and Dick Davis (London: Penguin, 1984).
Victoria Rowe Holbrook, *The Unreadable Shores of Love: Turkish Modernity and Mystic Romance* (Austin: University of Texas Press, 1994).
Elizabeth T. Gray, *The Green Sea of Heaven: Fifty Ghazals from the Diwan of Hafez* (Ashland, OR: White Cloud Press, 1995).
Frances W. Pritchett, *Nets of Awareness: Urdu Poetry and Its Critics* (Berkeley: University of California Press, 1994).
Walter Andrews et al., *Ottoman Lyric Poetry: An Anthology* (Austin: University of Texas Press, 1997).

ISLAM AND THE MODERN WORLD

• Mark Juergensmeyer, *Terror in the Mind of God* (University of California Press, 1998). A valuable book that talks about the global rise of religious violence in comparative terms, thus moving the conversation beyond the singular association of Islam with terrorism.
• Bruce Lawrence, *Shattering the Myth: Islam Beyond Violence* (Princeton: Princeton University Press, 1998).
• Malcolm X, with Alex Haley, *The Autobiography of Malcolm X* (New York: Grove Press, 1965).
• Michael Sells, *The Bridge Betrayed: Religion and Genocide in Bosnia* (Berkeley: University of California Press, 1996).
• Roy Mottahedeh, *The Mantle of the Prophet: Religion and Politics in Iran* (Oxford: Oneworld, 2000).
• Tayyib Saleh, *Wedding of Zein and Other Stories* (London, 1968).

Bruce Lawrence, *Defenders of God: The Fundamentalist Revolt against the Modern Age* (Columbia: University of South Carolina Press, 1995).

Wael B. Hallaq, *Authority, Continuity and Change in Islamic Law* (Cambridge: Cambridge University Press, 2001).

Dale F. Eickelman and James Piscatori, *Muslim Politics* (Princeton: Princeton University Press, 1996).

Ghassan Kanafani, *Palestine's Children: Returning to Haifa and Other Stories* (Boulder: Lynne Rienner, 2000).

Suroosh Irfani, *Revolutionary Islam in Iran – Popular Liberation or Religious Dictatorship?* (London: Zed, 1983).

Tayyib Saleh, *Season of Migration to the North* (London, 1969).

Albert Hourani, *Arabic Thought in the Liberal Age: 1798–1939* (Oxford: Oxford University Press, 1962; reprinted, Cambridge: Cambridge University Press, 1983.)

Daniel Brown, *Rethinking Tradition in Modern Islamic Thought* (Cambridge: Cambridge University Press, 1996).

Tariq Ramadan, *Islam, the West and the Challenges of Modernity* (Markefield, U.K.: Islamic Foundation, 2001).

Fazlur Rahman, *Islam and Modernity* (Chicago: University of Chicago Press, 1984).

Fazlur Rahman, *Revival and Reform in Islam: A Study of Islamic Fundamentalism*, ed. Ebrahim Moosa (Oxford: Oneworld, 1999).

Ebrahim Moosa, "The Poetics and Politics of Law after Empire: Reading Women's Rights in the Contestations of Law," *Journal for Islamic and Near Eastern Law*, 2001–2, 1–46.

John Cooper, Ronald Nettler and Mohamed Mahmoud, eds, *Islam and Modernity: Muslim Intellectuals Respond* (London: I.B. Taurus, 1998).

PROGRESSIVE MUSLIM THOUGHT

• Charles Kurzman, ed., *Liberal Islam: A Sourcebook* (Oxford: Oxford University Press, 1998).

• Farid Esack, *Qur'an, Liberation and Pluralism: An Islamic Perspective of Interreligious Solidarity against Oppression* (Oxford: Oneworld, 1997).

• Abdullahi Ahmed an-Na'im, *Toward an Islamic Reformation: Civil Liberties, Human Rights and International Law* (Syracuse: Syracuse University Press, 1990).

• Abdolkarim Sorush, *Reason, Freedom, and Democracy in Islam*, trans. Mahmoud Sadri and Ahmad Sadri (Oxford: Oxford University Press, 2000).

• Mohammed Arkoun, *The Unthought in Contemporary Islamic Thought* (London: Saqi, 2002).

• Progressive Muslim Network, *Definition of Progressive Islam*, www. progressive muslims.com

Aziz Esmail, "Islam and Modernity," in *The Muslim Almanac*, ed. Azim Nanji (New York: Gale Research, 1996), 483–7.

'Alija 'Ali Izetbegovic, *Islam between East and West* (Indianapolis: American Trust, 1984).

Abdulaziz Sachedina, *The Islamic Roots of Democratic Pluralism* (Oxford: Oxford University Press, 2001).

Paul A. Bové, ed., *Edward Said and the Work of the Critic: Speaking Truth to Power* (Durham, NC: Duke University Press, 2000).

Amartya Sen, *Development as Freedom* (Oxford: Oxford University Press, 1999).

Mohammed Arkoun, *Rethinking Islam: Common Questions, Uncommon Answers*, trans. Robert D. Lee (Boulder: Westview Press, 1994).

Edward Said, *Reflections of the Intellectual* (New York: Vantage Press, 1993).

Noam Chomsky, *The Fateful Triangle: The United States, Israel and the Palestinians* (Boston: South End Press, 1983).

Russell T. McCutcheon, *Critics Not Caretakers: Redescribing the Public Study of Religion* (Albany: State University of New York Press, 2001).

Edward Said, "Impossible Histories: Why the Many Islams Cannot be Simplified," *Harper's Magazine*, July 2002, 69–74.

Ali Shari'ati, *Reflections of a Concerned Muslim on the Plight of Oppressed Peoples* (Houston: Free Islamic Literatures, 1979).

Ali Shari'ati, *On the Sociology of Islam*, trans. Hamid Algar (Berkeley: Mizan Press, 1979).

Na'eem Jeenah and Shamima Shaikh, *A Journey of Discovery: A South African Hajj* (Oceanview, South Africa: Full Moon Press, 2000).

SEPTEMBER 11, AND BEYOND

• Study of Islam Section at the American Academy of Religion, *Scholars of Islam Responding to the Tragedy of 9/11*, http://groups.colgate.edu/aarislam/response.htm

• Emran Qureshi and Michael A. Sells, *The New Crusades: Constructing the Muslim Enemy* (New York: Columbia University Press, 2003).

• Michael Sells, "The Interlinked Factors of a Tragedy," http://www.haverford.edu/relg/sells/interlinkedfactors.htm

• Eqbal Ahmad, *Confronting Empire* (Cambridge, MA: South End Press, 2000).

• The many essays of Robert Fisk, the noted journalist for *The Independent*. His essays there can be accessed by doing a search for Robert Fisk on *The Independent*'s website: http://www.independent.co.uk/

• Ahmed Rashid, *Taliban: Militant Islam, Oil & Fundamentalism in Central Asia* (New Haven: Yale University Press, 2000).

• Arundhati Roy, "The Algebra of Infinite Justice," *The Guardian*, September 29, 2001, http://www.guardian.co.uk/Archive/Article/0,4273,4266289,00.html

Arundhati Roy, "War is Peace," http://www.zmag.org/roywarpeace.htm. Both of the above essays by Arundhati Roy are reprinted in her recent volume, *Power Politics* (Cambridge, MA: South End Press, 2002).

"Islamic Statements against Terrorism in the Wake of the September 11 Mass Murders," http://www.unc.edu/~kurzman/terror.htm

Michael Sells, "on the UNC Approaching the Qur'an Controversy of 2002," http://www.haverford.edu/relg/sells/UNC_ApproachingTheQur'an.htm

Harvey Cox, "The Market as God," www.theatlantic.com/issues/99mar/market-god.htm

Khaled Abou El Fadl, "Islam and the Theology of Power," *Middle East Report*, 221, 2001, www.merip.org/mer/mer221/221_abu_el_fadl.html

Roy Mottahedeh, "The Clash of Civilizations: An Islamicist's Critique," *Harvard Middle Eastern and Islamic Review*, 2, 1996, 1–26. This essay by a leading historian of Middle Eastern history at Harvard is the most serious challenge to and refutation of Samuel Huntington's problematic – yet highly popular – theory of "Clash of Civilizations."

Edward Said, "The Clash of Ignorance," *The Nation*, October 4, 2001. This essay, Edward Said's most recent critique of Bernard Lewis and Samuel Huntington, can be accessed at http://www.thenation.com/doc.mhtml?i=20011022&c=1&s=said

Foreign Policy in Focus http://www.fpif.org

ISLAM AND GAY/LESBIAN/BISEXUAL ISSUES

• Stephen O. Murray and Will Roscoe, *Islamic Homosexualities: Culture, History and Literature* (New York: New York University Press, 1997).

Everett Rowson, "The Effeminates of Early Medina," in G. Comstock and S. Henking, eds, *Que(e)rying Religion: A Critical Anthology* (New York: Continuum, 1997).

Everett Rowson and J.W. Wright, eds, *Homoeroticism in Classical Arabic Literature* (New York: Columbia University Press, 1997).

International Gay and Lesbian Human Rights Commission is a non-governmental organization that responds to human rights violations of Gay Lesbian Bisexual and Transgendered people and anyone living with HIV or AIDS. The current director of the organization is a Muslim. www.iglhrc.org

Al-Fatiha Foundation is an international foundation based in Washington, D.C., for Muslims who are lesbian, gay, bisexual, transgendered, or questioning their sexual orientation or gender identity, and their friends. PO Box 33532, Washington, DC 20033, U.S.A. www.al-fatiha.net

Ahbab, the Gay and Lesbian Arab Society, claiming to be the "first gay Arab radio station," and based in New York features news, articles, and essays about gay Arabs. http://glas.org/ahbab/

Bint el Nas is a website and its e-zine is designed for gay, bisexual, and transgendered women who identify themselves ethnically or culturally with the Arab world. www.bintelnas.org

Al-Fitrah is a LGBTQ Muslim support group in Capetown, South Africa. To join the Gay and Lesbian Muslims in South Africa (GLMSA) list-serve, send a blank email to glmsa-subscribe@yahoogroups.com

HUMAN RIGHTS ORGANIZATIONS, CIVIL RIGHTS GROUPS, AND PROGRESSIVE NEWS SOURCES

Human Rights Watch	http://www.hrw.org/
Amnesty International	http://www.amnesty.org/
ACLU	http://www.aclu.org/
ZMAG	http://www.zmag.org/
Voices in the Wilderness	http://www.nonviolence.org/vitw/
The Independent	http://www.independent.co.uk/
The Nation	http://www.thenation.com
Counterpunch	http://www.counterpunch.com/

INDEX

Notes: (quoted) refers to a quoted passage which has not been named in the text. Locators in parentheses refer to endnote numbers.